Kindred by Choice

Kindred by Choice

Germans and American Indians since 1800

H. GLENN PENNY

The University of North Carolina Press *Chapel Hill*

Library of Congress Cataloging-in-Publication Data
Penny, H. Glenn.
Kindred by choice : Germans and American Indians
since 1800/H. Glenn Penny.
pages cm.
Includes bibliographical references and index.
ISBN 978-1-4696-0764-1 (cloth : alk. paper)
ISBN 978-1-4696-2644-4 (pbk. : alk. paper)
1. Indians of North America—Public opinion. 2. Indians in
popular culture. 3. Germans—Attitudes. 4. Germans—Social
life and customs. 5. Public opinion—Germany. I. Title.
E98.P99P46   2013
970.004′97—dc23
2013001367

Parts of chapter 4 previously appeared as "The German
Love Affair with American Indians: Rudolf Cronau's Epiphany,"
Common-place 11, no. 4 (July 2011). Used with permission.

For Beatrice and Timmer

Contents

Figures

Preface

"Let me confess," said Charlotte, "that when you call all these
curious entities of yours affined, they appear to me to possess not
so much an affinity of blood as an affinity of mind and soul."

—JOHANN WOLFGANG VON GOETHE
  Elective Affinities, 1809

This book began as an effort to explain the abundant references to American Indians in contemporary Germany as well as the staggering numbers of Germans one encounters in Indian country today. That explanation, I quickly realized, has deep roots. It turns around a striking sense of affinity for American Indians that has permeated German cultures for two centuries, and which stems directly from German polycentrism, notions of tribalism, a devotion to resistance, a longing for freedom, and a melancholy sense of shared fate. It also has much to do with Germans' historical interactions with the United States and the transnational world of German cultures that spread across the Atlantic during the nineteenth century—a world we too often forget.

Germans' affinities for American Indians were always elective. Throughout the nineteenth and twentieth centuries, many millions of Germans repeatedly chose to embrace a sense of kinship with American Indians that stemmed from affinities "of mind and soul." At precisely the time when this process began, Johann Wolfgang von Goethe turned to the notion of elective affinities developed in the natural sciences to explain the tendency of some chemical species to combine with some substances rather than others. He drew on these scientific theories in order to explore the attractions and emotional connections between particular individuals. Later, scholars such as Max Weber drew on Goethe's insights while seeking to understand relationships within and between human societies. Others, such as Walter Benjamin, critiqued them extensively.[1]

What Goethe and those who followed him most sought to understand were the shared dispositions revealed by elective affinities. That is also a central goal of this book. For behind those affinities lies an internal tension about the place of Germans in the modern world that ran across multiple generations and persisted through all the political regimes and the most radical ruptures in modern German history—from the early nineteenth century through the so-called Age of Extremes.[2]

Scholarly efforts to engage the relationship between continuity and rupture in modern German history have long been plagued by teleologies. Most recently, for example, Helmut Walser Smith sought to expose the "profound roots" of what took place in Nazi Germany by sketching out the "chronological depth and the historical connections" of nation, race, and religion from the Nazi period back to the sixteenth century.[3] However, as Alon Confino and Dieter Langewiesche astutely noted, Smith's "narrow method" was so focused on revealing the historic roots of the National Socialist discourse of annihilation that it often ignored narratives and evidence that might call that putative continuity into question.[4]

A central problem with Smith's project was his desire to reach back in time for the antecedents of a historic event and his willingness to label continuity what might better be thought of as repeated similarities, each of which had singular meanings defined by their particular contexts. To Confino's mind, a preferable approach to the problem of continuities in German history would be to "conceive of German culture as made up of a repertoire of symbols and memories that were differently adapted, adopted, and changed as each generation chose certain elements within the constraints of the evolving tradition."[5] The first example he suggested, as someone who had written extensively on the topic, was the idea of *Heimat*, which persisted across the modern era, and which, as he and others have demonstrated, took up radically different resonances in different political eras.[6]

This book engages the problem of continuities and ruptures as well. For what began with an interest in Germans' persistent fascination with American Indians ended with an appreciation for how analyses of consistent or persistent dispositions within German (and, by implication, other) cultures can inform our investigations of particular events. There is no question that Germans' affinities for American Indians resonated differently within different historical contexts; but there is also no question that these affinities retained certain consistent characteristics that reveal persistent dispositions, moods, and attitudes within German cultures over a long period of time and across a geographic space that extended far beyond Germany's national borders.

Indeed, behind these elective affinities was an ongoing conflict within German cultures about Germans' place in the modern world—a conflict that was driven, to some degree, by the melancholy recognition that Germans were both victims and proponents of the homogenizing forces of modern Western civilization. This is not the kind of ideological continuity sought by Smith and so many others, and allowing this and other persistent dispositions to emerge and inform our historical examinations is not an attempt to describe how earlier actions necessarily lead to later ones. Rather it is an effort to underscore how consistent, repetitive actions by people associated with a culture can reveal equally persistent dispositions within that culture, which not only have an explanatory power that is often overlooked but also, in turn, unveil histories long overshadowed by those driven by nations, states, and scholars' all-too-frequent focus on political ideology.

Acknowledgments

If I had known that this book would take so long to complete, I might well have pursued something else: a life history, a state history, a take on an era, something with a more explicit beginning, middle, and end. There were many times when I cursed myself for not choosing a topic with a finite set of sources located in a tidy, accessible archive. Transnational and transcultural histories, I quickly learned, pose particular challenges—but they also offer significant rewards. Pursuing this project, for example, forced me to engage a range of unanticipated topics: German settler colonialism in the American Midwest, the rise and fall of German America, and the transnational world of American Indian performers and postwar activists, not to mention comparative genocides, persistent notions of masculinity, and the ways in which a range of American Indians helped to channel and shape German notions of human difference. Perhaps most importantly, this project has pushed me to think hard about the relationships between continuities and ruptures in modern German history and to rethink the ways in which we conceive of and write cultural history.

I am grateful that I had the chance to engage in this research, particularly because it put me in contact with so many generous people. I am also thankful for the institutional support I received and for the insights I gleaned into American Indian studies, American history, and many new realms of German and European history. Those areas were only at the margins of my earlier inquiries; they were simply sparks of ideas I had gleaned from conversations with Peter Fritzsche and George Mosse, until I had the opportunity to pursue them directly.

That opportunity was created through the support of the American Philosophical Society, the Center for Contemporary Historical Research (ZZF) in Potsdam, The George A. and Eliza Gardner Howard Foundation at Brown

University, the German Academic Exchange, the German Historical Institution in Washington, D.C., the Max Planck Institute for History in Göttingen, and the National Endowment for the Humanities. The University of Missouri Research Board supported my initial inquiries, while the University of Iowa's International Programs and Arts and Humanities Initiative proved crucial along the way. I could never have completed all the necessary research trips without them. I am particularly indebted to the University of Iowa for granting me a Faculty Scholar Fellowship. That fantastic program allowed me to develop the project to its full potential. Without it, this book would have taken much longer to complete.

The number of people who eagerly assisted me is so large that I cannot list them all here. Countless archivists and librarians aided me, and many scholars helped me along the way. I am grateful for their assistance. I benefited from comments on earlier versions of these chapters during meetings of the American Anthropological Association, the American Historical Association, the American Indian Workshop, the American Society for Ethnohistory, and the German Studies Association, as well as presentations in Berlin, Erfurt, Konstanz, Minneapolis, Munich, Montreal, New Orleans, Philadelphia, Potsdam, Seville, Washington, D.C., and Iowa City. The diverse and engaged publics that showed up to my presentations on the Dakota Conflict at St. Cloud State University in Minnesota were especially heartening and instructive. So too were the students at the University of Minnesota in Morris.

Indeed, the striking number of people from outside academics who have assisted me has been humbling. They have greatly enriched this book. People such as Ted Asten, Bernd Damisch, Joachim Giel, Max Oliv, and Wolfgang Seifert invited me into their homes, fed me, looked through materials with me, and introduced me to numerous interlocutors. Chuck Trimble offered me much more of his time than I ever could have expected. So too did Arthur Amiotte, Klaus Biegrt, Curtis Dahlin, Ann Davis, Joe and Janice Day, Richard Erdoes, Roswitha Freier, Andre Köhler, John LaBatte, Nick McCaffery, Lindberg Namingha, Angelika Powell, Uli Sanner, Cindy Sapp, Milo Yellowhair, Joe Whiting, Gerry Wunderlich, and so many others. A special word of thanks has to go to Hartmut and Heidi Rietschel. Their kindness and generosity seems boundless, their enthusiasm for the topic endless, and Hartmut's knowledge of American Indians' activities in Europe is simply astonishing; he never ceases to amaze. *Respekt.*

A number of my colleagues also deserve special thanks. Everything would have been much, much harder without the openness and assistance of Peter Bolz, who I suspect knows much more about this topic than anyone else. I also learned a great deal from Eric Ames, Randall Bytwerk, Siegrid Deutschlander, Christian Feest, Curtis Hinsley, Greg Johnson, Petra Tjitske Kalshoven, Karl Markus Kreis, Bradley Naranch, Mark Peterson, Paul Chaat Smith, Alina Dana Weber, and Thomas Weber. All of them happily shared their work with me. Others went to even greater lengths. Maiken Umbach has been tireless in her support. Fred Hoxie, Suzanne Marchand, and Lynn Nyhart read the entire manuscript and flooded me with critical suggestions. Chuck Grench was patient enough to wait for years for the book to be completed, recognizing its importance when it was only an idea. Andrew Zimmerman provided me with critical insights during the final phase of writing, and so too did two anonymous reviewers for UNC Press. My family deserves my thanks as well. They have put up with a lot: being dragged across the Dakotas, the Southwest, and much of Germany, being left alone for long periods of time, or being ignored during far too many nights when all they heard from me was the annoying typing in another room. That is, unfortunately, part of the enterprise, but that makes me no less grateful for their patience.

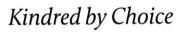

Kindred by Choice

Introduction *Beyond the Buckskin*

Germania is separated from the Gauls and from the Raeti and Pannonii
by the Rhine and Danube rivers, from the Sarmatians and Dacians by the
barrier of mutual fear or mountain ranges. The other parts, with their broad
promontories and vast islands, are surrounded by the Ocean; in recent times
war has revealed the existence there of nations and kings unknown before.

—TACITUS, *Germania*, 98 C.E.

In August 2006, I arrived in a forest clearing outside of Cottbus, a German
city near the Polish border, to join approximately a thousand Germans
dressed like nineteenth-century North American Indians. Hundreds of teepees, many of them quite old, were set in clusters around the meadow. As
I walked to my hosts' teepee, small children in breechcloths or buckskin
dresses ran past me with bows and arrows to swim naked in the nearby lake.
Their grandparents, in similar attire and with the same intention, trailed
closely behind. Traders had already set up tables on the side of the encampment, selling the porcupine skins needed for the quillwork that adorned
many of these peoples' garments, as well as newly tanned leather, a variety
of horns, hatchets, knives, trade beads and cloth, and the latest literature on
contemporary American Indians, their ancestors, and their arts and crafts.
Men dressed as Cheyenne Dog Soldiers patrolled the perimeter, keeping
tourists at bay, and ensuring that no one, with the exception of myself, entered the area in present-day clothing. Cars and trucks used to transport
these people, their belongings, and the thousands of teepee poles required
for the meeting were tucked behind a hill at a distance. Once settled in the
clearing, these hobbyists spent a week gossiping and socializing—exchang-
ing information about their handicrafts, rituals, and historic events; trading
artifacts; and taking classes in leatherwork, beadwork, and Lakota. They participated in daily gatherings that allowed them to demonstrate their knowledge of artifact production, dancing, or drumming, and they held a special

1

FIGURE 1. A group of Kit Foxes announcing the beginning of the opening ceremonies at "The Week" during the summer of 2006. Near Cottbus, on the German-Polish border. (Photo by the author)

ceremony to commemorate this thirtieth annual gathering of the hobbyist clubs in the former East Germany (GDR).

"The Week," as participants call it, is not an isolated event. It is one accentuated manifestation of the pervasive fascination with North American Indians among Germans. Shared by men and women alike, this fascination cuts across political, confessional, social, and generational boundaries. It is also much more than a current, postmodern enchantment with "the primitive." It has persisted across a strikingly *longue durée*.

During the early nineteenth century, stories set among American Indians became popular in German-speaking Central Europe. Literature about them became ubiquitous. The fantastic success of James Fenimore Cooper's *Leatherstocking Tales* is perhaps the most poignant example: the first volume was quickly translated into German in 1826, and it was ultimately condensed with the four following volumes into a single tome, released in abbreviated versions for children, and put through countless new editions during the next decades. It became, in fact, a classic of German literature, familiar to the literate classes in all German states across the nineteenth and twentieth centuries.[1] *The Leatherstocking Tales* was followed by a host of other, similar translations from English, French, and Spanish, which appeared in German periodicals and as swiftly consumed monographs. A series of German travel writers and novelists built on the success of those stories. By writing about American Indians, they became best-selling authors over the rest of the nineteenth century and well into the twentieth. The most prominent of these was Karl May, whose books sold more than seventy million copies by the 1980s, about twenty million more than the best-known American author of westerns, Louis L'Amour. The enthusiasm continued during the postwar period and moved rapidly into other media. May's books, for example, inspired West Germany's most popular set of movies; a similar set was fantastically successful in East Germany; and in 2003, after the fall of the Berlin Wall and German unification, *The Manitou's Shoe*, a spoof on those popular films, broke all records in the German film industry.

Such successes seem astonishing until we recognize that by the end of the nineteenth century thinking about American Indians had become integral to German cultures. They not only were a popular subject among German novelists and other writers but were incorporated into the production of toys, theater, circus, high and low art, and the new cinema. Across Imperial, Weimar, and later Nazi Germany, children of all ages and both genders "played Indian," emulating the characters from Cooper and May and the people they encountered in Buffalo Bill's Wild West, in German circuses, and with other impresarios who sought to capitalize on Germans' fascination with Native America. Adults "played Indian" as well, and not simply those individuals who joined the first hobby clubs in the early twentieth century. Artists such as Georg Grosz, Otto Dix, and Rudolf Schlichter, for example, turned to their childhood engagement with American Indians while dealing with their personal crises and the crises of modernity.[2] Art historian Aby Warburg traveled to the Hopi and Zuni Pueblos for the same reason;[3] the artist Max Ernst, the psychiatrist Carl Jung, and ethnologists Karl von den Steinen and Paul Ehrenreich followed. Adolf Hitler remained in Germany; but he continued to read Karl May's *Winnetou* for insights into crisis situations, recommending it to his general staff during the battles of World War II.[4] "Indians," in short, became deeply ingrained in German cultures during the nineteenth century, their stories became ciphers for modern struggles during the twentieth century, and that long cultural history continued unabated through the postwar era, resurfacing during Cold War clashes, peace protests, environmental movements, esoteric musings, and the persistent settings of backyard play and hobbyists' camps. The unrelenting breadth and depth of this preoccupation are astounding.

It is also well documented. Journalists have been writing about it for decades. Indeed, they have repeatedly discovered it with elation.[5] The spectacle of Germans emulating American Indians is particularly titillating and hard to resist. Writing about this obsession, especially the hobbyist meetings, is guaranteed to generate smirks and laughter among readers, even righteous anger from some, and that is a recipe for publishing success: those reactions have allowed reporters as well as scholars to reap attention from the sensation and then position themselves to disclose astute revelations.

Spectacular Copy

In August 2000 Daniel Rubin, a reporter for Knight Ridder Newspapers and the *Kansas City Star*, attempted to harness the spectacle produced by a group of hobbyists near Stolpe, Germany, by focusing on one man, Jörg Diecke, forty-four, whom he found "dressed in the handcrafted clothing a Hidatsa warrior might have worn on the Great Plains 150 years ago." As Rubin showed, however, Diecke was neither a social misfit nor insane. His wife was a dentist, and his compatriots included "doctors, engineers, cooks, and scholars." He was, if we were to believe the reporter, the product of an odd national politics. As Rubin explained, Diecke and other East German hobbyists had been weaned on state-sanctioned history books that endorsed viewing American Indians as freedom-loving heroes struggling against oppression; they watched movies in which "Indians were the good guys" and claimed to be engaged in serious business. As Diecke put it, "'We do not "play" at being Indians.'"[6] Rather they sought to learn from them, and they were eager to act in solidarity with American Indians whenever possible. Eccentric exhibitionist behaviors shaped by a wayward socialist dictatorship? This was spectacular copy indeed.

Diecke's rhetoric and actions, however, were old news; so too, for that matter, were Rubin's queries. East German reporters wrote similar essays about these clubs in the 1970s and 1980s.[7] West German reporters recorded essentially the same answers from hobbyists near Cologne in the 1960s;[8] American reporters had already been there as well. In the 1950s, Charles Belden, the "cowboy photographer from Wyoming," traveled to Germany in search of the hobbyists, establishing a tradition of inquiry and response around the sensation of the clubs that continues until this day.[9] Indeed, in 1996 alone, the *Boston Globe*, the *New York Times*, and the *Wall Street Journal* all ran similar essays on Germans' fascination with American Indians; and Elizabeth Neuffer's piece on hobbyists in the *Globe* also appeared under different titles in the *Rocky Mountain News* (Denver), the *Commercial Appeal* (Memphis), and the *St. Louis Dispatch*. She too quoted Jörg Diecke (then only forty), stressed the putative seriousness of his group's endeavors, and covered essentially the same terrain that Rubin would cover four years later.[10]

Spectacular Clichés

Despite hobbyists' explanations for their interests and behavior, and the possible implications those explanations could have for our understanding of the production of knowledge, the continuing importance of self-edification in German cultures, or even Germans' persistent interests in non-Europeans, the sensation has always appealed to reporters much more than the sober discussions. It is the spectacle that continues to drive journalists to hobbyist camps and their annual meetings in order to posit the same puzzled questions again and again until many hobbyists, irritated by the visits, much like some of the American Indians they emulate, have grown accustomed to the attention and have learned to receive their inquisitors with well-rehearsed answers, if they agree to receive them at all.

One characteristic of these reports is typical of even the most scholarly analyses of Germans' interests in American Indians: they harness multiple enticing clichés. As Susanne Zantop noted, such analyses are replete with a focus not only on clichéd and stereotypical depictions of American Indians by hobbyists and others but also on "stereotypical accounts of Germans and their national character or alleged (sinister) motivations."[11] Literary scholar Katrin Sieg's essay on West German hobbyists, written about the same time as Rubin's column, is exemplary. Theoretically sophisticated and analytically incisive, Sieg nevertheless assumed that some sinister notion of "Germanness" was being worked out through hobbyist actions. On the basis of a small number of interviews, and eschewing the kinds of ambivalences at the heart of Eric Lott's masterful work on ethnic transvestitism in antebellum American minstrelsy,[12] Sieg attempted to argue that Germans' "impersonations" of American Indians were essentially masked "attempts to cope with the guilt of the Holocaust as well as the widespread shame and resentment provoked by the accusations brought against Germans in the international war crimes tribunals and the denazification procedures." Embodying Zantop's lament, Sieg argued that donning American Indian garb from the nineteenth century somehow "allowed Germans to align themselves with the victims and avengers of genocide, rather than its perpetrators and accomplices." That was an unfortunate conclusion. For Sieg's assertions not only lacked a historical understanding of the many motivations that drove German hobbyists, before, during, and after the period of National Socialism but also failed to recognize the long history of German condemnation of the United States' efforts to eradicate American Indians, which predated the 1950s by a century.[13] She has hardly been alone.[14]

As Rubin showed, explanations driven by links to historical guilt and diabolical states are also easily, and sometimes all too gleefully, tied to the GDR. Friedrich von Borries and Jens-Uwe Fischer's recent book on hobbyists in former East Germany, for instance, is driven by the assumption that the GDR's ominous character best explains East German hobbyists' actions and behaviors. Dependent on a small number of extreme statements by a few participants (they too interviewed Diecke), and spurred by their fascination with the secret police (Stasi) and its interest in these groups, the book's conclusions that East German hobbyists were drawn to the study of American Indians because the GDR was its own kind of reservation are foregone in the first pages. Much like Sieg, they leave little room for either historical continuities or social and cultural explanations unhinged from the parameters of nation-states and national identities. Indeed, they seem blithely unaware that the hobbyist scene is a phenomenon that has persisted across many chronological and political borders, including the so-called Iron Curtain.[15] Despite that, and because of their eagerness to exploit the sensation of East Germans dressing in feathers, their book has been quite successful; the German television network ZDF even based a special on it.[16]

It is my contention, however, that the German fascination with American Indians has much to teach us about German cultures, transnational and transcultural histories, relationships between Europeans and non-Europeans, connections between state-sponsored efforts to gain influence and territory and informal settlement projects, and more. At the very least, it should remind us that German history is not always already driven by nations and states—even if it does flow through them—and it promises to help us rethink, even respatialize, the understanding of "Germany" and German history by connecting the indeterminacy and incompleteness of the German nation-state inside Europe with the sprawling diversity of the German presence abroad. Achieving those ends, however, requires moving beyond the immediate spectacle of Germans in buckskin, beads, and feathers and outside the parameters of hegemonic historical narratives. Tied as they are to the spectacular lure of German *Bürger* dressed in buckskin dancing in open fields, and dependent on the limiting parameters of nationalism and the nation-state for their explanations, journalists and scholars continually overlook these people's actual motivations for reproducing the material culture of another time and location and coming together to exchange information about places and peoples they may never see. There are, in fact, long historical explanations for their choice of kinships, if one looks past the glitz and the national paradigm, and critical implications for how we conceive and write cultural history.[17]

To reach those explanations and implications, however, we have to overcome many of our own prejudices about the very notion of adults "playing Indian" or thinking about American Indians and take these endeavors seriously. We have to be willing, for example, to soberly observe the behavior of German enthusiasts eagerly studying Lakota in a field outside Cottbus, listen to them asking their instructor the kinds of astute questions about grammar and pronunciation that would make any teacher's heart swoon, and understand that so many of them have managed to gain enough knowledge of the language that people working in places like the Red Cloud School on the Pine Ridge Reservation no longer find it surprising to encounter groups of Germans speaking Lakota in their courtyard. That is not only curious and out of the ordinary; it is, by any estimation, impressive. The fact that many of the hobbyists who achieve those goals are also from the working classes, never attended a university, and yet have found the time and energy to devote themselves to such endeavors with verve and success make the implications all the thicker.

Such engagement with non-European languages and cultures has a long history in the German-speaking lands, and so too does the search for community embodied in the creation of associations such as those established by the hobbyists. Beyond the buckskin, teepees, feathers, and beads, one finds not only an insatiable interest in all things Indian but also multigenerational communities that have persisted through a series of political regimes in which people meet, marry, raise children, and learn and create rituals that gain critical importance in their lives. Indeed, an ethnographic view into these meetings provides a glimpse into the broader phenomena of Germans' interests in American Indians, and an initial sense for the multifarious ways in which thinking about Indians has been a transcendent part of German cultures for a very long time.

On the most basic level, for the participants at The Week in Cottbus, who came overwhelmingly from the "new German states" of the former GDR, their particular community has persisted for generations, originating in the wake of World War 1 and continuing through the most radical ruptures in German political history. For many of them, that community is one thing, sometimes *the* thing, they were able to hold onto during times of repeated radical transformation, and it is something they have elected to do with great self-reflexivity. As with most groups of reenactors, or people engaged in revitalization movements, there is a hierarchy of authenticity and commitment that often holds sway in their meetings; but among many German hobbyists today there is also a growing sense of tolerance, a realization through decades of experience, that Europeans approach the study and emulation of American Indians in many ways, depending on their needs, and that those methods and the goals can change within individuals, not just from one person or one group to another. Their hobby is, in other words, both didactic and flexible, and a microcosm of the broader interests and needs that have fueled Germans' long fascination with Native America.

Not all Germans who share that fascination have been moved to fashion teepees or moccasins. Indeed, most have not. Nevertheless, the eager consumers of the Cooper novels in the nineteenth century, those who poured over May's books in the twentieth, the Weimar-era artists who returned to those narratives when trying to make sense of a fractured world, the Socialists and the Nazis who found different aspects of May's work to admire but who all esteemed his central characters shared certain assumptions about the world—about nobility, masculinity, modernity, tragedy, and, most importantly, the human condition.

Those shared assumptions have been articulated in a variety of ways and with countless anecdotes. For example, during a public debate in 1956 over the suitability of Karl May's books for socialist citizens of the GDR, one man recalled that "in the spring of 1945," when "Czech soldiers were searching houses in villages between Carlsbad and Eger," "five young soldiers" stormed into the house of "an old man who had traveled much of the world" and collected many things. They terrified the man and his wife, who expected the worst, until "one of the soldiers suddenly stopped in front of his bookshelves, called to the others," and pointed to the "sixty or so volumes of Karl May books" collected there. The old man began to talk about the books "until the first soldier sat on the arm of his chair with one of the books in his hand." They were captivated as he "recalled visiting the old Karl May in Radebeul" some forty years earlier. And when he "spread out photos, maps, and books in front of them," the "young men listened enthusiastically to his words" because "they had all read Karl May's books in either Czech or German." Only after they realized that much time had passed did they remove themselves from this old man, returning his property to him, "parting as friends," and "leaving him with a comforting memory of this difficult time."[18]

The veracity of this particular tale is difficult to determine, but the general assertion that people could relate to each other in the most trying of circumstances through shared interests in particular topics and texts is indisputable. Indeed, a central position of this book is that such shared points of reference—texts and tales about American Indians, knowledge about fictional characters and historically prominent individuals, the notions that run through those shared ideas, the intersubjectivity they create, and the experience of thinking about American Indians and the American West—have provided consistency across individual Germans' experiences of flux, rupture, and ebbing change that historians seeking to define and understand those changes often overlook.

It might strike readers as strange that many Germans felt such a strong affinity for American Indians over the past two centuries and that many of these Germans could and did turn to thinking about American Indians as a mode of dealing with crises and conflicts. It should not. Given American Indians' extensive presence in German cultures over the past two centuries, thinking about them offered a wide variety of individuals a method of grounding themselves in particular moments, and in successions of moments, over extensive periods of time. And that is another point of the book: in many ways "playing Indian" or simply thinking about American Indians goes to the very base of being "German" during the modern period, perhaps even more so than being American.[19]

Origins

My own interest in this topic stemmed in part from growing up in a family that came largely from Oklahoma and claimed a variety of American Indians in its genealogy. Like many Oklahomans with a Caucasian phenotype, my mother told tales of growing up in a family with relatives who were American Indians. I heard much about the collection of objects—knives, bowls, bows, guns, and in particular a fine beaded vest—in my grandfather's home, and of the tribal membership lost when his brother Wiley Gunter went drinking with the money meant to put the family on the Cherokee roles.

Genealogy is complicated. Moving back only five generations produces thirty-two ancestors, some of whom, in my family's case, were tied to one or more of the tribes forced into Indian Territory during the nineteenth century. Somehow, even as a child, I knew that did not make me an "Indian," but it did expose me to many personal stories from relatives like my aunt Maude, who reminisced about her childhood visits to Ben Whiteshield and his fam-

FIGURE 2. Charles E. Gunter and his vest near Pawnee, Oklahoma. (Property of the author)

ily near Canute, Oklahoma. I loved hearing how her father, whose hair extended to his waist, always "let it down when he went to sit with the Indians in their teepees," and how "the smoke from their fires almost burned out" her eyes. Maude's grandmother, and thus one of my great-grandmothers, was Maggie Triplet, a Cherokee, and according to Maude, "a beautiful lady."

Perhaps Maggie was the Indian princess my mother occasionally boasted about in ways that would have been familiar to Vine Deloria Jr. After World War II, he and other American Indian activists and scholars began noticing large numbers of "whites" eager to "proudly proclaim that he or she was of Indian descent." "Cherokee," he remarked, "was the most popular tribe of their choice," and people found them all over the United States, "from Maine to Washington State." Most of these "whites," he noted, also located those ancestors "on their grandmother's side." The reason, he argued, was that a male ancestor has too much of the aura of the savage warrior, the unknown primitive, the instinctive animal. . . . but a young Indian princess? Ah, there was royalty for the taking." At least Maggie Triplet was on my grandfather's side and lived in Oklahoma. But she was a she, as Deloria would have expected, and what I learned in college from reading his *Custer Died for Your Sins* was not only that many white Americans wanted to claim a connection to American Indians but that the family of my childhood embodied a stereo-type and lived a cliché.[20]

In the early 1990s, while conducting the research for my book on the history of German ethnology, Deloria's pronouncements made me sensitive to Germans' reactions to my ancestry and to similar clichés and tropes about American Indians in Europe. German academics, archivists, and others commonly asked about my family's origins when they learned that I spoke German and was interested in German history. When I confessed that I had no German lineage but rather stemmed from a mishmash of northwestern Europeans together with some smattering of American Indians, the reactions to the last bit were always the same: delight at being in the presence of "a real Indian." My discomfort with that reaction quickly taught me to change my answer to simply "some combination of English, French, and Welsh," even as I learned to pay more attention to Germans' interests in all things Indian.

After a short time in Germany, I also began to puzzle about a conspicuous absence in my research. During the nineteenth century, German ethnology produced the world's largest and most extensive ethnographic museums, some of its most impressive researchers, and even Franz Boas, the father of American anthropology, who went on to attract a number of equally famous German American disciples, such as Alfred Kroeber and Robert Lowie. And yet there was a striking paucity of material from Native North America in German ethnographic museums.[21] So few German researchers had traveled to the United States and Canada, and so much more attention had been paid to South America during the heyday of these institutions. In Cologne, for example, which placed its ethnographic collections in a building with a facade that included equal representations of an Asian, an African, and an American Indian (all male), only 3.4 percent of the collections came from North America. Those collections, however, were by far the museum's greatest attraction in the postwar era.[22] Conditions were initially similar in Stuttgart's Linden-Museum.[23] In Berlin, with the most extensive collections from North America in Germany, which included materials from Frank Hamilton Cushing, Alice Fletcher, Fred Harvey, Clark Wissler, and one of the richest assemblies of nineteenth-century Pacific Northwest artifacts in the world, its North American collections were, if we are to trust the guidebooks and curators' reports, overwhelmed by the rest of the collections. Indeed, it was not until the late 1990s that Peter Bolz was able to create a standing exhibit from those collections.[24]

Later, I understood that this absence was a product of the history of ethnology and ethnological theory rather than a lack of interest among Germans of any class or character. I also learned that there are many things such elite institutions fail to tell us about the production of knowledge in a given culture or its relationships with particular groups of people.[25] In fact, focusing on them can be misleading. Nineteenth-century German ethnologists believed that more could be gleaned through expeditions to the relatively "untouched" areas of South America and the Pacific than from North America. As a result, the directors of the American collections in German museums almost always specialized in Central and South America, or sometimes the Arctic, while North America received only limited attention in those institutions despite the popular interest.

Indeed, it was only after unification when popular interest became critical for the funding of German ethnographic museums that those institutions began harnessing American Indians and their artifacts for pedagogical purposes, popular entertainment, and increased revenues.[26] Thus, when I returned to Germany to begin this project in 2001, I not only found Peter Bolz's impressive exhibition on American Indian material culture and German cultural clichés in the Berlin museum;[27] I also found Hamburg's ethnographic museum encircled on one side by teepees and a sweat lodge, while on the other side, in front of the corner closest to the street, the museum had acquired a new twelve-meter-long totem pole fashioned by David Seven Deers out of a six-hundred-year-old cedar tree. In those teepees, the director of the museum, Wulf Köpke, faced with an impending funding crisis,[28] had begun hosting overnight campouts for children, complete with authentic "Indian tales," dance and drum lessons, a sweat, a mock bison hunt, and buffalo soup. The kitsch was astounding: "With the old ceremonies and the smoking of the pipe," their advertisement promised, the children "will be admitted into the Morningstar tribe."[29] Combined with that kitsch were overbearing gestures toward science, cultural exchange, and well-worn notions of authenticity—a Blackfoot artist from Montana painted one of the teepees for the museum.[30]

In its bookstore, I was also able to buy one of the remaining copies of the picture book issued to accompany the most recent exhibition on the museumgoers' favorite topic: Plains Indians.[31] That controversial exhibition, which ethnologist Christian Feest deemed "disgracefully underwhelming,"[32] touched all the most popular cords. It took place while Seven Deers, acting as his own living display, was completing his totem pole in the museum's courtyard, and as the exhibit came to a close at the end of August 1997, his pole was set in place in front of the building with great fanfare.[33] To distance the exhibition of historical artifacts from the (some argued) dubious character of the Western sciences that had brought them to Hamburg, to decrease the protests of local activists, and to increase its claims to authenticity and political correctness, the exhibition was consecrated by a prayer from Buster Yellow Kidney, characterized as "a wise, old medicine man from the Blackfoot nation in Montana," who had "advised [the museum] during the creation of the exhibition." Yellow Kidney also granted the museum two interviews for the exhibit's accompanying guide, in which he discussed his background and spiritual viewpoints, expressed his gratitude for being included, and explained how he, his wife, and David Seven Deers had prayed for the museum. He also discussed his concerns about Germans, whom he felt were in the midst of losing their traditions, and helped create a popular show out of a "disgracefully underwhelming" exhibition and boost visitor numbers, catalog sales, and the museum's revenues as well.[34] It took museum directors in Germany much longer than other people to realize that they could effectively utilize Germans' fascination with all things Indian for their own purposes. That action has been hotly debated. Yet there is no question that their successes spurred me to explore what was behind this enduring fascination: what were its origins, its characteristics, and its implications? The answers were more complex and poignant than I anticipated.

Elective Affinities

Many American Indians have long been aware of Germans' interest in them.[35] For generations, American Indian performers have returned from Germany delighted with their substantial salaries and exceptional treatment.[36] They spread the word. At the same time, however, even residents of Canadian reserves and American reservations who never left their hometowns have also become keenly aware of Germans' peculiar fascination for all things Indian—and not just through travelers' tales.[37]

Feel free to try this experiment: Ask a random selection of non-Native Americans about Karl May and his books and note the number of people outside of a university setting who have heard of him (probably not many). Then travel to one of the major reservations in the United States, such as the Pine Ridge Reservation in South Dakota, and ask the same questions. The chances are excellent that you will hear plenty, and with good reason. As sociologist Siegrid Deutschlander concluded in her study of aboriginal tourism in Canada, "If foreign visitors are present at Aboriginal tourism sites, they most likely are German."[38] American Indians living in those areas today have had Germans around them for most of their lives.

As a result, Germans' interest in all things Indian has begun to be reciprocated: many American Indians have become fascinated by the German fascination with them. Indeed, many wonder why the waves of Germans keep coming to the reservations full of idiosyncratic knowledge and penetrating questions. As one Hopi woman told me at Grand Canyon National Park in Arizona, "I always wonder why they look at me that way and what they are thinking."[39] Or, as a member of the Lakota Studies Department at Sinte Gleska University on the Rosebud Reservation asked me: "What about us interests them?" "Why do they come here?" "Is it because they are so lost?" "Did they also lose what we had before civilization?"[40]

Answering those questions and identifying the sources of affinity between Germans and American Indians is a critical part of this book. Such feelings of affinity have been widespread among Germans for generations, and increasingly during the twentieth century those feelings have gone both ways. It was not uncommon, for example, for German veterans in the 1950s or German peace activists in the 1970s to hear from groups of American Indians that they shared a joint victimization at the hands of the U.S. military.[41] Nor was it unusual for American Indians such as Buster Yellow Kidney in Hamburg or the American Indian Movement activist and International Indian Treaty Council member Jimmie Durham to note how both Germans and American Indians had lost their traditions to similar impersonal forces.[42] Other American Indians stress that Germans too came from a warrior society, an insight that embarrasses some contemporary Germans who have been schooled to reject militant nationalism,[43] while still others point to a similar connection to nature, or similar origins in powerful tribal cultures.

While scholars have acknowledged the prominence of such notions of affinity among Germans, they generally regard them as Germans' projections and fantasies.[44] Few have been willing to explore that sense of affinity as something other than self-delusion. Instead, they are more comfortable casting it as yet another manifestation of misguided national development or evidence of some limitation in German self-awareness. Moreover, very few scholars entertain the possibility that some American Indians might sense similar affinities as well. That has undermined their scholarship. For the fact that some American Indians have shared and do share some Germans' notions of affinity, and that they eagerly initiate discussions of the interconnections between Germans and themselves, makes it clear that there are good reasons for approaching those ideas of affinity as reasonable and rational connections before relegating them to fantasy, projection, and further telltale signs of German misdevelopment.

Tribal Polycentrism

Not all claims to special relationships between Germans and American Indians are equal, nor are any such claims universally valid. For example, some years ago, while demonstrating that German immigrants to North America lacked any particular or special relationship to American Indians, historian Colin Calloway reminded us that the German-speaking immigrants to the United States arrived from Austria, Hungary, Russia, Rumania, Yugoslavia, Switzerland, and Alsace, as well as from Imperial Germany after it was founded in 1871. Those immigrants, who made up about one-sixth of the new arrivals between 1830 and 1930, differed widely in religious denomination, politics, class, and culture, and they spoke a variety of dialects. "They entered Indian country," he stressed, "as individuals, families, and groups," and they "approached Indian country for much the same reasons as other Europeans did and behaved in much the same way as they did, and Indians responded to them accordingly."[45] Occasionally their marginal existence in colonial America allowed some Germans to develop particular relations with Indians, but those were generally based on highly specific contexts and were often fleeting. Germans, in short, never acted as a block. Their ostensibly unitary character was something other European immigrants and Anglo-Americans often imposed on them after they arrived, not something they brought with them, and because interactions between German immigrants and American Indians essentially ran the gamut, there could be no general claim for special affiliations.[46]

Calloway's point is well taken, but for more reasons than he may have imagined. So much of the scholarly analysis of German history has been framed by states, nations, and notions of nationalism that even the most sophisticated explorations of Germans' connections with American Indians (as well as most non-Europeans) have been dependent on the perception of Germans as a unitary group, as a national body, or a set of individuals who longed for inclusion in a nation-state. Calloway demonstrates the limitations of such conceptions. The irony, however, is that the fractured, composite nature of the German nation-state that took shape in the nineteenth century, with its motley collection of German speakers claiming a range of distinct connections to different indigenous traditions and particular locations and an aggregate unitary identity based largely on negative integration,[47] may be one of the things nineteenth-century German immigrants, as well as many of the Germans who remained in Central Europe, most shared with American Indians. Indeed, it may be a central point of affinity.

There was, of course, a general fascination with American Indians among Europeans. As ethnologist Christian Feest has repeatedly pointed out, the nostalgic pose or identification with the defeated, yet noble Native was never limited to Germans, and other Europeans continue to "play Indian" today as well.[48] There is, however, something different, perhaps profoundly different, about the Germans' consistent fascination with American Indians over the past two centuries that stems in part from the national experience, or rather the nonnational experience, that Calloway begins to illuminate, as well as other, longer trajectories in German cultural history. It is the polycentric character of German national and cultural identity combined with a history of resistance (putative and actual) toward Roman imperialism, Christianity, cultural homogenization, and a profound sense of loss stemming from that history that makes the German position particular.

During the process of transformation at large in Native America during the nineteenth century, many Germans saw an affinity, a loss of self, not unlike what many believed they and their ancestors experienced beginning with the hegemonic power of Roman civilization and the influx of Christianity and continuing through the oppressive modern structures that accompanied each successive economic system and state. Those structures had pressed Germans away from nature, away from more direct links to their ancestors, from the land and other species, from a more natural spirituality, and from an essential masculinity made explicit in Tacitus's descriptions of *Germania*, and into an increasingly material and often atomized world. Convinced that they too had experienced a kind of ethnocide in the past, and facing the creation of new, demanding states with almost every generation, many Germans were particularly sensitive to the mixed implications of assimilation facing American Indians during the past two centuries. Indeed, that sense of shared fate in the increasingly impersonal and hypermodern world of global capitalism may be the greatest affinity of all, and thus the central reason why so many Germans developed and retained an empathic fascination for American Indians.

Categories

As Robert Berkhofer noted long ago in *The White Man's Indian*, there was no unitary group of "Indians" awaiting or resisting European conquest in the Western Hemisphere. Nevertheless, from their earliest encounters, Europeans thought of American Indians as a collective entity, and regardless of what they learned about "the social and cultural diversity among the inhabitants of the Americas," the generic idea of "the Indian" took hold. According to Berkhofer, "general terms embracing stereotyped characteristics made sense to Whites" at the time, and these terms easily existed "alongside knowledge of specific societies with individual characteristics or of individuals with varying qualities." That coexistence was possible, he argues, because, for Europeans, "nations, races, and cultures were all basically seen as one interchangeable category for the understanding of peoples, and individuals were usually judged as members of their collectivity rather than as different, separate humans."[49] Hence one could experience a variety of different indigenous American peoples and cultures while still thinking of American Indians as a unitary group.

That tendency has continued among many Europeans and non-Native Americans to the present day. As Blackfoot author James Welch noted, modern readers are often dismayed to learn about battles between American Indians that worked so well to white advantage. Favoring the underdogs in the historic struggle for dominance in the Great Plains, these readers are just as often surprised to learn that Crows and Arikaras were on the "wrong side" of the righteous Battle of the Little Bighorn in 1876 and perplexed to discover that the Crows were eager to help the U.S. military find Lakota camps in the 1870s. Because they had been the victims of Lakota transgressions, Crows worked with the U.S. Calvary in a bid to get the best reservation lands after the Lakota had largely driven them from those territories. Later, in the 1880s, Cheyennes and even Lakotas helped to track and capture other Lakotas who had remained free and bring them onto reservations.[50] "The Indians," in other words, never acted in unison. In many cases, they were even decidedly fractured at the tribal level. And yet throughout those periods, and through continual descriptions of those periods in the twentieth century, scholars and laymen alike persisted in their use of the general term "Indians" to portray a varied assortment of people, to think in terms of "Indian wars" and "Indian resistance" when describing conflicts between Europeans and various groups of indigenous Americans. This persistent "use of the general term," wrote Berkhofer, "demanded" a general definition, "and this definition was provided by moral qualities as well as by description of customs. In short, character and culture were united in one summary judgment."[51]

Much the same could be said for Germans. During the nineteenth century, the Germans who remained in Central Europe were similar to those immigrants identified by Calloway. They were diverse and fractured, sometimes even tribal in their local orientations, often speaking mutually unintelligible dialects, and for much of the nineteenth century they were just as likely to find themselves on opposing sides of a European battlefield as united under one flag. That was the case even after the formation of Imperial Germany in 1871. The borders created by this new political entity excluded people who were German speaking, incorporated many who were multilingual, and contained many more whose identities were ambiguous.[52] In some cases, the new borders excluded German speakers living outside them, while including other language and ethnic groups within them—groups that were ultimately expected to assimilate and be absorbed.[53]

That process of nation making was never smooth. Indeed, James Retallack and David Blackbourn have convincingly argued that, across the nineteenth and twentieth centuries, "the political entity called Germany was so protean that German-speaking Europe seemed almost to serve as a laboratory for testing out different forms of state: Holy Roman Empire, German Confederation, Second Empire, Weimar Republic, Third Reich, Federal and Democratic Republics. Over the same period, the borders of Germany moved in and out like a concertina." No European nation-state shifted and changed as much as this one, and thus the label of "the Germans" remained ambiguous at best. For within that general term "German" (which, like "Indian," both required and defied definition) were various forms of collective identification—confessional, ethnic, national, political, and regional—combined within the minds of individuals in a variety of ways. Within the political borders of the different states, there were also always regions "whose inhabitants saw themselves, and were seen by others, as having a quite distinctive character" and who were not eager to assimilate. Thus there remained in Germany areas that were simultaneously frontier zones and heartlands, places where connections to local landscapes, communities, cultural practices, and dialects remained critical components in any negotiation. Resistance to any complete assimilation into a national unity, particularly within the cultural sphere, remained strong, and thus, during the imperial period, cultural affairs were left in the hands of the individual states, and cultural unity remained elusive.[54]

Resistance

That American Indians' resistance to assimilation has appealed to many Germans is perhaps understandable. A central trope in German fiction and nonfiction, and a critical characteristic that has long set American Indians apart from most other non-Europeans in the German imagination, is their ostensible unwillingness to be dominated and their committed resistance, stemming from their basic sense of freedom.[55] As the majority of Germans grew to understand them, American Indians could be conquered, but they could not be subjugated, they could not be made into a class of slaves or servants. Most preferred death.

As the philosopher Johann Gottlieb Fichte noted at the outset of the nineteenth century, Tacitus had reported much the same about the Germans in the first century C.E.:

> A Roman writer has their chieftains speak thus: "Is anything left for us but to assert our freedom or to die before we are enslaved?" Freedom meant to them that they remained Germans [Deutsche], that they continued to move forward in their development, and that they passed on this independence to their posterity. Slavery was the name they gave to those blessings that the Romans offered them, because by accepting these they could not but become something other than Germans; they would have to become half-Romans. It went without saying, they assumed, that every man would sooner die than become thus and that a true German could wish to live only in order to be and remain forever a German and to bring up his children as German also.[56]

The idea that American Indians, like these Germans, could be obliterated but not subjugated appears already in the early reports on conflict during the nineteenth century, on the so-called Indian wars that raged across the century until 1890, and on the precipitous decline in numbers of American Indians during the same period. In 1831, for example, the popular periodical *Das Ausland* reported that the declining population of *Indianer* in the United States was not only the result of the depopulation of wild animals by the fur trade and the ravages of European disease and alcohol but also the unwillingness of these truly free men to forsake that freedom and adopt a necessarily arduous and servile life under European American civilization. The essayist regarded philanthropic attempts at drawing them into that regimented lifestyle through the education of their youths as admirable, but considered it almost certainly doomed to failure because these youths all shared "an indifference to death and an immutable tenacity of will" that makes them difficult to guide toward a more docile existence under the auspices of some political state, especially when so many tribes' men had been raised "completely for warfare and the hunt." Anything else, he wrote, is beneath them, and they will not conform. To do so, the author implied, would be to lose their very sense of self.[57]

Across the nineteenth century, German periodicals reported, or rather purported, the unwillingness of American Indians to accept European or European American *Herrschaft* [domination] in much the same way, with a combination of melancholy and admiration, and with occasional outbursts of condemnation over the United States' Indian policy.[58] In this sense, nineteenth-century Germans shared Euro-Americans' more general conviction that American Indians were essentially "a vanishing race." The difference, however, is that Germans often wrote about this ostensible demise with more anger, with an admonishing tone, and with more remorse than their positivist counterparts. Moreover, they tended to attribute that demise to a set of admirable characteristics rather than essential limitations inherent in these people.

Furthermore, the way in which German periodicals reported the conflicts between American Indians and the U.S. military, captured for decades under the rubric of "the Indian wars," made it easy for German readers to imagine the unitary resistance of American Indians across a long period of time in different parts of the continent. The periodicals portrayed each conflict as the most recent battle in a long and terrible war, making it difficult for German readers to see these conflicts as a succession of subjugations of unique peoples who were largely unaware of similar conflicts in other parts of North America.

To Germans, however, it seemed that American Indians, while losing many of these battles, were nevertheless holding out somewhere. During the final decades, that was on the Great Plains. When these "Indian wars" came to an end with the Wounded Knee massacre in 1890, most Germans accepted that the frontier was indeed closed as the last resisters succumbed, and as a result, the coverage of American Indians in German periodicals waned precipitously. The overriding assumption was that the remnants of the resisters would ultimately fade away in seclusion on their reservations now that any chance of armed struggle had ended. Indeed, that assumption was almost universal, and thus reports from the "last of the plains warriors" remained popular for quite some time, and people claiming to be those "last warriors" were eagerly received as popular guests in Germany for decades.

In the middle of the twentieth century, however, as increasing population numbers demonstrated that claims of American Indians' demise had been premature, many Germans responded with elation to American Indians' resurgence on and off the reservations. Not only were they delighted to learn that the objects of their affections were still there in the postwar period, but they also began remarking that these survivors, indeed, these ultimate resisters who had persisted essentially under everyone's radar, had much to teach Germans. For example, in one 1963 history of Native America from the Ice Age to the present, Berndt Banach wrote that, although "it was said at the end of the last century that the Indians must be characterized as a 'dying man,'" it had become clear that the population of "different tribes was increasing." "The Indian," he wrote, "is not conquered." Their "heroes did not suffer in vain. Their sacrifice was not senseless," and their "self-preservation is a proud example for humanity!"[59]

Indeed, the example of long-term American Indian resistance and resurgence gave many Germans like Banach the hope that they too might overcome similar challenges in the modern world. Therefore, in the following decades German peace activists and environmentalists, the emerging Green Party, and others sought to harness the experience and knowledge of American Indian resisters, and brought some of them to Europe to advise and teach willing listeners. Representatives of the American Indian Movement (AIM) were welcomed in East and West Germany alike. Germans cast both street fighters and traditionalists as sage teachers who might aid them in their modern struggles with their own states to salvage their landscapes, combat corporate power, and protect their own individuality from the corrupting powers of so-called civilization. And as they did that, they acted within a rather long German tradition.

Organization, Methods, and Goals

This book has two parts. Part I proceeds in a roughly chronological fashion, sketching out the origins and development of a sense of kinship for American Indians embraced by many Germans across the nineteenth and into the twentieth century. It stresses that these Germans' attractions to American Indians were channeled and shaped by people living in a transatlantic sphere of Germanophone cultures, which I designate as an ebbing and flowing *Kulturkreis*,[60] who participated in a transcultural production of ideas, images, and notions about American Indians. It also demonstrates that Germans' contributions to this process were based not only on musings and fantasies about America and the American West but also on a wide range of experiences and realities on both sides of the Atlantic.

Part II, however, is organized thematically: it underscores the ways in which many of the consistent and persistent dispositions in the German discourse about American Indians that took shape in the nineteenth century remained relevant in the twentieth century, informing Germans' reactions to events in both Europe and the United States. It also draws out the implications of those consistencies for the ways in which we narrate German history, especially the degree to which that narrative is punctuated by radical cultural, political, and social ruptures. Essentially, it argues that we should push beyond such narrative structures and pay greater attention to the consistencies that flow through them and the alternative stories they reveal.

Much of the initial argumentation in this book harnesses the actions and experiences of individuals to illustrate the breadth and depth of German affinities for American Indians as they developed over time. While some of the individuals, such as Karl Bodmer and Maximilian von Wied, are included because they helped fashion German (and non-German) ideas about American Indians, many of the others did not. Quite a few, such as Rudolf Cronau, had no significant impact on what intellectual historians might term "German thought" or Germans' ideas about American Indians. Nevertheless, they remain important; their actions capture the impact of those ideas, which they often helped to channel and perpetuate more than to shape. Thus, Cronau's writings, for example, like many of the others that appear in these pages, are as much the output as the input of those ideas, and they should be regarded as part of the reception (quite literally the affirmation and promotion) of a German discourse on American Indians as well as one of the ways in which the affinities at the heart of that discourse were transmitted over time.

Similarly, I should underscore that this book is first and foremost about transnational German cultures and histories. I have gone to great pains to become familiar with American Indian history and the history of the American West, and I have pursued American Indians' reactions to Germans' interests and actions as well as their interactions with Germans wherever and whenever I could. That was often challenging, and I hope that people who are primarily interested in Native American studies and American history will find my analysis of the relationships between Germans and American Indians helpful. I also hope they will recognize, however, that this book turns around Germans' actions, interactions, and perceptions, and that my engagement with Germans' evaluations of the relationships between American Indians and the U.S. government, for example, should not be misconstrued as an objective rendition of those relationships.

That said, recognizing the sources of affinity and moments of exchange between members of these summative groups over a long period of time is a critical component of this book. It seeks to move past the kinds of binary models made popular by recent studies of German and non-German colonialism that depend so heavily on the notions of colony, metropole, and the formative roles of states. Instead, it tries to understand the joint recognition of a common fate that emerged out of ongoing discussions of shared characteristics among members of these groups over a long period of time. During the nineteenth century, those connections were often tenuous, primarily historical, and sometimes fanciful. By the end of the twentieth century, they became less curious and more urgent. Indeed, with the increased levels of communication and exchange among political activists at the end of the twentieth century, and with the overwhelming weight of military devastation in the memories of many Germans after World War II, this long relationship came to fruition. Germans and American Indians who were reacting against the dangers imposed on their lives by the precarious shifts of global capitalism and the machinations of their respective nation-states looked to each other for assistance while building on older notions of a shared fate for legitimization.

That led, for example, to fiery pronouncements by a young Winona LaDuke, who would later become the American Green Party's candidate for vice president in the 2000 presidential election, about the shared character, challenges, and goals of American Indian and German activists. Praising the seriousness of German activists, whom she stressed had experienced military and industrial devastation, she wrote in 1983 that "in North America it seems that only the Indian, who has also trod the path along the edge of national extermination, holds a similar perception of the true urgency of the contemporary [political and environmental] situation. The Germans have to an amazing extent understood this: hence, their affinity with things Indian." By the same token, she stressed: "Indians more and more are noting, 'Of all other peoples today, the Germans have recognized the danger of our peril, and they've tried to stop it.'"[61] Explaining the long-term development of these positions and the implications of their adoption in more and less radical forms by a wide array of American Indians and Germans is one of the central challenges engaged by this book.

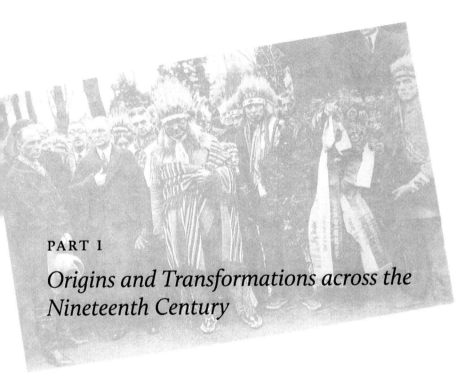

PART I

Origins and Transformations across the Nineteenth Century

In 1951 Hans Plischke's *From Cooper to Karl May* set the stage for a half century of literary analysis. Presenting a genealogy of German authors of "ethnographic novels" set in Native America, he argued that romanticism led Germans to develop an interest in these books at the outset of the nineteenth century. They "took readers into the past, into the communal life of earlier times," and "immersed them in natural landscapes." James Fenimore Cooper's *Leatherstocking Tales*, he explained, experienced particular success because of the quality of Cooper's writing and the fact that "a weariness with European politics and society" had increased Germans' interest in America and American Indians.[1] In turn, Cooper's success generated a long series of German emulators, including Charles Sealsfield, Friedrich Gerstäcker, Balduin Möllhausen, and ultimately Karl May. Plischke's narrative was marked by their personalities, but it was driven by evaluations of accuracy and notions of authenticity as much as literary skills, and it took its most striking turn in the shift from travel narratives and novels based on romanticized experiences to the pulp fiction and fantastic tales epitomized by May. That trend, in his opinion, was corrected only during the interwar years, with authors such as Fritz Steuben, who ostensibly strove for authenticity, and the translation of autobiographical books by the Santee Sioux Charles Eastman, which became immediate classics in Germany.[2]

There is, however, a story behind Germans' interests and eventual obsession with American Indians that informed the production, character, and reception of these novelists' tales, but it remains obscured by such genealogies. For the German fascination with American Indians took shape within multiple, shifting contexts in both Europe and the United States: America and Native America witnessed radical transformations during the nineteenth century; political structures in German-speaking Central Europe shifted mightily during this period as well; and during the later third of the century, so too did relationships between Imperial Germany (founded in 1871) and the United States. At the same time, the astounding influx of millions of German immigrants into the United States during the middle third of the century led to the expansion of a German Kulturkreis (an uneven linguistic-cultural area) across the Atlantic and a concomitant increase in many Germans' ease of movement within the United States and back and forth across the ocean.

Consequently, as the next chapter shows, the production of ideas, notions, and beliefs about American Indians within this Germanophone world were not so much transnational (for they predated the creation of the German nation-state considerably) but transcultural: many of the most iconographic images of Native America, for example, were fashioned by Germans in America, or by German Americans on both sides of the Atlantic. Literature and art produced within the context of cultural expansion, however, were only part of the story. Indeed, by the end of the century, groups of American Indians themselves were traveling ever more frequently to Europe, helping to channel and shape the discourse on America and American Indians within Imperial, and later Weimar, Germany.

As the German fascination with American Indians emerged and developed within these contexts, it nurtured notions of affinity between Germans and American Indians—especially Germans' admiration for American Indian resistance. Those notions easily accommodated even the most violent clashes between members of these two conglomerate groups. Despite travelers' importance to this discourse, Germans were not always outside observers of either American settler colonialism or American Indians' efforts at resistance. Indeed, as chapter 3 makes clear, they could be both victims and perpetrators of the worst kinds of violence. But even the most terrible of those could be folded, sometimes quite quickly, into the German discourse on American Indians as it took shape in both Europe and the United States. Thus, those notions of affinity stemmed from neither Germans' putative colonial fantasies nor some Germans' experiences with harsh colonial realities. Rather they persisted in spite of those realities, and they owed much to many

German Americans' often-antagonistic relationships with their Anglophone counterparts in the United States, as well as the vision of "the Yankee" that took shape in German-speaking Central Europe.

Shifting cultural contexts, the end of the "Indian Wars," even radical transformations of the American landscape could be accommodated as well—although they left traces. In particular, the decline of German America toward the end of the nineteenth century and the watershed of World War I, which effectively truncated the transatlantic German Kulturkreis, had a tremendous impact on Germans' relationships with America and American Indians. People such as Rudolf Cronau, who pursued a transnational life through this transitional era, were keenly aware of the rising importance of national categories for their own subject positions. Some recognized that those shifts recast their worldviews. Thus, as chapter 4 shows, the transition in the literature identified by Plischke at the end of the century certainly took place, but it reflected a transition in possibilities as well as literary production—Germans and German Americans had fewer chances for lived experience among American Indians, there were fewer examples of American Indian resistance to celebrate, and increasing numbers of German Americans began regarding themselves as first and foremost American. The Kulturkreis was dissolving.

Thus, 1890–1936 was a transitional era in which many of the contexts that initially shaped German interests in American Indians changed: the end of the so-called Indian wars, the emergence of an increasingly nationalistic and belligerent German nation-state, the resulting decline in relations between the United States and Imperial Germany, the loss of World War I and the elimination of Imperial Germany, and ultimately the brutal division of the transatlantic German Kulturkreis all mattered a great deal for Germans' attitudes about America. These crisis situations, however, did not undercut German obsessions with American Indians, nor did they alter their most central characteristics. Rather, as chapter 5 illustrates, they facilitated their articulation in a new, more modernist key.

The purpose of these first chapters is thus twofold: on the one hand, they seek to explain the origins of Germans' affinities for American Indians and their development across the nineteenth century while sketching out their consistent characteristics; on the other hand, they also work toward respatializing our conceptions of "Germany" and German history during this period by acknowledging the important interconnections between the indeterminacy of Germany inside Europe and the sprawling diversity of the German presence overseas.

CHAPTER 1

From Cooper to Karl May—Recast

Germany's black hills, the Elbsandsteingebirge, are replete with picturesque sandstone pillars jutting out of pristine forests textured by wide valleys, steep canyons, and imposing mesas. Much like in the Black Hills of South Dakota, tourists flock to the forests during the summer and take to the trails that wind through the narrows and up the stone faces. Inspiring romantic painters such as Caspar David Friedrich and the earliest landscape photographers, the mesas, hills, and outcroppings between Dresden and Prague are littered with impressive monuments. The carvings in these stones, however, are nothing like Mount Rushmore. Instead, castles and their ruins abound.

Perched high above a bend in the Elbe River, for example, the Königstein Fortress covers an entire mesa and dominates the region below it. Drawing upward of 700,000 tourists a year, this medieval fortress, which was passed from Bohemian to Saxon kings in 1408, contained a monastery as well as a garrison, and with its constantly updated fortifications, it was considered unconquerable for centuries. Today, while drinking beer with tourists in the mesa-top gardens, it is easy to envision late nineteenth-century romantics embracing the more natural, medieval world of their forefathers as they walked through the surrounding forests and valleys, across the sturdy wooden bridges, and toward the outcropping of rock near Bielatal known as "The Apache's Face."

A sign near that rock, which reaches up over the Felsenkeller Inn, explains that guests at the nearby spa, "Kurbad Schweizermühle," enraptured by Karl May's 1893 novel and his hero the Apache chief Winnetou, claimed to see his face in the "aesthetic profile" of the stone. The sign, however, tells us much more. It reveals that, in addition to reminiscing about European pasts while walking these romantic trails by medieval monuments, nineteenth-century

German tourists spent their time thinking about North American pasts and presents. They did so with a shared knowledge of North American landscapes and indigenous inhabitants, and that knowledge, acquired through images, texts, and conversations, allowed the majority to easily recognize the outcropping, familiar as they believed themselves to be with American Indians and their profiles.

One wonders, however, what these leisured classes actually knew about American Indians. What was the origin of the consensus that allowed the name on this stone to persist for more than a century after the first ambling Germans identified it in the 1890s?

It began with a triumvirate: Cornelius Tacitus, Alexander von Humboldt, and James Fenimore Cooper; but it took the ongoing interactions between Germans, America, and Native America across the nineteenth century to bring that consensus to completion.

Tacitus

"If you want to understand Germans' fascination with Indians, you should read Tacitus." I received this advice in 2003 from a German man who had been adopted by an Assiniboine family at the Fort Peck Reservation in Montana. It is a useful assignment. In *Germania*, written at the end of the first century C.E., the Roman senator Cornelius Tacitus portrayed Germans as a noble tribal people with a clear connection to the forests and lands of Central Europe, who suffered at the hands of an expansive, colonial civilization. Indeed, he wrote about Germans in much the same way German authors would later write about American Indians, as noble savages and formidable, violent warriors with painted faces, living in forest dwellings, whose most honorable qualities exposed the decadence and failings of the civilized world. And, like many Germans who later wrote about American Indians during the nineteenth and twentieth centuries, he got many things wrong.[1] Those errors and misunderstandings, however, matter less than the fact that his work became an influential point of reference for a range of Germans seeking to better understand themselves and their place in the world. Tacitus's portraits of tribal Germans as fearless, honest, unflinching, loyal, and physically powerful made comparisons to American Indians natural. Already in the seventeenth century, for example, German writers conflated the ancient Teutons portrayed by Tacitus with contemporary American Indians, and by the middle of the nineteenth century such comparisons circulated widely, coupled in many cases with the sufferings of the German populations during the Thirty Years' War (1618–48).[2]

Those comparisons were possible because Tacitus was rediscovered and introduced to German intellectuals in the fifteenth century during debates about the relationship between Germans and Rome. As Suzanne Marchand reminds us, the history of the Roman Empire "was fraught with fundamental questions about Germany's autonomy, identity, and world-historical role," and when Pope Pius II harnessed Tacitus's then unknown text *Germania* to criticize that role, German humanists took advantage of its exposure and quickly "mined it for their own purposes." Arminius or Hermann, who defeated the Romans in the Teutoburg Forest in 9 C.E., became the new Ur-hero, and the emerging humanist literature "dwelt on themes that were to prove remarkably durable." "The Germanic love of liberty, so passionate as to outweigh material or personal concerns, and so fatal to the creation of a united anti-Roman front," she writes, "was set against Roman tyranny, greed, love of luxury, and calculating pragmatism, all flaws that both explained the nation's success in conquest and prepared it for its falls from grace." During the second half of the eighteenth century, Protestant intellectuals drew again on Tacitus to oppose Francophile neoclassicism, and between 1807 and 1814 "attempts were made to found journals with names like *Germania*, *Hermann*, and *Thusnelda* (Hermann's Queen), and at least seventy-two publications were devoted to the Teutoburg Forest battle between 1809 and 1900."[3] German nationalists embraced these images and the conception of united German tribes with a superior character, and the popular reception of Richard Wagner's operas that turned around these themes demonstrates that by the 1880s a "descent from 'barbarians'" had become "less an embarrassment than a point of pride."[4]

It was, however, not simply nineteenth-century nationalists of Wagner's ilk who tapped into Tacitus's reports. Johann Gottfried Herder, Marchand explains, "ran ahead of his time in denouncing the enervating effect of Roman conquest on German culture,"[5] and he too made connections between the German tribes of the past and contemporary American Indians. In his *Philosophy of Language* (1772), for example, he argued that "we Germans would still, like [Native] Americans, live quietly in our forests, or rather still roughly war and be heroes in them, if the chain of foreign culture had not pressed so near to us and compelled us with the force of whole centuries to participate in it." With this proto-diffusionist argument, Herder painted that conquest of the German tribes as part of a regrettable but almost inevitable process, one that began long before the Romans rose to power and might "some day stretch over the earth."[6] The military and economic strength of well-organized and centralized civilizations, he realized, had ultimately won out again and again over loosely organized tribal peoples, even if the individual civilizations, such as the Romans, also faded away. Such broad historical trends ultimately brought a loss of distinctions, driven as they were by homogenizing forces. That, of course, was central to Herder's point; he sought out the distinctions being lost by both European and non-European cultures during his own time and attempted to use them to shed light on humanity and its character.

The sense of connection to tribal societies and warrior cultures facilitated by Tacitus's text and harnessed over the early modern and modern periods persisted well into the postwar era and continues today. Even during the imperial period (1871–1918), during the height of nation making, it was common for Germans to envision their new state as first and foremost an aggregate, based, in many cases, on a collection of tribes [Stämme]. These German tribes, defined in a variety of ways as regional, ethnic, linguistic, and cultural groups, were often evoked during political debates at the national and regional levels from the middle of the nineteenth century until well into the 1920s.[7] This rhetoric of German tribalism, with its references to Tacitus, also persisted through the period of National Socialism, even if it was turned to new, more exclusionary, racial arguments. That made the terminology fall out of favor, if not out of mind, in the postwar period. Nevertheless, its importance continued, and not simply for nationalists, but for a variety of people seeking to define German character by looking deep into the past.

Thus it has remained common to read statements by people such as Ursel Hahn in Erlangen, who wrote to a periodical in 1967 that "our own people in earlier times exhibited traits and characteristics similar to that of Indians." "Indian and German tribes," she continued, distinguished themselves through "a close bond with nature and a strong clannishness," and they "shared certain ideals," among which she listed: "boldness, bravery, honor, fidelity, and sincerity." Because of those connections, she wrote, she felt "a great sympathy for the Indians" after reading how they too had undergone "such a tragic fate in their history," moving from being "masters of their lands" to being "horribly displaced, often robbed of a sufficient means of existence," and "never recognized as equals in the world of the whites."[8] The similarity between her assessments and those of other Germans across the nineteenth and twentieth centuries demonstrates the enduring quality of the notion that German and American Indian tribes shared such clear affinities.

Bildung and Humboldtian Worldviews

Self-edification, or *Bildung*, a common goal among the German literate classes at the outset of the nineteenth century, combined well with the prevalent sense of Germans' destiny as a conglomerate of tribal peoples.[9] Indeed, in many cases it was the effort at gaining *Bildung* that led many Germans to read Tacitus in the first place and then encouraged them to seek out other means of exploring the German past.[10] A key component of Germans' attachment to *Bildung* was often a corresponding desire to gain and demonstrate a sense of worldliness, a characteristic that was present among literate Germans long before the nineteenth century.[11] They expected to glean that worldliness through the acquisition of knowledge from both study and experience. The person who most exemplified this ideal was the Prussian naturalist and explorer Alexander von Humboldt, who traveled to the Americas from 1799 to 1804 and produced a series of erudite and popular writings based on those travels until his death in 1859. The most notable of these was his five-volume work *Cosmos*, which began to appear in 1845 and went through innumerable editions across the Western world.

Humboldt's exploits captured the imagination of Germans in Central Europe and was admired and praised in the United States. Americans named countless towns, counties, forests, wilderness areas, bodies of water, and other things after him. His books quickly sold out, and he was incredibly influential. Indeed, historian Aaron Sachs argues that "almost all American scientists in the mid-to-late nineteenth century . . . considered themselves disciples of Humboldt," and "virtually all Americans who studied Indians in the first half of the nineteenth century" began with him.[12]

The same could be said about most German-speaking explorers and scientists.[13] There is no question that Humboldt's example encouraged many Germans to look to the Americas, to examine the materials about them carefully, and to travel there, if they could. Regardless of where they went, his example encouraged those Germans to consider the interconnections of the peoples and places they encountered and how they related to their own places of origin. He promoted open-minded voyages of self-discovery as well as explorations of foreign territory, and his example inspired many to pursue those efforts from a cosmopolitan position rather than from a sense of aggressive nationalism and conquest.

That is a critical point, because it opens up our assumptions about exploration and reminds us that not all explorers, German or otherwise, sought territory or possessions. Following a particular strain of Enlightenment thought that he shared with Herder, one that is too often overlooked among historians of Germany,[14] Humboldt took a strong stance against the excesses of empire, speaking out against ecological abuses and in favor of American Indians.[15] To his mind, the goal of exploration was not conquest but the accumulation of empirical data about the wider world and assistance in bringing that material together into a useful body of knowledge.

Humboldt's example had a tremendous impact on the methods and goals of German ethnologists as their profession took shape in the second half of the nineteenth century.[16] Even much earlier, however, the essays on America and American Indians in German journals such as *Das Ausland*, *Globus*, and *Über Land und Meer* showed indications of the same influence. They became more reflective, more interested in Humboldtian modes of inquiry, and more suspicious of reports that lacked them.

In 1830, for example, a translation of an English travel narrative titled "Adventure among the Indians," which appeared in *Das Ausland*, began with the translator's discussion of the author, John Tanner. The translator, sounding much like leading German ethnologists some fifty years later, stressed that most of the people who penned such travel narratives had little or no understanding of American Indian languages and thus produced "nothing more than the most superficial impressions of Indians, saturated with completely false assumptions about their character." As a result, he argued, "we first embellish these natural peoples with the magic of romantic poetry and then we see them debased as inhuman barbarians."[17] To the author's mind (already in 1830), such clichéd dichotomies of noble and ignoble savagery could be resolved only by travelers such as Tanner who were willing to spend "as much time as necessary" among a group of American Indians until the "understandable mistrust of the foreign disappears," and they can gain insight into "the colorful mixture of good and bad, of virtue and vice" that make up their personalities. With those insights and the accompanying information, one could surpass the kinds of impressions about American Indians commonly gleaned "through Cooper's novels," which "in some respects," give readers "a limited [or low] understanding of their character."

That argument is critical. It not only demonstrates the translator's call for information gleaned from superior empirical methods, imploring Germans to travel for themselves, to stay in faraway places, and to learn about other peoples, but also evokes and critiques James Fenimore Cooper, the man most responsible for transforming the interests of some elite members of German society into a widespread, popular phenomenon. It was indeed Cooper who gave most Germans a point of departure from which to engage American Indians.

Cooper

If Tacitus provided many Germans with a historic link between themselves and American Indians, and Humboldt offered an example for how to engage them, it was unquestionably James Fenimore Cooper who completed this triangle of origins by inspiring German imaginations with his finely crafted tales.[18] In the United States, Cooper was the first American author to support himself by writing, the first to produce a frontier novel, and the first to achieve international fame. He was easily the most translated American author in Germany and ranked in the top ten of anyone's list of popular foreign authors.[19] Through the countless reproduction of Cooper's novels, the German fascination with American Indians became heightened and widespread.[20]

Cooper's *Leatherstocking Tales* turns around the adventures of Natty Bumppo, a white man raised among American Indians. Like his Mohican 'brother' Chingachgook, he was a fearless fighter with extensive wilderness skills and great respect for the forests and their inhabitants. He was well known for his unmatched skill with his long rifle and was often referred to as "Hawkeye"; but he hunted only what he needed, and he fought only when provoked, and only with those engaged in wrongdoing. His life was framed by both the sublime beauty of nature and ethical and moral dilemmas that accompanied its veritable destruction by the forces of European civilization pressing across North America during the second half of the eighteenth century. In that sense, the *Leatherstocking Tales* offered readers a parable of modernity, one that had great appeal.

These were by no means the first stories about American Indians to be read in Germany; but for many Europeans, Cooper offered something new. In contrast to the more romantic tales of François-René de Chateaubriand's idealized American Indians, for example, Cooper's characters struck Europeans as more realistic and were regarded as truer to their subjects.[21] They also offered an alternative to the oppressive world of the Restoration, the period following the Napoleonic Wars during which Central Europe suffered under the yoke of reactionary rulers and the Austrian Chancellor Klemens von Metternich's Carlsbad decrees. That oppressive political environment led many republicans in the German states to turn to American themes to express their discontent, to set their notions of democratic freedom against the realities of the police states. Reading Cooper, who had no need to fear German censors, allowed these people to think about environments characterized by an almost Eden-like natural landscape and a world of uncompromising self-reliance and freedom.[22] Talking and writing about Cooper provided a means for communicating with each other about these virtues as well. Cooper offered them multiple points of comparison.

As some scholars have argued, Cooper's volumes also allowed some Germans to reflect on earlier periods of German history—on Teutonic knights, medieval legends, and times in which values such as chivalry and boldness played a greater role in society.[23] At the same time, he pressed them to think about their present and future, to juxtapose their own positions with those of Americans as well as other Europeans.[24]

Such contrasts resonated with German readers beset by radical social change. Many of Cooper's characters embody a quintessentially American pragmatism that contrasts greatly with the ideal characteristics of his heroic American Indians. Those contrasts informed the violent transformation of natural spaces he portrayed in his tales and, allegorically, many places Germans knew well. Indeed, Cooper was not only an idealist who could help German readers conjure up images of the past but also a witness to contemporary transformations on the other side of the Atlantic that reminded them of changes in Europe's past and present. He also provided them with an appealing contrast to the society and polity that circumscribed their lives. In addition, he offered them insights into America as well as American Indians, even as he placed those American Indians at the center of moral questions about the future of the world, of *their* world.[25]

What followed from this triangulation of origins of the German obsession with American Indians was a remarkable surge of inspiration and efforts at emulation, which spurred many Germans to travel like Humboldt, to write like Cooper, and to seek out the tribal peoples of North America, who had not yet succumbed to the fate of their own European ancestors.

German Humboldts and Noble Indians

Nobles were the first to arrive as independent travelers eager to emulate Humboldt's courage and adventures. Some, such as Duke Paul Wilhelm of Württemberg, who traveled more than one thousand miles along the Missouri River in 1821, shared Humboldt's dedication to scientific principles and his cosmopolitan perspective. They devoted themselves to acquiring exacting information about the peoples they met to share with erudite audiences across Europe and the United States.[26] They did this by traveling through landscapes in the midst of cultural and political flux, encountering tribes such as the Iowa and the Sauks, who were in the throes of negotiating and fighting with a range of other tribes, settlers, and representatives of the United States. On occasion, they also witnessed violent encounters between groups further up the Missouri, such as the Blackfoot, Cree, and Crow, which accompanied these tribes' shifting access to trade goods and the transformations brought on in their relationships, as some, such as the Lakota, gained more power with more horses.[27]

Prince Maximilian von Wied-Neuwied was easily the most influential of these nobles. A student of Johann Friedrich Blumenbach, who counted Humboldt as his mentor, he led a successful expedition to southeast Brazil from 1815 to 1817. Then, in 1832, when he was already in his fifties, he set out on what became one of the most important expeditions by a German naturalist to the Great Plains of North America.

His companion was essential to his fame. Having glimpsed some of the Great Plains' potential, Humboldt had called for an artist who could do justice to the vast American landscapes. Maximilian found that artist in Karl Bodmer. With the help of Maximilian's exacting eye and his commitment to Humboldtian science, this Swiss artist produced some of the most iconographic images of the people they encountered on North America's Great Plains.[28]

Beginning in St. Louis, they traveled up the Missouri as far as Fort McKenzie, near Great Falls, Montana. They remained at Fort McKenzie for three months, interacting almost daily with the different bands of Blackfoot camped around it and witnessing, at one point, a battle between a group of some six hundred Assiniboines and Crees who attacked the Blackfoot outside the fort.[29] Bodmer painted and sketched these encounters, and he became adept at convincing individuals to sit for his portraits. Maximilian took extensive notes on everything, while collecting examples of flora, fauna, geological information, and ethnographica.

Knowing that conditions would be too dangerous for them to travel further north, they spent the winter in miserable quarters down river near Fort Clark, in what is today North Dakota. There, Maximilian encountered the Mandan and their allies the Hidatsas, whom he termed "the most beautiful, powerfully built people of all ages and sexes." Both groups were under tremendous pressure from disease, more mobile tribes such as the Lakota, settlers, and the U.S. government.[30] When Maximilian met them, however, they had not yet been devastated by the infamous smallpox epidemic of 1837–38.[31] They were vibrant and impressive, dressed in "highly distinctive, finely worked and stylized costumes." "The Hidatsas," he wrote, "really are the largest and best formed Indians of the entire course of the Missouri; in this respect as in the elegance of their dress only the Crows can compare, though they perhaps exceed even them in the latter regard."[32]

These encounters and impressions were critical. For after Maximilian and Bodmer had published the account of their travels, Germans would understand what such comparisons meant, and over the course of the nineteenth and twentieth centuries the images they created of these formidable and handsome people would become a central component in the German lexicon of knowledge about American Indians.

In essence, Bodmer and von Wied codified the image of the noble plains warrior, the embodiment of Cooperesque Indians, by producing one of the last of the great, illustrated travel narratives of the era.[33] The two-volume narrative *Travels in Inner North America in the Years 1832 to 1834* was based on Maximilian's journals and was issued serially in Koblenz beginning in 1839. When complete, it was accompanied by "a deluxe atlas containing the finest engravings that Paris craftsmen could produce."[34]

It is worth noting how these highly influential volumes came about; they were a transcultural, or at least cosmopolitan, production. Just as Humboldt returned to Paris to write up his work, the Swiss artist Bodmer turned to French engravers in Paris to help complete the illustrations for his German patron's volumes, which were published in German, French, and English editions. The plates for the atlas took shape over a long period of time (some eight years after the journey itself) and many of them went through multiple revisions.[35]

There is also no question that Bodmer's images of sublime landscapes and noble warriors were in many ways a joint project. His plates were influenced by his patron, his publisher, and his initial audience and by the hands of the many craftsmen who produced the engravings. Maximilian, in particular, exerted great influence, approving and disapproving even minute changes to the plates. He was particularly critical of ethnographic details, but he was also interested in the aesthetics of the plates, making a point to exclude European artifacts and clothing from most of the portraits of American Indians and insisting on landscapes and individuals that were pleasing to the eye, setting the tone for subsequent artists of all nations.

Once released, the books and images took on lives of their own. Complete copies of the book first reached the United States in 1843, but they were not for the general public. The price of $120 (the equivalent of $2,855.89 in 2004) made them available only to libraries, government institutions, and the wealthy. The *Commercial Advertiser* in New York called it "the most elaborate and costly work on the geography and scenery of North America ever published."[36] Humboldt gave it a ringing endorsement.[37]

In the United States, where the images were not protected by copyright, the plates began appearing in periodicals and magazines. Some were copied in Mexico, and they could be found in German journals as well.[38] Indeed, over the course of the nineteenth and twentieth centuries, Bodmer's images (as drawings, watercolors, etchings, and prints) have appeared in museums and libraries across Europe and the United States, and they continue to be reproduced both legally and illicitly in a range of books, periodicals, prints, posters, and calendars.[39] His noble images had an enduring appeal.

In the wake of such ventures, came a host of lesser-known Germans from across Central Europe. Inspired by Humboldt's example, but lacking his and other nobles' access to wealth and influence, they quickly became integrated into American enterprises. Georg Karl Ludwig Preuss, for example, known as Charles Preuss in the United States, was a typical transitional figure, a Humboldtian without a noble pedigree who worked for, as well as in, the United States. Preuss left Prussia for America following the 1830 revolutions, and he accompanied the explorer John Freemont on a series of expeditions across the West—experiencing both the breadth of the continent and the intra-indigenous battles and "traumatic storms of expansion" described by Ned Blackhawk in *Violence over the Land*.[40] A talented cartographer, Preuss was with Freemont when he first glimpsed Lake Tahoe from a mountain pass in 1844, and he became well known for creating some of the most important maps of the West in the antebellum period. Indeed, he produced a map that was widely used among immigrants. It detailed the landscape, animals, grass, water, meteorological readings, and American Indians encountered on the trek from Westport Landing in Kansas City along the Missouri to the mouth of the Walla Walla and the Columbia. By any account, it was a tremendous contribution to the "closing of the West."[41]

Most important for the stimulation of Germans' broad interests in the West and American Indians, however, were those individuals whose talents also extended to capturing such moments, adventures, and transformations in words and images that could be circulated among popular audiences in the German lands. That took people who acted not only as German Humboldts but also as German Coopers.

German Coopers and Ignoble Yankees

The active participation of Germans such as Preuss in the history of the American West is well known. One still sees traces of them in popular renditions of westward expansion. For example, at a critical point in John Ford's *Cheyenne Autumn* (1964), the Cheyenne chief Dull Knife surrenders with a portion of his people at Fort Robinson after leading them on an epic trek from miserable reservation conditions in Oklahoma toward their homeland in Wyoming. The man who accepts their surrender is the German post commander Captain Oscar Wessels, played by Karl Malden. Before Wessels follows his superiors' orders to restrain the Cheyennes and experiences their violent escape as a result, he dines with Captain Thomas Archer, the sympathetic officer who has pursued the Cheyennes for hundreds of miles. Explaining to Archer and his other dinner guests that he "of course recognized James Fenimore Cooper's portraits of American Indians were inaccurate in many respects," he noted that Cooper nevertheless stimulated his interests in American Indians while in the Prussian army. Since then, he continued, he had made a point of learning as much as he could about Indians through Cooper's volumes as well as the many other books on the shelves surrounding his guests. When he lamented that others had not done the same, one of his officers pointed out that would have been difficult: most of those books were in German, which gave all of his guests a good laugh.

This scene, like the rest of Ford's film, has a loose historical base. By the 1870s, there were many Germans such as Wessels in the U.S. military, and it is easy to imagine that quite a few of the officers had read Cooper's *Leatherstocking Tales* before emigrating to the United States. It is also certain that by the middle of the nineteenth century they would have read the German Coopers as well. There were many candidates. Clearly the most popular, however, were Friedrich Gerstäcker and Balduin Möllhausen. They would have been on Wessels's shelves.

Gerstäcker and Möllhausen were adventurous, prolific, and spent many years in the United States. They wrote travel literature, essays, and novels, meant for popular consumption, which were widely read and well regarded. Indeed, Gerstäcker's *The Regulators of Arkansas* (1846) has been credited with being the first western novel, not just the first German western, and critics and scholars alike have praised the appeal of his books for adolescents. By the mid-1860s he was recognized as "one of the most beloved and admired of German writers."[42] Germany's oldest prize for children's literature is named after him.

There is little question that such authors helped to channel the popularization of ideas about American Indians among Germans. They built on Cooper's tales and the travel narratives from von Wied and others, and they legitimated their own stories with their personal experiences in North America. The status they gleaned as eyewitnesses gave them authority, and their willingness to critically engage the character of the United States in general, as well as American Indians in particular, made them quite popular.[43] Indeed, they articulated many of the essential ideals about the treatment of American Indians at the hands of "Yankees" that would be recapitulated by writers such as Karl May and reproduced in a variety of media well into the twentieth century.

One trope that gained great valence through their writings was the juxtaposition of corrupted and uncorrupted American Indians, who became ciphers for the loss of natural nobility, the impact of Yankee malice, and the tragedy of the United States. In 1846, for example, Gerstäcker wrote that, "for Europeans, a unique magic is contained in the very word and concept 'Indian.' Cooper's delightful tales, his good and courageous Mohawks and Delaware, his Mingos and Sioux, Tuscarora and Pawnee, with their battles and assaults, their nobility and sagacity certainly excite the highest interest in any wild tribe."[44] The realities, however, were often less magical. As he explained to German readers: the remnants of these great tribes encountered by squatters and pioneers in the frontier zones had often been so abused, cheated, betrayed, and mishandled by the settlers and the military that these people had changed not only their behavior toward whites but also their very characteristics. Indeed, in many cases, he continued, they had taken on the settlers' worst traits, as they were exposed to the violence, alcohol, and misdeeds of some. Through such interactions, they became "drunken, filthy, untrustworthy, and horribly violent," and as a result, he quipped, "it is no wonder that [pioneers and squatters] feel little sympathy for the Indian when they see how he is pushed back more and more, and how his tribe dissolves and finally completely vanishes under an ever more powerful civilization."[45] The process of their destruction, he underscored, had its own peculiar frontier dynamic; but the guilt lay with the Yankees.[46]

Only by moving past the frontier and away from those Yankees could one still find, as Paul Wilhelm and Maximilian von Wied had done, those tribes such as "the Pawnee and the Comanche" who had not yet been decimated by "the withering arm of civilization." Here, Gerstäcker continued, one could encounter the uncorrupted plains warriors who, as Pekka Hämäläinen reminds us, still controlled much of the Southern Plains under their own formidable empire.[47] To the eyes of a European, Gerstäcker wrote, that can be an "imposing sight:" glimpsing a "genuine chief of a western, still unspoiled tribe, when he is covered in war paint, with captured scalp locks hanging from him, adorned with fluttering, waving feathers, richly embellished buffalo robe, leather fringed leggings and shirt, beaded moccasins, sitting on a charger likewise adorned with feathers and scalp locks, the man and horse together as one unit . . . springing across the broad plain."[48] That, he even implied, is a vision worthy of Europeans' excitement, even Cooper's depictions.

Typical of such accounts, Gerstäcker concluded his observations with a Herderian lament about the loss of such distinctions: "How soon will the time come," he asked his readers, "when one speaks of these heroes of the prairie only as we speak of the ancient Spartans and Romans?" "The Eastern tribes," he noted, "are already almost eradicated." The "Mohawks and Delaware, the Oneida, Seneca, Yamasee and Algonquin live only now in the memories of the states they earlier ruled, and even the Sioux and Sauks, the Huron, Pawnee, Comanche, and Blackfoot have lost thousands and thousands of their warriors, they are continually reduced, pushed further and further into the wilderness, where even the number of buffalo, their only source of livelihood, are abating." Soon, he continued in a disillusioned tone, "the tomahawk and peace pipe" will come to rest. Soon, the buffalo that "tear the earth with their horns and hooves" and "storm across the plains," will be replaced by "fire spewing machines" and the "black abyss of squelching factories," which "digest the entrails of glorious mountains."[49]

The themes Gerstäcker captures in this essay became paradigmatic of the German literature on American Indians by the middle of the nineteenth century. They promoted the notion, evident already in the writings of the Humboldtian nobles, that there were corrupted and uncorrupted tribes of American Indians; that the uncorrupted tribes were under siege by industrial, urban civilization; and that while one could still find examples of free peoples among them, those peoples were encircled by the destructive powers of Western civilization, and that circle was closing. A similar sense of inevitable doom, to be sure, can be found in English-language literature as well.[50] But in the German-language texts, the loss is more poignant, more personal, more often tinged with empathetic anger. There is also more focus on blame.

Certainly, following Herder, many German authors recognized that the powerful historical forces, which favor larger, more centralized, and urban civilizations, were all but unstoppable and that many of the agents of this change, such as Gerstäcker's squatters, were ignorant of their actual role in that process. Gerstäcker's perspective as an outsider, however, allowed him to see that role, comment on that ignorance, and that outsider's perspective allowed a long line of Germans to place blame squarely in the hands of both local, greedy, evil actors and the U.S. federal government's "disastrous Indian policy."[51]

For if English-language writers might have argued in favor of the sacrifices that led toward "progress" with a belief that "the Indians' bones must enrich the soil, before the plough of civilization can open it," as one American travel book did in 1843,[52] German descriptions of that process frequently lacked the same active verbs. German authors generally included enough equivocation in their evaluations to make clear that the process of transformation was not so much "progress" as a predictable form of change driven by impersonal material forces and debased human motivations that could, with better leadership and higher ideals, be managed humanely.

These messages circulated through not only narratives and journal essays but also popular fiction. Balduin Möllhausen's writings are the perfect example. His exploits in the United States ranged from his ill-fated attempt to accompany Duke Paul Wilhelm on an 1851 venture into the Rocky Mountains to his assignment as topographer for Lieutenant Amiel Weeks Whipple's 1853 expedition across the southwestern United States, and ultimately to his appointment as "artist and collector in natural history" for Lieutenant Joseph Christmas Ives's 1857 expedition to evaluate the navigability of the Colorado River and investigate the Grand Canyon. All these trips informed his copious writings, and the last led to him producing some of the first-ever published illustrations of the Grand Canyon and some of the earliest images of the Mohave and Wallapai Indians.

The two books he published based on these expeditions, *Diary of a Journey from the Mississippi to the Coast of the Pacific* (1858) and *Travels from the Rocky Mountains of North America to the High-Plateau of New Mexico* (1861), were very much in the tradition of the epic travel accounts written by Paul Wilhelm and Maximilian von Wied, and both featured rare introductions by Alexander von Humboldt.[53] But they were more popular than the nobles' books. Indeed, Möllhausen's first volume was so popular that a cheaper edition followed two years after the first under a slightly different title. Moreover, his accessible writing style and the attractiveness of his tales led to a quick shift in genre: the same year he published the second travel volume he also published his first novel, *The Half-Indian* (1861).[54] Afterward, he wrote forty-five often multivolume novels, more than sixty-two novellas, and literally hundreds of shorter volumes and stories. Like Gerstäcker, his work was also serialized, and his essays could be found in essentially every major middle-class German periodical, and thus in most every middle-class home.[55]

For many literary critics, that oeuvre is disappointingly consistent. As Presten Barba describes it, Möllhausen "had opportunities for seeing western America as possibly no other German writer," but that experience did not drive him far from his initial impressions. His novels almost always read like spinoffs from Cooper, and he often borrowed from Cooper to narrate what he saw, happily creating, for example, multiple characters akin to Cooper's backwoodsman Natty Bumppo. Thus, while there was great realism in his depiction of places and things, even striking ethnographic details mixed into his stories, scholars generally agree that "he followed no new paths in fiction."[56]

This, however, is also telling, and in some ways typical of traveling Germans' encounters with Native America: rather than transforming the ideas he had brought with him to the West, his experiences confirmed them. Indeed, for Möllhausen, writing like Cooper was writing from experience. As he noted in his diary about his time stranded among the Otto Indians in 1851: "I learned to look with pride on my ragged moccasins and scarred feet, and to laugh at the icy north wind blowing on my naked breast. . . . I felt in the most joyous spirits, and seemed to be realizing the dreams of my youth when I sent a bullet through the skull of a bear, or gave some mighty stag the *coup de grace*."[57] These experiences pleased him because they allowed him to live out his fantasies about America that he had gleaned from literature: "I was happy," he wrote, "exuberantly pleased, because the dreams of my youth, called up by Cooper and Washington Irving, had become reality."[58] Indeed, later in life he wrote to Spencer Baird, director of the Smithsonian Institution in Washington, D.C., that "the happiest time of my life I have spent in the United States of North-America."[59]

As many literary scholars have pointed out, Möllhausen was able to have these confirming experiences because his America was a place distant from the eastern cities and limited to the 1850s. Wilderness, explorers, trappers, woodsmen, and various American Indians defined his America, and the American Indians that come forward in his travel books and especially in his novels are indeed Cooperesque.[60] Often overlooked, however, is another side to Möllhausen's portraits of American Indians, not derived from Cooper, not romantic, and repeated by a series of more activist writers before and after Möllhausen who were concerned about the conditions under which American Indians were forced to live. Much of his popular work channels this part of the German discourse on American Indians as well.

For example, in an 1863 excerpt that appeared in *Über Land und Meer*, Möllhausen describes a scene in Scullyville, Oklahoma, a community that developed around the Choctaw agency in 1832, while the forced removal of the Choctaw from their lands in the East was in full progress. Scullyville was located on the California road and was a stop on the famous Butterfield overland mail route. For a time it was the capital of the Choctaw Nation. The name Scullyville derives from the Choctaw word for money, and as Möllhausen explained to his readers, this is where the Choctaw received their annual payments from the U.S. government in return for leaving their ancestral lands.[61] The Choctaw, however, "profited very little from this arrangement." When the time for the payments arrived, he explained, the whites "get the poor Indians drunk and rob them thoroughly." That, he remarked "is one of the good deeds that Christian civilization has brought to the good Redskins." And yet these "Redskins" were not praying Indians in mission towns, nor were "these Indians" "so raw and wild, as one would have us believe": they were often skilled and engaged in agriculture, and at the outset of the Whipple expedition, when he encountered them, he met many Choctaws who were eager to partake in discussions of how best to link areas of the United States through the railroad."[62] There was, in other words, plenty of hard reality mixed in with Möllhausen's Cooperesque fantasy and considerable concern with the U.S. government's treatment of American Indians. By the time these essays appeared, that concern was characteristic of the German discourse on American Indians.

German Catlins and American Indian Resistance

The tropes of nobility, tragedy, Yankee malice, even American Indian resistance channeled by German writers circulated widely through German-speaking Europe in images as well. Those images were generally less spectacular than Bodmer's paintings, and few of the artists were as entrepreneurial as the American George Catlin, who toured Europe and the United States during the 1830s with his gallery of ethnographica and paintings of American Indians.[63] Still, a host of German artists helped to shape Germans' visions of the American West and American Indians.[64]

Reproductions of paintings from internationally celebrated artists appeared in the early issues of journals like *Über Land und Meer*, when such images were used as starting points for fanciful musings about adventures in the American West. One striking example is *Über Land und Meer*'s use of a virtual copy of Carl Wimar's highly acclaimed *The Abduction of Boone's*

FIGURE 3. Karl Bodmer, *Horse Racing of Sioux Indians: Near Fort Pierre*. Published as "Wettrennen von Siouxindianern," *Über Land und Meer* 15, no. 13 (1866): 204.

Daughter by the Indians (1855) as the point of departure for a short captivity narrative set on the wild Texas frontier in 1858.[65] Another is the same periodical's use of an image taken from Bodmer's *Horse Racing of Sioux Indians: Near Fort Pierre*, for a similarly fanciful essay on horse racing among Plains Indians in 1866.[66]

On rare occasions, images from such well-known painters were also used to illustrate more pointed essays that focused on the critical tensions inherent in American industrial expansion, which interested Germans so much. Perhaps the best example is the *Leipziger Illustrirte Zeitung*'s feature on the German American artist Theodore Kaufmann and his classic painting *Westward the Star of Empire* in 1869.[67]

The author of the accompanying essay lauded the American Indians in that painting, who were engaged in derailing an approaching train, as desperate individuals utilizing "the weapons of the weak . . . against the overwhelming power of their opponents."[68] For the author, the image showed German readers a moment in a tragic conflict, introduced to many of them decades earlier by Gerstäcker and others, in which "the homeland of these 'legitimate inhabitants' becomes more and more restricted," and in which "there is no hope to bring to a standstill this penetrating flood that, with its way of life, takes away the possibility of their continued existence."[69]

FIGURE 4. Theodore Kaufmann, *Westward the Star of Empire*. Published as "Indianer, einem Zug der Pacific-Eisenbahn überfallend," *Leipziger Illustrirte Zeitung* 52, no. 1336 (1869): 101.

These people, however, could and did resist their putatively hopeless situation, and thus "when nightly darkness lies over the prairie, the red men crawl like cats, pressed close to the ground, so that the high, stiff grass conceals the contours of their crawling bodies, as they move onto the track embankment." Because of the actions of these crafty warriors, the author continued, in just a few moments the train will lie "derailed, a heap of rubble, irredeemable in the wilderness, and the savages' knives and tomahawks will again celebrate their gruesome festival and fertilize the path to culture with blood."[70]

This was above all, if we are to trust the author's interpretation, a vision of a small and vengeful victory about to take place in a brutal battle that American Indians ultimately would lose. It was the kind of resistance to the impersonal material forces that so upset Gerstäcker, which he almost seemed to be calling for in his portraits of "fire spewing machines" that "storm across the plains." Indeed, it was the kind of report that would continue to have tremendous appeal among many Germans.

What one finds more frequently in the illustrated magazines, however, is less the dominance of artists such as Bodmer, Kaufmann, or Wimar than a striking variety of stories and images produced by numerous individuals about America that responded, one suspects, to an equally variegated range of interests among Germans.

It is reasonable to argue, however, that international artists such as Wimar still set a recognized standard in the more general production of images about the American West, and that both kinds of images, those easily reproduced in the magazines and those fantastic paintings that gained such renown in the nineteenth century, played critical roles in channeling and shaping Germans' interests in America and American Indians.

Indeed, art historians have paid considerable attention to artists from German-speaking Central Europe who helped create the image of the "West as America" in the United States,[71] and with good reason: a significant number produced iconographic images that became well known on both continents and, in turn, shaped the more popular, cheaper productions and their reception among Germans. There is, however, another critical reason for paying these artists such attention. They remind us that one of the central reasons Germans were so interested in America and American Indians during the nineteenth century is that so many Germans were there, not only shaping German ideas about the American landscape, beauty, wilderness, and nature but also integrating those ideals into Americans' self-image.

The Düsseldorfer and German Americans

It is striking how often art historians, when discussing the iconography of the American West, turn to artists who were German or German American or who spent time at the Düsseldorf Art Academy.[72] Take, for example, the popular subject of western art history, George Caleb Bingham. Many have termed him the first artist of Missouri and praised him for paintings such as *Jolly Flatboatmen in Port* (1857). Like many artists of the American West, Bingham spent several years at the Düsseldorf Art Academy (1857–59), where he produced not only his iconographic image of the jolly boatmen but also his full-length portraits of George Washington and Thomas Jefferson, which were commissioned by the Missouri state legislature. They are only a few of the classic images of America produced in Germany.

Although Bingham was already a mature artist when he arrived in Düsseldorf, he immediately sought out the highly regarded Emanuel Leutze. Leutze, typical of the transatlantic German American of the age, had been born in Schwäbisch Gemünd in Duke Paul's Württemberg, moved to America as a child, lived in Philadelphia and then Fredericksburg, Virginia, before returning to Germany to study in Düsseldorf in 1840, Munich in 1842, and then to Düsseldorf again to teach from 1845 to 1859.

While in Düsseldorf in 1850, Leutze painted both his highly idealized *The Last of the Mohicans* (1850) and his iconographic masterpiece *Washington Crossing the Delaware* (1851), which was much recirculated.[73] Toward the end of his tenure he also gained a commission from the U.S. government to paint *Westward the Course of Empire Takes Its Way* (also known as *Westward ho!*) for the U.S. Capital, which he produced in 1861–62. Leutze, the liberal, pro-revolutionary, German American, produced an image that he thought would represent the "grand peaceful conquest of the west." It was a commission much coveted by Bingham, and given its important subject and location, a clear testimony to the high regard in which Leutze and his academy stood in the United States. It is also a reminder of how important these German American artists were for the production of the iconography of the American West.[74]

Perhaps an even more telling example is Albert Bierstadt's *The Oregon Trail* (1869). Painted in the 1860s as a generic image of immigration, it "attempts to convey something of the spirit of hope which motivated the pioneering enterprise" of the mid-nineteenth century.[75] It was inspired by a scene Bierstadt witnessed in May 1863 when he and the prominent writer Fitz Hugh Ludlow departed from St. Joseph, Missouri, with an overland mail stagecoach to California, where Bierstadt hoped to encounter more mountain scenes and Western subjects. Near Fort Kearny, Nebraska, they passed a wagon train, which Ludlow described as "a very picturesque party of Germans going to Oregon." The Germans, he wrote, "had a large herd of cattle and fifty wagons, mostly drawn by oxen, though some of the more prosperous 'outfits' were attached to horses or mules." Many of the Germans, he continued, were from "the better class of Prussian or North German peasantry," but he also identified a "number of strapping teamsters, in gay costumes," who appeared to be Westphalians wearing "canary shirts and blue pantaloons; with these were intermingled blouses of claret, rich warm brown, and the most vivid red."[76] Ludlow was delighted by this spectacle in the middle of the plains and confessed that he could have followed the Germans all the way into Kearny.

While in Europe from 1867 to 1869, Bierstadt produced *Emigrants Crossing the Plains* and *The Oregon Trail*, the second being identical in subject to the first but only one-half its size. For historians of art, and indeed, in the public relations text created by the Butler Institute of American Art in Youngstown, which owns the painting, *The Oregon Trail* is deemed important because it transformed what to Ludlow was "a jolly encounter with a colorful band of

FIGURE 5. Albert Bierstadt, *The Oregon Trail* (1869). (Collection of The Butler Institute of American Art, Youngstown, Ohio)

emigrants into a spectacular allegory of westward expansion," and it captures a critical sense of nostalgia, because the second painting appeared just as the transcontinental railroad was being completed, effectively bringing to an end this particular aspect of the pioneer experience. According to this text, the key point is that paintings of this nature allowed disappearing aspects of pioneer experience such as the wagon train to "persist in myth for over a century as one of the iconic images of America's expansion westward." That is certainly true; but an equally critical point is that this "iconic image of American expansion" was created by a German American artist, on the basis of his observation of German immigrants in the center of the Great Plains, after he had returned to Germany. It reminds us, in other words, of the degree to which Germans were both intimately involved in making the West and fashioning its meaning through the production of images.

Bierstadt is perhaps best known for his gigantic paintings of Western American landscapes, such as his famous compilation *The Rocky Mountains: Lander's Peak* (1863). When he created this and similar landscapes of the West, American Indians often played important roles in them, melding into the scenery naturally and without conflict. In this way, his paintings often obfuscated the reality of conquest. Other German American artists, however, particularly Carl Wimar, who also spent significant time in Düsseldorf (where he read Cooper's *Leatherstocking Tales* for the first time), and who trained with Leutze, showed a good deal of conflict in their paintings.[77] Indeed, it was Wimar, who lived in Missouri after moving to the United States at the age of fifteen, rather than Bierstadt, raised from the age of two in New Bedford, Massachusetts, who produced the most classic images of wagon trains while he was in Düssseldorf in the 1850s.[78] The second version of his *Attack on an Emigrant Train* (1856), for example, published as a lithograph in 1860, became a widely circulated popular image, appearing not only in *Über Land und Meer* but in other illustrated magazines as well.

For many art historians, the most *German* aspect of the 1854 version of Wimar's *Attack on an Emigrant Train* is the black man included as an integral part of the emigrants' defenses, reaching for a rifle along with the other embattled men. His presence seems to express what some scholars might consider Leutze's liberal attitudes on the question of race and slavery, an attitude often attributed to German Americans in general because of their overwhelming support of the North during the Civil War,[79] and articulated in this case, some have supposed, through Leutze's student Wimar.[80]

Yet Wimar's paintings did not need to contain a republican message in order to express their putative Germanness; the very topic was a *German* one, and it had multiple variations. Thus, while Bierstadt, Leutze, and Wimar were all German Americans who spent formative periods of their careers in Düsseldorf and produced classical paintings of emigrants engaged in the process of American westward expansion, they did not create a homogeneous *German* view of the American West or of its conquest by the United States. For Leutze and Bierstadt, the conquest could be made to seem natural and peaceful; for Wimar, however, who had much more experience with American Indians and ultimately grew fond of living among them, that conquest was riddled with conflict.[81] Thus there was no unitary *German* vision of Western expansion, even among the Düsseldorfer; but there was an obsession with the topic among Germans, which the Düsseldorfer recognized, shared, and helped to perpetuate. And that is the point: by the middle of the nineteenth century, this obsession was well established; the key elements of interests and concerns in the Germanophone world were clearly articulated, and that engagement only grew as the German Kulturkreis rapidly expanded.

The Great Transatlantic Migration

German American artists were able to capture images of the American West because they, like the emigrants Bierstadt and Wimar portrayed, were part

FIGURE 6. Carl Wimar, *The Attack on the Emigrant Train* (1856). (The University of Michigan Museum of Art, Bequest of Henry C. Lewis, 1895.80)

of the mass migration of Germans from Central Europe to the United States during the nineteenth century. Millions of Germans moved back and forth across the Atlantic, and with them German cultural life spread across North America as individuals, groups, and communities took root and thrived. Over the course of the nineteenth century, a vibrant German America took shape, and German literature and art that focused on America in general, as well as American Indians in particular, flourished. Indeed, it is impossible to separate this movement of peoples from the production of ideas about America and American Indians in Germany.

Emigration from Germany to North America began during the colonial period. The first German families to come as a group founded Germantown, Pennsylvania, in 1683. Over the next century, perhaps another 100,000 followed, so that in 1790 one-twelfth of the population was of German descent. In 1751, Germans made up 30 percent of the Europeans in Pennsylvania, 10 percent in Maryland, 9 percent in New Jersey, and 8 percent in New York. For most of these immigrants, however, acculturation happened fairly quickly and many stopped speaking German within a few generations.[82]

By the time Cooper became popular in German-speaking Europe, however, Germans were engaged in what Mack Walker termed the "great mid-century transatlantic migration." From 1830 to 1854 Germans traveled "all but exclusively to the United States and almost entirely unsolicited."[83] Rising prices, European revolutions, a more favorable view of America, and the threat of diseases such as cholera in European cities were all factors that helped to initiate the movement. Once it began, it continued to grow yearly, until Germans became "the largest single group to enter nineteenth-century America."[84]

That growth, however, was not just a result of discontent and frustration with political and social situations. In many ways, it was a response to the emergence of what Walker calls "German outposts in America." There was a real, noticeable "accumulation of areas in Germany where *Auswanderung* [emigration] seemed a plausible thing to do" and a similar materialization of destinations where it made sense for Germans to go.[85] Although the numbers fluctuated with the changing political and economic circumstances, and different kinds of Germans (based on region, confession, political leanings, and other factors) came in different waves, the migration continued steadily across the nineteenth century. Between 1830 and 1930, about one out of every six immigrants to the United States was German-speaking.[86] Between 1871 and 1885 alone, some 1.5 million Germans, easily 3.5 percent of the population, emigrated. Over 95 percent of these went to the United States, and as a result, in 1900 first- and second-generation German Americans made up more than 10 percent of the population.[87]

The greatest concentrations of Germans were in Wisconsin, Minnesota, and Illinois. Nebraska, Iowa, New York, and Ohio followed closely. Indeed, in Nebraska, where Bierstadt saw his emigrant train, nearly half the inhabitants trace their ancestry to Germans. New York City, where so many of the immigrants arrived in the United States, always had the largest population of Germans. Indeed, as Walter Kamphoefner tells us, "around the turn of the century, more German immigrants lived there than in all but seven cities in Germany." Furthermore, if we include "the second generation, the 800,000 New Yorkers of German stock came second only to Berlin, and Chicago with its 400,000 Germans, was the eighth largest German city in the world. The cities with the highest percentage of Germans," however, were in the Midwest. Milwaukee was first. In 1860 more than half the heads of households and one-third the city population were German born. It maintained that position through 1900.[88]

With all the German people, came German literature, cultural traits, and an ongoing communication between German-speaking Europe and German America. In 1850, for example, as Leutze was producing his *The Last of the Mohicans* in Düsseldorf, New York City had more German dailies than

Berlin and Leipzig, and in 1872 the *New Yorker Staats-Zeitung* had a circulation of fifty-five thousand, making it the largest German newspaper in the world.[89] It remained central to German America through World War I, and it was often read in Germany as well as the United States. Between 1815 and 1850, Germans who had traveled to America produced more than fifty travel books. America, in short, was the place to go.

More than anything else, however, private letters informed Germans about life in the United States. Walker argues that this was already true during the 1850s; but by the end of the century the numbers of letters that crisscrossed the Atlantic were astounding.[90] Indeed, Wolfgang Helbich has argued that "with about 2.7 million German-born people living in the United States during the decade of the 1890s, and some four million letters sent from America to Germany every year," it would be "a very conservative estimate that an equal number of persons in Germany were direct recipients of letters from America over a five year span." Moreover, "the number of people to whom the news was spread by village or family networks may have been twice or three times that number."[91]

The end result is that America was an almost constant presence in the minds of Germans who remained in Central Europe. For many, it seemed like an extension of their homeland. And Germans who traveled to the United States often felt the same way when they arrived into strong German communities in which local societies had been set up to assist new arrivals and protect them from exploitation. These new arrivals also found other, more familiar associations and habits: singing associations, Kegel and Karten clubs, beer gardens, sharp shooting organizations, book clubs, workers organizations, military and fire fighting groups, peace organizations, gymnastic groups, and musical associations that Germans had spread across the United States. These immigrants also made Christmas trees, cards, and songs a regular part of the winter season, and after the middle of the century, through their participation in theater, music, and singing, and through the countless German-language periodicals, they spread other aspects of German culture as well. As Kathleen Neils Conzen has repeatedly argued, these German immigrants contributed much to the social organization in the United States.[92] That also included, as Bruce Levine reminds us, antagonistic politics and class divisions, which split many of these social organizations along material, political, and philosophical as well as ethnic lines.[93]

These arrivals were also part of the expansion of empire and not simply passive participants in Bierstadt's emigrant trains or Wimar's more embattled ones. Sometimes they came as missionaries. Moravians could be found across the colonial period just as the overwhelmingly German Catholic priests and nuns covered the upper Great Plains and especially the Sioux reservations in the Dakotas after the Civil War.[94] More frequently, however, Germans came as settlers, and they too eagerly flooded into the landscape that was opened up through treaties and the forced removal of many tribes. They were not only in Minnesota and other midwestern states but also in southern states, where the Cherokee and the Choctaw lived before removal to the places where Möllhausen encountered some of them later in the century. Charleston and much of South Carolina, for example, were full of Germans.[95] Moreover, Germans could be found in many of the critical historical moments in the history of the West. They helped to settle large parts of Texas, some died together with Jim Bowie and Davy Crockett at the Alamo, and thousands streamed into California after gold was found on the property of Johann August Sutter, the so-called king of California who was born in Baden in 1803 and began his kingdom in 1839.[96]

They also fought American Indians. Germans could be found in all areas of the American military, from the leading ranks of Union officers to privates in the most obscure western posts.[97] At one point some 10 percent of the U.S. Army in Arizona was German speaking,[98] and the oldest survivor of the famous 1876 Battle of the Little Bighorn, where combined forces of Arapahos, Lakotas, and Northern Cheyennes devastated the Seventh U.S. Cavalry led by George Armstrong Custer, was the German Charles Windolph, who won a medal of honor for his participation in that conflict. Indeed, he was not the only German to fight with Custer. Custer took a German band with him when he led his expedition into the Black Hills, many of the soldiers who died with him at the Battle of Little Bighorn were born in Germany, and in fact, the one man from Custer's entourage who was rumored to have survived by breaking through the Lakota lines with multiple wounds, Frank Finkle, was another German and a friend of Windolph's.[99]

On rare occasions, Germans also fought *as* American Indians. The most famous of these are the German children from Texas settlements such as Herman Lehmann, Rudolf Fischer, and Adolf Korn, who were captured by Apache and Comanche war parties, adopted into indigenous communities, and ultimately came to live and fight with them until the last Comanches were forced onto reservations in Oklahoma in 1875. As Pekka Hämäläinen, James F. Brooks, and many others remind us, captive raids had long been part of the southwestern economy, and many captured children were quickly incorporated into American Indian families.[100] Rudolf Fischer, in fact, became a formidable warrior, one of Quanah Parker's[101] right-hand men, and he refused to return to the German settlements or to his German family after the Comanches surrendered. Instead, he chose to go with them to Oklahoma.

Herman Lehmann's story was similar, if more tragic. He and Adolf Korn never completely adjusted to their forced return to the white world. As Lehmann remarked later in life, "How could I who was free as a bird be cramped up in a house and forced to toil for a livelihood?"[102] That was, to be sure, the critical question, one that resounded again and again in captivity narratives such as the famous *Blauvogel*, written by Anna Jürgen in 1950 and later made into a popular DEFA film in East Germany (1979). But it also remained a major theme in Germans' broader interests in American Indians across the nineteenth and twentieth centuries. How could anyone be "cramped up" and forced to toil for a livelihood? How could anyone—German, American Indian, or both—be forced to accept captivity over freedom?

There was great irony in this situation. On the one hand, the majority of Germans would have read with sorrow Gerstäcker's and Möllhausen's portraits of the railways leading to the destruction of the buffalo herds and the livelihoods of the last free American Indians. Many still do. When viewing Theodore Kaufmann's *Westward the Star of Empire*, the majority also would have felt sympathy for the plight of the American Indians seeking to derail the approaching locomotive and resist the inevitable onslaught of Western civilization. They might have read as well with great excitement the stories of Rudolf Fischer and Herman Lehmann fighting white settlers and be enraged along with these young men at the U.S. Calvary's destruction of Comanche villages, or the displacement of tribes ranging from the Choctaw in the East to the Dakota in the Midwest. But on the other hand, Germans themselves were eagerly engaged in mapping the landscape, riding the trains, building the factories, and settling the lands made empty for them by soldiers, many of whom were also often Germans. Thus, in many cases, as German readers were cursing the agents of progress and the Americans or, worse, the Yankees pressing their empire forward, they were actually, albeit often unwittingly, cursing themselves.

The Showmen and the Sioux

The showmen are the final critical component in this combination of factors and circumstances that shaped German interests in American Indians over the course of the nineteenth century. During the 1880s and 1890s, as ever-larger numbers of Germans became comfortable traveling back and forth across the Atlantic, as the steamships made the trip faster, and the distance became less daunting, American Indians came to Germany with a variety of showmen. By the 1880s, *Völkerschauen*, or what Sierra Bruckner has called commercial ethnography—the public display of non-Europeans for profit—became common in German cities. During that decade, a group of American Indians arrived almost every year, fulfilling childhood dreams and adult expectations.[103]

Initially, a variety of Indians came. In 1879, for example, Charles Reiche brought a troupe of what were purported to be Iroquois from around the St. Lawrence River in Canada: eight "good looking, strong" men with a "naturally proud bearing," one "graceful and fine" woman, one similarly endowed girl, and for some reason, one Comanche. Why he was included remains unclear.[104] Thousands came daily to see these "fellow tribesmen of the heroes they had read about in narratives and novels" as they performed harvest and snake dances, a burial ceremony, engaged in archery, rowed canoes, played lacrosse, and demonstrated their martial skills in mock battles.

In 1883 six Chippewas from the Great Lakes region were featured at the Berlin Panopticon and billed as the descendants of Cooper's characters and the fulfillment of childhood dreams. "From childhood on," wrote an author for the *Leipziger Illustrirte Zeitung*, "we Germans have a certain affection for 'Redskins.'" Indeed, "after reading Cooper, the life of a trapper seems the highest ideal" for many Germans. Moreover, through "countless travel narratives and books the lives and activities of the original inhabitants of North America have become familiar and in a sense sympathetic to us," and thus he was certain that it would be of "great interest for everyone" to see actual representatives of these people, watch them produce arrow heads and other things, and witness their performances, especially their dances.[105]

That connection was not possible for all American Indians. For example, in 1885 Carl Hagenbeck introduced Germans to a group from Bella Coola, along the northwest coast of North America.[106] The young Franz Boas and other ethnologists were particularly impressed, but for the large, popular audiences who attended the *Völkerschauen*, they did not seem like American Indians—their material culture was all wrong, there were no feather bonnets, no horses, and too much carving on wood and objects made from tree bark; most of all, "they looked like Polynesians," as many newspapers reported.[107]

Indeed, it became clear to the impresarios by the mid-1880s that, while the German public may have been weaned on stories of Cooper's Woodlands Indians, they had developed a keen sense for Bodmer's Great Plains, and they wanted to see examples of Gerstäcker's "still unspoiled people." They wanted

FIGURE 7. "Die Chippeways-Indianer im Panoptikum zu Berlin," *Leipziger Illustrirte Zeitung* 80, no. 2063 (1883), 41.

Plains Indians. Most of all, they wanted Sioux, those still embattled quintessential resisters who had displaced many rivals and often bested U.S. forces.

Their appeal was clear: as the Comanche Empire spun into decline in the wake of the Mexican-American War (1846–48) and then collapsed in the 1870s; as Kiowa, Osage, and other Plains Indians were forced, like the Sauks and Foxes before them, into reservations in Western Indian Territory; as the United States asserted itself with new vigor following the American Civil War (1861–65) and the Great Plains became the most violent place in North America, the Sioux, especially the westernmost division, the Lakota,[108] appeared to be particularly resilient. During this same period, as other tribes succumbed, Lakotas and their allies scored repeated victories against U.S. forces, culminating in the 1876 triumph at the Battle of the Little Bighorn.[109]

People in Germany took notice, and for that reason, even the Chippewas (sworn enemies of the Dakotas and other Sioux tribes) were linked to the Sioux in advertisements and essays; two of their group, for example, Black Bird and Sunshine, were purported to have been favorites of the Lakota Sitting Bull in the fight against Custer and to have "taken the scalps of more than one enemy." Similarly, in 1884 a group of Omaha from Nebraska was also featured in the Berlin Panopticon. But in order to attract the largest possible crowds, the Omahas too were billed as Sioux in the advertisements and news reports.[110]

In 1886 a group of fifteen mostly Oglala-Sioux finally arrived in Germany with Frank Harvey, and others have been coming ever since. Despite the fact that the Sioux had also been forced onto reservations by this time, their reputation in Germany held fast, and they continued to entice. In Dresden's or Leipzig's Zoological Gardens, for example, where they could set up camps for themselves and their animals in open fields and wooded areas, Germans flocked to gain a glimpse of actual Lakotas, members of the tribe that vanquished Custer, people who still embodied in the 1880s the vibrant possibility of resistance. Indeed, their presence raised Germans' awareness that such resistance was more than a myth. "The Dakotas or Sioux," wrote one correspondent, "have resisted the relentless forward pressing culture the longest of all the Indian tribes." "Soon, however," he remarked with the typical Herderian lament about the loss of distinctions, "they too will have to give up their old ways, and the flood of civilization will course over them and wash away their peculiarities."[111] According to the rhetoric of the day, this was the last chance to see these historical figures, revel in their distinctions, and even admire them as modern heroes.

Actually, the last chance to see them continued well into the twentieth century and long after the so-called closing of the frontier and the 1890 Wounded Knee massacre on the Pine Ridge Reservation. Indeed, 1890 was the red-letter date for seeing Sioux in Germany. That was the year Buffalo Bill's Wild West took Germany by storm, and the small *Völkerschauen* were eclipsed by Wild West shows that featured large contingents of overwhelmingly Lakota Indians engaged in thrilling displays of the skills necessary for surviving the conflicted history of the American West.

Doc Carver's "Wild America" set the precedent. In August 1889 Carver arrived in Berlin with a contingent of eighteen American Indian performers who embodied Gerstäcker's image of the Plains warrior on his mighty steed. By doing so, Carver accomplished a great task. He regained the public's imagination. According to one report, *Völkerschauen*, or what the author termed "caravans" of non-Europeans "that included even their house pets," had become so common in Berlin that "it appeared almost impossible to bring something new onto the stage," something that would capture Berliners' interests. But Carver did it. He brought American Indians dressed for

FIGURE 8. A group of Omaha in Berlin, advertised as "Tanz der Sioux-Indianer im Berliner Panoptikum," *Leipziger Illustrirte Zeitung* 82, no. 2118 (1884): 96.

war who demonstrated the skills of riding bareback, shooting, capturing a fleeing stagecoach, and engaging in mock battles that "really showed what it meant to ride a horse." They brought the so-called Indian wars to life, "fighting in circles" as they supposedly had when defeating Custer. And they impressed observers with their daring and elegance. Carver even included "two beautiful women," labeled "Indian princesses," who accompanied the "Chief" during the grand entry.[112]

Buffalo Bill did the same, but on a grander scale. He arrived in Munich on 19 April 1890 with a troupe of more than two hundred Cowboys and Indians, and continued through a series of major German cities until May 1891.[113] He was proceeded by well-organized and enticing advertising campaigns, and he stuck to a program developed over years of success in the United States and other countries, one that emphasized historical melodrama, sensational display, sporting exhibition, and, above all, authentic players. Dr. Carver was there too. Having returned following his incredible success the year before, his troupe often trailed Buffalo Bill, and in Hamburg he competed against them directly.

Buffalo Bill's three- to four-hour program was consistent across Germany. Spectators were entranced by the Pony Express, an attack on an emigrant

FIGURE 9. Postcard: Buffalo Bill's Wild West in Europe. (Karl Markus Kreis Postcard Collection)

train, a Virginia quadrille done on horseback, cowboys demonstrating riding and roping skills, an attack on the Deadwood coach, a selection of American Indian dances, and the final buffalo hunt.[114] This was a program that worked. In Munich the bleachers set up for five thousand spectators filled daily, and performances continued to sell out as they moved across the country. Even when the rain was pouring in Dresden, they had to turn people away. The very presence of the show was an excitement. People waited by the thousands to welcome the participants as they arrived in each city. They milled around their camps, transforming their occurrence into ongoing events, and engaging in assorted forms of admiration, celebration, and emulation.

Many scholars have written about the success of Buffalo Bill's Wild West. Most regard his cultivation of American Indian performers in the late 1870s as critical.[115] According to Louis Warren, however, Buffalo Bill's "boldest move" was not simply replacing white actors with actual American Indian performers. It was making "Indians more visible" during precisely the same moment at which "a consciousness of their supposed vanishing—along with all other vestiges of the frontier—became ever more pervasive." One of those vestiges was Buffalo Bill himself, whose experiences with the Pony Express, the military, and buffalo hunters made him an authentic piece of the frontier. The same was true for many of the American Indian personalities such as Sitting Bull, Black Elk, and Rocky Bear, who toured with him.

FIGURE 10. Buffalo Bill's Wild West in Dresden, 1890. Such advertisements of various sizes inundated German newspapers before and during Buffalo Bill's visits. (Property of the author)

Moreover, according to Warren, "Cody's intuitive sense of the public long-ing for noble savages as true, uncorrupted, honest primitives fading before the onslaught of modern, industrial commerce was the source of much of his success in the later years of his stage career and, of course, in the Wild West show."[116] If that was true in the United States, it was perhaps even more so in Germany, where the battle against Western civilization and the emerging global capitalism provided a parable of Germans' past as well as their present.

There is no question that Buffalo Bill's Wild West was a sensation, that it was fun and exciting to attend the performances. Much of its success stemmed from the fact that, as Albert Richter wrote in his review of the show's stay in Dresden, Buffalo Bill shared with Barnum an American mas-tery of promotion and advertising. He knew how to create an event.[117]

However, not everything that appealed was orchestrated. Much like the earlier *Völkerschauen*, Germans were already intrigued by these shows because of the immediate connections they made to the childhood readings of Cooper, of German Coopers such as Möllhausen, and of the many reports in illustrated magazines. Again and again, newspaper accounts began with the rhetorical question, "Who during his youth did not read with affection the Indian stories?"[118] And many, together with one contributor to the *Berliner Zeitung,* remarked that "it is actually nothing new that we see [at the performance of Buffalo Bill's Wild West]. We have all seen it before, admittedly not with our own eyes, rather only in the dreams of our childhood, when we read ourselves to sleep with the fantastic tales of Leatherstocking."[119] Buffalo Bill provided Germans with an opportunity to experience in real life, if only for a few hours, the events that had captured many of their imaginations during the most formative periods of their lives, and in some cases for much longer.

At the same time, however, if Buffalo Bill's Wild West encouraged Germans to relive their childhood moments with *Leatherstocking* and other tales, it also encouraged them to reflect critically on the situation faced by the Lakota and other American Indian tribes. Indeed, after relating the performances to childhood memories, the contributor to the *Berliner Zeitung* also noted that "whether it is pleasing at this moment that profit-hungry civilized humanity has waged such a war of extermination against the race of redskins is certainly another question." During the performance, "one had not time to think of that," even if "Buffalo Bill was also one of the lead scouts" and made "innumerable adventures out of battles with Indians," because one is whisked away by "memories of our childhood stories" that "play out before our eyes." And yet, he implied, there was plenty of time to contemplate this disjuncture after the show.[120]

There was also plenty of information to work with. Hand in hand with the many German news reports of the performances were also reports of another possible uprising in the United States, which was regarded as both understandable and tragic, given the desperate conditions in which Lakotas and other American Indians found themselves.[121] Some authors wrote about the "dying out of the Indians," but even more discussed their "extermination" with a bitter edge.

It was this current in the German fascination with American Indians, which swirled around the immediate, spectacular, even cathartic verisimilitude of the performances that made the German press so responsive to a spontaneous speech Rocky Bear offered during a dinner with the Munich Anthropological Society on 26 April 1890.[122] Seven American Indians attended the meeting. Rocky Bear took on the role of both their leader and a keynote speaker. Thanking his hosts for their attention, he explained that he was pleased to see "so many white faces" around him and "to know that they are friends." He greeted them from his family and ancestors and explained that Buffalo Bill had persuaded him to come on this adventure by promising that he would meet great men with an interest in him, and some of those men, he implied, were before him. Perhaps because he esteemed his audience, he took the opportunity to discuss his plight. Explaining that he had led a life that included much warfare, he stressed that he had "never fought for fighting's sake." "I was an enemy of the whites. But I had to be one." "I fought against them; I took their scalps, because they had taken my lands." "My people and I fought for our rights, for our freedom, our homeland and our fatherland." "We were beaten. But after we were beaten we did not hold a grudge in our hearts," and today, he noted as an example, we would treat a "white child" with the same love and affection as an Indian child. In contrast, however, "the American people have committed great injustices against us." They took the land and pressed his people into ever-tighter borders "until there was no room left for us to raise our tents." The same God, he noted, created all the people with their different languages and cultures, but he made them all people. "Look at my hand," he said, "it is black, but the heart in my breast beats like your heart." God also placed in "all of our breasts" a sense "for the difference between right and wrong." But what was he to do when "whites commit an injustice against" his people? What could he do when "the laws of the great American republic do not protect us?" His place, he stated, "was to negotiate between the white and red men, and that," he continued, "is a hard position" indeed.[123]

There is no specific discussion of how Rocky Bear's words were received among the members of the Anthropological Society or the readers of Munich's newspapers, which printed them in full. It is reasonable to assume, however, that given the large number of reports in German newspapers that underscored these same points of injustice, they were well received because they confirmed what most Germans already believed: those who should be honored for their resistance and incorporated into the American polity had been, and continued to be, mistreated.

After Buffalo Bill came to German towns, children were often seen in the streets with their own lassos, feathers, and makeshift tomahawks, and adults began to emulate the performers as well.[124] They continued to enjoy similar shows after Buffalo Bill was gone.[125] They organized some of their own, and when Buffalo Bill returned in 1906, the crowds awaiting him were even larger.[126] An entire industry of new books, magazines, and comics stemmed from his performances, and he became a household name. The German press also profited, and Germans witnessed a transformation in the production of toys, theater, and ultimately, as they drew near to 1914, the entire circus industry, which would learn to insist on the need for actual American Indians in their repertoire. It is fair to say that after 1890, with newer, cheaper forms of media, there was a veritable explosion of interest. Perhaps no one embodied it or capitalized on it more than Karl May.

The Explosion of Interest

Not everyone likes Karl May, whose famous Winnetou series appeared in 1893, directly after Buffalo Bill's successful first tour. Literary critic Jeffrey Sammons, for example, claims not to understand his success. He acknowledges that "May is by a large margin the best-selling imaginative writer in the German language." His "stunning success during his career" and "his endurance in German cultural life to the present day is beyond compare." Indeed, "since the expiration of his copyright in 1962, it seems hardly possible to count the number of copies published with any accuracy; estimates are approaching one hundred million, and annual sales a decade ago [1988] continued at around two million." For Sammons, however, "the magnitude of the phenomenon never ceases to amaze" because he regards May as a "meretricious" and "psychopathological writer," an author with a vivid imagination but little inventiveness. May's work, he argues, is "monotonous," his vocabulary was "limited to 3,000 words, like a tabloid newspaper," he "disclaimed any concern for style," and in the end his "Westerns lie somewhere between Cooper and comic book." Ultimately, Sammons argues, his success probably escapes all analysis because it was "over determined and, perhaps, to some degree accidental."[127]

For Sammons, May's success is also irritating, because he capitalized upon a powerful trend in German literature but contributed little to it. Even if he borrowed from them with great zeal, Sammons argues, he diverged from such authors as Charles Sealsfield and Gerstäcker: "He replicates neither the confrontational anarchism of the former nor the inquiring spirit of the latter." Instead, despite the "exotic, constantly excited tone of adventure, bounding from one crisis to another, May forms a utopia of conventional and substantially conservative values that have no detectable American dimension and contain very little challenge to the unexamined presuppositions of the German majority." As a result, he questions "whether May's fiction is in any intelligible sense about America at all, and whether the provincial introversion underlying its superficial exoticism accounts to some degree for the American lack of interest in it.”[128] May's books were never popular in the United States and were never translated into English during his lifetime.

What May did do was mine the literature produced by the writers who came before him and simplify Germans' efforts to engage it. Much of the serious scholarship on May stresses the ways in which he literally borrowed characters, plots, and entire pieces of other authors' work in addition to taking information from encyclopedias, travelogues, and many other texts on America for his fictions. These scholars have generally agreed that part of his success was due to his use of these already extant stories for the historical and factual backdrop of his adventures. That made them both familiar and authentic for his readers.[129]

As Karl Markus Kreis reminds us, however, the backdrop is the only piece of real America in these stories, which he and the Karl May biographer Helmut Schmiedt characterize as first and foremost the product of May's dream world. The beauty of the dream world is that the stories are essentially self-referential, that they “always follow similar and hence recognizable patterns: ‘duels, tracking, hunting for wild animals and taming horses, eavesdropping on enemies, and above all the endless sequence of being taken captive and escaping.’” The other key factor is that the characters in May's dream world are so familiar to many Germans, so predictably middle-class in their values. “All the heroes embody familiar traits in their origin and behavior: the stories are permeated with German figures, German associations of ideological or social nature—in short, the hero ‘is always a conventional German in a conventional environment.’”[130]

Thus, May's popularity stemmed to a large degree from the familiarity of both the American Indian theme and the German characters he placed at its center. It also owed much to the simplicity of plot that Sammons derides, the familiar patterns of behavior governing his characters, the clear (for Sammons monotonous) divisions between good and evil, all of which made the books easy to read and encouraged young readers to play out the parts, much as May himself had done. Indeed, Sammons recognizes this as well, noting that “it is easy to see how May's works could become the inspiration for generations of children's games, played anywhere there was, or could be pretended to be, a field, a hill, or a ravine.”[131] The parts are so easy to assign and to play. May's German hero Old Shatterhand “is also of great appeal,” because “even in the beginning, he knows everything, has nothing more to learn, and can outdo everyone in everything. He gained all his knowledge and skill by reading books in Germany.” And thus anyone reading May's books could do the same, indeed could do what May had done by reading others' books rather than actually traveling abroad and engaging in the kinds of adventures and experiences that shaped his literary predecessors." One has to be impressed. As Sammons stresses, "By a recursive, literal duplicity, the author builds into his narration salesmanship for his own product. For naïve shamelessness there is probably nothing quite like it in the history of popular literature."[132]

May's work never eclipsed Cooper's tales or the thrill of Buffalo Bill, but it did benefit from them and join them in perpetuating and broadening the German obsession with American Indians. His work also provided that tradition of interest on which it built with a set of easily accessible books that all children could, and most certainly did, read. That was largely possible because of his timing. May benefited greatly from the revolution in printing that led to a more general explosion in pulp literature, improved distribution systems, and rising literacy rates, which already in the late 1870s had led to an array of similarly sensational cheap westerns with increasingly simple plots in the United States.[133] As a result of that production, and the enduring interest in all things Indian among Germans, many scholars have noted that "there is scarcely a single autobiography written by male authors from this period that does not discuss reading Karl May's books before and during puberty or playing Indians."[134] And in many cases, with women as well, the interest continued into adulthood.[135]

There are other things that are critical about May's stories, particularly the ways in which they dovetail with nationalist ideals and ideologies. That connection would change many things, and we will return to it later in the book. The point for now, however, is that the reception of his work by the beginning of the twentieth century, combined with the ongoing interests and motivations that contributed to it, demonstrates how ubiquitous the German fascination with American Indians had become during the nineteenth century, the degree to which thinking about them had become an integral part of German cultures by 1900, and the ways in which Germans' fantasies about American Indians followed a long history of realities and of interactions with America on both sides of the Atlantic, and which derived from Germans' concerns with their own histories and futures as much as the tales that were told about American Indians.

After all, the identification of "The Apache's Face" in the rock above the Felsenkeller Inn near Schweizermühle in the 1890s was as much a product of those long histories, those interactions, and Germans' ongoing respect and admiration for the liberties enjoyed by such archetypal men as Sitting Bull and Rocky Bear and their powers of resistance as the more immediate celebrity of Karl May. And thus we should not allow May's success or the attention his fantasies have received to obscure the realities in which Germans' affinities for American Indians took shape.

CHAPTER 2

Accommodating Violence

In August 1862, while much of the United States was focused on the Second Battle of Bull Run in the American Civil War, the Minnesota frontier exploded. Dakota Indians began killing white, overwhelmingly German, settlers in southwestern Minnesota, leading to the "massacre"[1] of six hundred to eight hundred of those settlers and the depopulation of twenty-three Minnesota counties.[2] After the tide of violence turned, many Dakotas fled west. While the U.S. military pursued them, Minnesota's German American press joined the state's English-language newspapers to call for a "war of extermination" [*Vernichtungskrieg*] in response to the slaughter. Many Dakotas were captured and imprisoned over the next two months. Military court proceedings initially sentenced 303 to be hanged. Against local protest, President Abraham Lincoln intervened to commute most of those sentences; nevertheless, on 26 December 1862, thirty-eight Dakotas were put to death in Mankato, Minnesota, in the largest mass execution in U.S. history.

Within the context of American history, the Minnesota Indian wars have generally been regarded as yet another moment in the ongoing conflict between American Indians, the U.S. government, its military, and white settlers.[3] During the nineteenth century, that conflict was eulogized in the United States as part of the price Americans must pay for their manifest destiny. It was also condemned in German-language periodicals published in both the United States and Germany as exemplary of everything that was grotesque about "Yankee know-how." Indeed, for German polemicists on both continents, such conflicts stood as a cipher for the destructive forces of modernity that "Americans" had unleashed upon North America.

Such discourses, however, have a way of smoothing out complexities; for the brutal conflicts that raged around New Ulm, Minnesota, in 1862 remind us again that in many cases the "Americans" being condemned in the German press were Europeans, often Germans, many newly arrived in North America. Unlike the peaceful immigrants moving across the empty, sublime Nebraska landscape in Bierstadt's *Oregon Trail* (1867), these Germans dealt directly with American Indians on the Minnesota frontier, where they too offended, provoked violent reactions, fell victim to that violence, and later claimed the kinds of retribution that most scholars of Germany associate with German South-West Africa four decades later.[4] In that colonial situation, calls for extermination of the indigenous people, most notably the Herero and Nama, led to genocide.[5] In New Ulm, and across German-speaking Minnesota, similar calls went out as well, but only after these German settlers unwittingly moved into a colonial situation that predated them by centuries, and into a structure that was, in many ways, already inherently genocidal. There, they fell victim to what A. Dirk Moses has called "subaltern genocide: the destruction of the colonizer by the colonized."[6] This ritualized excess, which has accompanied indigenous resistance to colonialism in places as diverse as early nineteenth-century Haiti and twentieth-century Africa, drew German settlers into the classical colonialist response: widespread calls for extermination and removal.

That response is critical for several reasons. To begin with, when Friedrich Gerstäcker reported on the violent frontier dynamics in North America during the decade before the Dakota conflict, stressing the ignorant agency of many pioneers in the excesses of American imperialism, he, like many German travelers, did so as an outside observer of Yankees' misguided actions and policies. As German America grew rapidly during the middle of the century, however, more and more of those agents were Germans, and many, including the freethinking citizens of New Ulm, who eagerly channeled the German condemnation of the United States' Indian policies, appear to have been just as ignorant of their complicity in American imperialism as Gerstäcker's Yankee pioneers.

That ignorance had structural roots that went beyond the frontier dynamics. At the time of the conflict, such German American colonists were often poorly, or only partially, integrated into the American polity. Frequently aloof, they succeeded in living simultaneously in two different worlds: as insiders who were part of the immigrant society in the expanding U.S. territories, but also as outsiders who retained their distinctions, sought out isolation, and were not completely trusted by their Anglophone counterparts. Indeed, many more radical elements of American society continued to regard these Germans with suspicion, just as the German American settlers persisted in conflating their Anglophone neighbors with the Yankees decried in German-language publications.[7] Thus, the distinctions between German and Anglo-American (i.e., non-Irish Anglophone) settlers placed these Germans in multiple, often contradictory subject positions in their newly occupied land, and that contributed significantly to the striking disjuncture of cultural structures that produced much of the violence that ensued in 1862.

That complexity makes any effort to view this colonial situation through the lens of center-periphery arguments challenging,[8] if not impossible, and it implores scholars of German colonialism to develop their analyses of state-centered efforts at expansion to include the role of Germans as much as Germany in these broader global trends. The implications for German history, in other words, are quite broad.

Indeed, it is not only nineteenth-century discourse that smoothes out complexities of such relationships. For example, the map at the beginning of Jürgen Osterhammel's highly regarded theoretical overview of colonialism presents us with a striking image of North America at the beginning of the twentieth century. Canada is marked as colonial territory, while the United States is not. That makes perfect sense from the perspective of state-centered projects and theories; from the point of view of indigenous North Americans, however, the distinction would have been (and may still be) moot.[9]

Similarly, if we were to trust Sebastian Conrad's comparisons of Germans in nineteenth-century America and Brazil, which paint German immigration to the United States as overwhelmingly urban and filled with the perils of quick assimilation and Brazil as a place where Germans "encountered nature" and created "*Heimat* abroad," we might easily overlook the millions of Germans who established rural colonies in the American West and Midwest and pursued a distinct *Deutschtum* through the nineteenth century.[10] What we would miss, in fact, would be a significant proportion of Germans' nineteenth-century colonial situations and much of the context necessary for understanding those that have gleaned the most attention.[11]

Germans' colonial ventures in North America, in other words, have much to teach us about the kinds of colonial situations Germans experienced more generally, and they serve to remind us that any study of German colonialism that ignores the United States is partial at best. The critical point for this book's central argument, however, is that despite this extreme violence and the localized shock of this particular colonial encounter—which continues to resonate in popular renditions of German America today[12]—the fact that Germans were on the receiving end of American Indian resistance during the Dakota conflict (or in other moments of American history) did nothing to prevent this incident from being easily folded into Germans' celebration of either American Indians' admirable resistance or Germans' sense of affinity for the Dakota (and other Sioux). Just the opposite: the Dakota conflict helped the Sioux become Germany's exemplary American Indians.

Germans into Minnesota

Much of Minnesota was Indian Territory until the conclusion of the 1851 Treaty of Travers de Sioux, when the Wahpeton and Sisseton bands of the Upper Sioux ceded essentially all their lands in Minnesota, Iowa, and what became South Dakota for a fixed sum and a small reservation on the Minnesota River.[13] A month later, the Mdewakanton and Wahpekute bands of the Lower Sioux signed a similar treaty at Mendota, which placed them further down the river, and just a few miles away from what would become New Ulm.[14] Combined, these treaties yielded a gain of twenty-four million acres for the Minnesota territory, which Alexander Ramsey, the first governor of the territory, immediately opened for settlement. His hope was to populate the land with farmers who would produce cash crops for the national and global market and use that productivity as a means toward statehood.[15] The process was rapid. While only 6,077 whites lived in Minnesota in the year before the treaties were signed, there were 172,023 by 1860. And because that radical growth took place during a surge in German immigration, Germans composed the majority of settlers who arrived to take advantage of the moment.[16] Indeed, they remained the largest ethnic group in Minnesota until 1905.[17]

New Ulm, located on the territory's new western border, was founded in 1854 by two groups of German colonists, one organized by a handful of men who created the Chicago Land Company after meeting during an English-language class in Chicago,[18] and the other supported by the Turner[19] Colonization Society in Cincinnati.[20] Like many similar ventures, the colony was financed through membership dues, and the colonists envisioned creating a cooperative socialist settlement free of "attorneys and preachers,"[21] complete with commonly held mills and industry, and distinguished by equally distributed parcels of lands, which included lots in the town, farmland, garden plots, and timber for all of the original members.[22] Once founded, the town was quickly surveyed, plotted, streets were laid out, and buildings, many made of brick, rapidly rose up. Already in January 1858 the city had ninety-five houses, a school, the Turner Hall, which became a cultural center, six stores, one woolen cloth establishment, two blacksmiths, a butcher shop, a bakery, and two mills. And by 1860 it claimed a population of approximately

FIGURE 11. New Ulm promotional image 1860. Lithograph by J. Berndt. (Minnesota Historical Society)

635 people (only 2 of whom were non-Germans) as well as burgeoning industry and a freethinking newspaper, the *New Ulm Pioneer,* which boasted a circulation of more than twelve hundred.[23]

The unitary character of the city's cultural makeup was not accidental. In many ways it was a product of tensions between German arrivals and Anglo-Americans, especially those sympathetic to arguments of the anti-immigrant Know-Nothing movement.[24] Indeed, conflicts with the Know-Nothings were one of the central reasons Wilhelm Pfaender and his fellow Turners sought to move their families to a settlement away from the "mad, unworthy attempts at killing" they had experienced in Cincinnati.[25] These Turners were not impoverished laborers; like many German immigrants at the time, they were relatively well educated, highly skilled, even affluent.[26] They also lacked the kind of group political power that made the Irish the focus of Know-Nothing ire.[27] But they did constitute a distinct and ever-growing ethnic group whose fondness for beer and public socializing on Sundays upset many Anglo-American sensibilities, and the influx of so many skilled German workers during a period of economic decline heightened anxieties.[28]

Thus, the Germans who established New Ulm on the border of Minnesota territory regarded themselves as outsiders. They created a settlement that stressed socialist unity and German inclusiveness. They welcomed German speakers from across Central Europe,[29] and they provided them with a kind of safe haven against the exclusivity of the Anglo-Americans they had encountered further east. And as a result, they were largely unable to see themselves "through Dakota eyes," as part and parcel of a broader white-European expansion that threatened American Indians' resources.

German Colonists and the Dakotas before the Conflict

One of the most striking characteristics of the settlement of New Ulm for Germans, who had often learned about American Indians and the American West from James Fenimore Cooper and other novelists,[30] was the modern, industrial character of that colony. Unlike in the typical frontier stories they could have read in Germany, there was no wagon train, no joint suffering across the Oregon or some similar trail, no lightning attacks on the prairie captured by Carl Wimar and other German and German American artists of the 1850s and 1860s. Rather, most of the colonists traveled on trains and steamboats. Many were dropped off on the riverbank next to the settlement.[31] A minority walked the last thirty miles from St. Peter directly to the east. The town grew quickly because of those waterways as well, which swiftly delivered from St. Paul the finished goods and materials the colonists needed for their homes, stores, mills, breweries, and other industries and helped create a radical, almost immediate, disjuncture between the character of their settlement and that of the Dakotas who were just a few miles away.

That disjuncture would not have escaped the Dakotas. They interacted with the initial groups of Germans who surveyed the site and frequently returned to visit New Ulm from its inception through 1862: they came to trade and to spend money they received each year from the federal government; they passed by on hunting parties, war parties, and on their way to collect maple sugar; they came to town to perform dances and engage in celebrations; and in the years directly before the conflict, they often came asking for food.

The *New Ulm Pioneer*, which first appeared on 1 January 1858 as "an organ for the propagation of radical fundamental principles," reported many of these encounters.[32] Indeed, its editors promised in the initial issue to provide readers with insight into their neighbors, gleaned from trips to the nearby Dakota and Winnebago (Ho-Chunk) reservations, and with "reports over the Indian worldview, laws, customs, habits, tales, and warfare." And they did. Much of the paper reads like the popular travel narratives and ethnological reports about people in faraway lands that frequently appeared in German periodicals such as *Das Ausland*, *Globus*, and *Über Land und Meer*. Essays in the *New Ulm Pioneer* noted with great detail, for instance, the clothing, tools, and weapons of the American Indians who traveled through town, even their facial expressions and behaviors, and it often included notes on their family relations. It also issued current reports on the interactions between the Dakotas and the Winnebagos to the south, noted Dakota animosity and warfare with the Chippewas (Ojibwa)[33] further north, and provided ethnological discussions of the Dakotas' place in the broader Sioux nation, historical accounts of tribal movements, and even short reports about their language.[34]

A reader of the *New Ulm Pioneer*, in other words, would have been privy to considerable information about his or her neighbors. Ironically, however, much of that information was, like the ethnological travel narratives in German periodicals, descriptive knowledge stemming from studied observations of external markers and behaviors rather than the subjective knowledge that might come from intimate interactions and experiences. Thus despite the German colonists' physical proximity to their neighbors, as a group they retained a significant intellectual distance from them.

Much as in the popular stories one might read about American Indians in Germany, for example, titillating reports of intra-Indian violence also lurked within local accounts of Dakota, Chippewa, and Winnebago.[35] Such accounts accentuated German colonists' separation from these new worldly Others. One finds, for instance, discussions of war parties returning from the North with fresh scalps on their lances or, on one occasion, with a Chippewa captive destined for a torturous death. There were also reports of Dakota attacks on Omaha and Pawnee camps. Even the descriptions of Dakota visitors to New Ulm included such tidbits, referring in one instance, for example, to the number of scalps hanging in the lodges of Dakotas who briefly set up camp near town.[36] German settlers were clearly cognizant of (perhaps even enamored with) the warrior acts of these warrior societies; but those too were observed at a distance.

The only Indian-white violence reported in the paper took place in other areas of North America, in California to the west, among the Cherokee to the south, or in isolated incidents in Minnesota when Know-Nothings are reported to have attacked the property of an individual American Indian who had turned to farming. Indeed, on 6 July 1861, scarcely more than a year before the conflict, the paper issued an essay on immigration to the area that underscored its safety and explained that many colonists had lived miles from town for years in complete security. "Near New Ulm," they proclaimed, "the Indians had permanent homes" and were "overseen by agents" and they were not nearly as dangerous as the "rabble" and "thieves" one might encounter in St. Paul.[37] The notion that the violence they reported among American Indian adversaries might spill over in their direction was completely absent from the paper. It was also clearly missing from the minds of most residents in the area, as the testaments from German survivors of the conflict make clear.[38] They uniformly expressed surprise and confusion at having been attacked.[39]

In the years before the conflict, the chief concerns that circulated among German settlers about the Dakotas turned around notions of civilization, and its impact on their lives. In the *New Ulm Pioneer*, for example, romantic laments that "civilization is their death," or at least the death of the "authentic" Indians who lived a nomadic way of life, were occasionally intertwined with more systematic descriptions of Dakota visitors, especially those groups who traveled through the town in pursuit of the game that was quickly diminishing with the population explosion in Minnesota.[40] Such romantic images also drew directly on tropes popularized in German travel narratives, which the paper's authors would have known well.

More frequent, enthusiastic, and original, however, were comments about the putative progress of individual American Indians toward that very "civilization." These included, for instance, positive casual remarks about Dakota visitors to New Ulm greeting its residents on the streets with "how do you do,"[41] laudatory comments on such visitors' increasing interest in purchasing new household items and modern clothing in town stores,[42] special praise given to those people from the Upper Sioux Reservation who removed themselves from tribal rule and formed the Hazelwood Republic of farming Indians in 1856 with the help of the missionary Steven R. Riggs,[43] and vituperative condemnations of a Minnesota judge's treatment of nine of its members who sought state citizenship in 1861: the judge, they wrote, "knew about as much about the Dakota languages as a donkey knows about Latin." Dakota, they quipped, was in many ways superior to English in its clarity and thus ideal for many of the political purposes the judge had in mind. It was a rousing defense of both the individuals and their language.[44]

It was, in fact, the federal government's mistreatment of the Dakotas and other American Indians that gained the greatest attention in the *New Ulm Pioneer*. One finds, over the course of its less than four years in print, repeated attacks on the government and its agents' abuse of American Indians. In the issue of 23 February 1858, for example, one can read an essay condemning the government's treatment of the Yankton Sioux and the paper's argument that the government abused them with its treaties; there is a column detailing the ways in which the United States' repeated treaties with the Winnebago, each forcing them further west onto worse and less land, undercut their productivity and their livelihood and fundamentally transformed their culture, making them dependent on the government; and one can also read a more general essay titled "the demise [*Untergang*] of our Indian Tribes," which details the destruction caused by disease, alcohol, uncontrolled warfare, and the military and state officials' abusive and often violent treatment of tribes.[45]

In essence, the tone in the *New Ulm Pioneer* was complete dissatisfaction with U.S. Indian policy, which fit the radical principles of its editors and the town and mirrored the general tone of reports in German periodicals in Europe. Indeed, reports from 1859 on "the Indian wars" underscored the millions of dollars poured into them and argued that much of the money went directly into the "diverse pockets" of corrupt officials who encouraged the wars in order to generate those profits.[46] The wars, the *New Ulm Pioneer* exclaimed, "have no other purpose." Similarly, the paper detailed the illegal encroachment on American Indian lands across North America, and in 1859 a series of essays appeared on the corruption of Indian agents and other officials charged with upholding the federal government's treaty obligations.[47] Moreover, in July of that year, the paper reported the burning of an official's home that caused the death of his family in Tehama, California, by an American Indian boy reacting to the mass killing of his relatives in the area; the paper's sympathy lay on the side of the boy. It condemned the state of California's labors at "extermination" [*Aussrottung*] and argued that American Indians' "effort at revenge was only natural."[48]

It is thus not surprising that when word of protest and a possible uprising at the Upper Sioux Reservation in Yellow Medicine County was printed in the *New Ulm Pioneer*'s last issue on 9 August 1862,[49] it retained its descriptive intellectual distance and its polemical position. It focused on the neglect and responsibility of the Indian agents and showed no concern for the implications this might have for residents of New Ulm or other Germans spread across the nearby counties. Their principled opposition to U.S. Indian policy and their feelings of exclusion from Anglo-American institutions prevented them (the authors and readers of the *New Ulm Pioneer*) from seeing past their own sense of victimization and solidarity and recognizing their complicity in the broader process they had often condemned.

Tensions of Empire around a German Hometown

Tensions existed between Germans and the Dakotas, but colonists seldom saw themselves as a source of those tensions.[50] For example, New Ulm's German colonists considered friction over land a federal problem, a result of government actions divorced from their own. They knew they occupied land recently obtained through treaties with the Dakotas; but despite their condemnations of federal Indian policy, they evidenced little concern about the implications of occupying land acquired through those policies. Instead, they viewed their actions from a standpoint they shared with Anglo-Americans. They recognized their right to the land because they purchased it from the government in a transaction codified by U.S. law, but there is no evidence that they reflected on the government's right to sell that land or recognized the interconnections between their occupation of the territory and the government's actions toward the Dakotas before, during, or after its acquisition of the land and the Germans' subsequent purchase.

The Germans' lack of reflection was present from their arrival. Tensions arose with Dakotas when the first German colonists occupied Dakota lodges on what became known as the Milford settlement, cut holes in some of the walls, and refused to leave when confronted by groups of Dakota women and men. Instead, the colonists stood their ground as legitimate surveyors occupying and inspecting land the government had for sale and refused to acknowledge the Dakotas' claim over the encampment.[51]

These early confrontations took place largely because the borders of the reservation remained unclear to many Dakotas, who continued to move and live outside of them.[52] The German colonists, however, were unsure of the borders as well. In March 1859, for example, the *New Ulm Pioneer* printed an acknowledgment that land west of town, which had recently been marked off as a township, parceled up, sold off, and developed, actually belonged to the reservation and was not meant for sale. That error, however, generated no embarrassment among the colonists, and rather than immediately acknowledging the need to return the land, the essay stressed that the government must be forced to compensate the Dakotas for this further loss of territory. The reason it offered was economic, not moral or legal: it would be cheaper than returning the Germans' money and paying them for their labor. Placing the decision in the hands of the Dakotas, or recognizing their right to determine the fate of their land, however, was not an avenue it advocated or the colonists even appear to have entertained.[53]

The uses of the land continued to be a point of contention as German colonists, like most settler colonists, introduced new contexts for its valuation and use. Those contexts stemmed from the social, cultural, and political importance of property in Europe, and specifically in southern Germany. They were markedly different from the meanings the Dakota and other tribes had given to the landscape before the colonists arrived, and which continued to structure their relationship to the land afterward. As Gary Clayton Anderson reminds us, notions of assistance and reciprocity formed the basis for Dakota communal existence and all their relations with people. Their notions of reciprocity, for example, required mutual aid among friends and relatives and the sharing of resources in a variety of situations. Hunting parties, for example, might expect assistance—food, water, and information—from settlers they passed while looking for game, out of a general willingness to share resources rather than fear of their arms. Similarly, it was understood that people who possessed greater resources, especially food, would share with their friends who had less or none. To do otherwise would be impolite, would make it impossible for the settlers to be adopted into the Dakota kinship system, and could effectively constitute an end to friendly relations.[54]

Few of the German settlers recognized the implications of their willingness to either share or not share resources with the Dakotas or the broader impact their uses of the land might have had on their neighbors. One can read, for example, numerous accounts of colonists hunting widely around New Ulm. Rudolf Leonhart, for instance, a teacher who arrived in New Ulm only a year before the conflict, devoted an entire chapter of his *Memories of New Ulm* to the pleasures of killing diverse game, especially during a particularly successful outing with friends that filled their wagon.[55] He reveled in the freedom of the open land and his ability to take from it. But there is no sense that his actions might have contributed to the conditions that led many of the Dakotas to look to New Ulm as a source of food when they could no longer find game and the government neglected its obligations to provide for them. Instead, Leonhart wrote with great irritation that the Dakotas, whom he termed "red Hidalgos," were "on our backs" asking for food "almost every day."[56]

Such begging was constant, as was noted widely in the narratives produced by German survivors of the conflict.[57] Indeed, it was so common by 1862 that when John Other Day, who became famous for saving the lives of many colonists during the conflict, rode up on his horse and "kicked on the door" of Johann and Brigitta Pelzl's home to tell them to flee, "Brigitta gave her husband a loaf of bread and told him to go to the door, for most likely some Indians were in need of food."[58] When her husband told her that Other

Day warned they were in danger, she refused to believe him, left the house to inquire with her neighbor, and was killed as she approached the next farm. Clearly the intellectual distance evidenced in the *New Ulm Pioneer*'s accounts of the Dakotas played a role in the German colonists' intimate encounters with them as well. The Germans remained unaware of their complicity in undermining Dakota society and culture or the animosity it generated among their neighbors.

While few of the German narratives that recall life in New Ulm before the conflict demonstrate acrimony toward the Dakotas' frequent requests for food, and the vast majority imply that little or no tensions existed with their neighbors, essays in the *New Ulm Pioneer* reveal that friction over resources did exist. This was especially true when Dakotas helped themselves to goods or natural resources that Germans believed to be their own, including the plants and animals on their property. On 17 September 1859, for example, the *New Ulm Pioneer* included a letter from one of the town's residents that stated that their "red neighbors the Sioux Indians had recently committed many excesses against the property of the citizens of Milford Township." The author felt compelled to remind his fellow colonists that the "Indian laws" were on the residents' side: the Dakotas could leave the reservation only with permission from an agent; when they did, they had to conduct themselves according to the same laws as the Germans; they could not simply camp where they liked; they had no right to hunt or fish on other's property; and since local authorities could enforce those laws, the people in the upper settlement need not endure "further unpleasantries" at the hands of the Dakotas. Indeed, they could react against these violations with the help of local sheriffs or police.[59]

Increasingly, however, as a small number of Germans recalled, Dakotas engaged in reactions of their own during similar kinds of "violations." Minnie Carrigan, for example, wrote that in July 1862 a group of Dakota set up camp on her father's property, and cut some of his timber, and when he confronted them, "a squaw caught up a large butcher knife and chased him away." At the time, that confrontation caused Carrigan's mother great amusement; but in retrospect, it offered an epiphany. Carrigan recognized it should have been a cause for concern. We can also regard it, however, as evidence of one group of Dakotas reacting against a different set of "unpleasantries": the settlers' interference with their own use of the land and their stinginess and unwillingness to engage in reciprocation.[60]

Such reports, woven into the testaments, make it clear that colonists did, on occasion, experience the Dakotas' frustration when they were denied access to resources, and they provide a critical context for the incident that, according to most accounts of the conflict's origins, turned the Dakotas to violence: an argument among a small group of young warriors about their ability to take eggs from a bird's nest located on a colonist's farm, which led one, in frustration, to initiate the murders of the colonist and his family.[61] That story appears much less arbitrary when set against other, lesser-known examples that illuminate the disjuncture between the cultural structures in which the German colonists and the Dakotas made sense of their worlds. That disjuncture lay at the heart of the heartland's tensions of empire.

The Disjuncture of Cultural Structures

The great irony from the point of view of the New Ulm Pioneer's editors and readers is that in many ways the event that eradicated hundreds of German colonists in August 1862 stemmed from the disjuncture of multiple overlapping but autonomous cultural structures that occurred as German colonists became the victims of the interplay of Dakota categories with their own and were killed as the embodiment of American imperialism. We know this in part because Dakota narratives about the 1862 conflict are extant. Gary Clayton Anderson and Alan R. Woolworth located sixty-three of them for their book *Through Dakota Eyes: Narrative Accounts of the Minnesota Indian War of 1862*, and they drew directly on thirty-six of them as they reconstructed a chronological account of the conflict through those voices. In their introduction, Anderson and Woolworth argue that the central source of friction between the Dakotas and settlers came from the Dakotas' rapid and unwitting transformation from hunters to wards of the state. As I noted above with examples from German public and private sources, Anderson and Woolworth stress that the quick introduction of new cultural and economic structures into the Minnesota River Valley placed many Dakota, who "continued to hunt on lands increasingly occupied by white homesteaders," into repeated conflicts with farmers who regarded them as "intruders." The consequence that escaped the German colonists, however, was that "to a majority of the reservation Indians, all farmers, regardless of racial or ethnic origin, became threats to their existence."[62] That included the Germans, even those who were engaged in creating a socialist community based on industrial agriculture and who may have been sympathetic to the Dakotas' plight.

From hindsight, the disjuncture in those overlapping cultural structures is much clearer than it was at the time. For if the narratives and reports we have from German colonists fail to confirm that they all or always regarded the Dakotas who hunted on their newly acquired lands as "intruders," Dakota narratives reveal that this was the message they often received and the message that in turn affected what they thought of the colonists farming nearby.[63] It produced considerable hostility.

There were, however, other causes for the animosity that shaped many of the Dakotas' impressions of German settlers. Anderson and Woolworth list a series of flashpoints, some of which the Germans themselves had criticized in their local press: the unfair treaties, the government's subsequent failure to even abide by those agreements, the illegal sales of liquor, fraud by some Indian agents and other officials, and the government's failure to pay annuities on time were all denounced in the New Ulm Pioneer and later in German as well as Dakota narratives. Equally important, they argue, but generally unknown or overlooked by the Germans, was the impact of the punishment visited on Dakota war parties that acted against the Chippewa, the cutting of many men's hair, the rise of Christianity, the disrespect visited on shamans and medicine men, and the lack of protection against mishandled affairs between white men and Dakota women. A combination of all these factors, according to Anderson and Woolworth, generated a "growing ethnic friction in the upper Minnesota River valley" and contributed to "the outbreak of war."[64]

That friction, however, went beyond ethnicities and turned largely around the disparate cultural implications of farming. The Dakota chief Big Eagle made that explicit. He recalled in his account of the origins of the violence that "the 'farmers' were favored in every way." The government favored not only the German and Anglo-American farmers but also American Indians who took up farming—people such as John Other Day and the members of the Hazelwood Republic, who were lauded in the New Ulm Pioneer. Big Eagle stressed that these Dakota farmers "had houses built for them, some of them even had brick houses, and they were not allowed to suffer. The other Indians did not like this. They were envious of them and jealous, and disliked them because they were favored. They called them 'farmers,' as if it was disgraceful to be a farmer. They called them 'cut-hairs,' because they had given up the Indian fashion of wearing the hair, and 'breeches men,' because they wore pantaloons, and 'Dutchmen,' because so many of the settlers on the north side of the river and elsewhere in the country were Germans." Even for many of those who sensed the inevitability of the economic transformation of their lives, he noted, "it seemed too sudden to make such a change."[65] The pace was overwhelming.

The irony from our current perspective is that so many of the German colonists appear to have lived undisturbed by those tensions, unable to recognize their own role as the embodiment of the harshest forces that ruptured the Dakotas' social and cultural worlds. There are, however, cultural and structural explanations for that irony. One is the speed and scale of immigration, and the concomitant rapid introduction of the Germans' notions of land use and value, which they brought with them into the Minnesota River Valley from their towns and villages in Germany.

Most German colonists arrived with the intention of creating the kinds of farms they were unable to obtain in Germany, and given that opportunity, they focused almost all of their attention during their initial years in Minnesota on establishing their farms and creating a patrimony for their children. Their actions, however, were motivated more by an effort to preserve a world that European capitalism seemed poised to destroy than to build an entirely new world in Minnesota. As Mack Walker pointed out decades ago, many of these settlers "traveled thousands of grim miles in order to keep their roots, their habits, their united families and the kind of future they wanted for their families." They sought to conserve a way of life "they remembered or thought they did."[66] Therefore, these "peasant pioneers," as Kathleen Neils Conzen has deemed them, established tight ethnic communities in Minnesota that mimicked the cultural and social structures of their hometowns so completely that they effectively set themselves apart from both their Anglo-American counterparts and the neighboring Dakota.

Indeed, we know that their settlements were unique, often purposefully so, and created in many ways in opposition to their Anglo-American counterparts. Those who survived the conflict had significant economic success, acquiring little debt and building multigenerational farms, which they passed down for decades. In contrast, Anglo-American farmers often used their funds and lands less wisely, selling or abandoning the land after reaping initial profits. Their distinct interconnection between land, family, and community, drawn directly from their experiences in German states, is one of the central reasons why these and other Germans in Minnesota were so effective in creating what Conzen terms "phantom landscapes" for themselves, allowing them to live simultaneously in spheres governed by German and Anglo-American cultural structures. But the overlap of these structures and the immediate distinctions between Anglo-Americans and Germans remained almost unintelligible to the Dakotas, even though the distinctions between these white settlers created radically contrasting subjectivities. Therefore, while many Germans held the distinctions between themselves and Anglo-Americans as paramount, and those distinctions afforded German colonists a distance from which to rail against both the federal government and their white neighbors, the Dakotas did not seem to notice them at all.

By the same token, because German colonists were largely governed by their own cultural structures, they proved almost incapable of comprehending the meanings and implications of their actions within cultural structures they did not recognize or understand. Most of the German colonists who fell victim to the Dakotas' attacks had resided only briefly in Minnesota and interacted directly with only small numbers of Dakotas. As a result, many of the issues that surfaced in Dakota accounts of the violence were completely absent from both the German accounts of life before the conflict and the essays in their central publication, the *New Ulm Pioneer*.

For example, just as Dakotas were generally unable to discern the variety of Germans among them (Bavarian, Platt-Deutsch, Rheinländer, etc.) or to weigh the relative character of these new arrivals against that of the Anglo-Americans, neither the German narratives nor the essays in the *New Ulm Pioneer* recognized the critical role factions played among the Dakotas.[67] Attention to those factions frame most of the Dakotas' narratives. Internal divisions had heightened as the Dakota world split, as some, but only some, cut their hair and changed their clothing. And as Chief Big Eagle implied, all the white people, including the freethinking New Ulmers, played a role in intensifying this fractionalization. But there is no indication in either the public or the private records of the town that they recognized that their tacit support of Dakota farmers could also be regarded by many on the reservation as favoritism, inspiring jealousy and animosity there. Similarly, while German colonists noticed that some Dakotas took up Christianity (hardly a point of merit for the Turners), there is no evidence they were aware that Dakota religious leaders suffered as a result.

Despite the misgivings that the socialist-leaning Turners might have had at the revelation, many Dakotas regarded the German settlers as representatives of the forces that we would today recognize as global capitalistic forces, which were inherently ethnocidal and potentially genocidal, and which were compelling the Dakotas to either assimilate, react, or move aside.[68] Thus, for many Dakotas, only the wholesale elimination of those whites—German or otherwise—held the possibility of turning back that tide, and for many, like Little Six, who sang "the Dutch [Germans] have made me so angry, I will butcher them alive," the Germans closest to them became the focus of their anger. And when it was unleashed in a classic case of "subaltern genocide," they sought to kill as many as they could locate—men, women, and children.[69]

Vernichtungskrieg

Much has been written about the course of the killing that took place around New Ulm in August 1862.[70] Dakota warriors, emboldened by their observations that so many soldiers had left for the Civil War,[71] and eventually led by Little Crow, attacked the Lower Sioux Agency on 18 August, defeated a detachment of Minnesota militia and voluntary infantry at the Battle of Redwood Ferry, and then broke into bands that laid waste to the farms and small settlements in the Minnesota River valley, indiscriminately killing entire families, scalping and in some cases mutilating their bodies, pillaging and burning their homes, taking hundreds of captives, and causing hundreds more to flee to New Ulm, nearby Fort Ridgley, or further east toward St. Peter. Dakota warriors attacked New Ulm directly on 19 August and again on 23 August and nearby Fort Ridgley on 20 and 22 August.

The Dakotas were not well organized. They did not act in unison, and although they devastated individual farms across the region, they failed to take control of either the town or the fort.[72] The destruction they wreaked on New Ulm and its inhabitants, however, was extensive. Much of it burned, and after the second attack on the town, the survivors, close to two thousand people with 153 wagons, fled thirty miles southeast to Mankato. Dakota warriors also defeated a burial detail of 150 soldiers at the Battle of Birch Coulee on 2 September, and further war parties spread north and south from the Minnesota River valley in the ensuing weeks, ending only after the Dakotas' defeat at the Battle of Wood Lake on 23 September 1862. Many of the Dakotas surrendered soon afterward at Camp Release, but others, including Little Crow, fled west into Dakota Territory, pursued by General Henry Hastings Sibley, whose Minnesota regiments continued to fight with Dakota and Lakota warriors into 1864.[73]

The majority of accounts in the German-language press written in August and September 1862 emphasized the binary, essentially racial, character of the conflict as a war between Indians and whites[74]—perhaps with good reason, since this is precisely how many of the warriors around Little Crow framed it. Racial violence was not a new experience for North Americans, white or red. But it was new to many of the German colonists around New Ulm, and it precipitated dramatic shifts in their subject positions, which revealed the situational character of German colonists' identity as outsiders.[75]

That shift came through their exposure to the kinds of violence that were inherent in a structure they had unwittingly entered.[76] As Moses has taught us, "colonial war could mean total war on a local scale," in which entire societies were recognized as adversaries, and each side targeted men, women, and children almost equally. Victory, in most cases, was contingent on their elimination.[77] The more general, theoretical literature on the relationship between settler colonialism and genocide is particularly instructive in the case of the 1862 Dakota conflict, because it illuminates the degree to which that conflict followed a well-established pattern of violence, in which European "invasion," as Patrick Wolfe terms it in his work on Australia, can be seen as much as a structure as an event. Settler colonialism, he points out, is ultimately a zero-sum contest over land, in which the object of elimination endures apart from any subjectively held racist attitudes on the part of immigrants. Moreover, as Moses argues, "the mechanism of policy radicalization is the intensity of Indigenous resistance." Thus, rather than colonization being "genocidal tout court," it is often "a dynamic process with genocidal potential that could be released in circumstances of crisis," much as it was in Minnesota in August 1862.[78]

The implications of this structural argument are critical for our understanding of Germans' reactions to the Dakotas after the initial attacks. "The place to look for genocidal intentions," Moses argues, "is not in explicit, prior statements of settlers or governments," and thus not in the New Ulm Pioneer, "but in the gradual evolution of European attitudes and policies as they were pushed in an exterminatory direction by the confluence of their underlying ideological assumptions, the acute fear of Aboriginal attack, the demands of the colonial and international economy, their plans for the land, and the resistance to these plans by the Indigenous peoples."[79] Drawn directly into "the genocidal potential" of indigenous resistance, German colonists' subjective positions quickly gave way to the archetypical behavior of settler colonialists in similar crisis situations. It was a behavior shared by Anglo-Americans and German Americans alike.[80]

Once the violence of race war was unleashed against the colonists, a kind of negative integration took place in which Germans, whose identity had relied so much on the juxtaposition between themselves and Anglophone Americans, were quickly integrated into a suddenly more inclusive white Minnesota. Across Minnesota and surrounding states, the German American press (regardless of the respective newspapers' political leanings) reported on the conflict as a devastating attack of red against white, of "Indians killing white people," with little or no mention of the fact that the majority of the victims were fellow Germans.[81] Some German-language newspapers in other states also quickly printed rumors that further uprisings were taking place in Nebraska and Wisconsin, and they reported general concerns among the white populations of these states that the American Indians on local reservations might turn to violence as well.[82] In this broader discourse, New Ulm's specific ethnic and cultural character was immediately subordinated to its role as a site of white Americans' economic and political power, a point many Dakotas seemed to have understood much better than the German colonists.

Fairly quickly, however, the reporting in German-language papers became more textured, allowing for differentiation beyond the red-white binary, and acknowledging that this had been an attack of some Dakotas against most of the white people within their reach—not a wholesale race war. Even if race was a critical factor in many Dakotas' choice of victims, the press recognized that some Dakotas refused to participate. Some, the press also noted, warned settlers, and many of the French families were not targeted. Moreover, other tribes, the papers acknowledged, had stayed out of the conflict altogether, and a few, especially the Chippewa, were eager to join in the fighting against the Dakotas. In many cases, German-language newspapers reprinted translations of Chippewa requests to be included in the war that circulated in English-language papers.[83]

Across the Midwest, the German-language press searched for causality and sought to assign blame. Initially, some tied the conflict to the Civil War consuming the nation. Rumors spread through the German papers that agents from the South might have precipitated the attacks in an effort to undermine Minnesota's contributions to Union war efforts. Increasingly, however, the focus of the reports became more particular, and the conflict less glorious. Already on 2 October 1862, for example, the *Belleviller Zeitung* in Belleville, Illinois, proclaimed that the "government's deceitful Indian agents" were responsible for the "Indian atrocities." Its accusations stemmed from the testament of one farmer, John Schneider, who lived sixteen miles southwest of New Ulm but had "joined the [Union] army out of patriotism" and, while passing through Illinois, described in detail witnessing an Indian agent enriching himself by swindling the Dakotas on their payments. He blamed the greed and corruption of government agents for the loss of his farm and the suffering of his family. Similar accusations became ubiquitous after the conflict was over.

The broader implications of the agents' immoral actions and the Dakotas' violent response also quickly emerged in the German-language press in other states. As the *Nord Stern* in La Crosse, Wisconsin, argued on 30 August 1862, regardless of what sparked the violence, "a *Vernichtungskrieg* [war of extermination] had begun, one which could only end with the complete eradication of entire Indian tribes."[84] That prescient warning anticipated the general reaction in Minnesota's press, where demands for a *Vernichtungskrieg* became a mantra, and where contributors repeatedly argued that Dakota efforts to eliminate whites from Minnesota should be met with an equal, if not more powerful response: the complete elimination of the Dakotas from the state.

Indeed, St. Paul's *Minnesota Staats-Zeitung*, the leading German-language newspaper in the state, and the one closest to the political position of the *New Ulm Pioneer*,[85] began the call for a *Vernichtungskrieg* on the same day the *Nord Stern* predicted the reaction, losing no ground to the English-language press.[86] After arguing that "no words can do justice" to the acts that the "cannibals," "beasts," and "barbarians," committed "against men, women, and children" with their tomahawks and knives, it described the almost total destruction of New Ulm. "Hopefully," the paper opined in language typical of similar colonial situations, "the case of New Ulm will reach the ears of people in power" and encourage them to "arm the frontier and bring together a military force to pursue a war of eradication [*Ausrottungskrieg*] against the redskins so that we can win back the land that has been lost to Culture."[87]

While some scholars might be eager to regard this call for a war of extermination as a precursor to similar arguments in Germany's formal colonies decades later, it was not a uniquely German idea, nor uniquely Anglo-American or English, even if it was a fairly common retort in similar colonial situations.[88] It was, in fact, the position articulated by many in the state government, and government officials' willingness to embrace such an extreme reaction did much to elide the previous ethnic divisions among white citizens and tie them and their property together as a single concern.

Indeed, integration through violence permeated successive accounts in both the German- and English-language press. On 12 September, for example, the *Minnesota Staats-Zeitung* approvingly printed "The Governor's Message" to the state about the war. The first part detailed Governor Alexander Ramsey's plan to absorb the moneys that U.S. treaties had set aside for the Dakotas in order to compensate Minnesota and its white citizens for their tremendous loss of property.[89] The second part contained his plan for preventing further losses. Under the subtitle of "*Vernichtungskrieg*," he declared, in language typical of settler colonial governments, that "the Sioux Indians from Minnesota must be eradicated or forever driven over the borders of our state and kept away." His goal, he stated bluntly, was to make forever impossible "the return of even one of the murderers into the state."[90]

The editors of the *Minnesota Staats-Zeitung* agreed. Embracing the governor's message, they retained its racially violent tone during the rest of the conflict and its aftermath. And once the tide had turned, and large numbers of Dakotas were imprisoned, the paper pressed for immediate executions.[91] Thus, when President Lincoln commuted most of the death sentences, the paper raged against the federal government and declared that "peace" between the Dakotas and the state's white citizens could be achieved only by "the hanging of the 300 murdering red rogues" and the transportation of the remaining Sioux "thousands of miles from our border." Without those actions, it warned, the border would be transformed into a "bloody" war zone populated by Indian hunters, not unlike those found in Texas and California, who, because they were denied their due by the government, would act while proclaiming: "Vengeance is mine!"[92]

Those fears were not realized. A few Germans joined the military force that went westward in pursuit of the Dakotas, reveling in their own opportunity for vengeance, and staying with the army for the express purpose of fighting American Indians. But they were the exception. One was Jacob Nix, a veteran of the 1848 revolutions who had been sentenced to death for his role in that upheaval but had managed to escape to America. He was also an active member of the Turners, and a cofounder with Wilhelm Pfaender of the first Turner society in America. He followed Pfaender and the other Turners in 1858 to New Ulm and opened a general store. Because of his military experience during the revolution in Europe, he was appointed commandant of New Ulm when it came under siege in 1862, and he was wounded twice during the fighting. Afterward, he was made a captain in the U.S. Army and pursued American Indians until 1864.

Nix wrote a heated account of the conflict, which revealed that many of the tensions between Germans and the Anglo-American community had persisted beyond the moment in 1862 when racial unity seemed to trump ethnic division among Minnesota's white citizens. Indeed, Nix claimed in 1887 that he wrote his account in response to the "English-language works," which he found to be "full of errors and distortions:" they failed to acknowledge German contributions to "saving" the Minnesota frontier, and they often asserted that German colonists, with their strange manners, had been responsible for precipitating the uprising.

He countered those reports with an account that emphasized not only the strength of his German community but also the limits of the Anglo-American state and, by implication, of the Yankees in general, not just those in Minnesota. In that sense, he carried on the notion of German exceptionalism so prominent in the *New Ulm Pioneer*, while pushing back at the Anglophone press.

Nix attributed the extent of the destruction to the Germans' "tragic confidence" that "the Indians, with whom they had been on the friendliest of terms and to whom they had repeatedly shown kindness, would never consider the settlers living near the agencies responsible for their present miseries." The Dakotas, however, "betrayed" that "confidence." Initially, he attributed that betrayal to their nature, and Germans' overconfidence to their misunderstanding of their neighbors. He wrote with condemnation that he had read "in [my] youth," and "with much interest, the novels of [James Fenimore] Cooper. Especially *The Last of the Mohicans* aroused in [me] enthusiasm for the Redskins." But they had been poor guides to life on the frontier. Indeed, "had Cooper known the real nature of the Indian," Nix argued, "he would perhaps have preferred to put a bullet through his brain rather than writing such crazy nonsense about the red bloodhounds."[93] As he had learned, there were striking disjunctures between such colonial fantasies and colonial realities.

In his view, his fellow colonists, regardless of their race, were innocents undeserving of the Dakotas' "unforgivable hatred": they neither were tied to the longer history of racial conflict in the United States nor were representatives of the government, and they had conducted themselves fairly, even generously, with the Dakotas they encountered.

Because the Dakotas' violent anger was misdirected toward these "innocents," however, he joined the chorus of Minnesotans who demanded retribution, arguing that understanding the root of Dakota actions provided no grounds for forgiveness and that "immediately after the capture of the red scoundrels, one should not have wasted any time in shooting or hanging every one who took part in the horrible crimes."[94] Nor could anyone decry the strong military expedition that followed the Dakotas west. Their "objective" was simple and righteous: to protect the surviving settlers by taking "the remaining hostile Sioux out of action by either capturing them or, by what would have been best, completely annihilating them."[95]

Nix's eliminationist language was less a genocidal outburst than a righteous justification for the punishment of murderers.[96] It also stemmed from a perpetrator of violence who saw himself first and foremost as a victim; he believed that he and his fellow colonists had suffered dual indignities—from the Dakotas and the government. That position became endemic around New Ulm in the decades after the conflict. Indeed, Nix wrote that when word came to New Ulm that "the Indians had gone on the warpath," there was "a cry of horror, but also of indignation and righteous anger over the negligence of the Government, which had left the two agencies and almost the entire Upper Minnesota Valley at the mercy of the tomahawk and the red beasts."[97]

Furthermore, he argued, as did the majority of the authors of other narratives and the German-language press in 1862, that the ultimate cause of the conflict was not the Dakotas' "savagery." That explained only the character of their actions. Rather, it was the irresponsible, greedy, and inhumane actions of the government's agents. "No sensible human being," he argued, "could deny that a large number of the Indian agents might be worthy of the honorary title of 'rogue.'" Nor could anyone deny that the "Moloch of contemptible bane" arriving "in the shape of illegal enrichment appeared in a number of scoundrels."[98]

Stripped of its eliminationist language, Nix's narrative not only connects this and other colonial genocides but reminds us of the consistencies in the German colonists' subject positions before and after the rupture of the conflict. Those consistencies were in many ways codified by Alexander Berghold, a priest who arrived in New Ulm in 1866, and published *The Indians' Revenge* a decade later, which placed the conflict squarely within the more general German discourse on the history of Native America. Berghold studied the *New Ulm Pioneer's* accounts of interactions between the German colonists and the Dakotas and interviewed survivors before writing his book. When complete, his text, which shaped much of the local tradition and became quite popular in Germany, placed the German colonists overwhelmingly on the side of the Dakotas, as joint victims of the conflict, and then extended that narrative across the last decades of the nineteenth century.

Celebrating Resistance and Recasting Ethnic Memory

Berghold argued in his history that New Ulm, which he termed both a "genuine German village" and a German "colony," was the unfortunate object of the misplaced but righteous anger of the Dakotas, "whose treatment at the hands of the whites was at times that of a dog."[99] Placing the conflict into a broad historical perspective, he argued that "the history of the Indians in general, from the days of Cortez to our own, is the story of a continual defeat," one in which "the shrewd whites mostly followed the principle of a cruel Brennus, that justice is at the point of a sword." Indeed, while agreeing with Nix and many others that "the land belongs to the whites," he stressed that "it was mostly wrongfully seized," and that the "honest debt" the government incurred during its actions "was, with the exception of an insignificant portion of it, never paid." Moreover, what was paid "was embezzled," for "the superintendents, agents, etc., to whom the money was entrusted for distribution and payment, managed to keep the greater portion for themselves." This, he declared, "was the principal cause of the dissatisfaction and revolt of the Indians,"[100] and he held that these "agents who so shamefully defrauded the Indians ought to have been punished as severely as the Indians themselves [i.e., hung at Mankato]." Unfortunately, he explained, "the originators of the whole trouble, could not be reached by the laws of the land." Instead, "many of them are enjoying life in mansions erected by the money that they stole from the poor Indians, and the cement of those buildings is the innocent blood of hundreds of the unfortunate settlers."[101]

At this point in his argument, however, he diverged widely from Nix, leaving behind the righteous indignation of one who had suffered attack to take up that of the Dakotas themselves, reinforcing the act of displacement already apparent in Nix's narrative but strengthening it through the use of language that demonstrated the long-term avarice of the government and its employees and lauding more than condemning its first victims, the Dakotas. Indeed, Berghold lamented that the principle causes of the battles of New Ulm had continued unabated. While arguing that "the Indian outbreak of 1862 should have been the means of inducing the Indian departments to treat the redskins with more justice," he protested that "the same complaints and the same systematic swindles are the prolific cause of continual bloodshed, and probably will not cease till the last red man is dead."[102]

Further, rather than denouncing the character of the "red men" who reacted against these assaults, he repeatedly underscored that American Indians were justified in the violent reactions to these injustices. His response to the defeat of George Armstrong Custer and the Seventh Calvary at the Battle of Little Bighorn is perhaps most notable, given its proximity to the initial publication of his book. Lamenting that "a cry of revenge" had swept across the country upon learning of Custer's defeat, Berghold sought to strike it down by arguing that Sitting Bull and the Sioux had "in reality only defended themselves against encroachments upon their own lands."[103]

While those encroachments and the violence continued over the next decades, Berghold's position remained the same. When he reissued his book in 1892 he included an addenda that described the ongoing misdeeds of the government that had culminated in the massacre at Wounded Knee in 1890, and he argued that this latest massacre "was an example of the same kind of mismanagement by Government officers, and dishonesty, too, on the part of an agent. The Sioux, he reminded his readers, were suffering great privations—many actually starving," just as they had been in Minnesota in 1862.

And thus, for him, Wounded Knee was but another reminder that "the story of dealing with the Indians and the story of their wars is one of 'expense, barbarity, and shame.'"[104]

Transnational Circulation and Global Transformations

It is still possible to encounter people in New Ulm eager to debate the positions taken on by Berghold and Nix. The degree to which the Dakotas were justified in attacking New Ulm remains contentious and disputed, kept active to some degree by the recent protests that commemorate the events.[105] Most striking at the end of the nineteenth century, however, was the ways in which Germans in Europe came to regard the Sioux as the most exemplary American Indians, while pointing to the Dakota conflict as evidence of that fact. Indeed, the Sioux became the people who embodied the many positive physical and mental characteristics detailed in Berghold's book,[106] the people most willing and able to resist America's imperialist expansion.

Germans in Europe knew immediately of New Ulm's fate. Information from German-language newspapers was quickly reprinted in German periodicals like *Das Ausland*, which ran a series of three extensive essays on the conflict during the last months of 1862. Those essays began by portraying Minnesota as the romantic land of Henry Wadsworth Longfellow's "Hiawatha" and providing readers with extensive ethnological information about the character, population, and organization of the Sioux. Then it turned to the central issues in the German American press: the problems of the treaties, the Yankees' failure to deliver their payments, the duplicity and guilt of the Indian agents, the unfair treatment the Sioux suffered at the hands of the traders and some farmers, letters from the Minnesota governor, Little Crow, and the Chippewa, detailed reports of the attacks on New Ulm and the fort, and graphic descriptions of the dead found littered across the landscape. There were even discussions of the ways in which the conflict was instrumentalized by politicians like the governor of Wisconsin, Eduard Solomon, another veteran of the 1848 revolution in Germany. He responded to the outbreak in Minnesota by arguing that state troops must be sent to the borders, because southern agents had encouraged uprisings across the Midwest, and by agitating for protection against Wisconsin's own Indians, who might unleash similar bloodshed in their state.[107] The only thing missing from the reports in Germany's periodicals was the fact that the majority of victims were Germans. Much as this had been dropped from the broader coverage in Minnesota, it received little discussion in Germany.

Soon after the conflict was ended, the battles over New Ulm and the Dakota tribe's assorted victories, even the number of victims during the conflict, became a measure in Germany of the Dakota's or the Sioux's prowess as warriors rather than evidence of their inhumanity. Germans in Europe were impressed. Indeed, already in 1864 essays on American Indians in German periodicals such as *Globus* made special reference to the Sioux's strength, their greatness, and their danger. One ethnological essay devoted to their social and political organization began by calling them some of the "mightiest of the Indians" and underscored that point by reminding its readers that these were the people who had devastated New Ulm. Moreover, that devastation was portrayed in *Globus*, as in most German literature, as justified. It was never discussed as an assault on Germans, although their readers were certainly aware that it was. Rather, the periodical press continually portrayed it as a commendable reaction to the Sioux's treatment at the hands of the Yankees.[108]

Indeed, an essay that appeared in *Globus* just a few years later on the state of "the Indian wars" read much like the essays that had once appeared in the *New Ulm Pioneer*. It stressed that "no one can doubt that the responsibility for all of the Indian wars has fallen directly or indirectly on the Americans." Moreover, in recent years "their behavior toward the brown people . . . has only become more barbaric and detestable." To support his point, the author rehearsed a series of outrages committed by the military and the government against different tribes before focusing on the most egregious act: the indiscriminate murders of Cheyenne and Arapahoe men, women, and children during the 1864 Sand Creek massacre. The massacre of German men, women, and children two years earlier around New Ulm received no mention. And thus the Dakotas, or more generally the Sioux, shifted easily from being condemned in German-language texts as perpetrators of violence to being enshrined as the greatest of resisters, a people who cannot be enslaved, and the very embodiment of freedom.[109]

That was, of course, a renewed narrative rather than a new one. Characteristics commonly attributed to American Indians in Germany long before 1862 were now focused on the Sioux, and this remained the dominant narrative in the German press as New Ulm was transformed from a site of massacre to a site of resistance and victory. In the 1880s, for example, the artist and journalist Rudolf Cronau, while writing about his trip into Dakota Territory and his encounters with Sitting Bull and other famous Sioux, introduced his topic to his readers much as his counterparts had done twenty years earlier. He described them as the tribe that under Little Crow "had killed 800 whites" and "laid the German town of New Ulm to waste." As he did that, however, he argued that the Dakota victories in Minnesota had made the year 1862 as "unforgettable" as the Sioux's more recent victory at the Battle of Little Bighorn. The Sioux, he reminded his readers, were the tribe "that has offered the longest and strongest resistance" against the forces of "Yankee" imperialism, and that was the context that made them of great interest to his readers.[110] No wonder Germans were so enamored with the Lakotas who accompanied Buffalo Bill to Germany a decade later.

CHAPTER 3

Changes in the Lands

When Rudolf Cronau arrived in Minnesota two decades after the Dakota conflict, colonial encounters were no longer possible. The landscape had changed. A quest for "red winter wheat," which began "rivaling king cotton," had transformed areas once replete with meadows and forests. Farms had domesticated the landscape, and Minneapolis, he noted with wonder, had grown from 5,809 residents in 1860 to 43,053 in 1880. "When one observes the work of culture in Minnesota," he exclaimed, "it seems almost impossible that human diligence could achieve all this in such a short time."[1]

By the 1880s, German America was thriving. People such as Cronau could travel easily from New York City to Minneapolis and St. Paul speaking German all the way, reading German newspapers every day, staying in hotels and inns run by ethnic Germans, eating familiar food and drinking imported beer—or beer made much like it in one of the German American breweries. And many Germans did just that: traveling, crisscrossing the Atlantic, and easily living transnational lives in the United States through 1900.[2]

The 1880s also brought the end of the so-called Indian wars, and the armed resistance that had enticed German readers for decades. After the Wounded Knee massacre on the Pine Ridge Reservation in 1890, there would be no more reports of conflict. Titillating accounts from travelers among those free people ended as well. There was, in fact, a fundamental shift in the way in which the American West was portrayed in German periodicals—there were things about it that were still curios, and the landscapes remained wondrous, but as the century drew to a close, there was less and less about it that was wild.[3]

Cronau, in fact, was one of the last German artists and authors to draw on his own experience among American Indians who had engaged in armed resistance. He met many in Dakota Territory in 1881, and he wrote about them for the rest of his life. Over time, however, his tenses changed, as his subjects moved progressively into the past. The character of his writing shifted as well. Following the changes Hans Plischke identified in the production of German texts on American Indians, it moved from travel narratives based on experience to a cheaper kind of generic fiction and fantastic tales. In Cronau's case, however, it did so for practical reasons: it reflected the transition in the kinds of lived experiences among American Indians that were possible after the 1880s. They were not what German travelers had sought and found in the past.

As those changes in landscape, lives, and literature took place, other critical transitions were also underway. Imperial Germany rose into the realm of world powers and became ever more belligerent, while German American communities became further incorporated into Anglophone America. Many, particularly those who settled in rural areas, retained a local orientation that was ethnically and linguistically German. Nevertheless, those localities became increasingly integrated into American spaces. Regional, state, and national polities found ways to absorb them, and as the political and social structures shifted around them, the German Kulturkreis was circumscribed. That only grew more defined as antagonisms between the United States and Imperial Germany began to disrupt many Germans' transnational lives and this circumscription became a rupture that shattered the Kulturkreis in North America when those nations went to war.

This chapter uses the biography of Rudolf Cronau as a vehicle to sketch out the character of this transnational world in transition. Cronau is well known in immigration history because he did many things. He wrote a multivolume account of Christopher Columbus, which identified the explorer's final resting place and won an award at the 1893 Chicago World's Fair. He wrote a striking book on the history of advertising, another on environmental degradation in the United States, a multivolume account of Germans' contributions to American history, and a scathing portrait of British imperialism. As an American citizen, he became incredibly active in building, supporting, and documenting German American associations. He also took up an avidly anti-British position as nationalism threatened his transnational world. After World War I broke out, he saw his book on British imperialism impounded by the American courts and experienced the destruction of German America and the end of his transnational existence.

Cronau is best-known in Germany today, however, for the trips he took to the United States as a correspondent and artist for the German illustrated magazine *Die Gartenlaube* during the last two decades of the nineteenth cen-

tury. During those trips, he recognized, articulated, and helped to perpetuate a sense of affinity that had long been a part of many Germans' interests
in American Indians. He captured the excitement and melancholy of first
encounters that were often lost in the broader literature but characteristic
of individual experience. And even more than earlier German authors, he
juxtaposed the quintessentially hypermodern America in the East with Native America in the West, something that grew in importance in the German
discourse on American Indians by the interwar period. In that sense, he was
a quintessential transitional character, channeling the German discourse
on American Indians and experiencing the rise and fall of German America
while marking these transformations with the character of his prose.

Cronau's Vision: *Amerika!*

Rudolf Cronau was born in 1855 into a civil servant's family in Solingen, a
small Rhineland town just north of Cologne. He saw little of his father, who
died when Cronau was ten, and his mother left him an orphan just two years
later. Shuffled from one relative's home to the next, as each in turn passed
away, Cronau was increasingly isolated: his half brother and half sister left
him behind as each sought their fortunes in America, and his sister Anna
married and departed to Barmen in 1870. Afterward, he lived alone with
their aunt, until he too, at the age of fifteen, set off to attend the famous
Düsseldorf Academy of Art.

He did not stay long. Chafing under his mentors' strong Catholicism,
their focus on religious themes, and their insistence that he reproduce images from classical art, he left the academy, sought adventure in the Franco-
Prussian War, and returned to Solingen to work as a journalist while pursuing his passion: landscapes. He produced drawings of the Harz Mountains,
the Sächsisches Schweiz, the Riesengebirge, the valleys of the Elbe and
Oder Rivers, and other picturesque parts of Germany and Austria. He was
talented. He became a regular contributor to *Die Gartenlaube* by the mid-
1870s, moved to Leipzig and joined the city's Art Association, and eventually
became its chairman before gaining a commission to travel to the kinds of
"wonders" that dwarfed the landscapes he had seen in Europe: the geysers in
Yellowstone, the walls of El Capitan in Yosemite Valley, the vast prairies, and
the modern spectacle of American cities.

Cronau crossed the Atlantic in January 1881, and the wonders emerged
the moment his ship approached New York City. Copious notes from his
shipboard adventures fill the initial pages of his diary, but these detailed dis-

cussions of passengers, seasickness, and the ship's emergency preparations were quickly overshadowed by his excited first glimpse of the lighthouse on Fire Island, the quickening sensation that came with the early morning murmurs of land, and his impressions of their arrival in New York harbor. On entering the city, however, those reports gave way to silence. It took time to comprehend the wonder of New York—many days passed before he began recording it.[4]

When he returned to writing, he focused on the city's aesthetic. As many German artists and authors before and after him, Cronau discerned that aesthetic in the chaos and order of the city's architecture, the rhythm of its streets, and the purposefulness of its people. He described New York's harbor as a crisscrossing collection of ship's masts and towers, a throng of colorful confusion. His experience of the port was a mixture of quick images, of even quicker English, smatterings of various German dialects, and, above all, incessant movement. In New York, he explained to *Die Gartenlaube*'s readers, "the difference between the world that surrounds us here and the homeland is shocking; every step, every movement into the streets, brings something new and stimulating." "Everything is interesting," he wrote, "even if not all is satisfying. The construction of the houses, the deep red of the bricks, the chocolate color of the brown stone palaces, the number of colorful announcement boards" give the streets such a "special complexion" that one never tires of acting the flaneur.

There was no place in the city, however, for a European-style promenade. This was America, and in this world, "everything is pushed and shoved about." "Weak-willed," he explained, "the traveler pits himself against the current, only to be washed away and tossed up again just as submissively on the edge of some other street." Parts of the "vast crowd" filling the avenues are transported through them by "an endless procession of every sort of vehicle." "The brightly colored coach of a railroad king" works its way through the "melee" together with the more "heavily laden transports." "Omnibuses and horse carts" carry their occupants to their appointed destinations, while "over our heads thunder and roar the innumerable engines of the elevated trains, all filled with people" traveling from one end of this "huge city" to the other. Above and below the train tracks it seemed, thousands upon thousands of telegraph wires crossed from one side of the road to the other, houses appeared to overflow into the streets, and every corner was covered with fascinating announcements, giving the avenues "a singularly lively and active air."[5]

This was hypermodernity driven by commerce. In New York, he exclaimed, "everything, everything is business." People with nothing to do "are lost in this world." "Every minute," he wrote, "thousands hurry past us, no one has time to notice us, and only the street parasites focus their attentions upon us." Fruit handlers shouted out their prices, paperboys surrounded the slow-moving pedestrians, and advertisements were constantly pressed into their hands.[6]

While much of what he saw during his first weeks in America was wondrous, not everything was unfamiliar. This too is critical. In the eastern cities he visited, Cronau found monuments like those he sketched in the Rhineland, and he located deep and textured histories similar to what he had pursued in his hometown.[7] Most of all, however, he found Germans, innumerable Germans. His stepsister Mathilde Waldeck Stöcker greeted him on the docks and took him into her home. From that comfortable setting, he became acquainted with the city's diverse and fractured German community, but he moved among the political liberals and tended toward the social elites.[8] After only a few days in town, he met the editors of the *New Yorker Staats-Zeitung*, initiating a relationship that would continue until the last years of his life. Through them he gained access to the city's German art community and its German scientific association. The Schniewind family, whom he met on the ship from Bremerhaven, provided him with an introduction to the president of New York's German-American Association.

He was also introduced to Karl Schurz, a fellow Rhinelander and the U.S. secretary of the interior. It was Schurz who approved Cronau's idea to travel to the reservations in Dakota Territory and provided him with the documents that allowed Cronau to enter reservations and ensured the support of military and government officials after he arrived.[9] German American networks were vibrant and vast, and they carried him deep into the Midwest.

Sublime Landscapes and Emotional Projections

Traveling by train across the upper Midwest, Cronau saw endless woodlands, broken by occasional villages, zealously cultivated farmland, and burgeoning midwestern cities and towns. The distances were daunting. The trees in American forests seemed to grow more densely than in Germany, "everything," he noted, "struggling up towards the sky." The rolling landscape had a certain appeal, and he collected images, clipped from newspapers and magazines, in his diary. What most impressed Cronau during his journey to St. Paul, however, was the spectacle of Niagara Falls.

His arrival at Niagara brought him face to face with the natural sublime he expected to find in America, the antinomy to the cityscapes, and it evoked in him the essential longings that had inspired his trip. Staring out at the falls from Prospect Point he saw a vision "like that which had filled my fantasies since my early youth." Yet it was no fantasy, no rendering of an ideal in ink or oil. Rather it stood before him "in great incomprehensible reality," astounding in its veracity. Contemplating the gigantic whirlpool rapids, he reflected in his diary: "So wild and majestic had I imagined the American landscape, so was the nature in which I imagined the Indians, Cooper's characters, so was the background I pictured for [Washington] Irving's histories."[10] In primeval landscapes, he thought, one might find, indeed one should find, primeval people, original inhabitants: Indians.

Cronau's Melancholy

Cronau's first encounter with American Indians, however, took place much further west, and there was little sublime about it. It happened almost inadvertently near Fort Snelling, Minnesota, during a Sunday outing suggested by a German American family named Schäffer. Cronau met the Schäffers through the editor of the *Volkszeitung* in St. Paul, and they welcomed him into their home. On 22 May 1881, they suggested a visit to an Indian settlement, since it was only a few hours from town and an easy carriage ride away.[11]

It was a disturbing trip. He recorded in his diaries the initial excitement of seeing "the tops of brown tents" stretching up above the green forest as they approached the settlement. "On the edge of a small lake," he wrote, "the white tents, now browned from smoke, were a picturesque sight." Looking eagerly for details, he noted that "every tent was made up of a number of poles rammed into the ground whose ends converge at the top, so that they create a pointed cone, over which a covering of canvas is then stretched." He wrote too that these "wigwams," as he later identified them, were cleverly constructed to control the flow of smoke through the opening in the top, and they are quickly accessible through the door at the bottom; in other times and places, he remarked, they might also be covered with animal skins or the bark from trees. He included further ethnographic information in his notes, gleaned from his later inquiries, remarking upon the ease with which one can erect these structures, how they were generally spaced in a campsite, and that they were often located near lakes and rivers, and then he recorded similar information about their inhabitants: the Sioux.

He wrote that the Sioux were, as the Schäffers and others must have told him, "an Indian people who, through their ferocity and wild attacks, so fre-

FIGURE 12. Rudolf Cronau, "Lager der Sioux-Indianer bei Fort Snelling in Minnesota," *Die Gartenlaube* no. 9 (1882): 149.

quently placed their white neighbors in fear and terror." Around St. Paul, he noted, people always made reference to New Ulm, but the "redskins" he encountered near Fort Snelling "had been friendly minded for years" and "have opened the door and the gate to civilization's influence." That was immediately apparent in their clothing: most of the men "wore hats and bright shirts, pants and vests," while the women were clad in "jackets and skirts made of cotton and wool." Moccasins were the footwear of choice. Aside from their shoes, however, "there was no longer any sign of their national costume." That romantic element, and the link it documented to the natural sublime, the link he expected to find among Cooper's characters, was gone.[12]

Here one could have only postcolonial encounters. Thus the people he met were nothing like Cooper's free Indians, just as Minnesota was no longer primeval forest or sublime landscape. The forces that shaped and fed the hypermodern cities of the East, he recognized, had flooded west across Minnesota, fundamentally changing the land and its inhabitants—and leaving him disconcerted.

Indeed, for Cronau the Dakotas he met near Fort Snelling seemed more akin to the "wilting leaves" in Henry Wadsworth Longfellow's famous poem *Hiawatha* than to the bold characters in Cooper's *Leatherstocking Tales*. Thus he quotes Longfellow extensively for *Die Gartenlaube*'s readers, using

Hiawatha as a means of introducing his subjects and explaining their fate. He wrote that while standing by a waterfall near Fort Snelling, his imagination escaped into a time now past, into "Longfellow's wonderful poem," and into his portrait of "Minnehaha, the laughing water." "Wistfully," he told his readers, he reflected on the fact that the people about whom the poem was written were "scattered or all but exterminated, while a foreign language, the language of their destroyer, sings of their Gods and heroes." "That," he lamented, "is a cruel irony of history." For although *The Song of Hiawatha is a pearl in the crown of American poetry*," the conditions he observed in Minnesota in 1881 begged him to ask, "Who spared the heroes about whom the song sings in the horrible war of extermination," who spared "the poor Indian?"[13]

In the Dakota settlement, Cronau met Pa-Chu-Ta, the daughter of Aza-ya-man-ka-wan, a woman well known in St. Paul as old Bets. Because old Bets had shown kindness to many of Little Crow's captives during the Dakota conflict, and because whites credited her with saving some prisoners' lives, she and her children had been allowed to stay in Minnesota while so many other Dakota were forced to leave. Pa-Chu-Ta, however, had not thrived there. When Cronau entered her home, she was engaged in cooking eggs and potatoes over the fire. He noted the smile on her face and the sparkle in her eye but was most impressed by her size, describing her as "an enormous mass of flesh." Many of the women in the camp shared her condition, but none were as large as Tha-ti, a woman who took up her entire wigwam, and whose size was reputed to have quite literally pressed her last husband out of this life. The man who now lived in the margins of her lodge completed the depressing scene. Cronau described him as "a wretched old warrior, a strip of leather in a colorful shirt and torn leggings, who possessed no notion of manly dignity." The only thing impressive about him was the speed with which his hand grasped inside a bag of proffered candy. A young girl, whom Cronau judged to be about thirteen years old, was the only Hiawathan figure he could discern in the camp; slim, beautiful, moving lightly like a deer, how long would it take, he wondered, for her to become like Tha-ti?

For Cronau, these were people who had lost themselves. Dislocated from their pasts, isolated in the landscape, and marginalized in white society, they were neither fish nor fowl in the rapidly changing world. Evidence for that conclusion abounded in their tents. "There one found a colorful hodge-podge, which characterized," he felt, "the half-barbaric and half-civilized condition of their customs": "coffee grinders and peace pipes, rifles and bows, buffalo skins and old quilts." What most struck him, however, was "a gigantic map of the United States from Anno Tobacco and a true to life grandfather clock, whose hand covered an hour in only forty minutes, as a particular homage to progress."[14]

The German Mississippi

Cronau had traveled to St. Paul on his way to Dakota Territory in order to meet Captain Paul Boyton and accompany him twelve hundred miles down the Mississippi River.[15] Boyton, with whom Cronau became acquainted in Baltimore, had been experimenting with a rubber suit developed by C. S. Merriman of Iowa as a life-saving device, not unlike modern dry suits used today. To demonstrate the effectiveness of his suit, he took it on a series of sensational ventures, surrounded in most cases by considerable press.[16] Cronau went with him, seeking what was still wild in this part of the West, and becoming part of the spectacle.

His trip down the Mississippi from St. Paul to St. Louis only confirmed Cronau's impressions of the quick transformation of Minnesota's sublime landscapes and peoples. It too presented Cronau with a strange combination of the familiar German and the uniquely American. The Mississippi River was powerful and exceptional in its character. It propelled them quickly downstream, Boyton in his rubber suit with a kayak paddle, and Cronau in a boat with a young African American named Charlie Mangraff. Sometimes they camped on the riverbank, but most of their twenty-five nights were spent talking to reporters and residents in river towns and sleeping in hotels and inns.[17]

Indeed, they repeatedly came ashore to large banquets and German hospitality. In Lake City, for example, "the young ladies in this place decorated us with flowers, and our lunch table was about to break under the burden of the excellent food and deserts laid out for us."[18] Emerging from the roughest weather they encountered on the river into Fountain City, they were greeted by German voices. Along the way they met a hotelkeeper from Solingen who remembered Cronau's mother, and when they arrived in the town of Burlington, where one-third of the twenty-one thousand inhabitants were German, a German rowing club came out to greet them. Guttenberg offered perhaps the best reception. There they were "welcomed by men of true German mettle." They were encouraged to visit the best families, where "within less than an hour at least a dozen cups of coffee with accompanying pieces of cake were pressed upon us." In addition, they packed the boat with real German beer "several bottles of *Rudesheimer*, whose authenticity was confirmed as I saw the fasteners and the seal of the Casino society in Koblenz on the bottles."[19]

If these hybrid settlements, with their rapid American commerce and their German *Gemütlichkeit* (warm cordiality), offered Cronau a window into the transformation of life on the river, a single moment outside of Winona, Minnesota, caught Cronau as the most poignant. In his letter to *Die Gartenlaube,* he noted that they encountered a group of Winnebago on the river, who looked with wonder at Boyton.[20] During this encounter, he reflected on their birch bark canoes, their fishing implements, and their stature. But eight years later in his *Im Wilden Westen* he took the time to elaborate on this meeting and reflect on this iconoclastic American West he had witnessed and its significance: "Where on the earth could one again encounter such a sudden collision of the highest civilization and the lowest barbarity as offered by this image: over there the proud city with its churches, schools, smoke stacks, with its railroad bridges and photographers. Directly nearby, the giant river with its unbowed wilderness, in whose loneliness the aboriginals' paddle stroke and hunting call can be heard still today." Next to "the whistle of the trains" crisscrossing the continent, "beside the signal calls" from the steamers heading upstream, one hears the "strange voices of the redskins which, in a melancholy way, sing from the beautiful Winona," the girl in the American Indian "legend and tale." For a moment then, they seemed to escape "American society, with its confinement, its fervor, and its ruthlessness." They passed for a short time into a "dreamland," "so peaceful, so relaxing."[21]

Cronau's Epiphany

Cronau's melancholy, however, gave way to anger as he found what he sought in Dakota Territory. His goal, as he later wrote in his autobiography, was to "realize a long nourished and favorite wish to become acquainted with the original inhabitants of the New World, so gloriously portrayed in Cooper's *Leatherstocking Tales.*"[22] And he did. At Fort Yates and the Standing Rock Reservation, at the Pipestone Quarry and the Yankton Agency, and at Fort Randall, Cronau began to channel critical elements in the German discourse about American Indians: he began to take a strong position against the encroachment of white settlers on American Indian lands, to denounce the U.S. government's handling of Indian affairs, and to condemn widespread arguments about American Indians' inability to change with the times. He came to regard those arguments as nothing more than a rationalization for expropriating their lands and excusing their extermination, and his admiration for those who had managed to resist grew precipitously as he recognized an affinity between his ancestors and the people he came to know.

Here too he relied greatly on Germans.[23] Joseph A. Stephan, who was born in Gissigheim in the south German state of Baden, was the Indian agent at the Standing Rock Reservation when Cronau arrived. He welcomed his countryman to Fort Yates, introduced him to Crow King, Gall, Hump, and many other leading chiefs, and spent considerable time educating and advising him about Lakota culture and the government's policies.[24] Fort Yates's storekeeper was a German as well. So too was the quartermaster at Fort Randall, and his assistant, Fritz Schenk, was from Bern, Switzerland. Schenk guided Cronau through his initial meetings with Sitting Bull and helped him arrange an exhibition of Cronau's artwork for everyone at the Fort, including the Lakota. He also remained a key source of information about life at Fort Randall until Sitting Bull left for Standing Rock in the spring of 1883.[25] Moreover, throughout his time in Dakota Territory, and afterward while writing his essays and lectures in Milwaukee, Cronau drew on reports about Indian affairs in many German-language newspapers. They too helped shape his opinions and facilitated his channeling a distinctly German discourse.[26]

Most importantly, however, he gleaned information from his observations and from his conversations with the kind of men he had come to find: men of exceptional characteristics; natural men who had done great deeds; men who had not yet been corrupted by the myriad forces of civilization, and who need not be. These were men who could choose to accommodate themselves to those forces, but who were only then, in the fall of 1881, at the moment of choosing.

Cronau believed these men were an integral part of the landscape they inhabited. They were part of the natural sublime, and they harbored an essential masculinity. He saw it evidenced in their raw physicality, and he began rhapsodizing their magnificent bodies early in his trip. During his first excursion from Fort Yates to the "Hostile Camp," located just forty-five minutes away, he met with a series of chiefs who presented him with gifts, including an eagle feather from Pretty Bear, which he accepted as a token of great significance. Initially, his notes focused on recording these introductions and detailing the character of the camp. He described the weathered tents, some with painted exteriors, many decorated with scalp locks, bison skulls, and antlers, all showing evidence of the hardships that had brought their owners to the reservation.

His notes, however, moved quickly to the excitement of a dance that

seemed to begin almost spontaneously, and which overwhelmed him with stark and vivid impressions of perfect bodies in motion. Enamored with the dancers, he sketched out some of the patterns he saw painted on their faces in his notebook, and he described how they carried their weapons and wore their hair, and as the numbers of participants grew and they mixed into the light from the fires, he became enraptured, proclaiming them "indefatigable" and writing that "here, as I saw the dancers naked, I had the opportunity to marvel at the veritable athletic and superbly-built bodies of the Indians." "A large number," he added, "are six feet high."[27]

Such men easily fulfilled Cronau's hopes and expectations of American Indians. He regarded One Bull, whom he befriended at Fort Randall, as "the personified ideal of a Cooperesque Indian, an Unkas, but more manly, mature, complete, and noble in his movements." This "red warrior" with his "well-proportioned build," who surpassed in reality even the fantasy of Cooper's most notable young warrior, also carried a "true Apollo-like head on his shoulders" and, much as we might suppose, was the "favorite of the ladies" at Fort Randall.[28]

Although Sitting Bull was not as beautiful as the twenty-seven-year-old One Bull, Cronau described him as a "vision of pronounced manliness," and a "far more important personality than Cooper's Chingachgook," the father of Unkas, who was still the model of "authentic Indians" for Cronau's generation of Germans. In part, that "pronounced manliness" was embodied in his stature. He was a man "of average height, . . . with a massive head, broad cheekbones, blunt nose, and narrow mouth." When Cronau met him, his "shining black hair hung in braids wrapped with fur that were draped across his powerful chest," and a "single Eagle feather was placed in his long scalp lock." His entire body projected physical prowess, just as his eyes and his speech revealed his exceptional nature.[29]

Indeed, Sitting Bull and other Sioux leaders such as Hump impressed Cronau through their demeanor and words as much as their powerful bodies. Cronau arrived at Standing Rock during a moment of transition.[30] Stephan's tenure as agent was coming to an end; Major James McLaughlin had just arrived from the Devil's Lake Reservation to replace him, and Cronau was privy to the initial meeting between McLaughlin and his new charges. He recorded McLaughlin's speech to them, in which the new agent characterized the Lakotas as children who must learn to behave so that he, as their father, could care for their wants and needs and help educate them in the ways of white Americans. What Cronau witnessed in their responses, however, was not childlike.[31] It was inspirational.

Cronau documented in great detail the testaments of complete, independent, capable, brave, and self-confident men who commanded supreme respect when they spoke to a room. He recorded in his notebook, for example, the striking impression made by Rain in the Face, as he denounced the proceedings and the "crooked tongued" men who the "Great Father" sent them, and then he reflected on this man's participation in the Battle of Little Big Horn and the rumors that he had cut out and eaten the heart of Thomas Custer, the younger brother of George Armstrong Custer. Such men were not easily overcome. Even more impressive, however, was Big Soldier, whom Cronau characterized as a "felicitous speaker whose words rained down like a mountain storm" and who stood directly before McLaughlin, looking him in the eye, and explaining that the "Great Father" had sent many people to them with scores of promises, but they always disappointed.

Cronau's appreciation of American Indians changed as he witnessed these and other men, including Crow King, Fire Heart, Gall, High Bear, Hump, Running Antelope, and Two Bears face the agent and issue their complaints about the ways in which they had been misled, how whites had eliminated the wild animals, how settlers greedily pressed for more land and offered little reciprocation for what they took. He listened as the chiefs stressed that the agents had continually failed to do their jobs, failed to represent them well in Washington, failed to protect them against the encroachments of greedy settlers. And as he listened, Cronau began to develop his own understanding of a side of American history not present in Cooper's tales. He began to take a critical position on the history of U.S.–American Indian relations, and he gained further respect for these men.[32]

Thus Cronau's portraits of them, both his words and his images, not only emphasized their ferocity but also came to include their dignity, intelligence, and wisdom. As a journalist, Cronau understood the appeal of sensation, and he clearly enjoyed describing the most furious and indeed terrifying scenes he had witnessed during the dances.[33] More affecting, however, were his descriptions of the chiefs and their people during ration day: these men, "wrapped in colorful wool blankets or shaggy buffalo skins, with a Tomahawk on an arm," stood before the fort's commander "with the pride of Roman Senators."[34]

If Cronau's respect for these men emerged during the meeting with McLaughlin, it was solidified and deepened through his many conversations with exceptional individuals such as Crow King at Standing Rock, Struck by the Ree at the Yankton Agency, and Sitting Bull at Fort Randall. Cronau's relationship with Sitting Bull has received considerable attention in Germany, in part because Sitting Bull remains a celebrity there, and because Cronau was the German with the closest contact to him. He is well known for having painted Sitting Bull's portrait and for giving Sitting Bull a photograph of himself, which the Lakota leader allegedly kept with him until his death.[35]

Cronau met repeatedly with Sitting Bull and spoke with him at length.[36] Sitting Bull told him about his past, the drawings he had made that chronicled his biography, which had been sent to a museum in the East, the hard times and hunger in Canada, his dissatisfaction with living on rations, and his desire to have a farm, send his children to white schools, and have them learn trades.[37]

Sitting Bull also explained why he had gone to war: he had been forced after the 1862 Dakota conflict in Minnesota to fight back against the troops that streamed into Dakota Territory, abusing his people. He explained that he had fought against many American Indian tribes as well, refusing to attend the famous peace meeting in 1866 and effectively pushing the Crows, for example, off their lands. He also explained why he had led raids on the gold miners who invaded the Black Hills in 1875, and how he had tried to push the whites out of Lakota lands altogether. Sitting Bull became so animated during these stories that Cronau found it difficult to finish his portrait; but he did complete it, and during their discussions he experienced his epiphany about American Indian affairs as well.[38]

There are three places in his notebooks in which Cronau compares the fate of American Indian tribes to the fate of German tribes during the age of Rome: directly after watching the meeting with McLaughlin, after recording his discussions with Sitting Bull, and after his trips in Dakota Territory when he returned to his wife in Milwaukee and spent the winter writing lectures and essays for *Die Gartenlaube*.

In "The Denigrated Race," which he presented to German American audiences in 1882 and across Germany from 1884 to 1887, Cronau argued that American Indian tribes, much like German tribes more than a millennium earlier, suffered a devastating invasion from a better-organized and more technically advanced civilization. The consequences for American Indians, however, were more immediate and far greater. The German tribes were armed much like the Romans, and thus they did not suffer from the same disparity of weapons; they were less alienated than the various tribes of American Indians, they were not spread out across such vast terrain, and therefore they were able to unify much more easily in opposition to Rome. American Indians suffered all those comparative disadvantages and more: they were unable to anticipate the "formidableness or numbers" of their "overpowering opponent," and the character of the invasion was different as well. The "whites did not come with a large army" to America, as had the Romans to Northern Europe; rather they came in small groups, "fixed themselves on many different points," and much like a "slow, lingering, but certain sickness," much "like a bacteria" against which "there was no cure," they struck from multiple points of contact. In addition, they brought lethal diseases and alcohol. They also lacked men who thought "ideally and honestly" about the American Indians. Consequently, instead of encountering men of integrity, American Indians met the "dregs" of the white race, people who showed more "beastliness and meanness" than had the American "savages."[39]

Much like New Ulm's Alexander Berghold,[40] Cronau also denounced U.S. Indian policy. He raged against the constant deception, fraud, and the incompetence of government employees charged with maintaining treaties and reservations. He reviled the mean-spiritedness behind the ubiquitous swindles and abuses faced by American Indians who moved onto reservations, and he argued that it was the same mean-spiritedness that had permitted "frontier skirmishes" to develop into a "race war that is still not at an end today [1882]." He blamed the white settlers who lived close to reservations and who coveted American Indian lands for much of the bloodshed during the past decades, and he argued that "ninety-nine out of one-hundred times" violence erupted, it was due to "the same old story": "broken treaties, unfulfilled promises, and almost incomprehensible injustices." "Nowhere else," he argued, "has the collision between white people and another group of people" been so devastating as in North America, and thus he lamented that "the history of the red race in the territory of the Union" must be regarded as "one of the saddest chapters in world history."[41]

To underscore that point, Cronau devoted much of his lecture to describing in horrifying detail the treatment of several specific groups of American Indians by the U.S. government, its military, and its citizens. In an argument that anticipated by almost a century the seminal work produced by Dee Brown,[42] Cronau described the constant population transfers that had taken place under American auspices. The Delaware alone, he noted, had been forcefully removed on twelve separate occasions, each time leaving behind the graves of parents and children, much of their property, and their connections to the land. Each move winnowed away at their population until they had almost vanished. Most recently, he wrote, the Southern Cheyenne had suffered gravely at the hands of U.S. officials and soldiers in acts that could "only be regarded as criminal."

While the Anglophone reporters who attended his lectures in Minnesota characterized Cronau's portraits as typically German, "smacking" of idealized images from Cooper's tales, and wondered aloud at his audacity for being so critical of government policy while visiting their land, the Germanophone audiences greeted his condemnation with applause and reprinted his arguments in full in their papers. So too did the papers that followed his three-year tour in Germany, where Cronau provided Germans with authoritative confirmation of what they already believed.[43]

By all accounts, his efforts were well received among the Lakota as well. Before Cronau left Fort Randall and began his journey back to a middle-class lifestyle among Germans in Milwaukee, Schenk arranged for him to exhibit the portraits and landscapes he had made during his time in the Dakotas, sending out invitations to the entire garrison. The guests came eagerly, visiting the exhibit according to a strict hierarchy of rank and privilege: first the officers came with their families, then the soldiers, and then the Lakotas, who were pleased to recognize their friends from the North in his many drawings and paintings.[44] "It was without a doubt," he wrote," the first exhibit that these savages had been offered, and no one could wish for a more grateful public."[45] Sitting Bull walked through the images with his family, and then remained for some time with his warriors, uttering the names of their compatriots at Standing Rock as they viewed their portraits and paying Cronau respect for his efforts.[46] After returning to Milwaukee, Cronau also sent Sitting Bull copies of *Die Gartenlaube* that contained his essays about the Dakotas. According to Schenk, Sitting Bull was "quite delighted and probably even more flattered by the beautiful images in *Die Gartenlaube*," and he and his people demonstrated their eagerness to see Cronau again and confirm their friendship with their friend "Iron Eyes."[47] Although Cronau never returned, he remained aware of their movements and their fate; following Sitting Bull's murder in 1897 he received a letter from One Bull describing his end, which Cronau lamented in the *New Yorker Staats-Zeitung*.[48]

German Audiences

After spending the winter of 1881–82 in Milwaukee, Cronau returned to New York City to plan his next venture with two German American journalists, Udo Brachvogel and Charles F. Tag. They went seeking natural wonders, traveling across American deserts and mountain ranges, along the West Coast, and into Yosemite, Yellowstone, and other new national parks. Together with Brachvogel, Cronau produced another twelve illustrated essays for *Die Gartenlaube*, and he accumulated information that he would use for a variety of articles and books during the next decade.[49]

After three years in America, Cronau returned to Germany, where he was quickly reintegrated into Leipzig's art association and the city's cultural circles. His essays in *Die Gartenlaube* had already established his reputation among its readers, but he extended his audience considerably through the lectures he gave across Germany from 1884 through 1886. They were incredibly popular.

Crowds lined up to hear Cronau speak in educational and business associations in major and minor cities, geographic societies in places such as Halle, Karlsruhe, and Stuttgart, ethnographic museums in Stuttgart and Leipzig, and even at the Fifth National Meeting of German Geographers in Hamburg in 1885, which he considered a high point of his tours. Local notables such as Prince Hermann zu Sachsen-Weimar in Stuttgart often attended his lectures; so too did a wide range of others. Indeed, his lectures were often sold out, and portions of his audiences were forced to stand in hallways and aisles in many venues.[50]

Cronau offered his audiences a choice of five lectures based on his travels;[51] but "Three Months in the Land of the Sioux" was clearly the most popular, and its reception is particularly telling. Cronau spoke to his audiences for two or more hours, surrounded by some fifty of his landscapes and portraits as well as ethnographic objects (tools, weapons, and clothing) he had assembled during his travels. He divided his lecture into three parts: he always began with a discussion of the landscape and the nature of the wilderness between the Missouri River and the Rocky Mountains, before turning to the character of the people who lived in these landscapes, and then, ultimately, reflecting on their fate.

We know this because of the depth and consistency of the newspaper accounts. The coverage was striking. Unlike Buffalo Bill, who came to Germany less than a decade later, and whose efficient advertising organization was well known for bombarding each succeeding city on his tour with pamphlets, placards, and well-rehearsed statements about the importance of his show, Cronau traveled alone, with little fanfare and even less advertising. Nevertheless, much like the journalistic accounts of Buffalo Bill's Wild West, the reactions to his lecture were amazingly consistent.

Most journalists began, as they would when describing Buffalo Bill's Wild West in 1890, by connecting the subjects of Cronau's lecture to the characters in Cooper's *Leatherstocking Tales*. Drawing on that intertextuality, one journalist asserted that an evening with Cronau was sure to reconnect any visitor to "the sweet dreams of our youth—a period in which our favorite pastime was to sit in a corner of a room with an Indian tale and read about the deeds of chief Chingachgook." Indeed, many journalists wrote that Cronau's stories came to them "like a fairytale from a long faded and ancient time," awaking in them "memories from childhood."[52]

The consistency of these reports, combined with Cronau's endurance, circulated his thoughts on the Sioux and his opinions about the relationship between the U.S. government and American Indians across Germany. The literate public learned thirdhand about the "Dakota warriors' impressive appearance." They heard from reporters about the large number of Sioux who stood "over six feet high," and they were told as well about their strong bodies, their "graceful, energetic movements," and the ways in which they resembled "Roman senators."[53] Functioning as a kind of addendum to Cooper's texts, these widely distributed news accounts further codified German notions of American Indians' origins in sublime landscapes, the powers of the Sioux, and their misgivings about the mistreatment of American Indians at the hands of the particularly dangerous modernizing forces that poured out of America's hypermodern cities.

At the same time, however, Cronau's lectures also offered something new. His tales still bore the authority of an eyewitness, which corrected a number of popular impressions even as they reinforced and gave more authority to others. For example, journalists eagerly latched onto the sensational stories of Sioux warriors who married easily, who often stole and purchased women, and who enjoyed multiple wives. They readily repeated the story of Long Dog, who had twenty-three women listed among his conquests, but who could only recall for Cronau the blankets they brought with them rather than their names. Such titillating details played on tropes of such men's untamed sexuality, but the journalists' accounts did not end in cliché. They also reported Cronau's argument that the Sioux's masculinity stemmed from much more than their physical prowess and open sexuality. It also included a responsibility to their women. Cronau, the journalists stressed, argued during his lectures against the widespread belief that Sioux men overburdened their women with work and responsibilities.[54]

In short, Cronau's lecture offered German listeners and readers a more complex and textured understanding of the Standing Rock Sioux and their culture even while it reaffirmed popular notions and clichés promulgated by texts such as Cooper's and periodicals like *Die Gartenlaube*. Newspaper columns consistently reported, for example, his insights on courting and marriage, on raising and naming children, on how boys became men, and on the ingenious ways in which the Sioux had learned to use mirrors, smoke, and blankets to communicate across vast distances.[55]

Through his lecture series and his publications, Cronau established himself as an authority on Native America, which allowed him to take part in further encounters with American Indians in Germany. Indeed, when the Bella Coolas brought to Germany by Adrian Jacobsen traveled to Leipzig in 1885, Cronau was asked to give a lecture on their history, their culture, and the aesthetic qualities of their wood carvings and other crafts for members of Leipzig's art association. During this event, he acted as a kind of interlocutor; the Bella Coolas and Jacobsen listened to his introduction, and afterward they engaged in an exchange of information about European and American Indian art, demonstrating the ways in which they produced their artwork, tools, and other objects while members of the association listened attentively.[56]

Similarly, when Fred Harvey brought one of the earlier groups of Sioux to Germany in 1886, Cronau was invited to accompany them. He lent them his authority as a German who had lived among a group of Sioux for a short time, and he defended their origins during a debate over their authenticity that took shape in Berlin. He also wrote his own essay about the group for one of Germany's most popular illustrated magazines, and produced and distributed a short book on the Sioux during this tour, further enhancing his credentials.[57] Indeed, when many Sioux arrived in 1890 with Buffalo Bill, journalists in Leipzig recommended that people read Cronau's newly published *Im Wilden Westen* for background information.[58]

More Changes in the Land

By the time he published *Im Wilden Westen*, however, Cronau's representations of American Indians had already changed considerably in response to their fate in the United States. When he wrote about the Apache for *Die Gartenlaube* in 1888, for example, his description was more historical than ethnographic, based less on his contact with Apaches after their subjugation than on information about their struggles against the United States, which he gleaned from other texts. Similarly, in his 1893 essay on Kansas, American Indians were most notable for their absence.[59] From Cronau's perspective, by the 1890s life on the prairie was exemplified by loss and succession. "Today," he wrote, if one were to ask while crossing the "sea of grass in a train," "what happened to the enormous herds" of buffalo, he would receive "the laconic answer: 'exterminated!' Yes, exterminated are the buffalo herds," Cronau wrote, "disappeared like the red man, who is also unable to find a homestead in this land that belonged to him."

Even the postcolonial encounters he had experienced at the outset of the decade were impossible to relive when he returned at its end. So much had changed. The world inhabited by buffalo and American Indians, a world he had glimpsed, had already been replaced by a new wild west, one populated by famous outlaws such as Billy the Kid, unnamed horse thieves and other desperados, the chaos of cattle towns like Dodge City, and their inhabitants' vigilante justice. That new "raw" life, however, was also ephemeral. Cronau already saw it giving way as well to the farms of Mennonites, who were settling the tamer edges on the eastern side of Kansas near the dry town of Topeka. They began arriving from Prussia, Russia, and Poland in 1873, and by 1885 they had already transformed some 300,000 acres of land into farms. Thus in the images he made to accompany his essay on Kansas, the cattle town he placed at its center and the empty dilapidated teepee on its edge, were both objects of passing ages in his narrative of the plains.

For that reason, Cronau's *Im Wilden Westen* began with a disclaimer that it would be of little use to readers as a travel guide; so much had changed since he visited the American West less than a decade earlier. The book, he stressed, was little more than a snapshot of a phase of American expansion and development.[60] Yet it was not simply the West that had changed, his book and his later journalistic accounts of American Indians are very different from his initial lectures and essays. *Im Wilden Westen* is a compilation of his experiences. At times, it fleshes out his earlier travel accounts, but it also combines them with stories, images, and information taken from other authors, much of which, as Peter Bolz has noted, introduced errors into those accounts and pushed Cronau's work well into the realm of cliché.[61] That tendency grew even stronger as he became an American.

German American Life and Fears

Shortly after attending the Chicago World's Fair in 1893 as a reporter for *Die Gartenlaube*, Cronau became the American correspondent for the *Kölnische Zeitung*, one of Germany's leading newspapers. He took up residence in Washington, D.C., where he was quickly integrated into the city's high society and its thriving German American community. In 1898 he shifted easily to New York City, working as an independent journalist for Germanophone publications, becoming an American citizen in 1904, and capitalizing on the breadth of German America while worrying about its future.

By 1917 there were at least 520 German-language periodicals in the United States, more than all the other non-English periodicals combined. In 1910 there were 92 million Americans, 2.5 million of whom had been born in Germany, another 3.5 million had two German-born parents, and 1.8 million had one. In total, first- and second-generation Germans amounted to about 8 million people, which made them 8.6 percent of the population. That does not include all those who were descended from earlier German immigrants, nor does it consider the fact that Germans had long been the second-largest language group in the United States. New York City had one of the largest urban populations of Germans in the world, while in the Midwest their presence was marked: in Milwaukee, for example, first- and second-generation Germans made up 44.4 percent of the population. They also accounted for some 24.3 percent in Cincinnati, 20.1 percent in St. Louis, and 19.5 percent in Chicago.

As a result, in all of these cities and others as well, one encountered thriving German theaters, opera houses, symphonies, hundreds of associations, brewers, and at least two major newspapers. And thus, on the eve of World War I, America was covered by an array of heterogeneous, overlapping German American communities with a rich transnational culture, which most of the other Americans regarded as a net gain. Germans, most acknowledged in 1900, were thrifty and hardworking, an asset to local and national communities.[62]

Cronau certainly championed their value. Already in 1897, he completed a fourteen-part series of essays on the role of Germans in American history for the *Kölnische Zeitung*, which foreshadowed the heroic tone of his later work on the subject. The ways in which he engaged both German America and Native America, however, shifted simultaneously, and at times dramatically, over the next two decades, reflecting the changes in his subject positions that resulted from the nationalization of his transnational world.

As Cronau continued to write essays on different aspects of the American West, for example, they took several forms. Some focused on prominent characters and types of people who had passed away with the transformation of the West into an industrial, agricultural market economy: pony express riders, trappers, scouts, stage drivers, outlaws, even the cowboys received his attention.[63] In addition, he wrote about historical figures such as Lewis and Clark, George Armstrong Custer, Buffalo Bill, and Zebulon Pike, as well as a number of equally famous American Indians.

The overwhelming thrust of these essays was a celebration of independent courage and exceptional ability, but also loss: the loss of untamed lands and peoples (both white and red); the loss of lifestyles on the frontier; the loss of adventure; and, in many of his essays, the loss of great opportunities. That continued even after the editors of the *Kölnische Zeitung* concluded from his essays on American actions in Cuba in 1898 that Cronau had become much too American to continue working for them, and he became an independent journalist in New York City.[64]

While writing his essays on the American West, Cronau retained his critical opinion of the U.S. government's treatment of American Indians even as he continued to embrace clichés about them. He developed, however, a different tone. In 1904, for example, he wrote "The Last Great Chief" for the *New Yorker Staats-Zeitung*, which commemorated Nez Perce Chief Joseph (1840–1904) and his nearly successful, and ultimately renowned attempt to evade U.S. troops across 1,400 miles of rugged territory in 1877. This essay was fundamentally different from his essays on the Dakotas from the 1880s. Here, Chief Joseph became a stand-in for many great leaders—Osceola, Tecumseh, Black Hawk, Spotted Tail, Sitting Bull, Red Cloud, and others—who resisted Yankee avarice to the bitter end.

In Cronau's narratives, the tragic fate of such great men and their people underscored the central shortcoming of American history, politics, and character: material greed was the motor of American history, and the result had been the terrible mismanagement of both the land and the people. Indeed, this argument framed his 1901 essay on the twenty-fifth anniversary of the "Custer Massacre" as well, which he painted as the clear consequence of American lust for gold in the Black Hills. The "great Sioux war" that followed, which he blamed on the government's failure to control the corruption of white settlers and soldiers, resulted in "gruesome tragedies," the loss of "many peoples' lives," the destruction and dismemberment of the "once mighty Sioux nation," and a "cost of more than 35 million dollars for the American government!"[65]

In short, the theme of mismanaged cultural conflict that had so permeated Cronau's earlier lectures and writings on Yankees and American Indians continued through the period in which he gained American citizenship; but there was an added twist, a German American element he had not highlighted before. Indeed, in an essay on the U.S. government's Carlisle school for Indians in Pennsylvania, which he wrote for *Die Gartenlaube* in 1904, Cronau returned to his earlier statements about the ability of American Indians to embrace civilization, to learn in schools, to acculturate, and to assimilate. In the 1880s, he had condemned the refusal of many Americans to acknowledge those abilities because it provided them with an excuse for dispossession and violence. Twenty years later he used much the same language, stressing again that "nowhere else was the collision between the white race and another so ruinous as here." It was "one of the most somber chapters" in his new country's history, where "frontier battles turned into race war." But in 1904 he was able to add that decades of success in the Carlisle Indian School and similar schools advocated by his countryman Karl Schurz had proved the more mean-spirited Americans wrong, and he sketched out the history of these schools' grudging success as illustrative of what might have been.[66]

In short, while Cronau became a proud American citizen he remained a critical, and often-disappointed German who pushed back against what German authors had long identified as Yankee excesses while championing liberal German alternatives. Those criticisms and endorsements came out vociferously in his writings, the most arresting of which was perhaps his book on American environmental degradation and the essay he produced for the radical *McClure's Magazine*, which was based on the same material.[67]

His first work in English, *Our Wasteful Nation*, achieved two primary goals: it underscored the limits of American husbandry and pointed to Germany as a model of redress. In chapters on the waste of water, soil, timber, mineral resources, wild and domesticated animals, sea mammals, fish, birds, public land and property, and ultimately human lives, Cronau wrote a tour de force that demonstrated the lack of foresight and undeniable irresponsibility with which Americans despoiled their environment. He praised Theodore Roosevelt's attempt to initiate conservation efforts, recalled the ridicule Karl Schurz had received for trying to manage the forests, and drew on successful German examples to demonstrate that viable alternatives existed. In Germany, he wrote, forestry was "a real science," and no one engaged in *Raubwirtschaft*, an economy of despoliation.[68]

Americanized Indians

As Cronau adopted this increasingly staunch German American position, both celebrating the potential of his new country and unapologetically praising the achievements of his homeland, his written work achieved something else as well. It reduced American Indians to generic people in the landscapes who had learned to live with the environment rather than despoiling it completely. They became, much like the animals and plants he championed, part of a lush background on which American history was written. Thus the textured tales of individuals and incidents he told in the 1880s to German audiences gave way to tropes common in American literature.

Always present in his writing, these tropes about "wild Indians" became dominant, effacing the actual experiences, details, and variety he had once recorded. Even the individuals he had met were harnessed for this purpose. American Indians such as Sitting Bull became ciphers for wilderness and anticivilization; so too did the adventurers, like Boyton, Buffalo Bill, and even Cronau himself. Modern market forces had destroyed the land of adventure that once hosted American Indians and courageous white men, exhausting the resources on which they once thrived. His concern with those external forces changed his perspective on American Indians, but his shifting subject positions were critical as well: as he became more American, so too did his portraits of American Indians.

Objectified in his writings, American Indians not only became more and more like the buffalo, his anti-eliminationist arguments became less humanist and more materialist as he described the ways in which young American Indians could have been educated as workers. Just as the buffalo need not have been eliminated but could have been managed and harvested, American Indians could have been educated, assimilated, and put to work. While presenting his case, Cronau calculated the loss of the buffalo in dollars and cents, comparing their low maintenance to the costs of raising and driving cattle, estimating the financial burdens on the settlers who were unable to turn to the buffalo as a source of food. Despite those calculations, his argument remained anticapitalist, or at least it constituted an objection to the excesses of unregulated and mismanaged industrial growth; he argued that because of the unmanaged harvesting of resources "America is rapidly becoming the continent poorest in animal life. Its forests and plains are silent and dead, our streams barren and lifeless. Instead of the happy song of birds, we hear the shrill noise of devastating locusts and grasshoppers, or the hum of innumerable swarms of mosquitoes, who long for our blood, and load us down with the germs of malaria and other dangerous diseases."[69] In these material calculations and pointed arguments, American Indians were reduced to one-dimensional wise men, at times custodians of the wilderness. In his environmental writings, they became much like the crying Indian in American television and movies from the 1970s;[70] they became generic natural men, counterpoints to white America's wastefulness, agape at the extinctions surrounding and facing them.[71]

As his subject positions in America shifted during the following decade, Cronau continued to instrumentalize American Indians to make a series of political and cultural arguments, abandoning his criticism of the United States' Indian policy and forsaking the people he once championed. For example, while making a plea in 1910 for the preservation of old forts and battlements from the colonial era, which he argued would bear witness to "acts of bravery and noble heroism" that gave birth to his adopted nation, Cronau cast American Indians generically as the vile associates of the British, savages used to attack "bold Germans" and other settlers on the frontier.[72] In a striking shift from his 1884 lecture on the decimated race in which he had cast American Indians as the victims of the European "bacillus" that was the colonial settlements, these same American Indians became, in his new rendition of colonial history, the beastly tools of slaughter in the service of British aggression. Meanwhile, German and other settlers became innocents engaged solely in defense rather than an infuriating theft of land. Similarly, when he wrote *Women Triumphant* almost a decade later, which traces the achievements of women from Babylon to postwar Europe, American Indians, when they make their cameo appearances in his book, play the role of "wild" and "ferocious savages" against which women persevere together with other settlers.[73] Indeed, during the years leading up to World War I, as he became drawn deeper into American discourses, Cronau, the erstwhile pluralist, increasingly harnessed such negative clichés and, more and more, he adopted a strikingly racist rhetoric.

Nationalizing the Transnational

The shifts in Cronau's prose reflect the changes in his subject positions that accompanied the transformations in international relations, the rise of national antagonisms in the decades before 1914, and the consequent threats to the transnational world that had nurtured his adult life and shaped Germans' interests in the United States. Before 1914, Cronau's America was an exceedingly transnational place in which Germans were involved in all aspects of American life, while many remained connected to Europe in myriad ways. Cronau himself traveled extensively. As an independent journalist, artist, and author, he made his living giving lectures and publishing essays on both continents, and by the early twentieth century his quest for adventure was more likely to take him to North Africa, Spain, and the high mountains of Switzerland than into the American West.

That lifestyle remained possible right up to the outbreak of World War l. What changed, however, during the first decades of the twentieth century, was the ever-increasing pressure upon people like Cronau to abandon their hybrid positions and move away from national indifference and toward a national camp. Indeed, as James Retallack reminds us, when Germany emerged as "the dynamo of Europe" at the end of the nineteenth century, "its economic and military power were pre-eminent; German science and technology, education, and municipal administration were the envy of the world; and its avant-garde artists reflected the ferment in European culture."[74] Americans responded positively at first, but opinions shifted noticeably from general approval of the new state in the 1870s to ever-heightened concerns with Prussian militarism and authoritarianism by the turn of the century. Even American academics, often the same people who benefited so greatly from their excursions to German universities during this period, increasingly saw their German counterparts as arms of a militant state. As a result, during the decade preceding the war, heightened American nationalism and international self-confidence, a diminished respect for the German government among American elites, and Germany's increased bellicosity in international affairs combined to reinforce those impressions and undercut many earlier interconnections between the two states.[75]

In response to the nationalization of his world, Cronau devoted much of his time to building up German American organizations and attempting to remind his contemporaries of the critical role Germans had played in American history. For Cronau, America was a great nation that owed many of its achievements to the kinds of German men and women he had encountered in the 1880s, but whom the English-language histories had all but forgotten. Indeed, Cronau was increasingly convinced that Anglophones and Anglophiles had purposefully obscured German contributions. Thus, as he set out to resurrect those contributions and bolster German Americans' reputations and self-awareness, he took on a decidedly anti-British position, similar to that shared by many of New Ulm's inhabitants in the 1860s when they faced similar anti-German prejudice. At the same time, he became an ever-greater apologist for Imperial Germany, its colonial expansion, its disposition toward Poland, and its actions on the international stage.[76]

In 1909 he published his most comprehensive effort to redress the historical imbalance. His history of Germans in America over the previous three hundred years located Germans on the initial voyages of discovery, in early settlements, in major conflicts, and across the entire history of the nation-state. In this book, he gave voice to German Americans who had taken a stand against slavery, underscored the roles of German political refugees who, like Schurz, had become instrumental in shaping progressive public policy, and celebrated the many hardworking German settlers who had not only supported the United States in its conflicts but also played a critical role in "opening" and "colonizing" the middle and far west."[77]

Ironically, as Cronau engaged in these debates, he saw no disjuncture between his celebration of Germans' many contributions to American settler colonialism and his earlier condemnations of it. Nor did he evidence any difficulty distancing himself from his earlier concern for the fate of American Indians during that process of colonization. Just the opposite; as his subject positions further shifted and he sought to defend German Americans as Americans, and as he became an ever-stronger denouncer of British imperialism and British foreign policy during World War I, he abandoned his earlier cultural pluralism altogether, adopting the kinds of racial language that were circulating in the United States at the time, and which were increasingly directed against German and Irish Americans as well as other ethnic groups.[78]

Indeed, when war broke out in Europe, Cronau penned a series of essays and pamphlets that championed German Americans' loyalty to the United States, advocated for American neutrality, and condemned the British aggressor.[79] Most importantly, in a shift of rhetoric that was even more astonishing than his adoption of clichéd images of American Indians, or his sudden, enthusiastic support of settler colonialism after the fact, Cronau drew on a new set of clichés to argue vociferously that Britain's greatest sin was to engage in race suicide.

With broad and damning strokes, Cronau painted a picture of English aggressors focused for generations on systematically destroying European states and colonies by harnessing "savages" to do their bidding. In these new narratives, his portraits of American Indians underwent another fundamental change. While describing the border wars between the French and British colonies in the New World between 1689 and 1763, for example, he argued that "these wars reached an appalling character when the English as well as the French persuaded the Indians under their influence to help in the mutual murder," and "in this savage butchery, German emigrants from the Palatinate, which the English had settled at the most exposed points, had to bear the brunt of hostile assaults."[80] In Cronau's new narratives, such assaults came not from well-seasoned warriors such as Gall, or "visions of pronounced manliness" such as Crow King and Sitting Bull, men who, much like German tribal leaders had engaged in a righteous assault in response to egregious ills. Rather these were assaults from inhuman "savages" in the pay of America's "false friend," the British, against real Americans, against German Americans.

Such assaults, Cronau claimed, continued even after the War of Independence. The British returned with similar methods in the war of 1812, and in Cronau's new rendition of that story, he gave the British much of the credit for Tecumseh's rise and success. Casting off the last vestiges of German narratives about American Indians, he portrayed Tecumseh—a particular favorite in Germany, who Cronau had once lauded together with Sitting Bull—as a bloodthirsty destroyer of white settlements rather than the valiant defender of his own lands, and he recast American colonial history as a nineteenth-century precursor to current British efforts to commit "race suicide" by enlisting colonial troops to combat German forces.[81]

What are we to think of this transformation in Cronau's writings, of the shift from German journalist and traveler who returns from his stay with the Standing Rock Sioux in the 1880s to condemn American imperialism and settler colonialism and champion a position of cultural pluralism and then, only a few decades later, uses the strongest racial language to vilify and denigrate non-Europeans? It reflects the desperate state of German America as much as Cronau's shifting subject positions. In the 1880s, Cronau denounced the race war unleashed against American Indians by white Europeans and Americans over the course of several centuries. At that time, the

American Indians he portrayed were individuals and groups of people with whom he had sympathy, even empathy, equating their plight with that of Germans in several historical situations. Two decades later, as he became an American citizen and initiated his struggle for the recognition of German contributions to American history, he shifted his allegiance away from the victims of American capitalism and imperialism and aligned himself with the forces of "progress" and "civilization" he had once called into question. During that move, he adopted common tropes from American literature to replace the American Indians he had once written about with generic images on the landscape, equating them with the other dangers of nature that must be subdued.

Cronau's willingness to adopt racial language and radically shift his own positions on colonialism was a response in kind to what he termed the "un-American American press," which whipped up a racialized anti-German sentiment during the years of neutrality and vilified German Americans after 1917.[82] Indeed, Germans who became American citizens faced serious dilemmas during the outbreak of the war. Numerous but heterogeneous, German Americans were divided in politics and on their positions toward the war. At the outset, many went into the streets in support of Imperial Germany; others volunteered to fight against it. Still others focused their efforts on fighting another battle at home.

An impressive number of German Americans felt compelled to rally together with Rudolf Cronau during the noxious debates about "hyphenated Americans" that accompanied Anglophiles' rising jingoism during the first years of the war. These German Americans and their supporters called attention to the disjuncture between the generally positive images of German people who settled in the United States and the increasingly negative images of the German state in the years preceding the war. They fought against the anti-German image in the English-language press, which quickly extended its anger with the German state to all things German. And they advocated strongly for neutrality once the conflict began. The sheer number of people who sent letters and telegrams to the U.S. Congress pleading for America to stay out of the war is staggering.[83]

The battle to define German Americans' place in the United States raged across the country until Woodrow Wilson's electoral victory in 1916 and the end of American neutrality in 1917. Afterward, German Americans, regardless of their positions on the war, became pariahs, and abuses were quick and widespread. As Frederick Luebke recounts, the so-called Committee of Public Information "created a national mood of aggressive patriotism as it attacked dissent as disloyalty, extolled British culture, and fostered hatred for Germany." Other organizations, such as the American Defense League, "intensified the anti-German hysteria through indiscriminate attacks on German Americans' churches, schools, societies, and newspapers, describing them as inhibitors of assimilation and as agents of a worldwide Teutonic conspiracy." They also encouraged the public burning of German-language books.[84] The enthusiastic response was astounding, and not simply where German Americans were vocal minorities.

In the Midwest, for example, where German American culture had thrived since the states were founded, the state governments set up councils of defense that issued prohibitions against the use of the German language in any public place—including in many cases German associations, churches, and schools where German had been spoken since their inception decades earlier. The mean-spiritedness that erupted among Anglophone Americans and their supporters directed at communities like New Ulm in Minnesota represents a black mark on American history.[85] So too does the widespread assault on the Midwest's exceptional bilingual schools, the maltreatment of German-language instructors who worked in them as well as in other public schools and universities, the harassing and veritable destruction of the German-language press, and the public call in many cases for a few "first-class hangings."[86]

Speaking in the language of American politics, Cronau joined many others (especially German Americans and Irish Americans)[87] in their attempt to counter the attacks on German culture and the loyalty of America's "hyphenated citizens."[88] In a desperate attempt to not simply resurrect Germans' historical contributions to the United States but rather to save their seriously threatened position as full citizens, Cronau, not unlike Jacob Nix and other German Americans before him, embraced a language of white racial unity that would allow him to plea to his fellow citizens and his government to free America from British intrigue and retain German Americans as full members of the polity.

That Faustian bargain gained him little. In the end, the laws against sedition silenced Cronau. Hauled into court following complaints by the English about the contents of his *British Black Book*, he was warned away from producing any further "anti-British propaganda." The remaining copies of his book were seized and burned, and Cronau turned to working for relief organizations during the remainder of the war and the decades that followed.

At the same time, the thriving German America he had embraced was crushed.[89] The fate of the German language alone makes this clear. As Walter

Kamphoefner explains, "Not only were the last surviving German language programs in public elementary schools abolished, but cuts at the secondary level went even deeper." Before the war, "German was by far the most important foreign language in the high school curriculum." Two to three times as many students took German as French. "By 1922," however, "nothing was left of this dominance: only 0.6 percent were enrolled in German classes," and the language never bounced back. The war also cut the number of German periodicals in half and reduced their circulation by 75 percent. In 1919, only twenty-six dailies were still operating, and many of those that struggled through the 1920s collapsed in the depression.[90] At the same time, many families, businesses, and organizations changed their names to hide their German origins, and memberships in German American organizations "plummeted." Survival for those businesses and associations necessitated a transition to a nonethnic basis. So too did preventing "a recurrence of the persecution" against many people and their communities.[91]

Consequently, the transnational lifestyle on which Cronau's livelihood depended was destroyed as well. The second edition of his book on three hundred years of Germans in American history had been slated for 1916, but it was stopped by the war, and his inability to travel combined with the burden of relief work reduced his income considerably. So too did the fact that the topics that most interested him as a journalist, as well as the language in which he wrote, had become largely taboo. Those conditions depressed him greatly. He and his wife took their last trip to Germany in 1931, where the harsh conditions of life and the fact that few of his old friends were to be found alive in either Solingen or Leipzig drove his wife to a nervous breakdown from which she never recovered. She spent the last decade of her life in a sanitarium.

Cronau, increasingly impoverished, was forced to move into the basement of his daughter Margarete Hildegard's home, where he wrote his autobiography and organized his papers before succumbing to stomach cancer in 1939. His writings on American Indians had long since lost their resonance in Germany, where, perhaps ironically, the kinds of racialized language he had adopted remained out of favor. There, beliefs in affinities between Germans and American Indians continued to flourish, and many Germans persisted in looking to those original Americans for answers.

CHAPTER 4

Modern Germans and Indians

In 1903 W. E. B. Du Bois famously remarked that "the problem of the twentieth century is the problem of the color-line,—the relation of the darker to the lighter races of men in Asia and Africa, in America and in the islands of the sea." It was the color line that made him, as an African American, feel like a persistent "problem" everywhere and always, "save perhaps," he noted, "in babyhood and Europe."[1] In Europe, Du Bois felt treated almost as an equal, and it was at the First Universal Races Congress held in London in 1911 that he "heard Felix von Luschan, the great anthropologist from the University of Berlin, annihilate the thesis of race inferiority."[2] In Germany, where Du Bois studied at the University of Berlin from 1892 to 1894, he became enamored with Germans' pursuit of *Bildung* and *Kultur*.[3] His enthusiasm, however, was mixed, as it was when he listened to Luschan. For in the same speech in which Luschan dismissed race as a meaningful construct, he also questioned the wisdom of racial mixing and sang the praises of German imperialism, exemplifying the very contradictions that troubled Du Bois about Germany and his mentors:[4] while he was fond of German erudition and the pluralism he had encountered there,[5] he had been troubled by the belligerent militarism on the streets and in the classroom.

Through the complexity and contradictions of Luschan's positions, Du Bois was exposed again in 1911 to the fact that the color line might not be so black and white. Indeed, Steven Conn has pointed out that although Du Bois was clearly the United States' "most profound thinker on matters of race" at the outset of the twentieth century, "it is not at all clear" that he spent much time thinking about "the third race," American Indians, which had so occupied European travelers for centuries and had been such a critical part of racial discussions in the United States during the most formative decades of his life. Du Bois was born in 1868, but by 1903 he, along with many other white and black Americans, seemed to regard American Indians as all but invisible.[6] Thus, by 1903 he could focus on the persistent division between black and white because, as Conn put it, "the 'problem' of the Indian had been finally 'solved.'"[7]

Conn's point is well taken, but perhaps not taken far enough. For as Rudolf Cronau might eagerly have pointed out when he embraced a defensive racism while Luschan was "annihilating" it, stark lines of prejudice and violence cut across the colors as well; some even tied different colors together. Indeed, if, in fact, American Indians had become invisible to people as astute as Du Bois by the first decade of the twentieth century, so too would German America during the decade after World War I. It was still there, but no longer so prominent: another problem solved.

Moreover, in Germany, it was not the color line that would divide most people; whiteness was certainly no guarantee of equitable treatment in Weimar Germany or under National Socialism.[8] Rather, the racial lines condemned by Luschan and the anti-Semitism he characterized as "disgusting and shameful" would cut across Europe in a horribly deadly fashion.[9] Red, however, would remain a strikingly consistent color in Germany, one that even Nazis could embrace, as long as it was tied to the phenotype of American Indians rather than the stars worn by Communists.

Indeed, as a new, more nationally unified Germany rose out of the horrors of World War I and the repeated crises of the interwar period, as National Socialists battled other Germans to win control of the state and reshape it along racial lines, America remained on German minds. If the United States stopped being the central and most natural point of emigration for many who sought an alternative *Deutschtum*, it remained a critical point of comparison for the emerging states of Weimar and Nazi Germany, and a site for Germans to pursue modernist variations of old themes: celebrating affinities between Germans and American Indians, admiring American Indian resistance, and emulating American Indians in striking new ways.

Modern Indians

Many non-Native Americans in 1900 could regard the so-called Indian problem as solved because the majority "did not expect Indians to adapt to the modern world." As Daniel Francis has argued, and as many have repeatedly said, the only hope for American Indians "was to assimilate, to become White, to cease to be Indians." For most non-Native Americans, "any Indian was by definition a traditional Indian," and thus "a relic of the past." "The image could not be modernized," because a "modern Indian" was "a contradiction in terms."[10] American Indians were history.

Occasionally, however, as Philip Deloria has remarked, American Indians resurfaced in rather "unexpected places." Indeed, if American Indians had ceased to be a "problem" in the United States, many had nevertheless survived the massive efforts at acculturation and assimilation, and some of those people began to play new roles in America by seizing on modern opportunities. After the turn of the century, as interests in cultural primitivism rose and gained prominence in the United States, American Indians could be, as Deloria puts it, "objects, not simply of racial repulsion, but also—as they reflected nostalgia for community, spirituality, and nature—of racial desire."[11] That opened doors, allowing many to move into a variety of quintessentially modern places even when they were categorized as traditional, historical people.

American Indians found opportunities in entertainment and especially in early films, before American westerns settled into a static genre. They also moved seamlessly into athletic events, churches, and into a variety of endeavors in the United States that tied the essential primitive to whatever was current, new, and modern. Advertisements for technology, particularly for cars, and for their use in a new kind of tourism, provide Deloria with one of his most powerful examples: "In the late 1910s, tourism boosters explicitly linked American Indians, the frontier, and automobility in their hype for the Black Hills–Sioux Trail, a route that midwesterners took through Chicago and across the Rosebud and Pine Ridge Reservations on their way to Yellowstone National Park."[12] Protected from the contamination of the modern world, the new owners of technology could visit these historic Indians at and during their leisure. Because these American Indians were billed as preserved on the reservations, the owners of the new automobiles could get to the past in the seat of the present, in the epitome of technical innovation.

Yet, as Deloria also points out, Geronimo drove a car. In fact, at the 1905 "Oklahoma's Gala Day" organized by the Miller Brothers' 101 Ranch in Bliss, Oklahoma, Geronimo shot a bison from the front seat of a car for the audience's pleasure.[13] That, however, was a different kind of tourism; but the image is critical. Images of American Indians in airplanes and automobiles became incredibly popular by the 1920s. People loved them because they were iconoclastic: they merged antinomial objects of primitivism and modernity in one image. They also made it clear that in an age of fashionable existentialism and expressionist and surrealist art, technology could meld the past with the present, the primitive with the modern, and bring historical American Indians to the consumers of cultural primitivism wherever they might be. Technology, like a time machine, could place the historic and primitive in the center of the hypermodern.

Wild West shows in particular, Deloria argues, "left behind a trail of similar stories of Indian modernity," of American Indians appearing in traditional costumes in exquisitely modern places. The stories "appeared in images of Indians in the gondolas of Venice or playing ping-pong backstage." One finds pictures of American Indians filing onto airplanes in Frankfurt as well, and driving cars in Berlin. For Deloria, these stories of American Indians on the move demonstrate their agency. They document moments in which American Indians seized on modern opportunities, and they demonstrate how modern American Indians themselves had become, and how wrong non-Native Americans had been and continue to be in their assumptions about American Indians' exclusion from the modern era. Thus, he argues that "when Wild West Indians hopped into cars or learned to ride bicycles" they were demonstrating the similarity between themselves and other non-Native peoples, and "when performers, such as Hampa Nespa (who willingly worked in European circuses between 1887 and 1909) abandoned Cody for long-term careers in Europe, or when Wild West–seasoned actors joined up with one of the many groups performing as part of the Kickapoo Medicine Show, Indian people were crafting, not simply their own inferior version of modernity, but a shared global world."[14]

Modern Indians in Germany

Germany provided American Indian performers with ample opportunity to help "craft" that "shared global world." Indeed, if the transnational world based on the German Kulturkreis facilitated the transcultural production of iconographic images and ideas about American Indians during the nineteenth century, a transnational world of performance facilitated the perpetuation of these ideas and provided a place for American Indians to help channel and shape them within Germany.

American Indian performers were incredibly popular in Germany during the years leading up to the war. Indeed, they were easily as popular as the performers who came with Buffalo Bill in 1890. Germans' expectations, however, had changed. By the end of the century, even the stories about cowboys, outlaws, and ranchers were fading in prominence in the illustrated magazines. Increasingly, accounts of travel across the Great Plains focused on the ease of transportation on the most modern of trains, which could cut

Carl Hagenbecks Tierpark In Stellingen.
Sioux-Indianer: Begrüßungs-Szene.

FIGURE 14. Hagenbeck's Oglala Troupe (1910). (Karl Markus Kreis
Postcard Collection)

through high drifts and connect vast distances even in the dead of winter.
Hardships were relegated to the challenges German tourists faced negotiating Americans' strange rules and regulations as they visited America's cities,
towns, and national parks.[15]

Germans, in short, knew that the West had been won, that the "Indian
problem" had been "solved," but they also knew, like the tourists enticed to
take the "Black Hills–Sioux Trail," that not all American Indians had been
vanquished. They knew this because they kept reading about current conditions on reservations, because the showmen told them, and because American Indian performers just kept coming.

Of all Carl Hagenbeck's many *Völkerschauen*, the most successful was the
five-month exhibition of forty-two Oglala-Sioux in Hamburg in 1910. Together with Texas Tex and his ten cowboys, they participated in a ten-part
program much like that organized by Buffalo Bill, which turned around "real
events" from the 1870s, such as ambushes, horse stealing, and the thrill of the
Pony Express. They included historical individuals as well: Thomas American Horse, whose father had worked with Buffalo Bill, was among them, so
too was Edward Two-Two, Little Wolf, Bad Bob, Kills Enemy, Little Weasel,
and John Rock. These were people who could claim knowledge and experience of those past events.

To underscore the authentic, historical character of these performers, the organizers offered the 1.1 million visitors who came to see them a pamphlet that sketched out the Oglala-Sioux's historical resistance against the U.S. military and included biographies of the oldest members of the troupe who had fought in the Indian wars. The pamphlet, as well as the news coverage, also connected the people and the events to Cooper's tales, much as the papers had done in the 1890s.

At the same time, however, it contained information about current conditions on the Pine Ridge Reservation, which interested Germans a great deal, perhaps much more than non-Native Americans.[16] From the pamphlet, they learned about the new social organizations, the police, the courts, the judges, the schools, and the transformation of lifestyles on the reservation. While the performers brought teepees with them to Germany, the pamphlet explained that most families on the reservations had moved into cabins and noted the unfortunate fact that this shift had increased the rate of some diseases, particularly tuberculosis.

What the pamphlet did not discuss was the difficulty Hagenbeck faced in recruiting the performers. When Adrian Jacobsen arrived on the Pine Ridge Reservation to recruit for Hagenbeck, five other agents were already there, and one of Buffalo Bill's men was on his way. By 1910, these performers were highly sought after and eager to participate in Wild West shows and other exhibitions across Europe and the United States. Between 1883 and 1914, participation in such performances was easily the most lucrative form of employment available to residents of the reservation. The food and wages offered by the impresarios had great appeal, but so too did the opportunity to travel, to learn about other people and places, and to demonstrate bravery by traveling. Many were also happy to have the opportunity to recapture the nobility of remembered lives and to perform elements of "Indianness" in places where it was appreciated. Some performers saw an opportunity to teach whites about their cultures; some, like Rocky Bear in 1890, even considered themselves dignitaries and regarded these tours as opportunities to refashion themselves abroad and perhaps at home. In most cases, they were also treated well during these international performances, and many, not unlike Du Bois, remarked on the sense of freedom and equitable treatment they received in Germany.[17] Many of them enjoyed it repeatedly.

The Wild West shows and the *Völkerschauen* had been occasional events, but by 1910, after Hagenbeck's tremendous success, circus impresarios, particularly Hans-Stosch Sarrasani, transformed some of these occasional performers into seasonal stars. Sarrasani established a permanent building for his circus in Dresden in 1912, and he sent circus contingents across Germany as well as Europe. He began including American Indians in his performances, and in 1912 he turned to recruiting the very performers who had worked for Hagenbeck. In a short period of time, Sarrasani, who counted American Indians as the most lucrative components of his show, began to set up networks of communication with American entrepreneurs who could supply him with American Indians, and particularly Lakota performers, who were recognized across the industry as being particularly well suited to these western roles. Germans remained especially enamored with the Sioux.

By 1913, business was booming. Joe Miller, one of three brothers who ran the Millers Brothers 101 Ranch in Oklahoma, even sent his brother Zach to Germany in 1913 to negotiate directly for a more permanent arrangement with Sarrasani.[18] In the summer of 1914 several contingents of American Indians were working as performers in Germany, and plans were unfolding for further events, but then the war broke out, stranding Bill Arthur and a group of Lakotas employed by Sarrasani in Hamburg and an independent group of Onondaga Indians in Berlin. After several misadventures, which included mobs of Germans mistaking some of the performers for Russian spies, both groups were able to return to the United States and were back in their homes by the end of the year.[19]

The war interfered in the business and forced a multiyear hiatus, but it did not destroy the connections created during those prewar years, nor did it undercut in any way the appeal of American Indian performers in Germany. Even with the extensive devastation and economic chaos unleashed by the war and the subsequent inflation, Sarrasani began negotiating for new troupes of American Indians in the early 1920s, and in 1924 he took a contingent of performers commissioned by the Miller Brothers with him on a major trip to South America.[20] By that point, Joe Miller had met Sarrasani personally and had visited his circus in Dresden. They had met in Breslau as well, and the two developed a strong bond that lasted until Miller's death.

That relationship with the 101 Ranch gave Sarrasani a tremendous advantage over his competitors in Germany. They recognized this, and they too approached the Miller Brothers in an effort to secure performers like those assigned to Sarrasani. Indeed, just as Sarrasani had sought to recruit the people who had worked for Hagenbeck in 1910 before the war, Sarrasani's competitors tried to recruit the people working for him in 1924.

Paul Schultze, representing Circus Krone in Munich, contacted Joe Miller directly. Embellishing Krone's position in an effort to undermine Miller's commitment to Sarrasani, he explained that Krone was the only circus to come out of the war and the depression with significant profits (accrued by working in Italy directly after the war) and was thus the only circus that could meet the Miller Brothers' expectations for the care and compensation of their performers. He stressed that Circus Krone, which he claimed rivaled Barnum's position in the United States, was eager to include American Indians as a significant component of its business. He explained that Circus Krone had followed Sarrasani's recent trip to South America closely and asked for the same set of performers who accompanied him on that trip to be sent to Munich for the next season. At the same time, Schultze negotiated for a contract that would give Circus Krone exclusive rights to performers organized by the 101 Ranch for the extent of the 1925 season. Miller agreed, much to Sarrasani's chagrin, and in response to being shut out, Sarrasani, immediately began lobbying for the same or similar performers to come to Dresden the following season. The Miller Brothers also received similar requests from Hagenbeck and the directors of other, smaller circuses.[21]

By 1926, the market for these performances was so good that the Miller Brothers were overwhelmed by requests for American Indian performers. For example, Julius Gleich in Cologne contacted the 101 Ranch looking for a "good band of Indians from Pine Ridge" and hoping for a "complete troupe" for what he claimed was one of Germany's largest circuses, one that would soon rival Sarrasani. Many smaller circuses began contacting the Miller Brothers as well.[22] Some turned to other freelancers; but there were only so many "good performers" to go around. As Joe Miller had explained to Krone the year before, "they are a very popular people," and not all American Indians were equal when it came to performances. Everyone preferred the performers from Pine Ridge, because they had developed a tradition of traveling as show Indians, and they retained the skills of riding and shooting that many contingents from the Northeast no longer had.

These performers' talents and purported scarcity only made them more essential to the German circuses, where the public increasingly demanded their presence. Essentially any show with American Indian performers was a popular and profitable one. Sarrasani wrote in 1926, for example, that despite his inability to charge high prices in interwar Germany, the popular enthusiasm for American Indians was allowing him to make great profits: his circus could hold up to ten thousand people, and Miller's performers kept the seats full.

The challenge was to keep the performers coming, and in order to retain their shares of the market, Sarrasani and Krone battled out their respective positions in the German courts.[23] The Miller Brothers, inundated by requests, and recognizing the appeal of performers, considered traveling to

Germany themselves with their own Wild West show, which had been operating in the United States since 1907.[24] As Joe Miller wrote to Paul Schultze in 1926, they were doing such good business organizing troupes for the Germans that "we might as well do it ourselves."[25]

In order to prepare for that eventuality, Miller began to limit the number of circuses he would supply with performers in an effort to ensure that the market could not become saturated and the appeal would not wane. Thus, he began turning down requests from smaller circuses and started managing the flow of American Indian performers across the Atlantic, even using his connections with the Indian agents on reservations to prevent others from hiring performers for German circuses.[26]

However, the flow of American Indian performers back and forth across the Atlantic only grew. New entrepreneurs began approaching German circuses with promises that they could provide them with more, better, and cheaper performers, and the Miller Brothers began receiving letters from their clients quoting offers from this competition. Indeed, when Circus Krone ran afoul of Joe Miller's efforts to control the flow of performers into Germany and found itself without a contingent of American Indian performers for its 1926 season, it hired another agent, Charles L. Sasse, to go around the 101 Ranch. He found a group of American Indians from New York. In response, Joe Miller offered Krone's agent a primer on performers: "These Indians were New York Indians and not at all the real type of Western Indians, which I think Mr. Krone would have preferred; but I presume this was the best Mr. Sasse could do under the circumstances." Stressing that he had "succeeded in blocking" its efforts to get performers from Pine Ridge by speaking to the Indian agent there, he nevertheless noted that he regretted losing Krone's business and advised Schultze to keep an eye on the "New York Indians": "My own experience with Indians from the North," he noted, "has not been satisfactory."[27]

Sarrasani quickly saw why: while they arrived in Germany with "fine costumes," they "did not have the Indian face that the European people expect to see." Sasse clearly recognized this as well. Thus, when Clarence Schultz arrived in Hamburg to pick up Sarrasani's performers, he learned that many of them had been offered double salaries to leave with Sasse's people and work for Krone, forcing Schultz to track some of them down and, in at least one instance, turn to the police to help enforce the contracts.[28]

Joe Miller died on 21 October 1927, and that same year the 101 Ranch feel deep into debt, ending its role as a kind of clearinghouse for American Indian performers in Germany.[29] Nevertheless, the shows did go on. The performers demanded it. German audiences could not get enough of them; and many entrepreneurs had established good reputations and their own connections in Native America. Thus Sarrasani immediately harnessed his connections with the American consul in Dresden, hired Clarence Schultz directly to travel to Pine Ridge for him, and began negotiating with the U.S. State Department and the Indian agent E. W. Jermark on the Pine Ridge Reservation to keep the performers coming.

In support of that effort, A. T. Haeberle, the U.S. consul in Dresden wrote the State Department: "The Indians with whom I have spoken during my residence in Dresden stated that they were well satisfied with the treatment they received and as far as I remember there has never been any difficulties with the Indians that in any way involved Mr. Sarrasani. Owing to the general interest manifested in the Sarrasani Circus even by the most cultured classes, largely because of a representation of the 'Wild West,' I take the liberty of presenting this matter to the Department for such consideration as it might deserve."[30]

Many performers confirmed Haeberle's endorsement. Indeed, in his effort to gain more performers, Sarrasani had the help of people like Thomas Stabber (also known as White Buffalo Man) and Sam Lone Bear in the town of Porcupine, as well as George R. Nothing in Manderson, all on the Pine Ridge Reservation. These men wrote directly to Sarrasani seeking employment, and in the years that followed, they wrote to other Germans as well.

It worked. Clarence Schultz continued to organize troupes to go to Germany, Sarrasani continued to showcase American Indian performers, and individuals such as Lone Bear continued to sell their services there. Indeed, in 1931 Stabber again wrote to Sarrasani looking for work for himself and others, and Sarrasani, in turn, again contacted the commissioner of Indian Affairs and explained that "Mr. Thomas Stabber (aka White Buffalo Man), the chief of the party, and Sam Lone Bear, the interpreter, have writte[n] and cabled me intimating their desire to re-new their engagements with me. These Indians have been employed in my Circus periodically since 1915, having last returned to USA in December 1930."[31] As a result of these negotiations, Stabber was able to work with Sarrasani another season in the 1930s, and afterward he continued to negotiate for further opportunities to return to Germany, if not to work with Sarrasani, then with other companies, like Circus Krone in Munich, which his friend the German artist Elk Eber helped him and Lone Bear secure. Eber and Stabber had an ongoing correspondence during the 1930s, and in several of his letters to Eber, Stabber made his desire to return explicit. In 1936, for example, he wrote: "My country is no good.

No work and no money. . . . I don't want to go to American show, no good, I like to go to Deutschland show." Both he and Lone Bear preferred to work in Germany, and Germans were eager to have them.[32]

Modernist Indians

The transnational world of Native American performers from which German entrepreneurs and audiences so benefited took shape during a shift in aesthetics among Germans and other Europeans, marked by an increased interest in juxtapositions of the primitive and the modern identified by Deloria in American advertising but taken to a dramatic extension by German intellectuals and artists during the interwar era. They not only regarded American Indians as allegories for change and symbols of freedom and individuality but continued to identify them as resisters, while recasting older notions of affinity in a new, modernist key.

Aby Warburg's reflections on his experiences among the Hopi are exemplary. Warburg, the son of a wealthy German Jewish banking family in Hamburg, was a well-known if controversial historian of art and culture, with a keen interest in the Renaissance and a fascination with iconography. Indeed, he is often credited with establishing iconology as a separate field of study. He was also obsessed with the ways in which the classical world influenced the modern world, and he had an epiphany while visiting Pueblo Indians in Arizona and New Mexico in 1895–96, which became the basis of a lecture some twenty-seven years later that captured the juxtaposition between tradition and modernity in a way that has intrigued people ever since.[33]

"What interested me as a cultural historian," Warburg wrote, "was that in the midst of a country that had made technological culture into an admirable precision weapon in the hands of intellectual man, an enclave of primitive pagan humanity was able to maintain itself and—an entirely sober struggle for existence notwithstanding—to engage in hunting and agriculture with an unshakable adherence to magical practices that we are accustomed to condemning as a mere symptom of a completely backward humanity."[34] What he found, in other words, were survivors: people who had not been acculturated, individuals and groups who had resisted the Faustian temptations of modern Western civilization and who retained a part of themselves that Warburg felt most, if not all, Europeans had lost.

It was not that the modern world had failed to intervene in their lives. The point for Warburg was that the Hopi appeared to have resisted the modernizing, homogenizing forces of Western civilization, even if they had not kept it entirely at bay. Marveling, for example, at the totems in their dwellings, he described the "small dolls" he found "suspended from the ceilings" much like "the figures of saints that hang in Catholic farmhouses." These were "the so-called Kachina dolls: faithful representations of the masked dancers, the demoniac mediators between man and nature at the periodic festivals that accompany the annual harvest cycle." They "constitute some of the most remarkable and unique expressions of this farmers' and hunters' religion." Still, "on the wall, in contradistinction to these dolls, hangs the symbol of intruding American culture: the broom."[35] Of course, the image of the "intruding" broom was nothing like the scene in the Minnesota wigwam described by Cronau decades earlier. This was no mishmash of oddly unrelated things, the remnants of multiple cultural clashes; rather it was a hint of awareness of the world outside the mesas, and a disturbing threat to the alternative he had found.

Warburg's references to paganism among the Hopi were complimentary, not derogatory. He meant to underscore their vibrant, rich, and productive world of mythology. That mythology, while present under the deep coverings of European cultures, was alive among the Hopi in a way that contrasted sharply with the rest of America. When he wrote, for example, that "the American of today is no longer afraid of the rattle snake. He kills it; in any case, he does not worship it. It now faces extermination," he was not making the typical German quip that Cronau had made about the Yankee's destruction of wilderness and mismanagement of natural resources. Rather he was pointing out the poverty of life that had accompanied the triumph of Western, empirical science. Thus he argued: "The lightning imprisoned in wire—captured electricity—has produced a culture with no use for paganism. What has replaced it? Natural forces are no longer seen in anthropomorphic or biomorphic guise, but rather as infinite waves obedient to the human touch." While many of his contemporaries celebrated the capturing of electricity as a positive or progressive development, Warburg was concerned with the price: "With these waves, the culture of the machine age destroys what the natural sciences, born of myth, so arduously achieved: the space for devotion, which evolved in turn into the space required for reflection." In the modern American world, there was no time to think and nothing left to worship except material progress and perhaps oneself.[36]

Indeed, Warburg was convinced that people paid dearly for their technology: "The modern Prometheus and the modern Icarus, Franklin and the Wright brothers, who invented the dirigible airplane, are precisely those ominous destroyers of the sense of distance, who threaten to lead the planet back into chaos." In the modern world, Warburg saw distance foreshortened, space undone, indeed: the "telegram and telephone destroy the cosmos." For Warburg, "mythical and symbolic thinking strive to form spiritual bonds between humanity and the surrounding world, shaping distance into the space required for devotion and reflection." But this is "the distance undone by instantaneous electric connection."[37] This is the price.

What Warburg found most of all among the Hopi was insight into Europe and European history. Indeed, he later wrote to James Mooney at the Smithsonian Institution in Washington, D.C., that it was their civilization, because of its paganism more than its primitivism, which helped him better understand the Renaissance.[38] As he made clear in his lecture, however, he gained further insight as well into what irritated him most about contemporary Europe, into its deficits, and perhaps even more, into non–Native America.

He was not alone. Scores of German intellectuals and others turned to American Indians during the interwar period as a means of thinking through the challenges posed by technology and their modern, "machine-age" world.[39] Indeed, a string of ethnologists and artists such as Karl von den Steinen, Paul Ehrenreich, and Max Ernst followed Warburg to the Hopi Mesas and other Pueblos in search of what he had found.[40]

Much like Warburg, for example, the Swiss psychiatrist Carl Jung traveled to New Mexico in 1924 and visited the Taos Pueblo. His goal was to gain some insight into himself and other Europeans by conversing with the residents, and he later wrote about the rich and revealing conversations he had with Ochwiay Biano (Mountain Lake). Discussing whites in general, Mountain Lake said to him: "See how cruel the whites look. Their lips are thin, their noses sharp, their faces furrowed and distorted by folds. Their eyes have a staring expression; they are always seeking something. What are they seeking?" It was clear to him that "the whites always want something. They are always uneasy and restless. We do not know what they want. We do not understand them. We think that they are mad." The problem white Americans and Europeans shared, Mountain Lake explained to Jung, the thing that made them "mad," was whites' tendency to think with their heads and not with their hearts. Thus they have no intimate connection to the natural world. They have no place in it.[41]

Jung later wrote that his conversation with Mountain Lake provided him with a great revelation, a window into the mental stress he had seen in so many patients, and perhaps also in himself. "For the first time in my life," he wrote, "someone had drawn for me a picture of the real white man." Nothing about the typical European had been so clear to him until "this Indian had struck our vulnerable spot, unveiled a truth to which we are blind." Europe's was a history of colonialism and conquest, long in the making, with incredible breadth, and Europeans suffered from this condition, as did many other people in the world. Jung recorded those revelations as he contemplated these insights: "I felt rising within me like a shapeless mist something unknown and yet deeply familiar. And out of this mist, image upon image detached itself: first Roman legions smashing into the cities of Gaul, and the keenly incised features of Julius Caesar, Scipio Africanus, and Pompey." The conquests were endless: "I saw the Roman eagle on the North Sea and on the banks of the White Nile. Then I saw St. Augustine transmitting the Christian creed to the Britons on the tips of Roman lances, and Charlemagne's most glorious forced conversions of heathen; then the pillaging and murdering bands of the Crusading armies." The pillaging, he knew, crossed German Central Europe as well as the Middle East, so too did the forced conversions. "With a secret stab I realized the hollowness of that old romanticism about the Crusades. Then followed Columbus, Cortes, and the other conquistadors who with fire, sword, torture, and Christianity came down upon even these remote pueblos dreaming peacefully in the Sun, their Father. I saw too, the peoples of the pacific islands decimated by firewater, syphilis, and scarlet fever carried in the clothes the missionaries forced on them." Europeans, he concluded, were "a race" of pirates and highwaymen, whose "eagles and other predatory creatures that adorn our coats of arms" seemed to accurately capture the "psychological representatives of our true nature."[42]

Jung too recognized the importance that myth and mythology played in the Pueblo people's lives. He also wrote about how much its absence in European society accounted for many of the ills that occupied his own mind, and he recognized Mountain Lake's commitment to mythology as the thing that had allowed him to resist the onslaught of Western civilization where others, including many Europeans, had failed. During a discussion of religion with Mountain Lake, he asked his interlocutor if he thought what he did with his religion benefited the whole world. To Jung's amazement, Mountain Lake answered in the affirmative, explaining that his people were "the sons of the sun" and that "with our religion we daily help our father to go across the sky. We do this not only for ourselves but for the whole world. If we were to cease practicing our religion, in ten years the sun would no longer rise. Then it would be night forever." Jung's reaction was not unlike Warburg's reaction to the Hopi. Mountain Lake's sincerity made Jung realize "on what the 'dignity,' the tranquil composure of the individual Indian, was founded. It springs from his being a son of the sun; his life is cosmologically meaningful, for he helps the father and preserver of all life in his daily rise and descent."[43]

That revelation provided Jung with the critical insight into the limits of Europe's technological modernity and the price that Europeans and non-Native Americans had paid for it: "If we set against this our own self-justification, the meaning of our own lives as it is formulated by our reason, we cannot help but see our poverty. Out of sheer envy we are obliged to smile at the Indians' naiveté and to plume ourselves on our cleverness; for otherwise we would discover how impoverished and down at the heels we are." Then, sounding much like Warburg as he contemplated the price of electricity, Jung wrote: "Knowledge does not enrich us; it removes us more and more from the mythic world in which we were once at home by right of birth." "'God and us,'" he wrote, "even if it is only an unconscious *sous-entendu*—this equation no doubt underlies that enviable serenity of the Pueblo Indian. Such a man is in the fullest sense of the word in his proper place."[44] The implication, of course, is that most Europeans were not.

Such revelations attributed to encounters with American Indians were poignant articulations of a more general discourse on modern civilization within Germany. Ideas about America were inseparable from that discourse, and as John Czaplicka reminds us, in many cases American Indians stood in for loss of purpose, loss of competence, loss of both individuality and community, even loss of self-sufficiency and agency. He finds this, for example, in German magazine images where American Indians functioned as allegories for change in the wake of industrial modernity.[45] Such images of loss articulated more general concerns voiced by scores of intellectuals and artists about the social transformations at large in Germany during the first decades of the twentieth century. During that period, as Mary Nolan has written, "ambivalence, not unequivocal enthusiasm, characterized Americanism and its proponents." "Americanism," was a term that came to symbolize the changes in production, consumption, and social organization that accompanied rapid industrialization. Underlying the term, however, "was not Locke's belief that 'in the beginning, all the world was America.' Rather, it was the simultaneous hope and fear that in the end all the world would *become* America."[46] In that sense, the Pueblos gave Jung, Warburg, and other Germans a sense of hope, and a belief in the continued possibility of resistance.

Modernist Indians in Germany

From 1910 through 1925, self-reflexivity resounded through a generation of German modernists. As the circuses were focused on gaining troupes of American Indian performers, theaters were also providing Germans with a

FIGURE 15. Otto Dix, *American Riding Act* (1922). (Chazen Museum of Art at the University of Wisconsin–Madison)

flood of images and stories about America and American Indians; new, violent westerns were increasingly popular in modern theaters. Both the circus and film offered inspirational alternatives to the limits of living in Imperial Germany and the horrors experienced during World War I.[47] Both easily connected as well with childhood fantasies about America and American Indians shared by this generation and combined with them to shape these artists' visions of their worlds.

Not all of these artists stayed in Germany. Some, such as Max Ernst and Julius Seyler traveled to the United States and sought out groups of American Indians for inspiration.[48] Many more, however, remained at home and drew on their childhood fantasies, their engagement with Cooper and May, as well as their experiences with American Indian performers, who brought those visions to life. Indeed, Otto Dix created an entire series of drawings focused on these performers, capturing the excitement of their movement and skills in images such as *American Riding Act* (1922). But many more of these artists took American Indians as generic allegories for violent transformations, and they drew as much on the new western films explored by Deloria as the American Indians in the circuses among them.

That was easy to do. Films about the Wild West surged into Germany after the postwar import embargo was lifted in 1921, and they became a favorite among artists who harbored anxieties about the course of modernization. According to Lutz Koepnick, these westerns "served as discursive injunctions to reduce symbolically the vicissitudes of modern politics and economics to questions of morality." They often did this by counterposing "American greed with true German spirituality," much as Karl May had done, and that had great resonance with May's many readers in an age when "Americanization" was on everyone's minds.[49]

At the same time, these westerns appealed not only because they spoke to anxieties about modern transformations but also because many of them articulated "ideas about the home: individual authenticity, unfragmented temporal continuity, undistorted spatial closure, and idyllic harmony between a homogeneous social body and its natural environment."[50] These ideals were the counterpoint to the modern anxieties that concerned many artists and intellectuals. They could be found in other kinds of films at the time as well, particularly in *Heimat* (homeland) films.

The westerns, however, were even more popular, because they tied into common childhood experiences of reading Cooper, May, and others. As Koepnick argues, the "Far West" evoked in these films "invited one to embark upon a passage through space as much as it allowed for a voyage through time—a voyage not simply to an imaginary past of unhampered individualism and archaic nature, but also to the artists' or film makers' own childhood fantasies shaped by reading of adventure literature."[51] In that sense, the westerns were much like the *Völkerschauen*, Wild West shows, and the circus—but bloodier.

This was certainly the way many modernists received them. For example, Rudolf Schlichter had eagerly consumed the works of Cooper and May as a child, and he became obsessed with the challenges of technological modernity.[52] At the end of the war, Schlichter was a force in Karlsruhe, particularly in the southern part of the city where he and a group calling itself "the friends of the Indians" acted in ways meant to upset middle-class proprieties. The author Carl Zuckmayer, so impressed with Karl May that he named his daughter Winnetou, recalled that already in 1919 people referred to Schlichter as "Chief Wigwamlance," and that during the period of the German revolution directly after the war, Schlichter led an artists' group that deemed itself the *Rih*, an offshoot of the Berlin November Group, which sought to democratize the art world. Schlichter's group, however, was also largely enamored with the writings of Karl May, and chalk graffiti that proclaimed their presence marked the streets across the city in 1919.[53]

Enticed by the violence in the Hollywood and German westerns as well as Karl May's novels, Schlichter painted scenes of ambushes, battles, and vicious, even sadistic assaults in which the good and evil elements were difficult to sort out, and killing was "a mechanical act."[54] For him, it was the violence that connected the theme of American Indians in his childhood readings to the characters he saw in the films and the ways in which he experienced the decadence of urban Germany.

Similarly, the painter Georg Grosz, who wrote that "James Fenimore Cooper was the first slice of America I took to my heart," erected a teepee in his studio, smoked pipes there with friends, and took to dressing up at times as an Indian or as a cowboy. Grosz too eagerly acknowledged that it was precisely those childhood interests that informed his adult fascination with America and also explained his penchant for dressing in western costume and including Indians on his canvases during and after the war.[55]

We find similar testaments from other Germans of this generation as well. The war hero Ernst Jünger, who interacted with Schlichter and his circle, reflected on how much his understanding of the world had been shaped by Cooper and May. In his case, however, that reflection emerged as he was facing desperate circumstances during World War I. While Schlichter framed his battles with German culture within the context of May's dream world, Jünger, a multiply wounded and decorated war hero, took that framework with him into the field of technological warfare.

This was new, but also old. In many ways Jünger experienced the war much in the same way that Möllhausen had claimed to experience his life of natural subsistence among the Otto Indians near the banks of the Missouri. Jünger, like Möllhausen, filtered his experience of battle through his reading of Cooper and his fantasies about Cooper's characters. Thus, while crawling through the perils of no-man's land and moving through the trench-scared landscape of World War I, he imagined himself acting as an American Indian. That was by no means unique; Carl Zuckmayer recorded similar wartime experiences.[56]

The fascination for American Indians among modernists was so clear and intense during this period around World War I that it affected the work of some American artists as well. Marsden Hartley is the classic example. Although he had shown little interest in American Indians before traveling to Germany, his interactions with German modernists inspired him to discover them there. Thus, while in Berlin before the war, he created a series of paintings he called *Amerika*, which were based on the popular German notions of the American West, American Indians, and perplexing modernist concerns about technology and rapid change. These paintings, however, were based no more on personal experience among American Indians than those of his German counterparts. Indeed, it is fair to argue that he had less experience, having spent less of his youth obsessed with the topic. Nevertheless, once he returned to the United States, he became one of the artists who followed Warburg to the Southwest, joining the many American modernists who were discovering it at that time. Then, when he returned to Berlin in 1923, he took up painting pictures of the American desert for German audiences, based, this time, on his observations as well as his knowledge of what those German audiences wanted to see.[57]

The Hobbyist Scene

While the largely left-wing modernists from the interwar period have captured scholars' attention for generations, they represented only one of the ways in which Germans' interests in America and affinities for American Indians were recast during the period around World War I. Avant-garde artists and intellectuals were not alone in their obsession with America and American Indians or their eager consumption of films and novels about the American West. Nor, for that matter, were they alone in their introspection. For many Germans, however, especially those who became involved in the new hobbyist scene, that introspection was less dark, less about rebellion against existing norms and resisting troubling social and political transformations. For hobbyists, the goal was to experience some of the freedom of the American West, expand their knowledge of American Indians, and develop a broader understanding of themselves through that process.

They did that through the emulation of American Indian performers. In the wake of Buffalo Bill's visits, Germans who were eager to experience what they had seen during the performances began forming clubs where they could engage in acts of mimesis and become cowboys and Indians. These clubs were generally composed of men, although many came to include entire families in their memberships, and most hosted periodic meetings or even small festivals that became much broader in orientation, occasionally drawing upon a wide segment of their communities.

Ultimately, these clubs were concentrated around Cologne, Dresden, Freiberg, and Munich.[58] The Rhineland clubs owed part of their impetus to the prevalence of Carnival, where American Indian motifs had long played a role. Those in Dresden and Munich, however, did not. They were indebted to the Wild West shows and to the circuses that brought the performers into their cities on a fairly regular basis and allowed many Germans to come into contact with American Indian performers, observe them closely, engage them in conversation, and in some cases, develop significant relationships and friendships.

In Dresden in particular, enthusiasts were able to have direct and fairly regular interactions with the American Indians who worked for Sarrasani, and in some cases they took part in their performances.[59] Those lucky few were able to join American Indians in "playing Indian," as Rayana Green once put it; and after the troupes of American Indians left, the Germans literally went on with the show.[60]

Indeed, quite a few of the postwar members of the Dresden associations recall being inspired by these shows as children. Johannes Hüttner, for example, joined the oldest club in the area, Old Manitou, before World War II and took charge of reconstituting it during the postwar era, securing it legal status in East Germany. In his later years, he recalled how he had been inspired to become a hobbyist after meeting Chief Black Horn at Sarrasani's circus when he was only twelve years old. That meeting influenced the ways in which he pursued his hobby, just as similar meetings influenced many others.[61]

Dresden had other connections as well. Karl May lived in the nearby town of Radebeul, where people like Georg Grosz traveled to see him until his death in 1912.[62] Radebeul is also the site of the Karl-May-Museum, which was opened in 1928 and later became a meeting point for hobbyists from the area. It was also the place where many people, especially children, came to meet Patty Frank, who helped create the museum and acted as its director through the war years and well into the German Democratic Republic.

For three decades, Frank hosted countless visitors of all political persuasions and told them stories about American Indians, about his experience working for Buffalo Bill's Wild West during its 1890 tour of Germany, his repeated trips to the United States, his season with Barnum & Bailey, and his many interactions with American Indians throughout his circus career. They could also have learned about the objects in the museum, most of which Frank had collected himself, and all of which had a story he was eager to tell. On frequent occasions, he gave lectures to large groups of adults as well as children. A favorite topic was the Battle of Little Bighorn, which he often held in a room devoted to the topic. He even wrote a well-regarded book on the subject.[63]

This museum's striking combination of fact and fantasy made it incredibly popular. During its opening days in 1928, journalists characterized the objects and displays within the museum as "distant but not strange" to Ger-

FIGURE 16. Big Snake in Radebeul at Karl May's grave. (Karl Markus Kreis Postcard Collection)

mans. Indeed, they characterized those displays much as German journalists had characterized Cronau's lectures in the 1880s or American Indian performances over the previous five decades. They identified the artifacts on display as the "scientific evidence" that supports the "Indian romance" that "fills our days of youth."[64]

In the cabin that housed the museum, they recalled, "one sits for a while with Patty Frank in front of an open fire, dreams of Winnetou and of the great *Chingachgook*, the last of the Mohicans." Afterward, one could venture through the collections and take in the models of American Indians and the objects from their lives that everyone already knows through their books. One could even gaze at a collection of seventeen actual scalps, five of which had blond hair, and through the guidebook and the displays one could also learn about the European origins of scalping. One read about the premiums the English placed on such scalps during the colonial wars and the fact that the Vandals and Scythians collected similar trophies from their enemies, "as Herodotus and others remarked."[65]

A lucky few managed to experience even more at the museum: on 17 January 1928, Sarrasani turned the museum into a spectacle of the first order by bringing a group of Lakotas in his charge to the gravesite of Karl May. While at the grave, one of them, Big Snake, gave a speech in Lakota about his ap-

FIGURE 17. The Munich Cowboy Club hosting a gathering, Großhesselohe, 18 June 1934. Photographer: Schödl. (Stadtarchiv München)

preciation for May, before they returned to the new museum for a tour, a short meal, and a dance performance.[66]

Other hobbyist groups outside of Dresden, such as the Munich Cowboy Club, had contact with American Indians as well. They not only traveled to performances in other cities, visited those who came to Munich, and met the performers who came to work for Circus Krone but purchased clothing and artifacts directly from Sarrasani's performers and used them to create their own costumes, to fill their showrooms, and as models for their own craft production.

By 1930, the Munich Cowboy Club had a showroom in its clubhouse that boasted "original moccasins, real tomahawks, medicine bags, hunting shirts, feather bonnets, and similar things," much of which came from their connections in Nebraska and the Pine Ridge Reservation in South Dakota. Local newspapers reported that they collected these things "because the purpose of the club" was not only to engage in sporting activities, such as horse riding contests, knife throwing, and shooting, but also to pursue "the study of Indian customs and the collection of authentic objects." One of their members, the press explained, had even worked on a ranch in the United States, and he helped the others to understand the purpose and use of many of the things they collected. The members also had their own horses, which they borrowed from a local riding school. In addition to the various festivals they hosted, they also offered English classes, riding classes, and demonstrations of various dances and sign language learned from books.[67]

The Munich Cowboy Club, the oldest of these clubs still in existence, was founded in 1913 by a group of fifteen men who wanted to emigrate to the United States but could not afford to go. It was refounded after the war by the five surviving members, who remained completely enamored with America, and by 1930 it was quite popular, hosting celebrations in local parks for children and families, complete with teepees set in open spaces, riding demonstrations, and a host of activities among a smattering of lederhosen and American flags.[68]

These activities continued well into the period of National Socialism. In 1938, for example, the press coverage of the club's activities was much the same as it had been in 1930, and its members continued with their meetings, festivals, and demonstrations. During the twenty-fifth anniversary celebration, for example, journalists described the ways in which the exhibits drew in local children, irritating some mothers, because "the boys require a good deal of time afterwards before they will settle down," stop playing Indian, "and allow themselves to again be convinced that they have actually been appointed to be a mechanic's apprentice rather than an Indian." In fact, the press noted that their fathers often had the same problem after the show: "when they are back to sitting dutifully in a swivel chair, completing statements of accounts and calculating estimates," while thinking, "what a life that must be to spring over the prairie and crawl through the high grasses after an enemy."[69]

The romantic appeal of the club's activities was clear, and so too was the impression made by its clubhouse, which by 1938 boasted a long row of well-used saddles on the walls, including "a number of original Indian saddles, mostly from Colorado and often purchased by trade with eagle feathers." These, the press stressed, were not simply there for display, "they were taken down and ridden!" Nearby "in a glass case" were the club's most precious items: "a cradle board," a bow and quiver collected "by a well-known professor" who was a member of the club, weapons of all sorts, including Winchesters, and many other items that were praised by Patty Frank and the American artist Robert Lindneux, who had painted Buffalo Bill's portrait and who had come for the occasion of the club's twenty-fifth anniversary. The journalists also remarked that the collection and the club's library had impressed "actual Indians," ostensibly circus performers, who had been invited to visit.[70]

FIGURE 18. Elk Eber, *Custer's Last Battle* (1926). (Karl-May-Museum, Radebeul)

Some of the club's members and associates developed strong relationships with performers. The German artist Elk Eber, for example, who gained some notoriety for his unique painting *Custer's Last Battle* (1938), which now hangs in the Karl-May-Museum and has been used over the years by the U.S. National Park Service at the Little Bighorn Battlefield National Monument,[71] maintained a correspondence from at least November 1933 to December 1938 with Thomas Stabber (White Buffalo Man) and Sam Lone Bear.

Eber befriended Stabber in 1929 while he was working for Sarrasani. After a performance in Munich, Eber and the members of the Munich Cowboy Club invited Stabber and his wife to spend an evening with them, and during the following days Eber made paintings of different members of the Lakota troupe, including several of Stabber.[72] After Stabber returned to the Pine Ridge Reservation, Eber sent Stabber and Lone Bear money, medicine, eagle feathers, satin, calico, dye, trade beads, and other objects in exchange for older artifacts (e.g., a rawhide shield, bows and arrows, a scalp), finished clothing (e.g., moccasins, a dance bustle, leggings, bead and quill work), and

FIGURE 19. Elk Eber in his Munich studio where he produced his paintings of show Indians. (Karl-May-Museum, Radebeul)

in one case, drawings. Unable to travel to the United States as other artists had done, but eager to ground his images in authentic details, Eber turned to Stabber for information about Lakota culture. He sent Stabber outlines of warriors' faces and asked him to color in the drawings in ways appropriate to dances, celebrations, and warfare. Once Stabber returned those drawings, Eber used them as templates for his paintings.[73]

In addition to being an avid "Indian friend" who painted the portraits of many of the members of the Munich Cowboy Club and a number of Sarrasani's performers, he was also a close friend of Patty Frank, who helped create many of the Karl-May-Museum's initial displays and became a professor of art at the University of Munich. Perhaps even more important, Eber was also a Nazi. He was a *Blutsordnungträger*, a decorated member of the SA from 1921 until his death in 1941. He was also a favorite of Adolf Hitler. Indeed, if Eber is most often remembered today for his painting of *Custer's Last Battle*, which celebrated American Indian resistance by placing American Indian warriors rather than Custer at the center of the scene, his best-known paintings in the late 1930s were of German soldiers as resisters—for example, *The Last Hand Grenade* (1937) and *So Was the SA* (1938).[74]

Hitler's America and American Indians

Nazis understood the appeal of "playing Indian." In general, they supported it. In 1934, for example, the *Völkischer Beobachter*, the party's central paper, portrayed a gathering of the Munich Cowboy Club much in the same way that other German papers did. The paper included photographs of one member riding a bucking horse rodeo style, several members sitting and smoking in front of "three authentic wigwams" copied in part from teepees in German ethnographic museums, and a portrait of "the beautiful squaw of the chief," Fred Sommer, dressed as an Indian maiden. It also praised the club's collections, acknowledged with admiration the thousands of people who attended its recent festival without having to pay a penny, and remarked that anyone could see from the "truly valuable pieces" the "proficiency," "high artistic sense," and the "spiritual, cultural, economic, and military development of a great people." It lauded the club's members for their persistence and sacrifice while creating their collections and then added that "one can even recognize," through the collections, "a certain similarity in the lifestyle, in the conception of morals and customs, in the bravery [*Kampfesmut*], and in the positive development between the old Indian tribes and our ancestors."[75] Thus, for the Nazis too the affinities were clear: Germans "playing Indian" were ultimately playing themselves.

It is no secret that Adolf Hitler was an admirer of Karl May.[76] Many of his compatriots, such as Albert Speer, wrote of Hitler's enthusiasm.[77] Others, such as Klaus Mann, condemned it.[78] It is also well known that American Indians continued to be welcome in German circuses until the outbreak of war in 1939, and that the hobby clubs continued to fly their American flags and pursue their activities, until the National Socialists banned the activities of all clubs.

Indeed, initially, National Socialists retained an ambivalent position regarding both America and American Indians. From 1933 to 1936, the Nazis treated America cordially, even if they used Franklin Delano Roosevelt's "New Deal" as a point of comparison to make National Socialist efforts to energize the German economy in the wake of the worldwide depression look good, even superior to what they projected as America's failings.[79] As Nazi foreign policy became clear, however, tensions rose, and the United States was increasingly regarded as both a model and a threat. This was different, however, than the threats embodied in the *Americanism* of a decade earlier.

By the late 1930s, National Socialist ideologues began engaging in curious overtures toward American Indians—particularly the Sioux. In 1938, for example, the government in Berlin granted citizenship and Aryan status to the grandson of a Sioux woman and a German immigrant to the United States. Soon afterward, Nazi officials extended the recognition to embrace all Sioux Indians. This was not a completely original notion. American Indians had been labeled Aryan before.[80] But the Nazi argumentation was unique, drawing on older notions of affinities between Germans and American Indians and respect for their persistent resistance.

According to Kenneth Townsend, government officials in "Berlin claimed that the personality and the traditional military character of the Sioux clearly resembled those features found among true Germans." They even went so far in their explanation to advance "the idea that a lost tribe of Germanic people had wandered into the New World in the distant past and bred themselves into the native population, thus building a link to German ancestry." The act, however, was perhaps less ideological than political, albeit somewhat impractical and even naive. The hope, Townsend notes, was that "identification of Native Americans as Aryans would encourage the reception of Nazi ideology by a larger Indian audience." In order to reach beyond the Sioux to other tribes, "propagandists pointed to the literary works of German novelists such as Karl May, who, in the late nineteenth century, asserted the notion that Indians could adopt and bear German culture—a concept similar to Hitler's view of Japanese society." As Townsend notes, "the inference suggested the elevation of Indians in the German racial hierarchy," and it derives directly from the sense many Nazis shared with other Germans that Germans and American Indians had a similar origin in warrior societies, with similar characteristics, abilities, and morals.[81] For the propaganda ministry it made sense.

It also made enough sense to the U.S. Bureau of Indian Affairs that its director John Collier and his staff responded with a campaign on reservations meant to counter Nazi propaganda. He and Aleš Hrdlička, the first curator of physical anthropology at the U.S. National Museum and the founder of the *American Journal of Physical Anthropology* argued that American Indians were not Aryans, and Collier "warned Indians that Hitler planned to deal with them as he dealt with Jews."[82]

The Nazi's overtures toward American Indians gained little traction in the United States. For Hitler, however, such efforts were worthwhile because he believed that the United States was ultimately the greatest threat to German prosperity in the world. Many scholars have noted that much of Hitler's decision making, the timing, the kinds of military commitments he entertained, even the breadth of his war plans and his desire to turn Eastern Europe into the heart of Germany's agricultural economy, stemmed from his studies of the United States. He was convinced that America's wealth of natural and human resources placed it in a position of tremendous, almost unassailable economic and political power, which both impressed and worried him.[83]

Most scholars point to Hitler's unpublished second book for insights into his attitudes toward the United States.[84] In that book, he argued that already in the nineteenth century, with rising technological standards, higher life expectancy, and populations increasingly concentrated in urban centers, the quest for reliable supplies of food had become a primary concern. That had led to conflict and warfare, and to Hitler's mind, that was good. Warfare, he argued, was productive, and the imperial acquisition of land was righteous: "This earth," he wrote, "is not allocated to anyone as a gift, it is given as destiny's grant to those people who possess the courage in their hearts to conquer it, the strength to preserve it, and the diligence to till it."[85] People like the Americans.

According to Hitler, "The point of a healthy territorial policy lies in the expansion of a people's *Lebensraum* (living space) by allocating to the excess population new areas for colonization" that would "maintain close political and national relations with the mother country." That was difficult with overseas colonies, and for that reason, he argued, Imperial Germany's bourgeois politicians should have engaged in "an expansive territorial policy within Europe itself," following the American model.[86]

While Hitler lamented that so many Germans had been lost as "cultural fertilizer" to the United States, he credited the Americans for luring them there. They had acted as smart racists and good eugenicists "by making an immigrant's ability to set foot on American soil dependent on specific racial requirements . . . as well as a certain level of physical health of the individual himself." In that way, "the bleeding of Europe of its best people has become regulated in a manner that is almost bound by law."[87] That action gave the United States an incredibly powerful base of human resources with which to act, and combined with the wealth of natural resources at its disposal, it had become a tremendous threat to Europe.

"The only state that will be able to stand up to North America," he argued, "will be the state that has understood how—through the character of its internal life as well as through the substance of its external policy—to raise the racial value of its people and bring it into the most practical national form for this purpose."[88] Thus, Hitler posited a new racial empire modeled on the successes of the United States, one that would push east across Poland and into Russia much as Americans had pushed west.

As Adam Tooze reminds us, Hitler declared that the Volga "would be Germany's Mississippi." He argued again and again that "the bloody conquest of the American West provided Germany with the historical warrant it needed to justify the clearance of the Slav population." There too, "'in the East a similar process will repeat itself for a second time as in the conquest of America.' A 'superior' settler population would displace an 'inferior' native population opening the way towards a new era of economic possibility." And as a result, he exclaimed, "'Europe—and not America—will be the land of unlimited possibilities.'"[89]

According to Hitler's vision, the conflict that ensued would be harsh as Germans eliminated the indigenous elements, much as they had been eliminated in the United States' westward expansion. As Hitler's young men went east as a proud imperial force, however, space would be opened up for a flourishing German culture that would benefit from both its own European material resources and its ever-growing and purified population. The transatlantic German Kulturkreis truncated by World War I would expand in the opposite direction, across land to the east as a newly cast national entity, which would unify rather than disperse its superior population. In this vision, the Aryan Lakota in the United States, posited by the National Socialist propaganda machine, would have no counterpart in Eastern Europe. Curiously, Hitler and his followers never seemed to notice the contradiction in their ideological constructs, which embraced both the myths of Karl May and the reality of American Westward expansion: for National Socialists, American Indians became diametrically opposed models, people who were both good to emulate and good to eliminate.

PART II

Consistencies across Twentieth-Century Ruptures

Hitler's fascination with Karl May, his concerns with the United States, and National Socialists' interests in American Indians, even the ways in which the Nazis harnessed the American past to rationalize their efforts to colonize Eastern Europe, did nothing to undercut the widespread sense of affinity for American Indians among Germans during the twentieth century. The enthusiasm that developed across the nineteenth century and persisted into the interwar period never dissipated, and the material traces that flowed from it simply grew. The circuses kept running, American Indians kept traveling to them, and the hobbyist groups kept growing until the outbreak of World War II. More than two thousand people dressed as American Indians assembled in a camp outside Taucha, near Leipzig in 1938, where one group of Germans slept in a replica of a teepee they had seen in Berlin's Völkerkunde Museum. National Socialist newspapers reported eagerly on such assemblies—just as their predecessors had done, and just as the newspapers after the war would do.

Indeed, quickly following the war, older clubs, such as the Munich Cowboy Club, were reconstituted while new ones were created. The Western Club Dakota Karlsruhe, for example, was officially registered in 1948. In 1951 the annual national meeting of these clubs under an umbrella organization, the Western Bund, began taking place across West Germany. Each year, it moved from one host location to the next, until the late 1980s, when

FIGURE 20. Encampment of two thousand near Taucha, outside of Leipzig (1938). (Courtesy of Joachim Giel)

members secured a permanent spot for the annual meeting in the Wester-wald forest next to Hundsdorf, a small town near Koblenz. The first meeting boasted only 3 teepees and some 40 participants; but the numbers more than doubled the next year, and by the mid-1970s literally thousands of participants and hundreds of teepees appeared every year: the organizers counted 170 teepees in 1979, 209 in 1981, 306 in 1986, and 439 in 1993, after which they became increasingly concerned with finding parking for the more than one thousand cars and trucks needed to transport all these teepees and the people who occupied them to the annual event.[1]

In 1982 the number of clubs that participated in the meeting surpassed 100. By 1998 there were 156 clubs associated with the Westernbund and 53 former East German clubs connected to its eastern counterpart, the Indianist Union, which organized The Week.[2] In southwestern Germany, the city of Freiburg alone boasted 10 such associations in 2004.[3] Dresden, in former East Germany, claimed 12. Those numbers, however, are only part of the story. There have always been clubs that were not registered and clubs and individuals who did not participate in the annual mass meetings, and while everyone involved in these movements recognized a steady growth through the postwar era, no one has ever been in a position to accumulate exact figures. Thus during the last decade of the twentieth century, estimates of active hobbyists in Germany ranged widely from 40,000 to upward of 100,000.[4]

Hobbyist meetings, however, were only one of the many manifestations of Germans' obsession with American Indians that persisted across the twentieth century. Germans, for example, continued to eagerly read Cooper. Indeed, Hitler had read Cooper before turning to May, and Cooper's *Leatherstocking Tales* continued to be published and purchased under every political regime. Eventually, the *Leatherstocking Tales*, which had been made into a two-part film starring Béla Lugosi in 1920, appeared again as a four-part series in West Germany in 1969, following the tremendous success of the eleven Karl May westerns produced between 1962 and 1968. Given the crisis facing the West German film industry in the 1960s, their success was astounding.

The production of Karl May volumes across the twentieth century, however, boggles the mind. During the early years of National Socialism, the Karl May Press (Karl-May-Verlag) used a questionnaire to determine that 81.6 percent of German youth were reading May's books between 1931 and 1935.[5] At its twenty-fifth anniversary in 1938, the press exclaimed that it had sold 7.5 million copies of May's books. By the time the war was over, and the new German states were established, that number stood at more than 10 million.[6] By the end of the century it had risen to 100 million.[7]

Twentieth-century Germans, however, read far beyond Cooper, May, and other nineteenth-century authors who had written about American Indians. Many new German authors of westerns emerged, and continued to emerge, to compete directly with the classic texts for the ever-growing audience. For example, Friedrich von Gagern and Erhard Witteck, who used the pen name Fritz Steuben, became tremendously successful under National Socialism. Copies of the books in Steuben's eight-volume series on Tecumseh (1930–38), for instance, topped half a million by the end of the war, and repeated editions continued to be produced and praised in West Germany into the 1980s, pressing the publication numbers to over a million.[8] That, however, paled in comparison to the books published by Liselotte Welskopf-Henrich in both East and West Germany. Her books, in turn, inspired the now famous series of East German *Indianer* films staring Gojko Mitic, which appeared from 1966 to 1983 and were regarded as the East German alternative to the May films. They were every bit as successful.

American Indian authors competed as well. Mirroring the success of Charles Eastman during the interwar period, American Indian authors such as Scott Momaday became incredible hits during the postwar era. We should not be surprised. As Hartmut Lutz reminds us, from the late nineteenth century to the late twentieth century, books about American Indians were "the most widespread form of German children's literature,"[9] a fact that greatly facilitated Momaday's success among adults. It certainly facilitated Eastman's as well.

The traces that flowed from Germans' ongoing fascination with American Indians, however, traveled far beyond hobbyists and books, and even beyond the material. As Thomas Kramer has demonstrated, American Indians were a topic and point of reference and inference in a vast array of comic books, magazines, and small booklets as well.[10] They could also be found in the many open-air theaters that proliferated before and after the war. Out of the dozen or so theaters that currently feature Karl May productions, for example, the most famous is nestled in the Elbsandstein region near Rathen, in "Saxony's Switzerland," not far from the ominous Bastai. That theater was celebrated by the National Socialists, and scholars often refer to the Hitler Youth who crowded into the theater during the first Karl May performances in 1938,[11] although they generally neglect to recall that an array of other Germans were there as well: workers, school classes, soldiers on leave.[12] The town of Rathen staged the 1938 events in cooperation with theater groups, Sarrasani, and others, and their appeal was widespread. It still is. But the best-known of these theaters today is probably in Bad Segeberg, in Schleswig-Holstein; the theater holds over 7,000 people and entertains upward of 300,000 visitors a year. Pierre Brice, the actor who played Winnetou in the West German films continued playing that role in Bad Segeberg for years afterward. Following unification and Brice's retirement from the stage, Gojko Mitic took his place.

There were, and still are, many smaller institutions that also continued operating across the century. The Karl-May-Museum in Radebeul, to name just one, remained incredibly popular before, during, and after World War II. Indeed, despite its modest size and location, it was one of the most frequented museums in East Germany, remaining popular after Frank's death in 1959 and through unification.[13]

American Indians remained present in other, less obvious ways as well. The youth organizations that proliferated in the interwar period, for example, drew directly on tropes about American Indians as these groups turned to hiking, camping, and scouting activities and adopted notions of "tribal education," which led Walter Scherf to comment in his 1975 social and psychological study of youth groups that "'the fever and salvation of the youth movement' was probably 'influenced more by Winnetou than by the resolutions at the various association meetings.'"[14] One could say something similar about education in general, given the degree to which thinking about American Indians, talking about them, and playing Indian became "a fixture of professional pedagogical activities, especially in preschool and primary school" in West Germany.[15]

The more alternative, and sometimes violent, youth groups also embraced American Indians across the twentieth century, tapping into Germans' traditional admiration for their resistance. This was evidenced in the actions and rhetoric of not only the Edelweiss Pirates and the Navajos of Cologne, who fought Hitler Youth groups on the streets before World War II, but also those youth groups in postwar West Germany who took on the sobriquet of *Stadtindianer* (City Indians). How predictable, we might cynically remark, that a self-proclaimed *Stadtindianer*, "the Mescalero of Göttingen," was credited with the infamous obituary of Chief Federal Prosecutor Siegfried Buback, which appeared in the *Göttinger Nachrichten* in 1977 expressing sympathy for his murder at the hands of the West German terrorist organization, the Red Army Faction. As Karl Markus Kreis has noted, the only Mescalero most Germans knew was Winnetou, and everyone understood the subtext of resistance inherent in that signature.[16]

Intertextuality works that way, particularly when it crosses so many generations and political divisions. Indeed, in the 1930s, it was not only the Navajos of Cologne who channeled German ideas about *Indianer* while resisting the Nazis. Nazi ideologues taught Hitler Youth to embrace precisely the same tropes as they trained for future clashes. Thus, much like Jünger and Toller before them, many of the boys in the Hitler Youth, and the young men who emerged from it, recalled taking their thoughts about American Indians with them into training and, later, into combat.[17]

Such consistencies and continuities matter a great deal. Indeed, if one of the lessons of Germans' persistent affinities for American Indians during the nineteenth century is that German history was often made outside of Germany and beyond the reach of formal German institutions, one of the most telling lessons from the twentieth century is that this history flowed easily through the ruptures of war, revolution, regime change, and economic catastrophe that so often punctuate our historical narratives. That has great implications.

As the chapters in this second part of the book show, the degree to which our narratives depend on such ruptures has often led to misinterpretations and even myopic readings of chronological periods defined by political regimes. In some cases, that dependence has also resulted in scholars' inability

FIGURE 21. Patty Frank with Hitler Youth in the Karl-May-Museum. The exact date of the meeting is unclear, but it was sometime during the twelve-year period that followed his five years of telling his tales to Germans in the Weimar Republic and before his decade of telling those same tales to citizens of the German Democratic Republic. (Karl-May-Museum, Radebeul)

to see either the breadth of German history or the motivations of particular actors when they stem from long-term concerns. Both have been too easily obscured by our fetish for characterizing distinct historical eras and focusing our greatest attentions on moments of sudden change.

There are, however, alternative ways of conceptualizing and narrating German cultural history. Thus, while the next chapter begins by sketching out the ways in which American Indians were harnessed to support political ideologies in Nazi Germany, East and West Germany, and the unified Germany that succeeded them, it concludes by offering an alternative way of thinking through those differences and recognizing some of the consistencies that persisted through all these regimes. In turn, the three thematic chapters that follow press that point further by pursuing some often overlooked consistencies in several controversial areas: questions of race, character, and masculinity; narratives of genocide; and, finally, the hidden dialogic at the heart of American Indians' reception of Germans' interests in them.

Instrumentalization across Political Regimes

At first glance, the Karl May Indian seems to be the image that dominated German imaginations in the twentieth century. It was, after all, his books and the movies based upon them that outsold everything else. Scholars have posited countless theses for his continued success. Mary Nolan has argued, for example, that Karl May transformed America into epic fiction, creating an America that was "so different from nineteenth- and twentieth-century Germany that readers young and old, male and female, could project both a range of adventures and an ensemble of virtues impossible to imagine in Germany." His fiction and fantasy, she notes, were based in an illusory past that, by the beginning of the twentieth century, became a "prominent object of German nostalgia for lost clarity and simplicity."[1] That simplicity, however, actually lacked clarity; it was easily malleable, almost effortlessly instrumentalized, and thus the "range of adventures" that could be projected onto May's America and his American Indians was much broader and more diverse than Nolan indicates. Indeed, if Karl May's fantastic portrayal of America and American Indians encouraged readers to immerse themselves in his dream world, it also provided them with rarified characters, polysemous Indians, who quickly became vehicles for promoting multiple ideologies.[2]

As a result, ideologues across the political spectrum used his books to advance their arguments about the human condition and their conceptions of what constituted progress. During the 1920s and 1930s, Nazis and Communists alike found much to admire in May's books.[3] Ideologues in every German regime, in fact, were able to harness American Indians for their own purposes, and they continued to do so across a strikingly longue durée and through a series of radical political ruptures.[4] Focusing on that diversity of meanings, and the many ways in which Germans instrumentalized American Indians across the twentieth century, however, has its limits. It can obscure the core set of values and interests at the heart of that malleable exterior that also persisted through the political ruptures of those same decades, and which reveal shared dispositions, moods, and attitudes among many Germans across the political spectrum and over a strikingly long period of time. Those persistent concerns and values emerge when we compare the different ways in which Germans instrumentalized American Indians during various political regimes, or when we follow, as we did with Rudolf Cronau, a biography across those landscapes. In order to underscore the hazards of relying too heavily on narrative cultural histories punctuated by political periodizations, this chapter does both.

The Fascist Indian

Because it was the Nazis who ultimately seized control in the political struggles of the interwar period and then wreaked havoc on Europe in the twelve years that followed, their uses of Karl May, as well as their support for more explicitly fascist authors such as Friedrich von Gagern and Fritz Steuben, have gained much more scholarly attention than the musings of alternative youth groups or even such prominent Communists as Karl Liebknecht.[5] Hartmut Lutz, for example, has argued that May's Winnetou novels espoused petite bourgeois morality. That morality, he suggests, was embodied most clearly in his character Old Shatterhand—the prompt, clean, cultivated Saxon named Charlie, who was respectful of authority, antirevolutionary, and proudly German, and played the Natty Bumppo role in May's Winnetou series. At the same time, Lutz argues that Old Shatterhand and other May characters also acted as vehicles for a rather insidious nationalism, one that embraced the German hero from provincial Saxony as an inherent man of the world, a super being with natural talents that easily eclipsed those of other men.[6] Such attributes, he claims, could evolve into general German characteristics in the minds of May's readers, and the National Socialists were easily able to transform those characteristics into racial traits. Indeed, according to Lutz, May's tales were essentially protofascist.[7]

May, however, was too malleable and contradictory to be proto-anything. National Socialist ideologues recognized that; but they also realized that so many Germans read his books that May afforded them an opportunity to tie Nazi values to his popularity and harness that esteem for their purposes. Thus despite the fact that some Nazi ideologues were put off by his Christian pathos and the pacifism of his later works, they nevertheless recognized his propagandistic value.[8] In order to maximize it, they engaged in a process of sorting through his work, recommending and promoting some of his books, such as the *Winnetou* volumes, while discouraging the further publication of others. They even attempted to "improve" some of his texts through direct editorial intervention.[9]

The Nazi effort to exploit May's work for ideological purposes was part of a much broader program of censorship, in which controlling what young people read was particularly important.[10] Thus the Nazis strictly regulated the publication of youth literature through the National Socialist Teachers Association and the Reich Youth Leadership. In order to control the books circulated through libraries and used in schools, they produced yearly lists of books they endorsed as well as those they had banned, and they controlled the publication of new books through a system of ideological assessments [*Gutachten*], centralized through Berlin. They eliminated not only books based on content and topic but also those that had been written by Jews or other suspect persons. Thus, German ethnologist Julius Lips's highly regarded *Tents in the Wilderness* was first published in English in 1942 while he was in exile in the United States. It appeared in German only after the war. Lips was Jewish.

Once the Main Editorial Office for Youth Literature in the Office for the Propagation of Literature [*Schrifttumspflege*] made its selections, the party used its (albeit select) endorsement of May to set itself apart from the Weimar Republic's elite and proclaim the freedom of its National Socialist vision. Indeed, around the turn of the century, German elites condemned May's stories as the product of a criminal mind: debased, trashy, and unsuitable for children.[11] They set out to censor him indirectly, to isolate him in the world of uncultured pulp literature. In early 1934, however, Dr. Bernhart Scheer announced in the nationalist newspaper *Siegerländer* that the era of bourgeois sensibility had ended and that along with its demise had gone the elitist disapproval of May's books, and the limitations they had placed on the youth's adventurous spirit. Under National Socialism, he exclaimed, "every German youth can now read Karl May's books without deliberation or compunction, freely and happily." The "German youth of today," he declared, "have been freed from the bourgeois mindset of schoolmasters." Cultural Minister Schemm, he explained, the Reich's director of the National Socialist Teachers' Association, had declared in late January 1934 that "German boys and girls must possess more than the so-called fine school comportment"; they also required "courage, initiative, moxie, thirst for adventure, and Karl-May spirit!"[12] Such calls were echoed in Joseph Goebbels's newspaper *Der Angriff* as well, but with reference to soldiers, not just children.[13]

FIGURE 22. Swastika display in the Karl-May-Museum. (Karl-May-Museum, Radebeul)

With Karl May's books properly vetted, sorted, and endorsed, German youth, and particularly Hitler Youth, were encouraged by the party to visit Patty Frank and hear his fireside tales at the Karl-May-Museum. In order to accommodate them, the museum was transformed. In 1937 it was expanded, reordered along more scientific principles, and gained new displays. The most notable was the collection of American Indian arts and crafts that included swastikas. Recognized as a storm symbol by the Navajo and other American Indian tribes, artifacts that included this symbol could be easily reinterpreted to link the Nazi regime with tales of American Indians and the virtues they possessed in May and other authors' books.[14]

The virtues that were most important to the fascists included heroism, a martial bearing, a diminished fear of death, the mythification of war, a willingness to engage in brutal physical violence, an aggressive chauvinistic masculinity grounded in a joy of adventure, faith in one's own mental and physical strength, honesty, and truthfulness.[15] Readers could, if they searched, locate such characteristics in May's Winnetou and his white brother Charlie.

FIGURE 23. Sarrasani Indians at Karl May's grave. (Karl-May-Museum, Radebeul)

But there were other authors who made such values more explicit without the inconsistencies one found in May.

According to Hartmut Lutz, there were more than 650 titles on the United States published in Nazi Germany, and quite a few focused on American Indians. Indeed, Barbara Haible identified 77 books on American Indians published in Germany between 1927 and 1945, which the National Socialists recommended as good for Germans to read; 67 were written between 1933 and 1945.

Endorsing the Cooper volumes and other classics from the nineteenth century, the Nazis also recommended newer texts from American Indians. Charles Eastman's *Ohiyesa* and *Winona*, for example, became popular among Germans during the Weimar period, and they continued to be published and read through World War II and the postwar era as well. The Nazis also recommended translations of the largely fabricated autobiographies from White Horse Eagle and Buffalo Child Long Lance, and they even encouraged Germans to read Alexander Berghold's book on New Ulm, which was published again in Berlin and Stuttgart in 1935.[16] Older arguments about American Indians' resistance against the British and the United States fit in well with the Nazi program—even one that turned around the slaughter of Germans in Minnesota.

The Nazi's strongest advocacy, however, was reserved for those authors who took older tales of struggle in America and recast them to fit National Socialist ideology. Following a long line of German authors who attempted to legitimate their narratives by claiming a greater historical and ethnological accuracy than their predecessors,[17] these writers focused their tales on the biographies of great leaders who, during moments of crisis, attempted to unite individual tribes in acts of resistance. Emil Engelhardt, for example, celebrated Pontiac in his *Pontiac in the Great Indian War* (1935). Otto Kindler did the same in his *The Red Arrow (Pontiac's War)* (1941), and so too did F. L. Barwin in her *Pontiac* (1943). Similarly, Georg Groll cast Sitting Bull as a "Red Napoleon" in his *Dakota: The Sioux's Struggle for Freedom* (1931), *Dakota in the Fire* (1936), and *The Demise of the Dakota* (1940). By focusing on such leaders, these and other authors employed American Indians who were already German household names to endorse the Nazi's notion of the leadership principle and to transform American Indians' struggles into a parable of nationalist awakening.

In essence, these new authors were able to instrumentalize Germans' well-established interest in American Indians' formidable resistance to underscore Germans' need for national unity under a strong, even dictatorial leader. In this new parable, American Indians' demise became a direct result of their failure to unify behind a powerful leader against the oppressive forces that encircled them—a clear object lesson for young Germans preparing for war.[18]

The most eagerly endorsed of these historical figures was Tecumseh, the Shawnee warrior who attempted during the first decades of the nineteenth century to unite American Indian tribes from Florida to the Great Lakes against the continual pressure of the United States' westward expansion. Von Gagern and Steuben used him to promote explicitly fascist principles. So too did a number of others.[19] As they recast his biography, they seized on older arguments about the parallels between American Indians' fight against European invasion and German tribes' struggle against Rome. Von Gagern, in fact, termed Tecumseh the "Arminius of the Red Race"[20] while Steuben extolled the links between the valor and organization of German and American Indian tribes.[21] Similarly, in his *People without Land* (1935), Frank Sander preached that American Indians' failure to unite behind Tecumseh prevented them from replicating Arminius's victory and allowed white Americans to overpower them. Nevertheless, there was still much to admire: American Indians' "longing for their homeland," Sander claimed, had pressed them to resist; Tecumseh's valiant character led him to sacrifice himself for the "land of his fathers."[22]

Within these texts, the principles of sacrifice and devotion to a valiant leader were enshrined as universal principles, just as they were in Robert Beholz's *Tecumseh the Last Shawnee* (1936), which proclaimed that "the will of the leader alone is law!"[23] In short, these books and the others like them were meant to teach German youths, through their affinity for American Indians, that they must fight for the independence of the German race, as Arminius had done against the Romans in 9 C.E., and as valiant American Indians such as Pontiac, Sitting Bull, and Tecumseh had attempted to do for their own race.[24]

These tales about Romans, German tribes, and American Indians were much different from those the young Rudolf Cronau had told in the 1880s. Indeed, Tecumseh (as well as King Philip and Pontiac) had already been a topic of interest for Germans for a century by the time Steuben began writing his books. But the portraits of Tecumseh that emerged in his eight-volume anthology during the 1930s, the portraits that won him the Hans-Schemm-Prize in 1938–39 for the best book for German youth, had many new twists.

It is worth returning to some older texts for a moment. In 1832, for example, *Das Ausland* contained essays on both King Phillip and Tecumseh. The essays glorified their resistance, their leadership and martial abilities, and their character, but they also underscored the point that, while Philip may have had a limited chance at repelling Europeans, Tecumseh's bid to resist the United States' expansion before and during the War of 1812 came after the United States had grown too strong to be repulsed by a loose confederation of tribes.[25]

Some thirty years later, *Das Ausland* ran further essays on Tecumseh drawn from historical accounts. Like the earlier articles, this series embellished his character and abilities and portrayed him as one of Native America's truly great men.[26] Underscoring his conviction and sense of justice, they portrayed him as the kind of man who paid a poor white farmer for the oxen he felt forced to seize to keep his warriors fed. He was a commanding presence, an impressive speaker, and singular in his leadership abilities. Driven by an endless emotional energy, he covered vast distances in his effort to unite various tribes. He was also a formidable warrior who carried the British in their battles against the Americans. But he was not a savage: rather he was a man of high morals who condemned the massacre of captives by his allies. "Such bestial slaughters," they argued "could not take place in his presence."[27] Indeed, he was such a superior man that even in 1860 his memory was still "respected by all the old Americans" who had encountered him. His death at the battle of the Thames in 1813 brought his martyrdom. The essays lamented it as a tragedy for humanity as well as Native America.

There is nothing particularly German about *Das Ausland's* 1860 portrait of Tecumseh. One can find the same stress on leadership, bravery, high moral bearing, statesmanship, martial ability, and tragedy in English-language accounts as well. Indeed, *Das Ausland's* essays were derived from them. The point, then, is that National Socialists did not need to reinvent the wheel when authors such as Steuben wrote books and essays about this or other historical individuals. Most of the glorious material was readily available. So too were the historical details. National Socialist authors simply needed to recast them slightly by making massacres more palatable, devotion to great leaders more imperative, and Tecumseh's failure to win out against his oppressors a function of his follower's lack of will, while introducing a notion of race that was exclusive, biological, and a product of twentieth-century thought.[28] That effort was completed with the addition of connections to fascist iconography, such as the fasces, a bundle of sticks featuring an ax that appeared in Steuben's pages. In essence, the move toward a fascist Tecumseh, much like the recasting of May's characters, was a subtle shift in a transnational tale, so subtle, in fact, that Steuben's books continued to be published well into the postwar period until West German leftists recognized that he and others had simply dressed the Nazi superman in feathers and braids and imposed him upon a historical figure in settings that were otherwise fairly accurate. That realization led to immediate revisions, which stripped away the fascist particularities from Steuben's stories while leaving the characteristics that had appealed since at least the 1860s.[29]

Such efforts flourished in German periodicals as well. Again and again National Socialists found it useful to tell tales about American Indians resisting and, in many cases, failing. In 1938, for example, *Der Pimpf,* a leading Nazi periodical for young people, produced an issue that featured American Indians. It melded photographs of American Indians and their impersonators who had recently performed in German circuses, theaters, and Wild West shows with an essay by Rudolf Jacobs, "The Sioux's Fight to the Death," and a second by Werner Kallmerten, "The Downfall of the Aztecs." The first, which told the tale of the "heroic battle of a *Volk,* that despite the keenest resistance were not strong or united enough to withstand the Whites' advance," articulated the same lessons as Steuben's extensive tales, but with the enticing notification that one could still find "something of the heroic spirit of a Winnetou and an Old Shatterhand" on the reservations set aside by the Americans for the "bravest ancestors of their land."[30]

Those ancestors' greatest moments, however, were clearly in the past. Why then, the editors rhetorically asked, would German youth want to hear tales about these people from Karl May and others? "It is the manly virtues of the Redskins that appear exemplary to us! Courage, toughness, fidelity, and self-education are their highest laws," and those are precisely the "character-istics we youths seek to emulate." They should be remembered, quipped the editors, as the "complete men" they were; but one must also bear in mind that "the Indian race had to die out, because they [sic] did not find the inner unity that a people absolutely needs to defend its freedom and rights."[31]

As National Socialists recast the history of American Indian resistance to teach ideological lessons, even anti-Semitism was easily folded into their tales. In 1937, for example, the youth magazine *Hilf mit!* contained a pedagog-ical essay titled "A German Saves the Last Indian." Illustrated with images of contemporary Pueblo homes in New Mexico and Arizona and a shot of three Hopi women near the edge of the Grand Canyon, it began by rehearsing ac-counts of the mistreatment and abuse long suffered by American Indians in the United States. Yet this familiar story of American Indians swindled out of their lands and left at the mercy of unscrupulous Indian agents offered an additional revelation: "The white hyenas, the contractors," who "inside twenty months" became "multimillionaires" were "not men": "Crooks" and "vultures" had appeared "from the Jewish quarter in Eastern Europe!" They purchased the contracts negotiated by the government and "then raked in millions from the sorrows of the red *Volk*." Happily, the author reported, a heroic "German Baron" appeared to solve their dilemma. He fought special interests in Washington, D.C., until he gained the ear of another German, Secretary of State Carl Schurz, who was able to "run off the Jewish contrac-tors" and replace them with "honorable men."[32]

Here too, recast historical tales became ideological parables for future ac-tions: not only did Germans face formidable and abusive forces similar to those that oppressed American Indians (an old idea indeed), but the very same (now racialized) oppressors were at large in Central and Eastern Eu-rope. To combat those forces at home as well as abroad, Germany not only needed the virtues of American Indian warriors but needed men with the same character as Schurz and the anonymous Baron.

Given the ideological potential of such widespread narratives, it is little wonder that German affinities for American Indians were nurtured during the era of National Socialism, that the Nazis accepted the hobbyist groups until they disbanded all associations, or that they were delighted with the enthusiasm of their members for the performances of Karl May's stories in Rathen in 1938. There, crowds of Germans streamed in to see their heroes take form; to thrill at the presence of a putatively authentic American Indian, the actor Oskoman, who danced during the shows; and to further embrace and promote their ideological tales. Indeed, *Der Pimpf*'s issue on American Indians, which appeared in October 1938, opened with references to the excitement of Rathen and a trip to the Karl-May-Museum.[33] It was a natural reference. So many people had attended the performances—more than fifty thousand by 1940—or heard about them from others that their resonance was easily appropriated.[34] To that end, and for their own self-promotion, the Karl May Press produced *Winnetou Lives!*—a picture book that made the plays famous, and later infamous, for the many pictures of Hitler Youth pressed into the theater's twenty-four hundred seats, the many Nazi uniforms and flags surrounding them, the recollections of many leading party members in attendance, and the acknowledgment that members of the SA and SS numbered among the performers as well as the audience.[35]

In that sense, the Karl May Press and the Nazis made the Rathen shows National Socialist after the fact. In her analysis of these events, Alina Dana Weber stresses that the shows originated for local reasons—the theater was built a few years earlier to promote tourism; Karl May's stories were introduced to improve attendance; the initial press releases were more comical than ideological; but, in the end, these plays were transformed into National Socialist events, which continued until the pace of the war intervened. After 1945, westerns returned to the stage, including versions of Mark Twain's *Adventures on the Mississippi*, Friedrich Gerstäcker's *Horse Thieves in Arkansas*, and Helmut Menschel's *Daughter of the Dakota*.[36] Karl May's tales, however, were absent between 1945 and 1983 because the context had changed. Rathen's theater became an East German theater, governed by a different ideology, and a different take on Karl May.

The Socialist Indian

If the malleability of the Karl May Indian allowed for its easy instrumentalization by fascists, that plasticity could also facilitate its denunciation. Indeed, Christian Heermann opens his book on the history of May's work in East Germany with a vignette on Wilhelm Fronemann, a German who found solid ideological reasons for denouncing Karl May and his books to both the National Socialists before World War II and the Socialist Unity Party (SED) that emerged to govern the German Democratic Republic (GDR) after the war.[37] Not everyone liked Karl May. But while his Christian ethos, pacifism, and anti-imperialism had failed to unseat him during National Socialism, the general popularity he had enjoyed among the National Socialists raised new opportunities in the GDR: it made May's work suspect and provided the SED with a tool in its war on fascist and bourgeois culture.

Under the GDR, May's books were neither officially forbidden nor allowed. They could not be purchased, brought into the state across its borders, or found in its schools and libraries. People still read them, but not openly, and the unofficial ban rankled even strong supporters of the new state, who recognized that just because fascists had read May's books, not everyone who read them was a fascist.

Indeed, many of the GDR's new citizens recognized the weakness of the SED's ideological opposition toward May. If Hitler loved May's books, so too did Karl Liebknecht, the cofounder of the Spartacist League, the German Communist Party, and a martyr who had been tortured and killed together with Rosa Luxemburg by right-wing militants in Berlin in 1919. Surely he could not have been duped by May. Nor, thought many of the GDR's new citizens, could they.

Thus in 1955, the Young Pioneers, the organization for children operated by the SED, openly inquired why there was no Karl May for them. That led to a vigorous debate in the public press, heated arguments in open meetings between panels of experts and the broader public, and considerable complaints, petitions, and letters that continued to be sent to the Cultural Ministry for decades after the war.

Indeed, the German Federal Archive in Berlin (Lichterfelde-West) possesses a remarkable and enlightening collection of these letters. The sheer number of people who were willing to criticize the government directly over its opposition to May demonstrates both the importance his books continued to play for Germans in the postwar era and the seriousness of East Germans' continued interest in American Indians. They also reveal yet again, the kinds of collective consciousness that coalesced around the experience of reading these and similar books that Germans first saw threatened with the ban during the GDR.

Consequently, many East Germans, such as Heiner Schmidt in Dresden, complained directly to the Cultural Ministry. Schmidt called the state's action against May a "cultural disgrace," and he reminded the president of the People's Parliament (Volkskammer) that the citizens of the GDR were not "underage children who needed to be told by the Cultural Ministry what we or our children should read." Fathers and sons in the GDR, he argued, "had the right to an unaltered version of Karl May," just as their fathers and grandfathers had, just as "Albert Einstein, Albert Schweitzer, Karl Liebknecht, Peter Rosegger etc."—all fans of Karl May—had had. Moreover, Schmidt condemned "the hate-driven" technical analyses provided by the panels of experts convened by the state to legitimate its prohibition against May's books; that, he exclaimed, was a tactic "reminiscent of the Inquisition."[38]

These were strong words; but they were hardly exceptional. Many East Germans regarded the SED's blanket assault on May as an attack on their most cherished childhood memories and a critical component of German cultural heritage. However, even as the public exposed the weakness of its ideological arguments, the SED refused to relent. Instead, it adopted a position of official equivocation, explaining to protestors that "there is no prohibition from the state against publishing the Karl May books," rather "the publishers decided for themselves what they wanted to print." In May's case, they demurred for good reasons: his books had been too popular among the Nazis, as "528,000 copies were printed in 1938 alone"; they contained "strong ideological failures and artistic limitations"; and, most importantly, the excellent new "adventure literature" being produced in the GDR had eclipsed them. There simply was not enough paper to print everything, and thus "no reason at this time to bring Karl May back into the light of day and place him on the same shelves with our literature."[39]

The Cultural Ministry also understood, however, that if Karl May was no longer good to read, American Indians were still good to think about. They could still be employed for political purposes. Thus immediately after Patty Frank, the unassailable cultural icon of German childhood, passed away in 1959, the state seized the Karl-May-Museum, placed it under the auspices of Peter Neumann, the director of Dresden's ethnographic museum, and symbolically renamed it the *Indianer Museum*. Neumann's new scientific organization directed the collections away from their previous focus on May and Frank (the swastika display had long since disappeared), and his improved guidebook followed suit. By 1962, it began including short additions on the plight of contemporary American Indians under the rubric, "How do the Indians live today?"—followed by the explanation that they were suffering on a network of reservations.[40]

Indeed, just as a series of Germans had done under every previous political regime, the authors of the guidebook took pains to detail the many broken treaties and the physical and mental abuses heaped on American Indians by the United States. By the 1960s, the museum's curators could also draw on the efforts of some American Indians who had begun initiating legal claims against the United States in federal and international courts. They featured as exemplary one Iroquois who denounced the United States in a petition to the fifth meeting of the United Nations in 1950 for its unwillingness to acknowledge the American Indian nations within its borders. Later editions of the guidebook broadened this rhetoric even further, harnessing the language of racism that became common in civil rights rallies in America. Eventually they spotlighted the rise of the American Indian Movement (AIM), which gained international attention when members occupied the Bureau of Indian Affairs offices in Washington, D.C., in 1972 and participated in a standoff with state and federal authorities at Wounded Knee, South Dakota, in 1973.

After three decades, the SED finally lifted the ban on Karl May. Together with figures such as Martin Luther and Frederick the Great, May was readmitted into the Parthenon of Socialism in 1983, and the museum's original name returned. That, however, made little difference. American Indians, rather than Karl May, remained the focus of the institution, which continued to be lauded for its presentation of American Indians' resistance against "exploitation, repression, and slavery."[41]

Those traditional German interests in resistance had persisted through the ban, articulated and developed by many other texts. Classics such as *The Leatherstocking Tales* continued to be produced, and an array of new authors such as Anna Jürgen and Liselotte Welskopf-Henrich emerged already in the early 1950s with prize-winning new books on American Indians that became popular in both East and West Germany. Many set themselves in direct opposition to May, arguing against the quality, character, and accuracy of his writings in both literary and political forums, and claiming (much as von Gagern, Steuben, and other National Socialist authors had done) to offer Germans an historically, ethnologically, and ideologically superior product.[42]

The state tried to guarantee the ideological superiority of these new books by requiring its publishers to send their manuscripts to state functionaries for evaluation. That process led to ideological rejections, to personal and professional dangers for authors and publishers alike, and, in some cases, to controversies. In 1958, for example, the Altberliner Verlag received permission to print ten thousand copies of Edith Klatt's book *Amaroq—or the Sleigh Journey*.[43] Klatt became well known for her children's books focused on American Indians, which sold well in both East and West Germany. *Amaroq*, a story about an Eskimo boy, delighted the initial reviewers, and it was nominated for a prize. The prize committee, however, reacted aggressively against the text. One member of the committee, Ursula Kroszewsky, denounced the book as "a portrayal of primitive, sleeping and eating people for whom the leader does all the thinking and negotiating." Indeed, she argued, a fascist leadership principle "runs like a red thread through the entire manuscript" and she accused Klatt of penning a story about a *Führerkult*, one that bordered on National Socialist ideology and required immediate repression.[44] In response to her evaluation, the state seized the remaining copies from the press and the bookstores, and the author and initial reviewers were castigated for their misdeeds. Revisions and future vigilance, they all learned, were imperative.

Even Rudolf Daumann, well known for books such as *Tatanka-Yotanka* about the life of Sitting Bull, and a recipient of the Bronze Fatherlands Medal for Service in 1956, had to tread lightly.[45] The problem, as one reviewer wrote during his evaluations of Daumann's *The Four Arrows of the Cheyenne* (1857),[46] was the classical "weakness of most Indian stories": when their authors wrote against "the colonization of the territory that was the Indians' homeland," and "against clearing the land over which the free nomads had ranged," they too often took up "a position against progress." Since there was "no doubt" that the "building of the Union-Pacific Railroad across the American continent was progress," and because the support of technological innovation and progress of this sort was a socialist principle, the key was not to assail technological developments or the clearing of the land per se but rather to attack the "inhumane, horrifying methods, through which one overran and eradicated an ethically and morally superior people."[47]

This, of course, had been the position of many nineteenth-century Germans as well. If some, such as Aby Warburg, feared and disdained technological progress, the vast majority, following Rudolf Cronau, condemned its abuses in the American West without deriding technological advances and innovations. The same was true for many National Socialists. Indeed, in every political context, as long as the forces responsible for the abuse were ideological opponents, similar tales could be told: even tales written by a surprising number of Americans.

For that reason, the state's reviewers responded positively to requests to publish the work of people such as the American Oliver La Farge, who had been president of the Association on American Indian Affairs from 1937 to 1942 and 1946 to 1963,[48] and they were particularly enamored with books such as Dee Brown's *Bury My Heart at Wounded Knee* (1970).[49] They termed Brown's book "a poignant indictment of the colonial and exterminatory politics of the whites in the USA," and they quickly approved the production of thirty thousand copies by the Berlin publishing house Neues Leben in 1976.

The fact that this book had already been successfully translated in West Germany three years earlier did not deter them. Stories of American Indian resistance were especially popular in East Germany, just as they had been during the nineteenth century, the Weimar, and the Nazi eras. Within the new international context of rising minority rights movements, however, they gained even more value. East German reviewers could see the critical interconnections between their own official state history—cast as the culmination of heroic struggles against a series of oppressors—and those of American Indians.[50]

So too could many others. Indeed, Brown's book was well received in the GDR because it fit into an established frame of argumentation. For example, films focused on the heroic efforts of American Indians to resist precisely the "colonial and exterminatory politics" that Brown portrayed were already a raging success in East Germany when Brown completed his book. In 1966 DEFA, the state-owned film company of the GDR, began its series of *Indianer* films[51] with *The Sons of the Great Mother Bear* [*Die Söhne der großen Bärin*], based on the 1951 novel by Liselotte Welskopf-Henrich.

The DEFA films contrasted radically with American cinema, which generally portrayed American Indians as primitive savages who attacked innocent settlers and were righteously repulsed. They also differed from West German films, which placed American Indians at the center and allowed good to triumph over evil. That evil, however, was generally embodied in a small group of men. In the DEFA films, American Indians were engaged in resisting broad economic or political systems. Indeed, by the time American film makers began producing movies like *Little Big Man* (1970), which was framed in a manner similar to the DEFA films, the East German group Roter Kreis was already working on its sixth movie, paving the way for *Little Big Man's* East German success.[52]

As the *Times* of London noted, one of the DEFA *Indianer* films' most redeeming characteristics was their honesty.[53] That honesty stemmed in part from the producers' efforts to portray the character and life worlds of specific tribes along with their stories of heroic struggle. Particularly in the first five films, the creators focused much of their energies on achieving historical and ethnological accuracy.[54] Ethnologists from Leipzig were even brought onto the sets in Yugoslavia to ensure the authenticity of the costumes, tools, weapons, and character of communal life in tribal villages.[55]

At the same time, these gestures to historical accuracy underwrote a polemic about the United States. That too was part of the honesty noted by the *Times*. The pamphlet that accompanied the release of the first film, for example, included an extensive discussion of life on various reservations along Route 66, listing the high infant mortality rates, lower life expectancy, and poverty levels found there. By 1968, the pamphlets and news reports also began making explicit comparisons between the historical struggles of American Indians and events in contemporary Vietnam. As one reporter noted in a Cottbus newspaper while reviewing *Die Spur des Falken* (The Sign of the Hawk) (1968), "This successful *Indianer* film from DEFA makes one aware of terrifying comparisons with actual events." When a "group of burning and murdering whites falls upon an Indian camp shooting women and children in a blind rage, as if they were on a rabbit hunt, and the tents in their camp go up in flames," who, he asked, "does not then think of Vietnam and the raids by soldiers of American imperialism with rockets and napalm?"[56]

Both conflicts, many East Germans agreed, revolved around struggles for freedom against American imperialism, and by placing the struggles and losses of American Indians at the center of their films, DEFA claimed to avoid the tendency of most Hollywood films before 1970 to excuse the actions of white settlers and soldiers. Instead, as the DEFA pamphlet produced to accompany *Spur des Falken* explained, "viewers cannot and should not become comfortable" with the fact that "the seizure of the land by the whites took place with the greatest brutality," or that "the capitalistic colonial politics was, and today still is, a politics of extermination of the people [*Völker*]." Rather than ignoring or excusing the conquest of the American West, they argued, one should recognize that conquest was an early failure of the United States, "one of the most advanced countries in the world," to live up to the claims for human rights it espoused on the international stage—a failure, they argued, that persisted into the present.[57]

While consistent with arguments made by Germans for a century before the creation of the GDR, the shifting contexts of international relations in the postwar era, as well as the experience of the Holocaust in Europe, made these facts and assertions particularly attractive to the SED leadership, which proved eager to use them in that context. This position, however, was hardly unique to the SED; increasingly activists, artists, and others did precisely the same thing in West Germany and even in the United States; they simply began a bit later.

The Democratic Indian

Most disconcerting for many readers who grew up outside of the GDR and remain invested in a clear Cold War distinction between East and West may be the strikingly similar ways in which East and West Germans instrumentalized American Indians during the postwar era. While the Federal Republic of Germany (FRG) lacked the organs of censorship established in the East, popular images of American Indians were nevertheless channeled and shaped in the FRG as well, and regardless of the different political systems, they often tended toward the same ideals and thus the same kinds of idealized American Indians.

Unlike the SED, West Germany's democratic government had no reservations about the continued publication and consumption of Karl May's books. The Nazis' use and abuse of his texts was immaterial, and largely ignored. In fact, May's books retained their popularity in the FRG throughout the postwar period, just as they did in East Germany. In West Germany, however, they were sold openly and with considerable profit. They were also well liked in a range of countries outside the United States; by the 1980s they had appeared in almost countless editions and as many as thirty-nine languages.

During the early 1960s, with the West German film industry facing a ruinous future, Harald Reinl capitalized on Karl May's continued celebrity by making *The Treasure of the Silver Lake* (*Der Schatz im Silbersee*) (1962), based on May's book by the same name (1890/1894). The most expensive film produced in the FRG, it cost 3.5 million marks and earned almost as much after expenses. It was an unprecedented hit in West Germany and a huge commercial success: an amazing amount of paraphernalia was sold to the public, and the film's title theme, "Old Shatterhand," composed by Martin Böttcher, topped the national singles chart for seventeen weeks. To this day, almost everyone in Germany can still recognize it. The film itself was ultimately released in sixty countries, and sixteen more Karl May films followed between 1962 and 1968.

The unprecedented popularity of the Karl May films is what spurred the production of DEFA's *Indianer* films, which were meant as a kind of counterpoint to their success. The May films inspired the famous spaghetti westerns as well. These too, however, much like the DEFA films, were quite different from the May movies. As Tassilo Schneider has argued, if "the spaghetti western may be said to *deconstruct* the genre, the [Karl May] films may be said to *reconstruct* it." The Italian films were focused on demythologization of the Wild West, whereas "the May adaptations seem to pursue the opposite objective: to construct, or reconstruct, a viable generic mythology."

Indeed, while placing the tragedy of American Indians' fight for survival at the center of the Karl May films set them apart from American westerns, they were not nearly as radical as the DEFA films. The May films were meant to soothe rather than provoke. Indeed, according to one critic, "the appeal of the May westerns resided in their restoration of the genre's classical mythology, their return to the representation of an ideologically unproblematic and deeply if simplistically moral universe," precisely the kind of appeal that Mary Nolan identified in May's books during the outset of the twentieth century. To that end, however, the films abandoned the focus on the national identities so prevalent in the books and offered viewers a more peaceful international orientation.[58]

All of that—the effort to play down nationalism, to soothe rather than provoke, to seek a return to a comforting, familiar world—fit well with other West German efforts to locate a sense of normalcy, free from the tensions of nationalism and capitalism and the horrors of the National Socialist past during the first decades of the postwar era.[59] By the 1970s, however, as the generational revolts of the late 1960s came to fruition, as peace movements, environmental concerns, and antinuclear actions increased, and as the United States seemed less able to secure West Germans a peaceful future in the nuclear era, such unproblematic glosses on May and the German past fell out of favor. As a result, the citizens of the FRG began to engage American Indians' past and present in ways quite similar to those in the GDR.

Throughout the 1970s and 1980s a series of West German authors began to scrutinize and condemn the books written by May, Steuben, and other Germans for their unrealistic, racist, and fantastic portraits of American Indians. Indeed, it was within this context that Steuben's books were revised and May's books were cast as horribly riddled with clichés (a point that East German critics had made decades earlier). This more critical West German literature followed East Germans' lead by underscoring the atrocities visited on American Indians during the nineteenth century, and it made clear connections between American Indians' past and present plights and, much like East Germans, connected those plights to acts of American troops in Vietnam. Increasingly, West German pedagogues also identified the topic of American Indians, so popular with German children, as the ideal site for instruction about the problems of racism, economic inequalities, prejudice, diversity, and stereotypes in both schools and museums. They also utilized their revised visions of American Indians to return to the rhetoric of heroic resistance, lauding many American Indians' persistent and successful refusal to conform.[60]

In many cases, these were international trends, most prevalent at first in the GDR but quickly apparent in the United States and West Germany as well. As Robert Berkhofer noted at the time, by the 1970s, left-wing American political discourse conflated the Viet Cong and American Indians, and an array of "counter-culture Indians" emerged as new tropes for criticizing the American government. These new tropes functioned much like the older notions of the noble savages in the eighteenth century. The critics used these new ideal types to critique American policy at home and abroad, to juxtapose the loss of a more natural way of life with the limitations of a capitalist and, many argued, imperialist society, and to underscore the ways in which the U.S. government failed to meet its own standards for the protection of human rights within its own borders as well as in places like Vietnam. Moreover, as new concerns developed among non-Native Americans, they found new things about American Indians to support their interest in drug use, communal and spiritual ways of life, ecological concerns, and almost any alternative lifestyle. American Indians proved quite versatile in postwar America.[61]

In West Germany, that versatility had even broader implications: it became fashionable for West German intellectuals to equate the Americans, or at least the American ruling class, with fascists. They regarded American military and political elites as a threat to world security, and thus "a wide array of articles in conservative and liberal newspapers used terms traditionally linked with Nazi policy to characterize American warfare in Vietnam: 'final solution,' 'totalitarian degeneration,' 'doctrine of salvation,' 'war of extermination,' 'scorched earth.'" Much as in East Germany, in other words, West Germans used America's failures in current events to demonstrate that "America had finally disgraced its claim to being a worldwide role model for democracy."[62] At the same time, those critics also used the history of Native and non-Native American relations to demonstrate that these were not new tendencies. They were old habits. Once practiced during the United States' westward expansion, those habits had been unleashed during the postwar era on the wider world.

Indeed, revisionist films such as Ralph Nelson's graphically violent *Soldier Blue*, which ran in West Germany in 1970 under the title *The Lullaby of Homicide* (*Das Wiegenlied vom Totschlag*), undercut the romance of the May films by focusing on the brutal elimination of American Indians at the hands of corrupt officials, soldiers, and settlers. Billed by West German promoters as the "harshest film in the world," *Soldier Blue*, much like *Little Big Man*, was a huge success, resonating with crowds in East and West Germany. In fact, *Soldier Blue*'s portrait of the 1864 Sand Creek massacre of Cheyennes and Arapahoes shortly after revelations of the 1968 My Lai massacre in Vietnam opened up broad debates about the original victims of American imperialism in the United States.

Already prominent in GDR books and films,[63] that discourse quickly reverberated through West Germany during the 1970s as well, leading to the publication of books such as Frederik Hetmann's *The Red Day*, a volume for adolescents about the famous victory of a combined force of American Indians over the U.S. Seventh Calvary at the Battle of Little Big Horn, which he dedicated to "the memory of the victims of Sand Creek (1864), Wounded Knee (1890), My Lai (1968), and Da Nang (1975), in anger and sorrow."[64] Incredibly popular among pedagogues, it went through four editions in the first three years and received the Friedrich Gerstäcker Prize for children's literature in 1976.

By the mid-1970s, in other words, West German portraits of Indian-white conflicts became increasingly similar to those promulgated much earlier in the East, where American Indians had consistently taken on the role of victims and resisters in both books and films, and where people like Welskopf-Henrich and her husband, who counted as "victims of fascism," and who lived in a state that drew a strict ideological line between itself and Nazi Germany, had been less reluctant than their counterparts in the West to talk about American imperialism and genocide.

Indeed, in 1976 West German political activist and journalist Claus Biegert responded to the American Bicentennial with his book *200 Years without a Constitution. 1976: Indians Resisting*. Biegert maintained that his book was first and foremost an "engaged documentary," a book about "a variant of modern genocide [*Völkermord*] and resistance," which had "taken shape through direct contact with surviving and, in the mean time, dead Indians like Pedro Bissonette"—an Oglala who was credited with bringing the American Indian Movement to Pine Ridge before he was fatally shot there in 1973.[65]

Throughout the book, Biegert characterized Bissonette and other AIM members as warriors engaged in resisting generations of genocidal efforts by non-Native Americans. He termed earlier reservations "concentration camps" and argued that with the creation of the Bureau of Indian Affairs, "*Völkermord* [genocide] lay in the hands of the administration."[66] That administration, he explained, was determined from the beginning to eliminate the last vestiges of Native Americans by either destroying them physically or eradicating their culture through forced assimilation.[67]

Biegert's rendition of Native American history was driven by a self-defining dialectic between injustice and resistance, and much like the authors of East German books and films (as well as Nazi artists and authors), the resistance he saw stretching over centuries was narrated from American

Indians' perspective, through a series of strong-willed and persistent individuals who refused to conform. Much as in the GDR, that resistance was
judged to culminate in the creation of AIM, which he likened to organizations of freedom fighters in Vietnam and elsewhere, including young radicals
in Germany.[68] Indeed, in the final section of his book, titled "Indians and
us: Wounded Knee is everywhere," Biegert began with a 1967 citation from
the student radical Rudi Dutschke talking about democracy as it should be:
an amalgamation of individuals free from capitalistic or Stalinistic bureaucracy that was organized from the lowest levels of society by councils. Biegert argued that "what Dutschke was striving for was already being practiced
by Indians" over four hundred year ago and was "still practiced in part" on
some North American reservations.[69] American Indians, he asserted, knew
about real democracy, just as they knew about real socialism, just as they had
known, as earlier authors professed, about real National Socialism.

Much like Hetmann's critical text for children, Biegert's book for adults
was also a tremendous success. Indeed, it became a virtual bible for the
many West Germans who quickly joined the AIM support groups that began
sprouting up across West Germany in the 1970s.

AIM Indians

The American Indian Movement's popularity across East and West Germany
belied the putative impermeability of the Iron Curtain. Indeed, in many ways
AIM helped to bridge the gap, as supporters on both sides of the border demonstrated their willingness to work together to help AIM's Red Power movement. Support groups in Hamburg and West Berlin, for example, sent fliers
and petition forms to their counterparts in East Germany, and together they
collected tens of thousands of signatures in support of individuals ranging
from Russell Means to Sarah Bad Heart Bull as they battled the American
court systems.[70] Representatives from AIM did much to develop these relationships. Clyde Bellecourt, for example, toured Europe in 1974 spread-
ing the word about their efforts, and Dennis Banks and Vernon Bellecourt
followed the next year, opening the AIM office in West Berlin. These men
traveled beyond the Berlin Wall as well, meeting with Liselotte Welskopf-
Henrich and members of East German support groups in her East Berlin
home, and speaking publicly to students and others while they were there.
The support groups even worked together across the border to finance repeated visits by AIM members,[71] and the AIM members, in turn came to West

Germany and marched in May Day parades, spoke in open forums to hundreds of people, and raised awareness, together with their supporters, about current events in Indian country.

At times, AIM members also traveled with Central and South American Indians to express international solidarity and discuss their individual efforts to gain self-determination. In 1977, for example, Clyde Bellecourt, Erroll Kinistino, and François Paulette traveled with eight other American Indians from North and South America supported in part by Amnesty International and the West German organization Gesellschaft für bedrohte Völker (Society for Threatened People).[72] More than eight hundred people came to hear them drum together and discuss the "concerns and goals of the Indian movement," in the Schwabinger Bräu in Munich, and even more attended their appearances in Bonn, Cologne, Bremen, and Hamburg.

During these trips, AIM members became precisely what had intrigued Germans in both these states, and what had long entranced their predecessors for over a century. As Dietmar Halbhuber wrote in an essay in the East German newspaper *Junge Welt* (Young World) in 1975, these advocates of Red Power "are just as one imagines Indians: proud, calm, and through their hair—long braids with feathers—and clothing clearly distinguishable as Indians."[73] In both East and West Germany, AIM members dressed the part, taking on the identifiable trappings of modern American Indians and presenting themselves less as victims than as resisters. Indeed, they portrayed themselves as warriors engaged in combating impersonal forces of repression, and many, such as Russell Means and Dennis Banks, took on the mantle of mythical leading personalities. As Halbhuber noted, this accounted for their ability to connect emotionally with members of the support groups. Their rhetoric touched Germans' nostalgia for childhood tales of past conquests and rebellions, and it combined that nostalgia with Germans' contemporary concerns about the impersonal forces of imperialism and capitalism that many felt were embodied in America. And as a result, as H. Guillermo Bartlet recalled, "the welcome mat spread for AIM."[74]

AIM members proved quite savvy, able to instrumentalize the Germans for their own uses, and initiating relationships and new tendencies in both East and West Germany that outlived their own movement and the existence of these states. AIM members organized some of the support groups themselves, but the broadcasting and publication of their rhetoric caused just as many to spring up spontaneously. Particularly in East Germany, groups of people came together to found associations geared toward solidarity with American Indians in an effort to assist them in resisting the homogenizing power of Western civilization. They also committed themselves to combating the depredations of poverty from the Mohawk reservations in the Northeast to the Lakota and Navajo reservations in the Far West.[75] Quite quickly, in fact, these East and West German efforts became much greater than AIM. Even as AIM began to falter,[76] Germans only increased their efforts to connect with activists in Native America in an attempt both to support them and to glean from their history and experience of resistance.

To that end, people such as Biegert helped organize delegations of American Indians to come to West Germany for dual purposes. On the one hand, they wanted the delegates to inform West Germans and their politicians about the continued plight of American Indians, and to ask the West German government for its assistance. On the other hand, they also sought to use these American Indians, and their putative deep and natural understanding of current environmental and political problems, to shame the West German government into ecological and geopolitical actions. In addition, they hoped that the American Indians' experience as resisters would aid in West Germans' own protests.

Thus, for example, a loose coalition of antinuclear and environmental activists teamed up with Petra Kelly and the Green Party in 1983 to bring a delegation of American Indians to West Germany because, as one put it, "they have so much to teach us."[77] That group attended debates over Pershing II missiles in the West German Parliament, participated in an antinuclear rally, took part in an environmentalist protest near Frankfurt, and talked to German peace and environmental activists and to sold-out crowds of enthusiasts across the Federal Republic.

It was these experiences that led Winona LaDuke to write a series of essays about the shared character, challenges, and goals of American Indian and German activists. "In North America," she wrote, "it seems that only the Indian, who has also trod the path along the edge of national extermination, holds a similar perception of the true urgency of the contemporary [political and environmental] situation. The Germans have to an amazing extent understood this: hence, their affinity with things Indian." By the same token, she stressed that "Indians more and more are noting, 'Of all other peoples today, the Germans have recognized the danger of our peril, and they've tried to stop it.'" That peril, she claimed, came from "two striking similarities between the situation of contemporary Native America and that of Germany. First, both are militarily occupied by the same nation (the United States). Second, both have been designated by the occupying power as an area/people to be consciously sacrificed in the interests of some mysterious 'greater good.'" That sacrifice, she explained, came in part by exposing both American Indians and Germans to the effects of the uranium pulled out of American Indian lands and then placed near German cities in the form of missiles—an argument West German activists eagerly embraced.[78]

At the same time, Petra Kelly took the case of the Oglala participants in that delegation to the West German parliament, asking the government to sponsor a resolution in the General Assembly of the United Nations calling on the World Court to issue an advisory opinion as to whether the United States illegally confiscated the Black Hills in violation of the 1868 Fort Laramie Treaty. While the parliament suggested that the Lakota should take the issue directly to the World Court, which could only hear issues between states, Kelly encouraged the Lakota to analyze the parliament's report for legal concerns and promised to bring it up to the parliament again.[79] Her efforts and advice were well received in Indian country. They demonstrated to many the promises of reciprocal instrumentalization.

Instrumentalizing American Indians in Unified Germany

The unification of the German states in 1990 changed little in terms of how Germans thought about or sought to support American Indians. Indeed, the very lack of thought among many of the most active support groups led people such as Peter Bolz, the director of the North American section of Berlin's ethnographic museum, and Richard Kelly, who had long been active in these movements, to exclaim in exasperation that the supporters were engaged in instrumentalizing American Indians in ways not unlike those promoted by the very people they often disdained.

In 1993, for example, Bolz reacted to arguments from a Munich-based support group about the role of the Max Plank Institute in a fight over the use of Mount Graham in the Pinaleño Mountains of Arizona, a holy site for the Western Apache, as the location for an international observatory. The members of the support group, he argued had learned little: "The battle over Mt. Graham," he wrote "turned originally and exclusively around white interests—here the environmentalists, there the astronomers." In a "tried and true colonial fashion," he noted, "it benefited both sides to draw the Indians into this conflict." "The 'good' Apaches stand naturally on the side of the environmentalists, the 'bad' ones naturally on the side of the scientists." But who decides between the good and the bad? "Especially those people who speak so grandiosely of the genocide of the Indians should perhaps at one point reflect on the traditions in which they are acting." "Since the early colonial period, there were whites who knew what was best for the Indians, and up to today nothing has changed." American Indians, he went on, were continuously instrumentalized in the name of progress, environment, and profit, and "everyone thinks that moral righteousness is on their side."[80] That righteousness is what most disturbed him about the support groups' position, for in the end it was no different from the righteousness of the original colonists, the missionaries, the Nazis, or the Communists.

Moreover, from the perspective of the 1990s, Germans such as Bolz, who had considerable experience with these movements and with the more general interests in American Indians shared by East and West Germans, were able to identify shifts and trends in the emphasis Germans placed on the character of American Indians even during the last few decades of the twentieth century. Dorothea Schmidt, for example, recalled watching during the 1970s as books about American Indians moved from the children's sections in German bookstores to the adult self-help section and then to the sections devoted to coffee table books. She also noted the explosion of other materials that hit the West German market soon afterward—American Indian jewelry, music, artwork in the form of paintings and blankets, old Edward Curtis photos with bits of sage wisdom stenciled below them, and then, of course, the many "medicine men" who traveled across Europe to groups of esoterics seeking spiritual guidance and who quickly recognized that West Germany was a particularly good place to ply their trade.

Schmidt speculated on a wide range of reasons why the "plastic shaman"—pretenders eager to sell knowledge they claimed to have of American Indian religions—were so successful in Germany before other American Indians and their German supporters shut them down. She listed the following reasons: social "instability, a religious vacuum, estrangement at the hands of automated technologies, fear for the future, an end to the belief in progress that accompanied the overpowering might of technology, environmental degradation, and a life-stifling concrete landscape in which so many urbanized Germans were forced to live."[81] None of these were new concerns, just new articulations of older ones generally lumped under the label of "crises of modernity," and thus the shift in emphasis toward the esoteric in Germany was but one example of a general trend that Berkhofer had observed in the United States and that people such as Marianna Torgovnick identified more generally.[82]

The point, then, is that the polysemous Indian offers a trope for almost any predilection, and it can be put to many uses; it can teach Nazi values of racism or democratic values of antiracism. It can be used to endorse liberal or socialist values, feminist or ecological values. It can address spiritual needs or explain material want. And yet in some ways what matters the most from a historical perspective is not the various purposes to which "the American Indian" can be and has been put but the consistent characteristics Germans assigned to American Indians across the longue durée. In that sense, Liselotte Welskopf-Henrich's biography provides us with critical insights into those consistencies, their implications, and some of the limits of focusing only on the varieties of instrumentalization within the contours of political regimes.

Persistent Concerns, Ideals, and Values

Welskopf-Henrich's biography (1901–79) stretched across the most prominent political ruptures in the twentieth century. By any estimation, she was an accomplished woman. Born into a barrister's family in Munich in 1901, she received her Ph.D. in economics in 1925 at the University of Berlin. Financial problems brought on by the depression prevented her from continuing her academic training in the 1920s, and her opposition to National Socialism caused her to refuse to return to the university in 1933 when a position became available.[83] Instead, she became a resister, delivered clandestine food packages to Jews and French POWs, assisted prisoners from the Sachsenhausen concentration camp who were brought into Berlin as laborers in 1943, and helped one, the confirmed communist Rudolf Welskopf, who later became her husband, escape in 1944 after ten years in captivity.[84] Indeed, she hid him in what was left of her home for the better part of a year, and during the last months of the conflict she helped him produce and distribute flyers calling for soldiers to lay down their weapons and embrace the Red Army.[85]

After hostilities ended, she became the personal secretary of the Charlottenburg mayor and head of his statistics department and translation office until April 1946. At that time, she chose to move into the Soviet zone of the city, where she and her husband felt they were "most needed."[86] She also became a member of the Communist Party (KPD) and soon after the Socialist Unity Party (SED). In 1949, during efforts to rebuild the faculty of the Humboldt University, she was able to return to academics as an *Aspirantin* (research assistant) (1949–52) and then *Dozentin* (lecturer) (1952–59) in ancient history until she became the first female professor of history at the Humboldt University in 1959. She also became the first female member of the Berlin-Brandenburg Academy of science, and she received a series of decorations from the East German state.[87] In addition to those impressive

FIGURE 24. Liselotte Welskopf-Henrich at her home in East Berlin in 1975 with two leaders of the American Indian Movement (AIM), Dennis Banks (on the right) and Vernon Bellecourt. *Junge Welt* 81, 3–4 April 1976.

achievements, she wrote two series of novels about American Indians, which were incredibly popular in both East and West Germany.

She conceived of her first book, *Die Söhne der großen Bärin* before the 1930s, completed it in 1940, published it in the GDR in 1951, and then saw it go through more than three editions by 1952.[88] That same book, awarded a prize for youth literature in the GDR, was reworked into the fifth and sixth volumes in her first series and remained a blockbuster that has sold more than a million copies internationally. It not only was the basis for the first DEFA *Indianer* film in the 1960s but was also rated one of the best children's books in the world by UNESCO in 1963, received the Friedrich Gerstäcker Prize for children's literature in West Germany in 1968, was translated into over a half dozen languages,[89] and is still in print and highly recommended as a classic today. It is, in other words, much more than simply GDR literature, and its origins turned around a striking combination of creative forces that cut across the political divisions and historical ruptures detailed in this chapter.

To a certain degree, those origins were tied to the tradition of tales written about American Indians in the German languages for more than a hundred years before she began her first novel. At the same time, however, the important context for its production was her cumulative experience in war-torn Berlin. Welskopf-Henrich, who, like other Germans of her generation, had also read Karl May as a child and played Indians with her friends, completed her first contribution to this broad component of German culture while living under National Socialism. During the last years of the war she came into contact with men she felt possessed those very characteristics and virtues she admired most among Indians she had read about and whom she felt Karl May had misunderstood.[90] Indeed, for the revisionist Welskopf-Henrich, the concept of "Red Power," as one that turned around committed notions of loyalty, conviction, resistance, and community, existed long before AIM members took up the phrase. She identified it first in her readings about their ancestors in the translated autobiographies of American Indian leaders from the late nineteenth and early twentieth centuries and then discovered it again among the communist prisoners from Sachsenhausen who were brought into her neighborhood as workers. In 1944 these heroic convictions in the midst of crisis situations seemed to her to be something the "red points" in the present shared with the "redskins" from the past,[91] and this is what she tried to capture in her books.

Welskopf-Henrich's first novel *Die Söhne der großen Bärin* (and the series of six books by the same name) revolves around the story of a group of Lakotas in the northern plains of the United States who, facing pressure from white settlers and later starvation and poor treatment on a reservation, rise up in 1862 and begin an odyssey across the northern plains that ends in Canada in 1878. The story is also focused on an individual, Tokei-ihto, the young war chief who leads his clan through a series of adventures and crises before the clan completes its odyssey north.[92]

It is a classic setting for such novels, but when Welskopf-Henrich wrote it, she sought, as a revisionist, to move beyond the "kitschy gloss" produced by Karl May and other German authors, combining instead the adventure of a western with historical and ethnological instruction and a pointed exploration into the actions and character of people faced with crisis situations.[93] Her timing was perfect. Her book appeared in 1951, just two years before an open discussion in the GDR about the suitability of adventure literature for children. And that timing, given the limited number of new titles available, the immediate popularity of her recently released book, and the official rejection of Karl May, placed her in the position of offering German youth the exemplary alternative. Indeed, both she and the press hoped that her book would "heave Karl May out of the saddle."[94]

It nearly did. It certainly paid the press great dividends for its risk. The initial run of 15,000 books disappeared in months, multiple editions followed, and by the eleventh edition in 1961 more than 200,000 copies had been printed. Already in the 1950s the book was licensed for printing in West Germany and Austria, and the letters she received from readers make it clear that their interest in getting new copies continued unabated. Indeed, it was the readers' incessant requests that led to the decision to rework the book into a series.[95]

There are literally thousands of letters in her collected papers at the Archive of the Berlin-Brandenburg Academy of the Sciences from readers who spanned generations, classes, professions, and political boundaries in both the East and West. Many of these readers praised her efforts to provide them with a historically accurate portrait of what one called the "staggering fate of the Indians," and just as many wrote to her about the importance these books had for their own lives.

The characteristics embodied by Tokei-ihto, especially his unflinching willingness to endure extreme hardship while working to save his community from overwhelming forces, and the strength of his personal conviction, had tremendous appeal among her readers, and he quickly became a role model for many East and West German boys and girls.[96] Moreover, her work spurred them on to further inquiry; a few even began trying to contact Indians directly. That shift to the present, however, became ubiquitous only after Welskopf-Henrich began publishing her second series of novels and encouraged her readers to become active in supporting the emerging American Indian Movement.

Focused on contemporary American Indians, Welskopf-Henrich's second series of novels, *Das Blut des Adlers* (The Blood of the Eagle), was also set in the North American plains among the Lakota. It too turns around a strong individual, Joe King, who lives on and off the reservation, and at the beginning of the first volume, *Nacht über der Prärie* (Night over the Prairie), has just returned with the hope of giving up a life of crime. Quickly married to an equally strong woman, their life together provides the red thread that guides readers through the five volumes, introducing them to the complexities of reservation life. These include the pair's violent confrontations with whites and other American Indians, Joe King's cleansing experience in the Sun Dance, the sacred birth of twins, encounters with peyote and the Native American Church, a group teen suicide on the reservation, the foundation of the American Indian Movement, which King joins, and the occupation of the island of Alcatraz in San Francisco Bay, which Welskopf-Henrich had witnessed. At the beginning of the fifth volume, the couple is murdered, removing these romantic characters from her narrative as she plunges into the many brutal events on the Pine Ridge Reservation that took place around the 1973 uprising at Wounded Knee and during the protests and tensions that followed.

This second series was, in short, a pointed excursion into contemporary American Indian affairs, and her readers made that transition to the present with ease.[97] Indeed, the reception of this new series of books remained much the same as the reception of the previous series. Young people continued to write that they were taking the characters as role models, and parents continued to write about the positive influence her characters had on their children.

The critical difference in this new wave of correspondence, however, was that, in addition to asking about the history of the Indians and the circumstances of her novels, they wrote that they had "learned through her books," as one reader put it, "not to see the Indians as something special, but as an oppressed group that, like many others, has the right to resistance."[98] Within that group there were, as Welskopf-Henrich made clear in one of her responses, "intelligent people who are pushed in crisis situations from passive to active characters."[99] These are not Nazi-style supermen—she reiterated this repeatedly in her correspondence—but among them emerged people "who, under exceptionally difficult conditions, remain courageous, honest, helpful, and honorable," and who "fight with all their strength for their people's right to live."[100]

She tried to capture these commendable traits in her character Joe King, whom many of her readers independently linked to the leading AIM activist Russell Means.[101] Welskopf-Henrich agreed with her readers' comparisons.[102] Means, she wrote, was "a man who in the middle of many difficulties and dangers has chosen a particular course in order to help his people," and "much like Joe King, he had a turbulent life until he returned to his people."[103] And just like the protagonist in her novels, the flesh-and-blood embodiment of his characteristics, Russell Means, soon became many of her readers' living "role model."[104]

Although the GDR limited its citizens' mobility and curtailed the flow of publications and goods from West to East, Welskopf-Henrich was surprisingly well informed and well connected in the United States and Canada. Her status in society and in the party allowed her to receive Native American newspapers and monographs, which she quickly consumed and illegally distributed. She was also allowed to travel to North America for professional meetings, after which she visited most of the major Indian reservations. After she returned, she acted: she worked to have Native American authors translated into German, collaborated with Lakota artist Arthur Amiotte to bring art produced by some of his students on the Pine Ridge Reservation to East Berlin for a show, and went out of her way to assist a surprising number of Native Americans who were trying to improve their material conditions.[105] After a visit to Akwesasne, New York, in 1975, for example, she sent books and blankets to the school there.[106] She sent packages of clothing to groups and individuals she had met while abroad, and although East German currency was of little use to American Indians, Welskopf-Henrich drew on the Western currency she received through royalties from books sold in the Federal Republic to send money to struggling individuals, to AIM chapters, and to the International Indian Treaty Council.[107] She also wrote to lawyers and public officials about the plight of Native Americans she had met in American prisons, offering on several occasions to help pay for their defense.[108]

The travels that followed her initial venture also took her into the thick of Native American activism. She brought water to activists during their occupation of Alcatraz in 1969.[109] She met with the people who published the leading activist newspaper, *Akwesasne Notes*. She attended the memorial of Pedro Bissonette, who had been killed in 1973 on Pine Ridge, and she accompanied a group of mourners to Wounded Knee afterward to pray for the victims of the conflicts there. Because of her open support for AIM, she spent a night in the Pine Ridge Tribal Jail and she was detained and interrogated by the FBI.[110] Such adventures, however, only increased her legitimacy among American Indian activists, who repeatedly turned to her for help.[111]

She was always eager to comply. For example: when Dennis Banks asked her to collect signatures in Germany for a protest in 1974, she wrote to organizations that had sprung up in Rostock, Berlin, and other East German cities, asking them to go out and collect signatures on a petition she drafted,[112] and during this action alone, Welskopf-Henrich was able to collect thousands of signatures in support of AIM's cause.[113]

She also took to the airwaves and went to the press in support of AIM, giving interviews and broadcasting statements about the conditions Native Americans faced in the United States. And whether they heard this interview, read other press reports, or were inspired by Welskopf-Henrich's books, a staggering number of her readers in East and West Germany wrote to her for tips about how to become involved in AIM's struggle.[114] She encouraged the better organized groups to set up information stands and print pamphlets to reeducate Germans about Indians;[115] but she also provided them, and her more general readers, with contact names and addresses for Indian schools and cultural centers,[116] suggesting that they send clothing, school supplies, or material for crafts, such as glass beads from Eastern Europe or porcupine quills and eagle feathers collected from German zoos, all of which the schools could put to good use.[117] By early 1975, she was able to report that there were children in the GDR saving money to send to AIM, groups who organized monthly packages for schools, and reports from AIM members that "they have received more letters of sympathy and support from the GDR than the rest of Europe combined."[118]

Welskopf-Henrich considered such letters and petitions particularly important, and she urged readers in both the East and West to participate.[119] But in her correspondence with people in West Germany, she also encouraged them to travel to America to see the conditions for themselves and, if possible, to pitch in. A nurse from Göttingen was perhaps the most exceptional. After beginning a correspondence with Welskopf-Henrich, she traveled to Pine Ridge, took up a volunteer position at the reservation hospital, became a strong supporter of AIM, and one of Welskopf-Henrich's most important sources of information as the violence on Pine Ridge started to escalate.[120] Together they helped deliver AIM's messages east into Europe.

Messages about cultural identity and even political struggles, however, also went the other direction, from East and West Germany to Native America. Like many of her predecessors, Welskopf-Henrich felt that Germans and Native Americans were drawn together because of certain shared characteristics that stemmed from parallels in their histories. Fascinated with Indians' purported connection to "mother earth," she often remarked that "earlier the old Germans also had this close connection with nature."[121] Writing in English to Lakota artist Arthur Amiotte on Pine Ridge in 1969, she explained that "all the tribes of Europe and Asia were earth-born peoples." When they lived as nomadic tribes, Germans too had gathered fruits and hunted, and "the German tribes—had a tribal constitution not so far away from the tribal constitutions of Indians tribes." She stressed that one could "still see relics of it—as the common ownership of meadows and woods in South Bavaria and in Tyrol/Austria by the villagers in the mountains."[122]

In a rather striking use of the past by a professor of ancient history, one that echoed older arguments from Rudolf Cronau and other nineteenth-century Germans and would have resonated well with her counterparts in West Germany, she argued that much like American Indians, Germans' love of nature also had been undercut by their conquerors. Writing to Ann Rourke at the Akwesasne Library in 1975, she explained that when the Romans arrived in Northern Europe, Germans "were living in tribal systems, pure, proud, brave, having big families, many children, living by agriculture, cattle-breeding and hunting inmidst [*sic*] of enormous woods and nice meadows, always in contact with nature; the oak was their holy tree," and they "did not yet know anything of Christianism [*sic*]." In principle, she stated, "the Romans admired their tribal customs and their courage," but "in practice they tried to get our country, to suppress our ancestors." And like American Indians, "our German ancestors resisted"; they defeated a large Roman army and kept the Romans west of the Elbe. As a result, "the German tribes were divided, the one were submitted [*sic*], the others free." But "the representatives of Greek and Roman civilization" persisted to combat the free tribes in other ways: "They sent their missionaries to our ancestors. Slowly the tribal system was abolished, the nature-religion became persecuted, the missionaries, the towns, the 'civilization' became victor."

She described the oppression that followed from the church, the ruling monarchs, and the resulting revolutions as her narrative dovetailed with a Marxist historiography and then diverged from it radically. Now, she explained, East Germans had created a new republic, "but we have not yet again enough brotherhood and solidarity. We have to learn that again. Seeking our own traditions we have to control and analyze all the Greek and Roman traditions having invaded our way of life [Greek and Roman not capitalist], our thinking, our feeling and we have to judge what is good and useful even now for us and what is bad and useless."[123] East Germans, she wrote (just like all the Germans who came before them), faced very similar challenges as American Indians.

Given these affinities and shared history, Welskopf-Henrich, like Biegert and other West German activists, was convinced that Germans had much to learn from their counterparts overseas about how to achieve a life worth living in a modern, technological, rational age.[124] Sounding much like Aby Warburg, Carl Jung, and a host of other German intellectuals around the turn of the century, she argued that in this "world-wide process" of self-reflection and rebuilding "the fate and development of the small part of the Indian people who live in the USA and Canada, that is, in those lands that are the most advanced in technology, organization, and perhaps in general," are particularly important. These "small groups of Indians," she explained, "must, in a few centuries and under the pressure of a terrible defeat, move from the stone age to the atomic age," and that effort had given them a critical perspective and distance. They have, she explained, the ability to "see us," in "the middle of our own development," from "outside" of that process. They have the ability, through their observations, to "identify the fractures" and the problems in that development, and thus, she argued "it would be very fruitful to speak to each other and listen to each other before it is too late."[125] Moreover, because they came "out of a prehistory and prehistorical democracy, in which they already mastered the special connection between individuality and community," American Indians were of particular importance for East Germany. People in the GDR, she wrote, were supposed to be engaged in "developing their own personalities without becoming egoists" and learning to "work with and for the whole" of society.[126] From her perspective, some American Indians still knew how to do that, and thus building up relations with them in order to learn from them was critical for this new state's future.

While Welskopf-Henrich clearly sought to harness what she had learned about American Indians and what she hoped to learn from them to improve conditions in this new German state, little of what she said about American Indians was particular to East Germany: not her focus on their heroic nature, their efforts at resistance, the connections between the American Indians' and the Germans' tribal character, or even the ways in which she identified their putative insights into coping with modern technological society. Because of her personal biography, however, because of her dedication to communism, her privileged position in the GDR, and her membership in the SED, it would be easy to criticize her actions, to undercut her achievements by painting her with a red brush in order to draw more attention to the limitations of the political system she chose to embrace rather than the implications of her actions and her successes. That is a common hazard of historical inquiry framed by political periodization.

Placed in a broader context, however, her biography reveals a set of interconnections that transcend geographic and chronological borders, and which she drew on and extended as she wrote her novels and made sense of her world. There is a striking dialogical relationship between her thoughts on American history and her experiences under National Socialism. Repeatedly in her collected papers we find reminiscences of her efforts to write that first book, *Die Söhne der großen Bärin*, which she completed in several drafts during the 1930s and 1940s but never felt was truly finished until she was faced with an exceptional crisis, forcing her to make difficult decisions in war-torn Berlin, and introducing her to individuals who seemed to embody precisely those heroic characteristics she imagined were most necessary for the Indians in her novel—as well as the people around her.

Her notion of the collective efforts Indian tribes required to resist the overwhelming powers of American capitalism and imperialism in the prairies of the nineteenth century informed her evaluations of the kinds of solidarity and resistance she discovered among the Sachsenhausen communists; those experiences in turn helped her rethink how she cast the characters in her first book and the others that followed. She recalls in her correspondence during the decade after the war devising plans for getting food to camp inmates while reading the autobiography of a Blackfoot chieftain who describes his struggles to survive persecution.[127] Each experience informed the other, and the kind of integrity required in both crisis situations seemed to her, but also to others, to be embodied in the man she helped escape and hide in the rubble, Rudolf Welskopf. The artist Hans Grundig, another inmate in Sachsenhausen, later described Welskopf in his memoir as "medium-sized, strong, with a face that, in its deliberateness and calm, always reminded me of an Indian chief. With his narrow, dark eyes, with the taut and almost colliding eyebrows, he resembled an Inca, whose word carried much weight with his tribe."[128]

Those characteristics, which both Welskopf-Henrich and Grundig had read about and imagined in their childhoods during the imperial period, which both believed to have witnessed in this man during the Nazi era, and which she felt she should emulate during her illegal actions at the end of the war and in the rest of her life,[129] became embodied in her novels' protagonists, and later in the living American Indians she sought to assist. In turn, the incredible success of those novels and the striking appeal of these American Indian activists across both East and West Germany and over several decades demonstrates the widespread and lasting attraction of the values and morals they represented. We know that not simply through the sheer number of editions of her books but also from the literally thousands of letters in her collected papers from a vast assortment of readers who articulate in clear text the joint reception, even consensus, across the political divide. The implication, of course, is that the meanings of these encounters in the 1960s were scripted decades earlier and drew on the revision of persistent tropes that retained their strength and salience across a broad span of years and stark political divisions.

Perhaps most suggestive, then, is the question her biography poses about how scholars narrate history, and the ways we might harness the reoccurring patterns, enduring characteristics, and consistencies that one finds in her biography to rethink the process of history, not just the repeated instrumentalization of American Indians. The transformation of her subject positions, that is, her own sense of self, during the crises of the final war years demonstrates the critical impact of experience on both her worldviews and her contributions to the century-old German discourse on American Indians.

But the war did not constitute a rupture for either, and that is the critical point. Instead, the war was a moment of shifting contexts in which actions and ideas coalesced in new ways, quickly regrouping before clear social and political structures reemerged—as they always do. But her interests in American Indians, their common use as a vehicle for embodying optimal human characteristics, and even many of those characteristics themselves retained their salience for her and many other Germans through a kind of synthesis for which those moments of crisis offered little deterrence and which historical analysis ignores at great peril.

CHAPTER 6

Race, Character, and Masculinity
before and after Hitler

On 7 July 1959, the *Süddeutsche Zeitung* gleefully reported the burning of three thousand books in a public square in Munich. The bonfire took place toward the conclusion of a successful "Indian-Exhibition" in Munich's Old Botanical Garden. About one thousand people, including U.S. military officers and public school officials, attended the incineration of these "bad books about Indians," while the muscular and dexterous U.S. Army sergeant Silkirtis Nichols, also known as Buffalo Child Long Lance, danced by the bonfire in full regalia. Organized by the Munich Cowboy Club, the books were obtained largely through children, who were encouraged to collect them for a reward. The most ambitious, such as Rudolf Wittmann, who committed 240 books to the flames, were allowed to ride the club's horses, offered a selection of "better books," and given free entry to the Indian exhibition, which had already attracted twenty thousand visitors.[1]

The mind reels at the spectacle of Nichols, a black man who claims a Choctaw/Cherokee heritage, dancing near a bonfire in which Germans publicly burned "bad books," while U.S. military personnel and the city's public school officials looked on. Capitalizing on Germans' well-known affinities for American Indians, the U.S. military command targeted West German hobbyist groups during its efforts to improve German-American relations immediately after World War II, and American Indian servicemen were encouraged during this period to take part in the hobbyists' activities. Particularly in Munich, the connections between Americans and the hobbyists were especially strong. Nichols was incredibly well received at this and other hobby clubs. He took part in many of their outreach activities, traveled with them to the annual gathering of West German clubs, and became a favorite of the hobby-

FIGURE 25. Burning "bad books" in Munich while Buffalo Child Long Lance (Silkirtis Nichols) dances in regalia. From "Feuer und Flamme für Schundheftl," *Süddeutscher Zeitung* 214 (7 September 1959). (Stadtarchiv München)

ist movement during the following decades. Nichols, in fact, felt so at home in Germany that he chose to remain as a kind of professional Indian. He became a fixture at hobbyist gatherings, public events, and Western shows into the twenty-first century. In 2009, well over eighty years old, he was still dancing on the German powwow circuit and at myriad other events.

It is hard to know what is more striking: U.S. military officers and West German school officials participating in a book burning in postwar Germany, the fact that an American service man became the darling of the ever-growing Indian hobbyist movement in West and eventually also East Germany, or the detail that Germany's favorite American redskin had black skin and very few people seemed to either notice or care. Indeed, in the case of Nichols, his physical presence, dancing talent, and character clearly trumped his phenotype and made the obscurity of his origins and the color of his skin all but immaterial. This has much to tell us about the relationship between notions of race, character, and masculinity long before and after Hitler.

American Indians and German-American Relations in West Germany

While I was working through the scrapbooks and other materials connected to Buffalo Bill's travels through Germany at the Harold McCracken Research Library in Cody Wyoming, the librarian asked if I was interested in the Charles Belden files. I had never heard of him. The cowboy photogra-

FIGURE 26. A postwar gathering of twenty-three West German hobby clubs in the Black Forest near Freiburg in 1953. More than four hundred people attended. (Charles Josiah Belden Collection, Harold McCracken Research Library, Buffalo Bill Historical Center, Cody Wyo.)

pher of Wyoming, however, had heard of the hobbyists, and during the late 1950s he had traveled to southern Germany in search of Western enthusiasts in Bavaria and Württemberg. During his visit, he took stunning pictures of their members, their clubhouses, and their encampments, including the large annual meeting of hobbyist clubs that occurred each summer in West Germany. Enamored with these Germans and their pursuits, he became a member of the Munich Cowboy Club, collected copies of their journals, flyers for different events, and bits of historical information about the history and purposes of their activities.

Unaware that the clubs had been so active directly following the war, or that the U.S. military had taken such a shine to them, I was particularly entranced by a hand-drawn flyer, produced and distributed in Munich, which announced an upcoming powwow on 9 July 1959 at the Munich American High School Auditorium under the auspices of Major General Paul A. Gavan, the acting commander of the Southern Area Command (SACom), and Major General Lloyd R. Moses, the former commander of SACom and, as I later learned, a Rosebud Sioux. The event included a variety of exhibitions, mostly dances, from a combination of German hobbyists and U.S. servicemen, including Silkirtis Nichols.[2]

Even without the context of the book burning that occurred days before the powwow, the notion of such high-ranking members of the American military sponsoring powwows in Cold War Germany enticed; but it was unclear how best to pursue it. Shortly afterward, during a trip to the Nebraska State Archives in Lincoln, archivist John Carter, after looking at a copy of the Munich flyer, suggested I speak with Charles Trimble. Trimble, a Lakota who was raised on Pine Ridge, was (among other things) the principal founder of the American Indian Press Association in 1969, the executive director of the National Congress of American Indians from 1972 to 1978, as well as a board member of the Nebraska State Historical Society and its president for three years. He also served in the U.S. Army, and he lived just down the highway in Omaha.

Trimble was incredibly helpful. After politely listening to my general description of Germans' affinities for American Indians and my experiences in Wyoming and Nebraska, he responded with some amazement to the copy of the flyer I presented to him. Yes, he told me, he was familiar with such events, which were fairly common when he was stationed in Germany. In fact, he had drawn the flyer I was showing him some forty years earlier, and he had taken part in the dances. He was listed among the participants on the second page by his Lakota name: Chun-Sha-Sah, Red Willow.[3] As he scanned the list of participants at the powwow he also remembered Silkirtis Nichols as "a black man who was an incredible dancer," and he recalled with some pleasure the many times he had interacted with Munich's hobbyists. He provided me with details about some of the people in the pictures I had located in Wyoming, and he explained that he had very much enjoyed their company.

The history of Germany during the years directly following World War II is seldom written as a time of pleasure or leisure. Historians generally characterize the immediate postwar period as one devastated by radical cultural, political, and social ruptures and defined by Germans' desperate instability,

FIGURE 27. Buffalo Child Long Lance among German hobbyists during a meeting of West German clubs. (Courtesy of Wolfgang Seifert)

their poverty, their consuming guilt, the "rubble women" picking through the skeletal cities, families without men, the emasculation of so many men who managed to survive, and the overwhelmingly depressing character of society at that time.[4] Nevertheless, amid that social, political, and economic wreckage many men—some with and some without their families—held on to a cultural continuity by quickly reorganizing into these peculiar social groups and spending large sums of evidently available money on meticulously constructed American Indian outfits made of materials that are even now difficult to obtain. They also printed journals about American Indians in their basements and kitchens; they traveled back and forth across the disjointed, occupied German states to ever-larger meetings, and they had, by all accounts, a lot of fun.

By 1948, Munich's hobbyists had already begun reconstituting their club and were meeting in the forests outside of the city to engage in their activities, and by 1951 their meetings were again attracting thousands of guests; two years later they celebrated the fortieth anniversary of their club with great fanfare.[5] In Berlin, the arrival of the American Berlin Brigade excited the surviving hobbyists' interests, and they quickly returned to their activities in response to the American presence. In Freiburg as well, survivors began meeting again in 1948, quickly reconstituted their clubs, and by 1959 they boasted more than four hundred members.[6] Similarly, Ernst Ditzuleit, who was born in 1892 in Bühl Baden, served as a pilot in World War I, and became a homeopath in the 1920s and an active *Indianist* in Karlsruhe during the 1930s, helped to establish the Dakota-Club Karlsruhe in 1948. He became its leader, and then helped his counterparts in other cities create the West German–wide International Club of Indian Friends in 1951, and directed its first publication, *Der Indianerfreund* and its sequel, the *Dakota-Scout*, which was founded in 1952.[7] Some twenty or more similar journals were established across West Germany during those years until they slowly merged in 1962 into a single primary publication titled *Kalumet*.[8]

These were activities that caught the eyes of the U.S. military's high command. Reaching out to the hobbyists and encouraging American Indian soldiers to interact with them was part of a broader effort to promote German-American relations in the new Cold War context in which American strategic interests necessitated transforming former enemies into friends and presenting the U.S. Army as something other than an occupying power. Their efforts were wide ranging. For example, they eagerly set up sports associations, such as the American Rod and Gun Club for U.S. servicemen, which would allow them to interact with German hunting and fishing societies and help them develop closer personal relationships with Germans around social events.[9] Once established, the U.S. military tracked those and other associations throughout the 1950s, producing ongoing reports about civilian affairs in Germany and stressing to their commanders across West Germany the need to encourage the kinds of socialization that would transform Germans and Americans into "one international family." That, the military high command hoped, would allow their "mutual problems" to be solved with greater ease.[10]

These were not covert activities. They were open efforts, and along with the official military reports on German-American activities in the government records, one also finds a considerable amount of German press that explicitly publicized the American goals. In 1955, for example, *Der Spiegel*, one of West Germany's leading magazines, ran an article that explained how this international socializing was good for everyone and noted that "Lt Col Frederick A. Zehrer, Psychologist of the U.S. Army in Germany, requested the wives of all U.S. Officers stationed in Germany to get into closer social contact with the Germans. They should not," he warned, "exclusively participate in social U.S. club meetings."[11]

According to Maria Höhn, these were also well-coordinated activities. The military high command made improving German-American relations a priority. It instructed its commanders that these relations "'be nurtured to the highest possible degree.'"[12] To that end, "a European Command board on German-American relations was established in 1950, and by August of that year a program aimed at improving the relationship between the troops and the German civilian population was initiated." After 1952, "military post commanders, instead of the Land Relations Officers (LROs) of the High Commissioner's Office, assumed responsibility for direct relations with German officials."[13] At the same time, the Department of State made its own inroads into facilitating these developments by creating and funding the so-called America Houses in many German cities, which promoted an astonishing number of activities. Indeed, as Alexander Stephan remarks, "no other country in Europe was blanketed after 1945 with such a network of American cultural institutions (Amerikahäuser): nowhere else were there comparable programs of the translation and dissemination of American books and films."[14]

All of this was good news for the hobbyists and other friends of American Indians, who flocked to the libraries in the America Houses and eagerly sought out U.S. servicemen for information about America and American Indians. In Munich, those servicemen were sent directly to the hobbyists. Nichols danced repeatedly at their events; three thousand people showed up to watch him one evening in August 1959.[15] Just as many attended a rodeo the next month, hosted by the hobbyists together with Native American servicemen who had been issued free passes from fall maneuvers to attend.[16] Lieutenant Colonel Charles E. Gilbert, chief of the U.S. press corps provided them with western-themed movies to screen at their club,[17] and Charles Belden and others publicized the club's activities in the Army's newspaper, *The Stars and Stripes*, to let American soldiers know where to go.[18]

This was not limited to Munich. A few months later in Düsseldorf, the Sioux-Nevada Club put on a public exhibition about the hobby with the support of the American General Council.[19] It set up a display of crafts, including "warrior costumes of Sioux-Indians," which, according to the local press, "the members of the Sioux-Nevada Club had crafted so well over many months of work that they could not be distinguished from actual Indian pieces." There was a large feather bonnet of a chief, "the leather dress of a squaw, toma-

FIGURE 28. Two German hobbyists captured by Belden near a Mercedes 300D with a Wyoming license plate. Attaching plates from Western states remains a tradition among German powwow participants to this day. (Charles Josiah Belden Collection, Harold McCracken Research Library, Buffalo Bill Historical Center, Cody Wyo.)

hawks, peace pipes, moccasins, bags decorated with bead work," and more. In "a large cabinet," stood the "masterwork of an enthusiastic craftsperson"; it was a model of an Aztec temple produced with exacting detail and accompanied by two pictures created by the Maya Indian Nan Cuz, who was living in Hamburg at the time and had attended several hobbyist meetings. Her work was also displayed in Hamburg's Museum für Völkerkunde and in similar locations in Munich, Kiel, Berlin, and Paris.[20]

Americans initiated such exhibitions as well. In Essen later that same year, for example, the America House set up an exhibit on "Indian traditions," and Louis Warrior, a Shawnee, took part in the opening.[21] The following year Leonid Massine choreographed a display of American Indian dances hosted by the America House in Berlin together with a more general exhibition titled "The Indians of North America."[22] Germans flocked to see them both. A few years later, when the America House in Berlin also sponsored an exhibition of around seventy-nine of George Catlin's famous paintings of Plains Indians,[23] it too was a raging success.

FIGURE 29. Performers from the St. Johns School in Berlin.
(Courtesy of Wolfgang Seifert)

During the same period, the Berlin-Brigade conceived of the German-American Folk Festival, which became an annual attraction in Berlin and a site for the re-creation of Western scenes, such as the 1963 Santa Fe–themed exposition in which hobbyists from Berlin populated the re-creation of a part of the Taos Pueblo. Navajo were flown in from the United States to demonstrate the fashioning of silver jewelry and wool rugs, and six young dancers from the St. John's Indian School in Arizona gave daily performances.[24] Such performances became recurring events.[25]

While the America Houses in Essen and Berlin eagerly created exhibitions of American Indian art and culture for Germans, the U.S. Army helped the Munich Cowboy Club build a house of its own. In July 1961, after American bulldozers, Army engineers, and members of the Third U.S. Pioneer Battalion had cleared out a space for the Munich Cowboy Club's new ranch house, the Lord High Mayor of Munich attended the ceremonial emplacement of the building's cornerstone together with Major General J. F. R. Seitz, the new head of SACom, a number of his officers, and Sergeant Nichols, who again danced at the ceremony in regalia. Both German and American military newspapers celebrated these events.[26] The following spring the U.S. military

FIGURE 30. Buffalo Child Long Lance dancing on 22 July 1961 at the ceremony in honor of the Munich Cowboy Club's new clubhouse. In attendance are Munich's High Lord Mayor and high-ranking German and American military officers. (Stadtarchiv München)

helped the hobbyists set up their twelfth annual council meeting outside of Mannheim. Nichols danced there as well.[27]

Clearly, West German hobbyists never missed a beat after the rupture of war; they quickly threw themselves back into their passions for American Indians, and the U.S. military's eagerness to exploit those passions made good geopolitical sense. But why were people like Nichols so popular and so enthusiastic? That answer has much to do with ongoing transnational assumptions about American Indians' character and the racialized opportunities that emerged through the U.S. military's efforts in two world wars.

Race and American Indian Servicemen in Germany

Like many African American soldiers, American Indian servicemen noted the greater freedom they experienced in postwar Germany than in the United States. Colin Powell famously remarked in his autobiography *My American Journey* that West Germany in 1958 was a revelation for him and many others: for "black GIs, especially those out of the South," he wrote, West "Germany was a breath of freedom—they could go where they wanted, eat where they wanted, and date whom they wanted, just like other people." Moreover, "the dollar was strong, the beer was good, and the German people friendly, since we were all that stood between them and the Red hordes. War, at least the Cold War in Germany," he quipped, "was not hell."[28] These were common observations.[29] Other African American servicemen made similar remarks, and so too did many American Indians. People such as the Lakota artist Oscar Howe, who had lived under such strident racism in South Dakota, were surprised to find much less of it in the U.S. military than in American hometowns, and even less among the Germans emerging from the twentieth century's greatest racial state. Indeed, Howe married a German woman he met there directly after the war.

Historian Heidi Fehrenbach has argued that West Germans' reception of people of color after World War II was mixed. Certainly, there were many like Howe, Nichols, and Powell whose interactions with German society were refreshingly simple and generally pleasant, especially when aided by their uniforms and dollars. There were, however, also negative reactions from Germans to the presence of African American soldiers. Indeed, the U.S. military showed enough concern with Germans' occasional comparisons between African American soldiers and the controversial African colonial troops the French had used as occupation forces following World War I that they closely watched the interactions between African American troops and the German population.

Indeed, the U.S. military dedicated itself to monitoring the German press and created extensive collections of German news clippings about the presence of African American soldiers in their towns, and they also generated lists of "incidents" between Germans and these soldiers. The extent of those collections, now held in the National Archives in College Park, Maryland, testify to their commanders' concerns.[30] As Fehrenbach notes, the reports of incidents swing between two poles: sometimes they include angry discussions of African American soldiers misbehaving, sometimes the focus is on sexual interactions, promiscuity, and accusations of rape, but just as often there are arguments about the mistreatment of African American soldiers by the U.S. military, condemnations of Jim Crow routines, racial segregation, and unequal punishments for misdemeanors and higher crimes.

Most striking, however, is that the problem of "race after Hitler," as Fehrenbach terms it, appears to have been so black and white. If discussions of African Americans and the mixed-race children that resulted from their unions with German women dominated the discourse on race in West Germany during the first decades after the war, the other races within the U.S. military are conspicuously absent. This is true in both the U.S. military records and the German press accounts. Indeed, one searches in vain through the files in College Park for racialized discussions of American Indians, Asian Americans, or Latinos interacting with German civilians. Nor can members of these groups be found listed according to their race in the files devoted to "incidents." In all of these records, black soldiers are identified by their skin color, but brown, red, and yellow soldiers generally are not.

To a certain degree, these records reflect a bureaucratic distinction created by the U.S. military's own policies on segregation rather than a sensitivity to questions of race. The segregated army that the United States sent to fight the Nazis was divided into two categories, black and white, or rather, black and everyone else. Soldiers such as Oscar Howe, as well as his Asian American and Latino counterparts, certainly carried the distinctions they knew in their civilian lives with them, even if those were often transformed when they put on their uniforms. Still, there is no question that they were integrated equally into white units and allowed to take part in all aspects of military activities and to rise into the commanding ranks.[31] Moreover, in the unique case of American Indians, the racial category they inhabited, and the stereotypes associated with it, gained a different resonance in military contexts. In many cases, the racial prejudices they experienced shifted from negative to positive, in the sense that their value for military operations was often judged to be superior to that of other Americans, either black, white, or anything else. Thus, American Indians were not only accepted into the ranks of the military along with white soldiers; they were eagerly embraced.

This was already true during World War I, when American Indians fought Germans in Europe for the first time. In 1917 the government, and especially the Office of Indian Affairs, deemed the integration of American Indians into the ranks of the military as both beneficial to their effort to assimilate American Indians into white society and advantageous for the American war effort. Some politicians advocated for segregated units of American Indians; but the historical precedents were weak. There had been a few short-lived attempts to create units composed solely of American Indians at the end of the nineteenth century, but they were disbanded. In stark contrast, the integration of many American Indian scouts into the U.S. military, where they served effectively and eagerly in exchange for horses, weapons, food, clothes, and wages equal to that of other cavalrymen, was well known. Such service and income had given many American Indians prominence in their communities during the nineteenth century, and when America entered World War I, many American Indian men sought to enlist for similar reasons.[32]

The fact that a majority of these men were not American citizens, however, led to bureaucratic hurdles and special categorizations that persisted through World War I and into the interwar era.[33] So too did the somewhat ambiguous racial categorization of many people who claimed American Indian identities. For example, draft quotas issued to the states during World War I were divided between black and white troops. That segregation led to debates about who was and was not black, as well as who could be counted white or American Indian. For quota purposes, American Indians and Mexican Americans were counted as whites, while African Americans alone were counted as blacks.

This was true even in North Carolina, where the Lumbee Indians had long been considered colored.[34] Because of the context of the new draft quotas and the disparity in the size of the large colored population versus the small white population in North Carolina, however, the white government officials recognized it as expedient to reclassify the Lumbee as white when fulfilling their quotas so that men from Lumbee communities could offset the number of previously recognized white North Carolinians who could be drafted. That tactical political maneuver thus allowed the Lumbee's racial categorization in World War I to shift them from the diminished category of segregated black soldier to the enhanced category of celebrated American Indian warrior. It also ensured more of their members would be sent to the war.[35]

Some ten thousand American Indians ultimately served in World War I, taking part in every major engagement, and both the American and the German military observed them with great interest and in ways that set the tone for decades.[36] Both assumed that American Indians would be formidable, even exceptional soldiers, because they possessed talents inherent in warrior societies. As Thomas Britten notes, "Unlike African American soldiers, who were frequently held in contempt and struggled to earn the respect of their white peers" during World War I, American "Indian soldiers entered the army with a degree of respect and acceptance already."[37]

Indeed, the secretary of the National American Indian Memorial Association, Joseph Kossuth Dixon, argued directly during World War I that American Indians had all the qualities of a natural soldier: "strength, courage, intelligence, loyalty, power of endurance, stoicism, sagacity, persistence and relentlessness of purpose."[38] In essence, Dixon and many others stereotypically considered Indians to be "'bloodthirsty warriors,' particularly eager to fight."[39]

There is some evidence that German officers agreed. At the end of the war, Lieutenant John Eddy conducted a now famous survey of American army officers concerning the performance of American Indian soldiers under their commands.[40] In his report, he cited captured documents that revealed the Germans' "appreciation of the value of the Indian as night worker and scout," including orders from a colonel of the Ninety-Seventh Landwehr Division "stating on account of there being numbers of American Indians used as scouts and runners among the American forces on his front, which he characterized as being greatly superior to the North African natives used by a certain specified French regiment, that additional German snipers be detailed to specifically pick off these dangerous men." Similarly, he noted that "the Germans closely questioned a captured American officer in the St. Mihiel drive, showing much concern to learn the numbers and disposition of American Indians among our forces." Faced with American Indians, many German soldiers felt a sense of despair because they too believed in American Indians' inherent martial abilities.[41]

Such characterizations of American Indians as exceptional, formidable soldiers continued into World War II, where their eager participation was celebrated even more than it had been during the first conflict. Politicians, such as Secretary of the Interior Harold L. Ickes, again found it useful to assert their "uncanny ability to get over any terrain at night," their "endurance," their "feeling for combat," and their "enthusiasm for fighting." Such arguments spread across the military ranks as well, and many, such as Major Lee Gilstrap, who had trained more than two thousand American Indian recruits in Oklahoma, argued that "the Indian is the best damn soldier in the Army." Boasting "long sleek muscles," they had superior endurance, an acute sense of perception, and a facility for bayoneting, shooting, tracking, and scouting. "Even General Douglas MacArthur commented on American Indian capabilities. 'As a warrior the Indian's fame is worldwide.'"[42]

Thus, there was a striking consistency across the two world wars in the stereotype of American Indians as formidable soldiers and the willingness of the American high command to believe in those stereotypes and exploit them. Because of their conviction, Allied commanders sought out American Indian soldiers for particularly challenging and daring tasks. And because the Axis troops and their commanders shared those convictions as well, they found the presence of American Indian troops intimidating and held them up as a standard of ferocity and skill. Indeed, because of American Indians' reputation, Adolf Hitler used them as a point of comparison when warning his eastern front divisions that "the Soviets fight like Indians."[43]

The other critical continuity was that American Indians were almost always inducted into white units during World War II. Sometimes there were tensions at the local level, when, for example, American Indians from tribes such as the Mississippi Band of the Choctaws, the Rappahannock of Virginia, and some North Carolina Cherokee, after being sent to black induction stations, refused to go; some faced penalties for their protests, while others were able to have their cases redressed. Overwhelmingly, however, American Indians of all shades and colors were placed in white units, and by most accounts they were well received because they were believed to possess stereotypically superior martial abilities.[44] Those continuities provided men such as Silkirtis Nichols with fantastic racialized opportunities: through military service in Europe they could transcend their phenotypes and their positions as second-class American citizens and become the embodiment of superior warriors, even quintessential men in war-torn Europe.

On Passing

"In the early decades of the twentieth century," as Philip Deloria reminds us, "Indian people opened a small window of opportunity in which they might be valued and included in American culture." Faced with that opportunity, "it should come as no surprise that black and Latino athletes sometimes passed as Indians" or that the "dark–skinned black tricksters like Buffalo Child Long Lance and Two Moons Meridas should claim redness rather than whiteness as their entrée into American culture and society."[45] Deloria, however, is not referring to Silkirtis Nichols. Decades before he took the sobriquet of Buffalo Child Long Lance, another man, Sylvester Clark Long, who came from North Carolina, was part Lumbee on his mother's side and part Cherokee, white, and black on his father's side, took up that same name. Classified as black or colored in North Carolina, but possessing facial features that many whites recognized as American Indian, Long began 'playing Indian' in a Wild West show. That opportunity became a means for improving his social position. To that end, he also worked to improve his knowledge of his Cherokee background and learned to speak some of the language from other Cherokee participants in the show. That knowledge in turn helped him gain admittance to the famous Carlisle school, where he was a classmate of Robert Geronimo and the athlete Jim Thorpe, and where he changed his last name to Long Lance. He graduated at the top of his class in 1912, attended several military academies, and petitioned President Woodrow Wilson for admission to West Point. In 1916, however, he left the United States, enlisted in the Canadian Expeditionary Forces, and was wounded twice while fighting with white troops in France. Like Nichols decades later, he too became a sergeant.

When Long Lance returned to Canada in 1919, he took up a position as a journalist in Calgary, learned much about life on the Plains, visited several American Indian reserves, and wrote essays for newspapers and magazines that exposed injustices and abuses there. Living in Calgary, he built on his American Indian identity while playing down his blackness in a society that discouraged black immigration from the United States. Gradually, he began enhancing his biography, claiming at first to be a Cherokee from Oklahoma while acting as an advocate for American Indian issues. He openly criticized Canada's Indian Act, and the Blood tribe, a part of the Blackfoot Confederation, adopted him in recognition for his efforts, giving him the ceremonial name Buffalo Child, which he used continually thereafter. He wrote many essays in journals such as *Macleans, Cosmopolitan,* even *Good Housekeeping,* and by the time he published his autobiography in 1927 he presented himself as a full-blooded Blackfoot, a chief, and the son of a great chief. That text contained much hyperbole and many untruths. Nevertheless, it was a tremendous success, and it made him an international star. As a result, he was perhaps the most famous American Indian of his day, and because of his stardom, he lectured for high premiums, gained wealth, attracted wealthy women, became popular in the New York party scene, was the first American Indian admitted to the prestigious Explorer's Club in New York City, and starred in the film *The Silent Enemy: An Epic of the American Indian,* which boasted a cast made up almost exclusively of American Indians.[46]

Throughout that rise he also continued to advocate for American Indian rights. His stardom, however, initiated his downfall. Investigations were launched into his ancestry. His father Joe Long, who had been raised as a slave and had not known his parents, was located working as a janitor in North Carolina. After his background was revealed to be mixed and unsavory, many of Buffalo Child's high society friends abandoned him. The short story writer Irvin S. Cobb remarked most explicitly (and famously): "To think that we had him here in this house. . . . We're so ashamed! We entertained a nigger!"[47] The pressures of these revelations led to his suicide in a friend's home in 1932 in Arcadia, California. All of his wealth was left to St. Paul's Indian Residential School on the Blood Reserve, which supported scholarships for American Indian children.

Many scholars have condemned Sylvester Long as an imposter.[48] More recently, however, some such as Eva Marie Garroutte have noted that the greatest of the many secrets revealed through his biography was not the inaccuracies he placed within it but the fact that so much of the American population possesses a multiracial ancestry that has long been underplayed or overlooked.[49] Long may have been passing as a Blackfoot and did fabricate a new biography as he left his father's home and rose in celebrity, but there was no doubt that some of his ancestors were American Indians. One could spend considerable time sorting out the truths and falsehoods about that biography in an attempt to classify him properly, to place him into one or another ethnic or racial box, but that would miss the larger point. As Garroutte argues, his biography underscores that, "while individuals certainly formulate ideas about their race, it is the larger society that ultimately invests their assertions with legitimacy—or refuses to do so."[50] What Buffalo Child Long Lance was able to achieve tells us as much about North Americans of all colors as about the man himself.

If this was the case with the first Buffalo Child Long Lance, it was also the case with the second. Regardless of their varied origins, American Indian servicemen were consistently endowed with a collection of admirable characteristics that came to dominate their identities and the identities of anyone who was willing to embrace the role of an American Indian in the service. Much like Sylvester Long decades earlier, Silkirtis Nichols was one of those individuals who was able to harness social conventions and ideals to move from his mixed-race background and a world of prejudice to a purified identity as an essential Indian worthy of great admiration. Unlike Long, however, Nichols has been able to hold on to that position for over fifty years by staying in Germany throughout most of the postwar era.

It helped that Nichols, much like Long, looks the part. He too has the strong facial features associated with American Indians in the popular imagination, and just like Long, who was termed "a captivating picture of chiseled manliness,"[51] Nichols's physical prowess is well known. During his time in the military from 1942 to 1963 Nichols measured 1.97 meters, possessed those "long sleek muscles" that Major Lee Gilstrap had described when characterizing American Indian soldiers, and demonstrated impressive strength and endurance. Indeed, he set a significant high jump record at the Military

Olympics in Berlin in 1947, and the strength in his legs continued to impress audiences during his dance performances over the next fifty years.

He also has talent as a performer and was soon able to combine his military background with the kinds of performances that had so endeared White Buffalo Man and other show Indians to German audiences during the interwar years. In that sense, his role in the U.S. military's overtures to German hobbyists was quite fortuitous. It allowed him to transfer almost seamlessly from a position as an American Indian serviceman and representative of German-American relations, to American Indian performer at large in West Germany. Indeed, after leaving the army in 1963 he played in the West German theater production "Annie Get Your Gun" for several years, playing the famous Lakota Sitting Bull at one point, and beginning in 1965 he took part in the Karl May Festspiel (open air theater) in Bad Segeberg; later, in the 1980s, he appeared in a similar production in Elspe. In 1966 he also took over the position of director of the Karl-May-Museum in Bamberg, which was created after the Karl May Press was forced to move out of East Germany, and he maintained that position until 1971.

During the years when he was a museum director, he also traveled to Leipzig three times, where East German hobbyists and audiences eagerly awaited his presence. On one occasion, the SED forbid him from dancing in East Germany, and one defender of the controversial decision argued that he was no American Indian but the director of a West German museum, and "a black man" rather than "a redskin." On another occasion, a group of Brule Indians in the U.S. military also argued that "he was a black rather than an Indian." Such opinions, however, were seldom voiced and quickly rebutted. So many Germans deemed Nichols's person and actions to be "so typical of an Indian" that he remained, as the *Indianermagazin* commented in 1993, "probably the best-known Indian in Germany," and by then "an unquestioned authority" on all things Indian.[52]

The displacement inherent in such discussions of race, skin tone, and character is striking for several reasons. Most importantly, it contradicts the fact that racial mixing had long been common among American Indian tribes before the outbreak of World War I. It was only with the institution of the modern, bureaucratic efforts at categorization (which continue to plague many tribes today) that blood quantum and ancestry began to be calculated mathematically.[53] Louis Warren notes this irony in his book on Buffalo Bill, arguing that Cody's show demonstrated both clear examples of racial mixing and an underlying message of white supremacy: there were many mixed-blood cowboys with Indian families on display in the encampments and

FIGURE 31. Buffalo Child Long Lance in his prime, after twenty years of performing in West Germany. (Karl Markus Kreis Postcard Collection)

even on the program. Warren notes that these facts strike some observers as contradictory because they fail to realize that "racial identities are cultural artifacts which masquerade as 'natural' categories." Racial identities are "an ongoing deception that the public practices every day," and which are most quickly unveiled in contexts like Buffalo Bill's Show, in which one can so easily scrutinize both the players and their masquerade.

Furthermore, "the ability of some people to 'pass,' to deceive the public into believing they are of one race when their ancestry supposedly consigns them to another," is considered dangerous by many, because it can subvert "the supposedly 'natural boundaries that defined America's racial hierarchies."[54] That fear of subversion is what made the truth about the first Buffalo Child's biography so disconcerting to his friends in high society; it was the counterpoint to the appealing and reassuring fiction of his crafted biography as a pure, royal Blackfoot. The lack of that fear of subversion in West Germany is one of the central reasons why the second Buffalo Child seldom faced such problems.

Moreover, across most of the past two centuries racial mixing was common among many American Indians because such racial distinctions made little sense to them. For example, among the Lakotas, as Warren has written, "the only thing that made marrying white women a strange concept was white hostility. Race was less a factor in Lakota identity than residence and behavior." This was true, for example, with the marriage of the Austrian nurse Louise Rieneck to the Lakota Standing Bear during his 1889 trip to Europe with Buffalo Bill. What she learned, and what the Standing Bear family demonstrated after she moved to the Pine Ridge Reservation in 1891, was that "by living among Lakota, and acting Lakota, one became Lakota." Indeed, as Warren remarks, many American Indian performers met white women in Europe, and some of them married. Rather than shattering a division between white and red, however, the Lakota warrior and Austrian nurse acted within a much older context of "a real frontier history of mixed blood" that "typified relations on the northern Plains for many people throughout the nineteenth century."[55] Thus, as Warren argues, "in some ways, Standing Bear's marriage to Louise was traditional."[56]

In addition, racial mixing was never limited to white and red; there were many black Indians as well in the United States,[57] and Germans accepted other black men as representatives of American Indians long before Nichols arrived in Germany. In 1929, for example, newspapers in Germany's major cities trumpeted the presence of the putatively 107-year-old Big Chief White Horse Eagle, who together with his white wife, "Queen" Wa-Te-Na, was receiving a royal reception in city halls and expensive hotels in German metropolises. Thousands of curiosity seekers showed up at central train stations when they arrived in each town, and their popularity was so great that Sarrasani, who was always able to detect a profitable opportunity, made a point of organizing a joint meeting between the Big Chief and his Lakota performers.[58]

In Munich, the performance was particularly grand. The Lakotas, surrounded by thousands of fans and accompanied by the American general counsel, greeted the ancient warrior in front of Munich's train station and escorted him to the Regina-Palasthotel, while policemen on horseback kept the crowds at bay. Described in the local papers as "an even deeper copper brown than the other members of his race" who greeted him, the Big Chief was not so big. He was of middle size, and he "hardly made the impression of a 107 year old man." For several months he traveled through Germany, "holding lectures about the history of North American Indian tribes" and meeting with dignitaries and royalty, and he expressed his delight at having arrived in Munich. In the evening, he attended the circus and greeted Germans from the five hundred tribes of American Indians before calling for a future in which all men could be brothers. He then suggested that he would name the Lord High Mayor an honorary chief, which met with great applause. Afterward, the Big Chief moved on to the famous Hofbräuhaus, where he drank profusely.[59]

In 1950 Gustav von Hahnke, the private secretary for Sarrasani, wrote in the 4 April issue of *Spiegel* that Sarrasani was in Bremen when he learned that there was a "105 [*sic*] year old American Indian named Big Chief White Horse Eagle" with his "white squaw, the 'Queen' Wa-Te-Na," in a luxury hotel in Berlin. They negotiated with Edgar von Schmidt-Pauli, who had helped the Big Chief produce a book about life on the Great Plains,[60] and they were able to book him for several venues at two hundred marks a day, plus expenses. "The first bomb exploded," however, "during the press reception at the Hillmann Hotel in Bremen." When White Buffalo Man, "the chief of the Sioux, saw the honorary guest he became pale." "'He is a nigger,' he declared to Mr. Clarence Shultz, who as cowboy directed our Indian troupe." "And in fact it became clear," von Hahnke reported, "that the 'prince' and head chief was no redskin, rather a mixed-race Mexican." "Our Indians were so incensed that they wanted to throw their coffee cups at the head of the pseudo Chief. They threatened to go on strike and did not want to be seen with him." Only by promising the troupe significant numbers of "presents," he explained, was Sarrasani able to convince the Lakotas to participate in the farce without conflict. After several appearances in towns such as Munich, von Hahnke recalled, the Big Chief abandoned a big hotel bill in Berlin under the cover of night and took his trade across the channel to England.[61]

A more famous and competent trickster was Charlie Oskoman, who took part in a number of Karl May pageants in Rathen in 1938. German papers noted that he studied in Paris and had performed in Berlin. Most of his performances, however, had taken place in Paris, where a woman known as Madame Clement, "a French composer who was enamored with 'things Indian,'" had schooled him in being an Indian. She promoted him as Charlie Oskoman, chief of the Yakima, and for years he was quite successful. Indeed, his success impressed the young Molly Spotted Elk, who wrote in her diary that he lived in an apartment that was "'big enough for a soirée.'" Molly, a Penobscot who had performed in the United States with the Miller Brothers 101 Ranch during the 1920s and played the leading female role in *The Silent*

Enemy together with the first Buffalo Child Long Lance, "doubted Oskoman's Indian and artistic authenticity almost immediately." Nevertheless, she recognized his appeal to Parisians and agreed to perform with him repeatedly. Together, "Chief Oskoman and Princess Spotted Elk" entertained in places such as the American Conservatory of Music in Fontainebleau. But already after the rehearsals for this first of many performances together, she noted in her diary that Oskoman "strikes me as a good showman, but ignorant of real Indian art, music, dances and mythology." She studied him closely and her suspicions were confirmed: "saw a picture of his father—typical negro type. Must be from the Carolinas or the southern Atlantic seaboard. . . . He's no more a chief than he is a Yakima . . . but I won't disturb him." Nevertheless, she noted, if he continued to put on airs and make a fuss at rehearsals she would confront him: "If he gets too mouthy, I'll tell him [I know] what he really is."[62] She, like White Buffalo Man, was one of the few people in Europe who had the authority and ability to do that.

Indeed, one of the further ironies of the displacement of racial markers among American Indians in Europe was that despite the great racial mixing among many American Indian tribes, it was often American Indians from reservations who were able and willing to expose the tricksters who were passing. They had more reason for concern, because if these tricksters were no threat to the racial hierarchies at work in Europe, they did have the potential of subverting other American Indians' advantageous positions within those structures. For that reason, people such as White Buffalo Man and his counterparts often reacted strongly against those who threatened their positions even if they did not condemn all tricksters uniformly or denounce all those with black skin.

It is striking, for instance, that Molly Spotted Elk, who worked closely with the first Buffalo Child Long Lance, spent so much time with him socially and professionally during the shooting of *The Silent Enemy*, and whose younger sister became his lover in New York City, was not party to the doubts conveyed by their fellow star in the film, Chauncey Yellow Robe, whose suspicions about Sylvester Long's identity initiated the first investigations into his sordid past.[63] Yet she immediately identified Oskoman as a fraud. The critical difference, it would seem, is that Oskoman did not play his part as competently as Long, nor was he able to harness the same virile masculinity that might make up for his other shortcomings. Indeed, in the case of both Buffalo Childs, the combination of their often-lauded masculinity and character generally trumped any concerns about their skin tone or their mixed race.

Real Men

I stumbled upon the Winnetou Gallery during the summer of 2001 when I was in Nürnberg for a meeting with the director of the city's Toy Museum. Nürnberg still has its old walls and an impressive castle up on a hill in the city center. Since I was early for our meeting, I took a walk up to the castle. When I arrived at its base, I discovered the Winnetou Gallery inside an old black-smith's shop, where the proprietor, Tim Sikyea, a Canadian Denée, claimed to offer Germans access to "real Indian art and culture" through the sale of arts, crafts, and the skills needed to make them.[64] The many brochures lying out in the shop were graced by his photograph: taciturn, shirtless, sporting a bone choker and feathered bonnet, the photo capitalized on a range of stereotypes and clichés about American Indians with which many Germans have been comfortable for more than a century. In addition, however, Tim Sikyea had also taken on a classic characteristic of hobbyist movements.[65] In the production of artifacts, the gendered division of labor among the peoples hobbyists emulate is often lost, as women's tasks become men's pleasures for those men seeking to escape the gender tensions of the modern world.[66] Fol-lowing suit, Tim Sikyea offered clinics where one could learn a range of skills, from how to create authentic musical instruments, to making moccasins, leather clothing (with fringe), and a variety of beadwork—a combination of male and female tasks. His overwhelmingly masculine image, in other words, was flexible even while it remained consistent. That is essential to its appeal.

Much has been made of the breakdown in gender norms and the "crises in masculinity" in Germany during the twentieth century—and with good rea-son.[67] The position of women shifted several times, family relations changed, men recoiled under the burden of their losses in wars and during the eco-nomic crises, and in the postwar era two radically different welfare states were established in the East and West that sent strikingly different signals to their citizens about the roles of men and women in society. Despite these political and social upheavals, however, many conceptions of manliness re-mained salient throughout these crises, even as relations between the sexes and the roles of men in society shifted and changed. Indeed, it is fair to argue that it is the salience of characteristics such as individuality, freedom, wis-dom, and physical and emotional strength in German conceptions of manli-ness that both account for these putative crises and for Germans' persistent fascination with the centuries-old tropes of American Indian masculinity, which Tim Sikyea embraced and people like Silkirtis Nichols embody.

In her oft-cited book *Manliness and Civilization*, Gail Bederman argues that because gender is by definition dynamic and always changing, "change in the gender system—even extensive change—doesn't necessarily imply a 'crisis.'" Indeed, she claims that simply pointing to moments in which "masculinity was in crisis" is problematic, because it "suggests that manhood is a transhistorical category or fixed essence that has its good moments as well as its bad, rather than an ideological construct which is constantly being remade."[68] In essence, for Bederman, masculinity is by definition in perpetual crisis, and there is much to support her position.[69] However, it is precisely because of our growing comfort with the idea that gender is protean, that it is also worth restating the rather unsurprising fact that there are, nevertheless, some persistent characteristics associated with men, masculinity, and manliness that return again and again.[70] And in that sense, perhaps Bederman is also wrong: some elements of masculinity may indeed be transhistorical.[71]

Moreover if, as Bederman argues, the term "masculine" often turns out to be a "rather empty fluid adjective—devoid of moral or emotional meaning,"[72] the character of the American Indian, embodied in people like the two men who took on the name Buffalo Child Long Lance, has proven to have a similar fluidity, one that can simultaneously retain a set of salient "masculine" characteristics while accommodating new ones as concepts of masculinity shift and change around a core set of ideas produced and consumed by women perhaps as much as by men. In that way, the liminal Indian has provided a nice wrapper for a rather fluid category (masculinity), and this seems to have been true for at least a century before the postwar era.[73]

Indeed, the German fascination with American Indians has always been androcentric in character.[74] The general absence of leading female characters in German narratives about American Indians, in fact, is remarkable. It is also consistent throughout nineteenth-century literature, the art of the 1920s and 1930s, the proto-fascist stories written by Fritz Steuben and others, and the films produced in both East and West Germany. It is also not limited to novels and films. Images of men, especially the Plains warrior, that symbiosis of man and nature, dominate the literature produced and consumed by hobbyists since the 1950s as well as the political support groups that spread across both East and West Germany during the 1960s and 1970s.

The consistent return to American Indians by people as diverse as Georg Grosz, Adolf Hitler, and the anti-American and anti-imperialist youths in both East and West Germany could suggest the type of primitivism that many scholars regard as quintessentially modern and essentially imperialist, and which most agree was already quite common among Europeans by the late nineteenth century. As Marianna Torgovnick and others have argued, however, that form of primitivism stems as much from an indictment of civilization's effeminacy among the men who embrace it as from their desire to suspend normative conditions of the Western self.[75]

In contrast, the desires and emotions behind many Germans' obsession with American Indians generally have been much different from what we now expect to find in Saidian Orientalism or Foucauldian explanations of colonial power, which so often stress gendered notions of domination and underscore the role of white frontiersmen.[76] The focus among the German men most attracted to American Indians has long tended to be on emulation rather than possession of an enticing Other; the desire has been to be more like American Indians, or—by implication—to become a more complete man.

At the same time, German men have not been alone in producing and embracing these tropes of American Indian masculinity. Women dominate many of the hobbyist groups in German states such as Saxony, and most of the political support groups in general. And the leading East German authors of texts about American Indians—Eva Lips and Liselotte Welskopf-Henrich—were women, even if their central characters remained men. Indeed, it was Anna Jürgen's award-winning novel *Blauvogel*, so lauded by Hartmut Lutz and many other West German leftists, that best captured this desire to go native and emulate the real men. In *Blauvogel*, the young white hero learns from his American Indian captors to work with rather than against nature, to face pain and discomfort with stoicism, to value cooperation over competition among individuals and groups, to recognize the limits of Western progress and, as his adopted father put it, "to learn to behave like a man and not a paleface."[77] It is a powerful transformation, which, once complete, causes him to reject the incomplete people in white society after he was returned to them by the military and quickly escape back to his American Indian family where he could be a whole man: free of imposed duties and service, free of oppressive social hierarchy, and able to realize the liberty of Tacitus's ancient Germans and to escape the servitude of the modern German *Knecht*.

In the German discourse about American Indians, real men are free men possessed of physical and emotional strength as well as an independent and proud bearing. The exposition of such manly virtues was not unique to books and films produced in the postwar era in either East or West Germany. It is worth recalling Rudolf Cronau's enraptured descriptions of Lakota dancers moving in the firelight at the Standing Rock Reservation in 1881, his delight in the "exquisitely-grown youths" who possessed "the most beautiful and noble builds imaginable." Superb in their bodies, they were also exceptional in their character. Even the older men, such as Sitting Bull and Crow King were termed "visions of pronounced manliness" by Cronau. So impressed was he by their dignity and independent spirit, that he was eager to equate the chiefs at Standing Rock with proud, accomplished, Roman senators.

It is striking how the fascination with these physical and personal characteristics and their attribution to American Indians persisted through the twentieth century unhindered by the creation of new states. This suggests that while there was, as a number of scholars have shown, an important dynamic interaction between gender and political systems in the various German states, there was also a broader cultural consensus about manliness that persisted under the surface in these new societies, and which was flexible enough to accommodate Winnetou's learning to sew in post-unification Nürnberg but still rather consistent over a long period of time.

Indeed, while many left-wing literary scholars in the 1970s relished unveiling the neofascist character of Fritz Steuben's popular novels, unifying in their lament that postwar German children had continued to be exposed to the same destructive racial stereotypes that their grandparents had consumed in their youth, very few said anything about the gender stereotypes. The virtues Tecumseh possesses in Steuben's stories are so similar to those in the stories from seventy years earlier because most of those virtues (his intellect, leadership and martial abilities, sagacity, strength, commitment, and talent) apply to his manliness, not the fascist characterization of it. Indeed, while racist characterizations were eagerly edited out of his volumes along with references to leader worship and fascist liturgy, no one has sought to edit the characteristics that make Steuben's still popular Tecumseh inherently manly. Those remain as consistent today as they did when he wrote his books in the 1930s or when Germans reported on Tecumseh in the 1830s.[78] Indeed, they are essentially the same characteristics that Dixon attributed to American Indian soldiers during World War I.

Probably the only author who made a pointed intervention into the manly characteristics of American Indians in German literature was Liselotte Welskopf-Henrich during her efforts to correct what she regarded as the terminal failings of Karl May. Like so many middle-class children of her generation, she too recalled being initially enticed by May, eager to read his books under the covers of her bed at night, and delighted to play out his scenarios with other children. Already as a child, however, she became disillusioned with his character Winnetou, whom she regarded as an inaccurate representation of a real American Indian chief. He was, she argued, much too submissive, "show[ing] a canine devotion" to his white friend Charlie. Moreover, he had too many "feminine traits." She was irritated by the references to his "Madonna eyes," and already as a child, she became convinced that "the author recounted Winnetou's tales untruthfully."[79] At the same time, she became enamored with the other American Indians in his stories, the Oglala-Sioux, "who killed Winnetou's white friends," and these experiences with May's books made her determined to learn "how it really was." Indeed, it was the deficiency in Winnetou's masculinity, one that has been noted by many literary critics as well,[80] that motivated her to pen her own tales about American Indians and to produce stories about a superior figure, one who was more true to himself and his people. Thus, she created Tokei-ihto, who submitted to no one, fought against the whites for his people, and returned in many ways in her second set of novels in the form of a modern hero—Joe King. These, of course, were also the characteristics she identified in her future husband, Rudolf Welskopf.

Her concerns about American Indian masculinity resurfaced again in a pointed manner when DEFA was preparing the first of its films about American Indians based on her first book, *Die Söhne der großen Bärin*. She was adamant that the producers cast the role of Tokei-ihto properly. Initially, not even the muscular and athletic Gojko Mitic, presented in East German newspapers as "Yugoslavia's favorite among the ladies and a hero of many Indian battles," could pass muster. Writing to the film's producer, Josef Mach, in February 1965, she explained that she had just seen a photo of Mitic in the latest issue of the *Neue Berliner Illustrierte*. She was disappointed and concerned. Welskopf-Henrich characterized him as a "truly handsome young man, muscular from sport, surely a favorite of the ladies, placed in a mannequin-like pose with a hand on one hip and his head held a little elegiac to the side—marvelous," she commented, "for Karl May's Winnetou," but "absolutely no war chief, and hardly a Tokei-ihto." "I don't know who posed the unfortunate in that way," she continued, while noting that she expected that one of Mach's employees would soon try to convince her that "he actually appears more manly than that," but she was worried and unsure if they could transform him into a Tokei-ihto: a hardened man who was "raised in battle," and who, by his twenty-fourth year belonged to a hunting people steeped in a pitiless frontier war and a bitter feud within his tribe.[81]

"The Dakota," she explained in a second concerned letter to Dr. Günter Karl, the head of the DEFA group *Roter Kreis*, "were a decidedly warlike and hard people, feared by their neighbors and the whites alike."[82] She did not want to idealize them, but she listed their qualities as "stoic, impenetrable in their dealings with strangers, proud, even haughty, bold to foolhardy, raised to be hunters and warriors." Among these men, "a Dakota War chief was the most manly one could imagine. And so was Toki-ihto." Eventually, she hoped that they could make their "young Yugoslavian" into a proud, fearless, stoic, and contemplating man." That would take time, but in the end they appear to have managed it. Once he was shed of his softer, Winnetou-type qualities, stoic and contemplative rather than elegiac and soft-eyed, she began to praise his portrait and to underscore that he not only was "good looking" but also had a good character: he was a good rider, able to do his own stunts, and he had begun to capture the proud and disciplined character of an American Indian.[83]

Her readers confirmed Welskopf-Henrich's sense for how to encapsulate the essence of American Indian masculinity. This too we know from the abundance of correspondence in her collected papers. Approximately 75 percent of those letters are from women and girls reacting to her novels and, in some cases, to the DEFA films. The letters reveal a consensus among East and West German readers that Welskopf-Henrich had successfully portrayed American Indian masculinity. They also reveal an eager desire among many of these women and girls to emulate those characteristics.

Indeed, while some women confessed their admiration for such men as men they would like to encounter, they just as often expressed their desire to take her characters as role models in their own lives. This should not surprise us. A number of scholars engaged in reader response theory have underscored the fact that women and girls often read books written for men and boys (much as Welskopf-Henrich herself had done) and participate in those stories in their own ways. One cannot assume a gendered response to a text.[84] Nor can we assume that women would seek only heroines in the novels they read, or that they would be either incapable or uninterested in reading themselves into a variety of parts of a play, poem, or novel.[85]

Thus, if one woman could write with delight from Munich in 1974 that her twelve-year-old son had become consumed by his reading of her books and had attempted since that time to emulate her hero Toki-ihto, other mothers wrote how their daughters did the same.[86] Already in 1956, for example, a woman wrote from Wittenberg about the deep impact that Welskopf-Henrich's first novel had had on her, how eagerly she read the second, and how her daughter now played Toki-ihto for her.[87] Over the decades, many children also wrote to her directly; in a number of cases, entire groups of young girls wrote expressing their enthusiasm and explaining how they engaged with her characters;[88] some sent her pictures of themselves dressed as their hero—dressed as men.[89]

During the same years that many women were corresponding with Welskopf-Henrich, others were becoming increasingly engaged in the West German hobby movements and in the various activist groups. The hobby journals that list the names of new members to their associations show a noted increase in female membership, and the essays in the journals include more and more penned by women.[90]

There is no question, however, that some German women were interested less in emulation of these men than admiration or even consumption. That has also been part of American Indians' appeal in Germany for a very long time. Many scholars, such as Louis Warren, have noted that American "Indian men" working with Buffalo Bill were practically overwhelmed with "offers of white women's companionship" while in Europe,[91] and news reports of Sarrasani's American Indian troupes make the same claims. Even for older men, such as Edward Two-Two, journalists reported, "the blond girls stood rapt before the windows of the Indians' quarters and rhapsodized sentimentally for the heroes of the prairie." In 1913, when Two-Two was in charge, some tried to use bottles of schnapps to lure them out of their Dresden quarters at night, and one could occasionally see ropes and strings lowered to the ground, and "bobbing liquor bottles instead of dangling fishes" being reeled up into their rooms. In one case, the police had to be called in to break up the mayhem.[92]

Similar escapades continued even in the stern home of Welskopf-Henrich when men like Dennis Banks and Vernon Bellecourt came to visit, causing her to reprimand the East German girls in the support groups connected to her for their peculiar efforts to promote "*Indianer* friendship."[93] At the same time, ethnologists across Germany and North America often remark of the weariness of meeting German women searching for American Indian men wherever they can be found. Most ethnologists keep these visits to themselves, but some, such as Christian Feest, have articulated what is already well known on many American Indian reservations and reserves: "A colleague at a museum in the Canadian Plains reports that every summer significant numbers of German females arrive on his doorstep asking for directions to the nearest eligible Indians whom they might take as spouses."[94] Some German women even advertise their interests in American Indian periodicals.[95] Others ask for advice in Germany, while still more circle around the American Indian men who visit and live there.

That consumerist impulse has also been part of American Indian men's appeal in Germany and part of what encouraged many of them to travel to Germany and stay for a time. And again, that appeal is not limited to the youths. As Ingrid Ostheeren, a reporter for the *Süddeutscher Zeitung* wrote in 1993 while describing a performance by Silkirtis Nichols in a German western-themed town called No Name City not far from Munich, the sixty-nine-year-old Nichols had not lost his touch. During the performance, a woman next to her remarked: "'Just look at him. That is a fine figure of a man! And he is 69 years old. . . . ' There was a moment of appreciative silence, and then another woman noted: "Oh my! . . . and now imagine our old men. Naked and on a horse! Then I could only say: Good Night!"[96] "Nicki," as Buffalo Child Long Lance has been affectionately known for decades, continued dancing, and impressing men and women alike, right through unification. Some, like the women cited by Ostheeren, were focused on the fantasy of possession. Over the years, however, even more revealed desires that continued to turn around emulating that set of characteristics that have long made Germans regard the kind of American Indian he projects as the quintessential examples of real men. Such desires remind us that consistent notions of masculinity and character repeatedly trumped concerns about race both before and after Hitler. They still do today.

CHAPTER 7

Comparative Genocides

During a recent meeting of the American Anthropological Association I had the pleasure of eating dinner with an anthropologist who works in Zimbabwe. We had just completed a panel on settler colonialism, where I had spoken on subaltern genocide and New Ulm. During the more general discussion of Germans' long fascination with American Indians that ensued over dinner, he offered an anecdote about an encounter with Germans in Zimbabwe that varied only slightly from those told repeatedly by non-Native Americans who have been in Europe. As he explained, when discussions between Germans and non-Native Americans turn to genocide (in academic settings, at dinner parties, and during a wide variety of casual conversations), many Germans are quick to retort: "Yes, but what about what you did to the Indians?" Non-Native Americans, such as the anthropologist, typically respond to this query with exasperation; those who later hear their anecdotes, much like our dinner companions, are generally amused, bemused, or both.

American Indians, however, are unlikely to be amused. American Indian activists, politicians, cultural critics, and others have been making such inquiries for a long time, and they have been harnessing the language of holocaust and genocide for decades. Indeed, when Paul Chaat Smith, an associate curator at the National Museum of the American Indian (NMAI) and a self-proclaimed cultural critic, published a collection of essays in 2009, it made perfect sense to him to describe his own grandfather, a Comanche born in Oklahoma at the turn of the century, as a "holocaust survivor" and to speak of American Indians in general as "the descendants of the greatest holocaust in human history."[1] It also made sense to Tex Hall, president of the National Council of American Indians, to argue during his "State of the Indian Nations Address" in January 2004 in Washington, D.C., that "the Indian plays much the same role in our American society that the Jews played in Germany. Like the miner's canary, the Indian marks the shift from fresh air to poison gas in our political atmosphere; and our treatment of Indians, even more than our treatment of other minorities, marks the rise and fall of our democratic faith."[2]

Such statements have become ubiquitous. Already in the 1980s it was common for American Indians, and not just well placed activists, professionals, and politicians such as Smith and Hall, to express their own indignant exasperation at the attention the United States had been lavishing on the crimes of National Socialism while ignoring those perpetrated in North America.[3] In 1983, for example, Red Hail (Wasuduta) from Porcupine South Dakota on the Pine Ridge Reservation wrote in a letter to *Lakota Times* that "recently the U.S./Government paid homage to members of the Jewish Tribe who survived a holocaust [sic] many years ago. We, the Native people have, for many, many generations lived a holocaust under the U.S. Government, here on our land." Listing a long series of grievances and arguing that institutional efforts at genocide had not stopped in the United States during the twentieth century,[4] he ended his litany with a point of comparison he thought was critical for the paper's readers to understand: "Adolf Hitler was a great admirer of both the USA and England." He "relished the way in which both countries applied positive suppression and genocide upon the indigenous peoples." "Hitler," he stressed, learned his lessons from the Americans and "then applied them well upon the Jewish Tribe." Consequently, he contended, "if the USA and England were to stand in front of a full-length mirror, both will [sic] see Adolf Hitler!"[5]

A decade after Red Hail's angry pronouncements, the United States Holocaust Memorial Museum was opened next to the Mall in Washington, D.C. It had nothing to do with American Indians, which rankled some. For them its opening underscored the disparity of awareness and memorialization voiced for many years by American Indians such as Red Hail. Indeed, many hoped that the NMAI would take up the task of consciousness building and memorialization of the crimes committed against American Indians when it opened on the Mall a further decade later in 2004. It did not. The curators eschewed the language of genocide and the notion of an American holocaust, even if they evoked the millions who had perished in the wake of 1492. Their language was affecting but circumspect.

Visitors who entered the permanent exhibit titled "Our Peoples" were able to read a panel titled "All My Relations," which displayed a statement composed by Paul Chaat Smith. Set next to a striking collection of names of tribes that survived and some that did not, it explained that "entire nations

FIGURE 32. Denton Fast Whirlwind, *13th Trophy of the Holocaust* (2008). This painting captures the character of the discussion in 2008. It combines images of both holocausts: thousands of moccasins from the past swirling out of the trophy of Mount Rushmore in the Black Hills. It received multiple awards at the 2008 Red Cloud Indian Art Show. The Heritage Center at Red Cloud Indian School in Pine Ridge, S.D. (Courtesy of the artist)

perished in the waves of death that swept the Americas. Even their names are lost to us." Visitors who read the panel learned that "nine of ten Native people perished in the first century of contact between the hemispheres." The panel, however, does not explicitly attribute those deaths to malice, and it places its greatest emphasis on the fact that "one in ten survived." Indeed the argument the curators chose to stress in this exhibit, and with the museum in general, was that those survivors "didn't fear change; they embraced it."

They grew, and they remain present. In short, the museum's staff focused on survival, continuities, agency, multiplicity, even, at moments, revitalization.

For many American Indian critics, however, the curators' laudable efforts to stress survival and persistence made the victims' fates and the survivors' daunting challenges much too implicit. For them, the museum's narrative folded too neatly into a victor's history that left non-Native Americans and many others unaware of past atrocities. As Dennis Banks, Clyde and Vernon Bellecourt, and Floyd Red Crow Westerman argued, it failed to "characterize" or "display" the "sordid and tragic history of America's holocaust against the Native Nations and peoples of the Americas." Indeed, on the day of the NMAI's opening in September 2004, those men called in the name of the American Indian Movement Grand Governing Council for the museum to be "named and referred to as the National Holocaust Museum of the American Indian." They were not alone.[6]

Many Germans evidenced a striking sympathy for the critics' position. They were keenly aware of the atrocities suffered by American Indians, and many have long wondered privately why there is a Holocaust Museum in Washington, D.C., that stakes out the history of the Nazi genocide in Europe and no counterpart that portrays the genocide that washed across North America. Their sympathy and wonder, however, are often regarded by non-Native Americans as self-serving and suspect, revealing, perhaps, a misguided sense of displacement, even a desire to underscore the fact that the Americans who had long sat in moral judgment of Germans' "unmasterable past" would do well to reflect on their own "sordid and tragic history"—hence the bemused reactions to Germans' queries. Both impulses were certainly present in the postwar era, but the point most Native and non-Native Americans often overlook is that these postwar impulses were only the most recent additions to a more general discussion of genocide that was as old as Germans' fascination with American Indians.

For more than 150 years, Germans have been concerned with what they regarded as the United States' persistent efforts to eradicate American Indians. There have been, in fact, a series of striking consistencies in their awareness of this history over a long period of time. The ongoing shifts in geopolitics, historical circumstances, and fluid contexts refracted those consistencies too much for them to be labeled continuities. Shifting contexts have given those persistent concerns equally shifting implications and meanings. Nevertheless, there is no question that Germans' postwar reactions stemmed from much older awareness, interests, and concerns.

Displacement and Condemnation

Relations between West Germans and the United States shifted and changed dramatically over the postwar period. Sometimes they were quite good, but they were not always rosy. Indeed, as Michael Geyer has argued, they often reflected West Germans' perceptions of the United States' ability to provide them with security during the unsettling years of the Cold War. Many felt concerned with their dependence on the United States, and not all were trusting. Already during the 1950s, for example, West Germans drew on older tropes of American savagery while portraying themselves as its victims. According to Geyer, the introduction of atomic weapons into West Germany "led to the fear of mass death and even extermination. In a classic act of displacement," he claims, "a near majority of Germans . . . was convinced that they would be the ones exterminated in a nuclear war." While Americans were "generally perceived to be peaceable and hence solid guarantors against a threat of war, German lore also held the opposing view that Americans had a way of smashing things and people they did not like." Everyone was aware of the "terror-bombing" of German cities during World War II, but "one did not even need to refer to Dresden, because there was a more traditional case that one 'knew': the Americans had exterminated the North American Indians. The only open side to the question was whether or not this was worse than what the Germans did (as Nazi propaganda asserted)."[7]

The "German lore" Geyer evokes took shape during the nineteenth century. While the term "genocide" was coined in 1944, the rhetoric of genocide appeared frequently in nineteenth-century German periodicals that carried stories about the "winning" of America's West. It was common to read not only essays in the 1860s and 1870s on "the slaughter [*Abschlachtung*] of Indians in North America" in middle-class journals but also articles in which authors argued that "the extermination [*Ausrottung*] of the redskins is being pursued in a completely systematic and business-like manner, so that one can hardly wonder about the extinction of individual tribes."[8] Newspapers too often used words like "annihilation" [*Vernichtung*], "extermination" [*Ausrottung*], and "destruction" [*Zerstörung*] when describing the conflicts between the red and white "races" in the United States. Much like the *New Ulm Pioneer* had done in the 1860s, and German travelers and immigrants such as Rudolf Cronau and Alexander Berghold did in the decades that followed, these German newspapers blamed the Indian wars on "greedy and unscrupulous agents of the government" and the excesses on the "barbarism of the soldiers."[9] Indeed, even the entry under "Indianer" in the 1876 edition of *Meyers Konversations-Lexikon*, perhaps the leading German encyclopedia of the age, details the sufferings of the 1838 "Trail of Tears," explains the tragic conditions on reservations, and laments that, for the Americans, the "solution" to their Indian question seems to have been the "extermination of the red vermin" [*Ausrottung des rothen Ungeziefers*].[10]

There is a telling consistency in these tales. Already in the 1830s, for example, essays in *Das Ausland* called for an end to the "inhuman system of butchery" that raged across American frontiers. They detailed the gratuitous killing and scalping of American Indians at the hands of irregular troops, who practiced a kind of "nefarious barbarism," which "far exceed" that attributed to "savages."[11] Throughout the decade, columnists and editors continued to report on the U.S. efforts to wage "unjust" wars and supported American Indians' attempts at resistance.[12] In the 1840s, *Das Ausland* reported on the "horrifying" "annihilation of the Mandan tribe," whose members, the author explained, were poisoned by traders with blankets infected by small pox. The few survivors, the column went on, were driven off by the Sioux or forced into slavery, and the famous Mah-to-toh-pa was left to "roll himself into his buffalo robe in despair," where "he passed away nine days later."[13] Such tales continued throughout the nineteenth century: in 1850 multiple essays appeared about the elimination of entire tribes,[14] which included reports on the Yankee calls for "wars of extermination,"[15] and by the 1860s contributors to *Das Ausland*, much like the editors of the *New Ulm Pioneer*, were detailing the "extermination of the Californian tribes" that followed the gold rush.[16]

By the 1870s the journal began casting the Indian wars as a long-term "race war," which had "continued with only short pauses since the founding of the North American Union." Indeed, in 1873 the journal contended that the current Modoc wars in the Northwest were simply continuing the pattern: they "again involved the extermination [*vertilgen*] of an American Indian tribe, because its members were unwilling for any price to learn the benedictions of American civilization." German readers also learned from *Das Ausland* that President Ulysses S. Grant and "General [William T.] Sherman" both advocated the "extermination" [*Ausrottung*] of the Modoc tribe after their resistance was quelled, in order to avoid future uprisings.[17] The following year, *Das Ausland* recorded more conflicts in this ongoing "race war." In each case, the contributors continued to blame the warfare on the "barbarism [*Grausamkeit*] of the Yankees," on their consistent mistreatment of American Indians. They underscored as well the understandable efforts of those people to resist and lamented the ways in which that resistance was met with "ghastly repression" [*schauderhafte Repressalien*] and systematic elimination.[18]

The angry rhetoric that accompanied such reports in *Das Ausland* and other German periodicals faded from prominence in the German discourse on American Indians with the putative closing of the frontier and the end of armed resistance that accompanied the Wounded Knee massacre in 1890.[19] It is easy to understand, however, how the rhetoric could return again in the postwar period, particularly after American Indians themselves began adamantly harnessing it while engaging in new forms of resistance, and popular portraits of Indian-white conflicts changed in the United States, as the public became sensitive to the oppression of minorities in a post-Auschwitz world.

Emulation and Colonization

The persistent discussion of eradication within the German discourse on American Indians was not limited to condemnation.[20] Some Germans, particularly those who were interested in territorial expansion through settler colonialism, looked with understanding, even enthusiasm on the United States' efforts to clear the land of indigenous people who failed to submit or conform. Red Hail was essentially correct in his assessment of Hitler's impression of American efforts at extermination. But neither Hitler nor other National Socialists who looked toward American conquests and eradication as a model for their own efforts in Eastern Europe fashioned their plans from whole cloth. There were nineteenth-century precedents for their perspectives as well, which existed alongside Germans' more general condemnations of Yankee actions.

Indeed, not all German periodicals followed *Das Ausland* and *Globus* in their condemnations of American efforts to clear the land of indigenous people. Some, such as the Anglophile *Minerva*, uncritically reprinted American accounts of conflicts with American Indians, which rationalized the violence and attributed it to the character of the people they sought to subjugate.[21] Even in *Das Ausland*, Germans could read uncritical translations of English-language essays that legitimated the removal and elimination of American Indians.[22] Thus German arguments and rationalizations for the United States' actions against American Indians were circulating together with German condemnations of those actions throughout the nineteenth century, and as a German nation-state was formed, and as that state sought expansion inside and outside of Europe, empathy for genocidal violence emerged among German nationalists. As Ben Kiernan notes, toward the end of the nineteenth century, "German expansionists increasingly seized upon U.S. wars with Native Americans as precedents or justification for colonial war and, eventually, genocidal tactics."[23]

In the German colonies in the three southernmost states of Brazil, for example, people such as Hermann von Ihering, the director of the Paulista Museum in São Paulo, reacted to Brazilian tribes' resistance to German colonists' ongoing expansion into their territories by calling on their countrymen to support "Indian hunters" who could clear out the resisters while pointing to the effective American example as justification for a policy of eradication.[24] Similarly, as Helmut Walser Smith reminds us, even the left-liberal politicians who took part in the 1913 Reichstag debates about the treatment of Imperial Germany's colonial subjects in Africa, looked to the United States as a model for controlling unruly populations, leading members such as Ernst Müller-Meiningen to argue in favor of American-style reservations as an effective means of dealing with recalcitrant colonized people and leading them down the road to assimilation.[25] Conservatives looked to the United States as well. In 1909, for example, German colonial newspapers were eager to draw parallels between German genocidal actions in South-West Africa and the measures taken against American Indians on the American frontier; the infamous explorer, cofounder, and later High Imperial Commissioner of German East Africa Carl Peters found inspiration in the United States' efforts as well.[26]

Within Europe, German nationalists drew on Prussian precedents of looking east with an eye toward the United States' westward expansion. As David Blackbourn has demonstrated, German settlers who moved east often saw themselves as importing culture and taming landscapes in ways completely analogous to other German settlers in places such as New Ulm, Minnesota.[27] Indeed, as the settlers around New Ulm became engaged in bitter warfare in 1862, Heinrich von Treitschke's history of the Teutonic Knights' actions in the east began initiating a trend: "After the 1870s," Blackbourn notes, "hundreds of books appeared on medieval and Hohenzollern colonization," which helped establish "a mental framework for viewing the East. The Germans" were set in stark contrast to the Slavic inhabitants: Germans reclaimed unhealthy marshland and created flourishing meadows. They "tended crops and animals; the Slavs stayed close to the water and lived by fishing."[28] In short, much like in the United States, the assumption was that the indigenous Slavs lived from the land, while German settlers improved it.

We often forget that during the nineteenth century, German-speaking states contained lands that were only recently subjugated by new industry, where nature was still being tamed. As a result, one could find frontier societies there as well, and as Germans thought about those European frontiers, they often harnessed language and ideas familiar to readers of westerns and other stories about settlement. As Blackbourn reminds us, these could be found in the travel narratives that portrayed Germans' movements to the European East as well as in the learned, theoretical treaties written on national expansion.[29]

Indeed, there were notable connections between German and American scholarly arguments about the growth of their respective states. As scholars have noted, Frederick Jackson Turner's 1893 frontier thesis, which argued that pioneers' engagement with the wilderness and the special character of frontier life shaped American values and institutions, not only "interested contemporary Germans" but was indebted to their work. Turner had learned much from Friedrich Ratzel's writings about the influence of geography on history. He even collaborated with Ratzel's American student, Ellen Churchill Semple. Moreover, "Ratzel, who originated the term 'living space' (*Lebensraum*), credited Turner with showing the dynamic effects of American westward expansion." Thus, as Blackbourn argues, "an imagined version of the American frontier resonated in Germany, because the American west seemed such an obvious analogue to the German east." Indeed, many other authors, such as Max Sering, who wrote a series of books on German colonization of the East in the 1880s, also took the American pioneer as "exemplars of hardy enterprise, a model for Germans."[30]

Within that German discourse of settling Eastern Europe, the Slavs remained the indigenous people who had to be overcome. This too has a long history. Frederick the Great had equated the Poles with the Iroquois, and that equation of Slavs with American Indians stuck. Indeed, it "persisted through the nineteenth century, becoming a 'favorite theme of Prussian politicians.'" "The Poles," they argued, much "like the 'American redskins'—were doomed to ruin": just as American Indians "were being pushed back into the 'everlasting wilderness' where they slowly perished, so Poles were 'pushed out of towns and landed properties as they yielded to Prussian civilization.'" Poles recognized this equation of Frederick's at work as well, and thus already in 1864 Ludwik Powidaj wrote an essay titled "Poles and Indians" that sketched out the fate of American Indians and asked: "'What Pole will not see the situation of his own country'?"[31]

These tropes of eastern frontiers, indigenous Slavs, and hardy German settlers bringing culture to a wilderness persisted into the interwar period, evidenced, among other things, through German travel writing.[32] Such discourses inspired National Socialists, and once they came to power, they quickly seized upon them and set out to pursue Prussian ideals about colonization on a much wider scale. As they did so, they too looked toward the United States as a model, tapping the rhetoric of frontier culture and excess as much as the language of living space, and combining it with the respect they had gained together with political theorists such as Carl Schmitt for the United States' Monroe Doctrine and its notion of manifest destiny.[33] The Nazis did not take everything; they also noted the mistakes made by Americans. Aware as they were of the devastating Dust Bowl, for example, they were careful not to drain every marsh for fear of turning the area into a steppe.[34] They were also more thorough and systematic in their efforts to clear out the indigenous Slavs. To that end, Blackbourn notes that Germans "projected on to them the [negative] qualities to be expected of wild people or 'savages': passivity, a childlike nature, above all cunning, cruelty, and undying hatred for the 'superior' race. They cast them, in short," he argues, "as Indians." Indeed, in 1941 Hitler stated that "there is only one task: to set about the Germanization of the land by bringing in Germans and to regard the indigenous inhabitants as Indians." When those inhabitants resisted, the National Socialists engaged in what they believed was a "real Indian war" in places like the eastern marshes, and as Blackbourn demonstrates, "there were indeed parallels. In the German East, as in the American West, the conquerors visited dispossession and genocide on indigenous peoples, all the while proclaiming their mission to 'civilize' the land; then they attributed 'hatred' and 'primitive cruelty' to their victims," who seemingly got what they deserved.[35]

National Socialism, American Indians, and the Logics of Genocide

Ultimately, the ways in which National Socialists conflated older discourses about the German colonization of Eastern Europe with those about the colonization of the American West explain why they came to regard American Indians as resisters who were both good to emulate and good to eliminate. On the one hand, the Nazis took up the mantle of Frederick the Great, looking east toward ostensibly wild lands and uncultured indigenous peoples whom they believed must be cleared away so that German colonizers could settle in the East and improve the lands, and Germany could prosper. In that sense, as Dirk Moses has argued, National Socialists were engaged in a "classical case of imperial genocide," one he traces back to Rome, but which many scholars now recognize was largely modeled on late nineteenth- and early twentieth-century German nationalists' understanding of American expansion.[36] On the other hand, however, the Nazis also drew on the legacies of Tacitus, on feelings of empathy and affinity with American Indians that had also built up in Germany across the nineteenth century. They too regarded themselves as an indigenous people who must react against invaders, most specifically, against Jews, principally from Poland, whom they believed had colonized German culture. As a result, and in a rather striking conflation of opposing historical legacies, the Nazis who set out to eradicate millions of people across Central and Eastern Europe were engaged not only in "a classical case of imperial genocide" as colonizers but also in "subaltern genocide," as people who believed they were resisting colonization by others.

Many scholars agree with Jürgen Zimmerer that "the German war against Poland and the USSR was without doubt the largest colonial war of conquest in history." Hitler, they note, regarded it as a war of territorial expansion. What set it apart from other colonial wars was the Nazis' ability to marshal unprecedented resources in pursuit of equally unprecedented aims.[37] In particular, the speed and extent of conquest took it beyond the complex and unplanned character of most colonial expansions, and past the society-driven violence that often characterizes colonial genocides.[38] Instead, this conquest was accompanied by state-led genocide and industrialized mass killing uncommon in most colonial situations. Thus, while it shared what Patrick Wolfe has called the "primary logic of settler colonialism," the elimination of the people who occupied the land the Germans hoped to settle, it also contradicted Wolfe's central contention that colonial genocide is best seen as a process rather than an event, and it stretched far beyond the territories meant to be settled.[39]

We can gain only so much by debating classifications. It is worth recalling, however, that according to Wolfe, settler colonialism is ultimately "a zero-sum contest over land," in which the object of elimination endures apart from any subjectively held racist attitudes on the part of immigrants. If we accept Wolfe's arguments that the primary logic of settler colonialism, the logic of elimination, is driven by the "zero-sum contest" over land rather than any subjectively held attitudes about race, then the National Socialists' racialized arguments and rationalizations would seem to disqualify the German war against Poland from the characterization Zimmerer gives it as "the largest colonial war of conquest in history." Moreover, if we also accept that, as Moses argues, "the mechanism of policy radicalization" that leads to genocidal actions in most settler colonial situations "is the intensity of Indigenous resistance," then the Nazi case, which was radicalized less by indigenous resistance than internal dynamics within the Nazi Party,[40] would also seem to belie the notion that this was indeed a "colonial war of conquest" that engendered a typical colonial genocide[41]—that is, however, unless we accept the Nazis' own vision of themselves as indigenous people under siege and recognize the dual nature of the Nazi's self-characterization as both colonizers and resisters and the ways in which that dual role informed their logic of elimination.

Moses is a strong and convincing advocate of this view. Indeed, he argues that the extermination of Jews "needs to be understood, to begin with, in terms of subaltern genocide." The evidence, he argues, can be found in Hitler's *Mein Kampf*, which portrays Germany as if it was under foreign occupation, specifically Jewish domination, since the middle years of World War 1. "Hitler," he notes, "was wont to speak of Jews in terms of colonists, mixing bacteriological and colonial metaphors," as Cronau had once done with Europeans invading North America, and he urged German resistance against their encroachment on German culture and the German nation.[42] Indeed, he believed that Jews were undermining both, and thus Moses argues that "the relentless drive to exterminate the Jews entirely, then, is best explained in terms of the subaltern's racist nationalism." The Nazis, he contends, "thought of themselves as a national liberation movement, a self-consciousness that continued the German policy during the First World War of supposedly liberating central European nations from Russian domination." If, however, "the Nazis' anti-Semitism was 'redemptive,' its particular intensity at this historical conjuncture cannot be read from centuries of anti-Semitism, which had not resulted in genocide like this before." The continuity that leads to mass genocide is something else: "In the Nazi mind," Moses argues, "the Second World War was a war of national liberation, and redemption inhered in the elimination of foreign Jewish rule." In short, their eliminationist racism stemmed more from their history of identifying with colonized subaltern groups such as American Indians than with any legacy of anti-Semitism in German culture.

If we accept Moses's contentions, we gain more than a solution to the kind of label that best captures the type of genocide that raged across Europe during the Nazi era. We gain some insight into the unintuitive ways in which seemingly contradictory, even competing discourses in Germany about the eradication of American Indians could be harnessed simultaneously and fused together into a single logic that allowed National Socialists to look to Americans for both models of indigenous resistance and models of colonial expansion, models of classical imperial genocide and models of reactive subaltern genocide.

Indeed, Moses reveals that there were multiple forms of genocide within the Holocaust that shook Europe, which resemble what one finds in other redemptive, postcolonial decolonization movements as well as the colonization movements stemming from European nationalism. Thus, Moses's ultimate contention is that one can reconcile both Wolfe's and Zimmerer's arguments that "the Holocaust was no colonial genocide in the common understanding of the term. It was an event, or multitude of events, that united four different, even contradictory imperial and colonial logics into one terrible paranoid mentality and praxis borne of a frustrated imperial nation struggling against a perceived colonizer." And in that sense, it was much different from what took place in the United States, where the circumstances and logics were less complex, if no less deadly.[43]

"Dare to Compare"[44]

It is not my intention to argue about the character of the Holocaust or reduce it to an imitation of North American examples. Certainly, efforts at understanding the dynamics that drove the Nazis into genocide have spurred scholars from a wide range of disciplines to engage in comparative analyses. The virtue of such analyses is that they often lead to the identification of general processes and shed greater light on the particularities of specific historical events. The danger arises, however, at the point of characterization, especially with the temptation to fashion hierarchies. The virtue of considering Moses's, Wolfe's, and Zimmerer's contentions together is not that they might generate a new label for the form of genocide in which the Nazis engaged. That is not the point. The benefit stems from the recognition of the ways in which National Socialists could draw on older, well-established discourses in German cultures about the eradication of American Indians to develop a vision in which they took on the mantle of both noble savages and noble colonizers against people they managed to cast as both ignoble savages and ignoble colonizers. Those insights are important for this study, because they substantiate the continual importance of these discourses through the Nazi era, demonstrate some of their unique manifestations during that period, and help us to understand how these persistent discourses could continue through the postwar era as well. Again, they help us bear in mind that East and West Germans' interests in American genocidal efforts were anything but new in the postwar era, even if the implications of those interests and the uses to which they could be put shifted and changed with the new geopolitical contexts.

Indeed, what we learn from a transnational, long-term perspective is how much the Holocaust recast the domestic and international meaning of nineteenth-century American efforts to eradicate various American Indians. The aura of Auschwitz created an entirely new context for the evaluation of those actions. The universal condemnation of the Holocaust, the increased importance of human rights in international and domestic politics, and the complete bankruptcy of racial arguments delegitimized the old rationalizations for American genocidal efforts accepted by German nationalists from Frederick the Great to Adolf Hitler. In doing so, those new contexts also created space for the discourse of condemnation of the United States' treatment of American Indians, evidenced for over a century in *Das Ausland* and other German periodicals, not only to return to the field of discussion but to dominate it. That was ultimately true in both East and West Germany, and eventually also in the United States, where essentially no one stood up in defense of the older rationalizations.

That did not happen immediately. The Holocaust received scant attention for decades after World War II. It was not ignored. As Michael Rothberg has pointed out, many people such as W. E. B. Du Bois engaged it directly in the immediate postwar years.[45] But as Peter Novick also makes clear, the "revolutionary changes in world alignments" directly after World War II made "talk of the Holocaust" "not just unhelpful but actively obstructive" to Western European and American interests in the new world order. In essence, as the Cold War began to take shape, "the Russians were transformed from indispensable allies to implacable foes, the Germans from implacable foes to indispensable allies." The "apotheosis of evil" was relocated from Berlin to Moscow, and because "public opinion had to be mobilized to accept the new worldview, symbols that reinforced the old view were no longer functional."[46] As a result, the talk was limited.

The term "genocide" came into being in this context. Coined by Raphael Lemkin, who was a Polish Jew, it rose out of his concern with the fate of the Armenians at the hands of the Turks during and after World War I. As he introduced it, it stood as a generic category. Indeed, taking shape in the immediate postwar context, the terminology of genocide was quickly used by people in the West to critique the actions of the Soviet Union more than those of the Germans. The Holocaust, as Novick notes, was the "'wrong atrocity' for contemporary purposes" and thus not the focus of Lemkin's efforts or of pointed discussion in Western Europe and the United States.[47]

By the 1970s, however, purposes had changed and a dramatic transformation had taken place. Postwar culture began loosening up, Western European and American interests became less unitary, and a combination of factors and events came together that allowed the Holocaust to gain prominence as both a commonly recognized term and a historical event with great resonance. The most important factor is generally accepted to have been the sensational trial of Adolf Eichmann before an Israeli court in 1961, which was "the first time that what we now call the Holocaust was presented to the American public as an entity in its own right, distinct from Nazi barbarism in general." From this point, the word "Holocaust," which was an Israeli translation of the Hebrew term Shoah dating from the Israeli 1948 Declaration of Independence, became firmly attached to the murder of European Jewry in American and European minds. With the concerns for the fate of Israel that emerged in the wake of the Yom Kippur War in 1973, that term was evoked ever more frequently in the United States and eventually internationally.[48]

As the notion of the Holocaust as a unique event took shape, it became a kind of moral reference point, which had many unanticipated consequences. To a certain degree, those consequences owed much to the broader cultural shifts in the United States that Novick has argued created a "cultural climate that virtually celebrated victimhood," one that led to a "culture of victimization" that "allowed" Jews "to embrace a victim identity based on the Holocaust." That is something he laments. According to Novick, within "the Jewish discourse on the Holocaust" that emerged during those years, and which continued well past the founding of the Holocaust Museum in Washington, D.C., there was "not just a competition for recognition but a competition for primacy." This, he notes, has taken many forms. "Among the most widespread and pervasive is an angry insistence on the uniqueness of the Holocaust," which he terms "vacuous" and, "in practice, deeply offensive."[49]

Indeed, many non-Jews were offended, and unfortunate debates ensued over whose victimization was greater, longer, and more tragic.[50] Such assertions had significant political implications.[51] As scholars have argued, the focus on the uniqueness of the Holocaust ultimately promoted the "*evasion of moral and historical responsibility*" by the U.S. government, which could now argue that, although the older rationalizations for past actions were no longer valid, "whatever the United States has done to blacks, Native Americans, Vietnamese, or others pales in comparison to the Holocaust."[52] Indeed, that position could be used by the state not only for "evasion" but also "for the purpose of national self-congratulation." The "'Americanization' of the Holocaust," Novick remarks, "has involved using it to demonstrate the differences between the Old World and the New, and to celebrate, by showing its negation, the American way of life."[53] That celebration and evasion not only left many American Indians who regarded themselves as current and former victims of New World genocide unimpressed, and at times downright angry; it also irritated many in the Old World, particularly Germans, who had long known better.[54]

It is perhaps true, as Michael Rothberg argues, that "the emergence of Holocaust memory on a global scale has contributed to the articulation of other histories—some of them predating the Nazi genocide." In some ways, Rothberg contends, other groups have benefited from this broad, international discussion of the Holocaust because they have been able to capitalize on the rhetoric of genocide developed during these extensive discussions to make their own local, national, and international claims. Increasingly, such groups have been able to learn from each other while pressing their claims, and many have even learned to work together and to pursue them jointly.[55]

The danger, however, of basing too much of a group's identity on grievances and notions of joint victimization has also been made clear by the debates around the Holocaust. Indeed, it was largely Novick's concern about those limitations that led him to write *The Holocaust in American Life.* As he put it, "turning the Holocaust into the emblematic Jewish experience" has not only "been closely connected to the inward and rightward turn of American Jewry" but has also "contributed to the erosion of that larger social consciousness" that was a "hallmark of American Jewry" during his youth. That, he feels, has been a regrettable loss. Moreover, the very prominence of the Holocaust in American Jewish culture, he argues, has displaced the role of the Jew in non-Jewish minds in America, where the "zealously promoted" proliferation of "Holocaust curricula" in American schools has "inscribed" "the equation Jew-equals-victim" into the young minds of Jewish and non-Jewish Americans alike.[56]

That is not necessarily the identity all Jews would like to maintain, but as Novick also explains, they may well be stuck with it. There is, he notes, little chance that there could "be a *second* Jewish institution on the Mall, presenting an alternative image of the Jew. And there certainly is not going to be *another* set of legislatively mandated curricula about Jews in American schools."[57] Given that perspective, it is hard not to appreciate the wisdom of Paul Chaat Smith and his fellow curators at the NMAI for recognizing the limitations of entering a competition of genocide monuments on the Mall, in which even a victory in that "zero-sum game" would be pyrrhic at best. There were better options open to them at the outset of the twenty-first century, and despite Smith's own ambivalence about the NMAI's effectiveness, emphasizing success and survival over victimization and genocide clearly provided American Indians with a much greater set of options for their futures.[58]

New Transnational Rhetoric of Genocides

In the immediate postwar period, Germans continued to think about and write about American Indians much as they had in the decades before the war. As the hobbyist associations were quickly reestablished, novels reissued, and new ones produced, Germans' respect for American Indian resistance persisted, and it continued to be articulated in books, films, theater, and a host of other media. Discussions of the eradication and destruction of American Indians during the nineteenth century persisted as well, changed little by the recent genocide in Europe. As Michael Geyer pointed out, Germans continued to *know* that "the Americans had exterminated the North American Indians," even if they refrained from broadcasting that knowledge in West Germany so long as they felt dependent on the United States. Indeed, Novick's contention that the new postwar political alignments inhibited an early public discussion of the Holocaust in Western Europe and the United States likely accounts for the fact that, initially, West Germans were less willing to discuss colonial and exterminatory policies than their counterparts in the GDR. East Germans followed a broader international trend. Rothberg notes that "communism provided one of the discursive spheres, both in the United States and elsewhere, in which the articulation of genocide and colonialism could first be attempted—and this long before the intellectual vogue for either Holocaust or postcolonial studies."[59]

It should not surprise us then that East German authors harnessed the new rhetoric of genocide much earlier than their counterparts in the West. The East German state's official position on its relationship to the Nazi past was one of resistance. Whether that was a foundational principle or foundational myth of antifascism, it nevertheless opened up space for this older discourse of eradication and resistance to reemerge much earlier in the GDR than in the West.[60]

It would be misguided, however, to think of that emergence as simply a political ploy or an act of displacement, an effort to cover up another tragic event.[61] East Germans felt no need to cover up the Holocaust, because they, as ostensible and actual resisters, felt no responsibility for it. Indeed, the official state rhetoric was that they, as communists, were joint victims in that calamity—the other, often forgotten, inmates in the camps. Moreover, while discussions of genocide in North America may have fit well into the Communist Party's rhetoric about the United States being an imperialist and aggressive power, and it could have been used to deflect condemnations of German character, those impulses were not its genesis. Rather, and this is the critical point, early East German authors of novels and stories about American Indians continued to work within and to promote a discourse of eradication and resistance that antedated the GDR considerably, which then gained new ramifications and political usefulness for the leadership of that state after its foundation.

It is worth returning to the censors for a moment because, although Lemkin's notion of genocide was used to critique Soviet actions during the early postwar period, and East Germans could have easily taken it up while writing about America's past, the first generation of East German authors continued to use the same language as its predecessors. So too did censors and state critics. Thus, while reviewing Rudolf Daumann's *The Demise of the Dakota* in 1957, for example, the censors continued to use the German word *vernichtet* (annihilated) when discussing the Dakota's demise and eschewed the new rhetoric of genocide.[62] Even as late as 1962, when Welskopf-Henrich's latest novel, *Top and Harry,* passed through the censors, they were still using the same old terminology while praising her portrait of the "rücksichtslos vernichtete Indianer" (ruthlessly annihilated Indians) rather than discussing that annihilation in terms of an American genocide or holocaust.[63] None of the censors pushed these authors to do that. In East Germany, much as in the West, that language would first become common during the aftermath of the Eichmann trial and the United States' involvement in Vietnam, and it came largely through contacts with American Indian activists in the United States.

Indeed, when the postwar language of genocide arose in East German discussion of American Indians' history and their contemporary conditions, it did so largely through Welskopf-Henrich and the networks of connections she had built up with American Indian activists during her trips to the United States. Those activists understood the political capital inherent in harnessing a terminology recognized by international bodies, and they used it during the occupation of Alcatraz in 1969, which Welskopf-Henrich followed with great interest. Two years earlier, in fact, when ABC released a nine-episode series on George Armstrong Custer that portrayed him in a positive light, Native American civil rights groups showed their understanding of the utility of using the new rhetoric of genocide to press their claims. Launching a massive protest, they termed Custer the "Adolf Eich-mann of the nineteenth century."[64]

Welskopf-Henrich picked up on this language, and thus in 1973 when she gave a thirty-minute radio interview in East Berlin, during which she sketched out the history of American Indian reservations, their demograph-ics and economic conditions, she adopted their new language while explain-ing that many American Indians regarded federal efforts at assimilation through the Bureau of Indian Affair's schools as tantamount to "cultural genocide" through "forced assimilation." She termed the education at these schools "brain washing" and argued, as did many of the AIM activists she supported, that this flew in the face of UN charters. She stressed that Ameri-can Indians had a right to their own language, schools, and colleges and to support for developing their reservations, and she adamantly proclaimed that "anyone who will destroy and depopulate the reservations facilitates genocide, because they are the centers of resistance for the younger genera-tion." Moreover she spoke of AIM and its activists with great reverence, as leaders in "a new phase in the struggle" that turned around "much more than civil rights," but rather "human rights in general" and the "rights of this minority to [live by the principles of the] UN Charter."[65] Her rhetoric was powerful, and for many AIM members it would have been quite familiar. So much of it came from their pamphlets.[66]

By the middle of the 1960s the connections between past crimes against American Indians and their current, generally impoverished conditions on reservations was common fare in both the East and West German press;[67] by the end of the decade, such connections were also being made in American and German films about American Indians, in books for German children, and in the activist handbooks produced by Claus Biegert and others.

In many cases, people such as Biegert in the West and Welskopf-Henrich in the East became willing mouthpieces for American Indian activists, much as Rudolf Cronau had been for Sitting Bull almost a century earlier. As they took up that task, they adopted much of those activists' language. There is no question that Biegert's successful book *200 Years without a Constitution. 1976: Indians Resisting* (1976), which he explained was meant to elucidate the long history of one "variant of modern genocide and resistance," and which eagerly compared American Indian reservations to the concentration camps of the Nazi era, owed much of its rhetoric and comparisons to his American Indian friends and informants. He makes that explicit.

There is also little question that he was not alone in adopting that lan-guage or a new comparative perspective stemming from the United States.

Other, less-connected Germans engaged in the same process. Indeed, before Biegert's book was published, Welskopf-Henrich was receiving letters from her readers in both the East and West that already drew on the writings of American Indian activists such as Steve Talbot to make the same arguments and comparisons that Biegert would make in the press. For example, in 1975 one woman wrote to Welskopf-Henrich discussing the denial of the American holocaust in the United States, which she had gleaned from reading and listening to Talbot. She also stressed that reading Dee Brown's *Bury My Heart at Wounded Knee* had reminded her of "what occurred during the Third Reich"; his descriptions of the Rosebud Reservation struck her as "essentially concentration camp conditions."

Welskopf-Henrich confirmed that Talbot's tales were accurate and that many reservations were precisely as Brown portrayed Rosebud in his book; she had "heard the same in many places from the old people, for example, from the Siksika [Blackfoot] in Montana. Their reservation was fenced in and no one could come or go." At the end of the nineteenth century, they were "threatened with extinction in their concentration camps," the numbers of Siksika dropping "from 8,000 to 400." In her opinion, she wrote, "the American public could have learned about these conditions, which continued well into the twentieth century, if they had wanted to." But then "there are also many millions of Germans among us who claim to have never known anything about the concentration camps; Sachsenhausen, for example," where her husband had been, "lay practically at Berlin's doorstep and a secondary camp was in Lichterfelde in the SS-Kaserne. But people put their heads in the sand, to avoid burdening their own consciences."[68]

Welskopf-Henrich's hope was that contemporary American Indian activism, supported by Germans and others, would make it difficult for people to keep "their heads in the sand," and thus she greeted with pleasure the letters from other readers in the East and the West who told her about their efforts to take up the challenge of advocating for American Indians. These readers discussed sending letters of protest to the U.S. government for the treatment of American Indian activists in the United States' courts and prisons, and to international bodies such as the World Health Organization and the United Nations, in which they argued, for example, that the forced sterilization endured among the Sioux during the twentieth century must be recognized as well as "acts of genocide."[69]

Thus what changed most about German discussions of American Indian eradication and resistance within the second and third decades of the postwar era, was not simply the use of new internationally recognized terms such as genocide and holocaust that could be harnessed to wage political wars for recognition of past and current injustices and crimes; nor was the lingering presence of the Nazi Holocaust in German memory the critical factor. Rather, it was the possibility of activism that came from the rise of a new international understanding of human rights and a new set of forums such as the United Nations, UNESCO, and ultimately the Working Group on Indigenous Populations in which Germans could move beyond local complaints and protests over the conditions faced by American Indians and toward a kind of assistance in a new international space that had not been available during the nineteenth century. And in that sense, Rothberg is certainly correct: international discussions of genocide and the Holocaust created a space not only for "multidirectional memories" and the "articulation of other histories" but also for greater transnational action.[70]

Beyond Displacement

The screening of *Der Letzte Häuptling* (The Last Chief) at the Museum of Ethnology in Berlin in 2004 had the potential to either demonstrate what was new about German concerns for the eradication of American Indians or provoke more bemused comments about displacement. Understanding the former required a long historical perspective, whereas submitting to the later would have been unlikely with that knowledge. The multimedia presentation by journalists Peter Hinz-Rosin and Dirk Rohrbach, which was also the basis of a book, offered the audience a multilevel documentation of some legacies of the 1890 Wounded Knee massacre.[71] Part of the presentation was focused on the efforts of a group of Lakota, led by Leonard Little Finger, to retrieve a lock of hair from a museum in the Woods Memorial Library in Barre, Massachusetts, which was taken from the body of his great-great grandfather, Chief Bigfoot, one of the better-known victims of the Wounded Knee massacre. It was about closure. At the same time, much of the film turned around the creation of a new tradition, retracing the journey of Big Foot's band from the site in North Dakota where Sitting Bull was killed south to the town of Wounded Knee on the Pine Ridge Reservation. That tradition began in 1986, it continues today, and it is generally regarded by participants such as Arvol Looking Horse and Birgil Kills Straight as a somber effort to connect the Lakota past to the Lakota future. In many ways, however, it also documents one phase of German interactions with residents of American reservations; increasingly Germans can be found involved in efforts by people like these Lakotas to reconstitute their lives.

The award-winning presentation by Hinz-Rosin and Rohrbach underscored the Lakota's effort to seek connections across time by tying the history of the Wounded Knee massacre to contemporary conditions on the Pine Ridge Reservation and to the wishes that many residents have for their future. It also celebrated their resistance, which was captured, for example, in Leonard Little Finger's opening line in their aesthetically stunning presentation: "They may have killed our people but they will never kill our way of life." That statement, which reconfirmed a traditionally German conviction about American Indians, was understandably well received by the German audience that watched the presentation with me; the audience was quite at home with the story of Wounded Knee, the discussion of holocaust and genocide that ensued in the film, and the emphasis that the film makers and the people they interviewed placed on the Lakotas' role as survivors. Indeed, seeking to return Big Foot's hair to his people and building connections between the past and the present through an arduous ceremonial ride over two hundred miles of winter prairie, were in many ways metaphors for processes many Germans have eagerly supported for decades.

The film's dual focus on the violence of the past and the violence that overwhelming poverty continues to inflict on Pine Ridge's residents underscored the legacy of genocide in North America that Germans have long captured in their writings, and which many learned to understand through contact with American Indian activists, their books, and their presentations decades ago. The American Indian music that made up the sound track and the testaments Hinz-Rosin and Rohrbach chose to punctuate their narrative underscored the many challenges these people still face in the contemporary world.

While detailing her own heroic efforts to redress some of that suffering, for example, Vashti Apostol-Hurst, executive director of the National Association for American Indian Children and Elders, described her "shock" at the poverty she encountered on the reservation. This, she argued, "is the forgotten minority in America." And that forgetting, she explained, was part of the long process of genocide that has been inflicted on these people: "What's going on here in America is wrong. The American Indian people on the North American continent have gone through the longest Holocaust for the longest period on the largest continent in the history of the planet and they have survived. That is a fact and not my opinion. We in America have almost managed to exterminate an entire race of people."

She believed, she added, that the United States was the greatest land in the world, and she could not accept that the American people would tolerate the situation she found on Pine Ridge if they were aware of it. Consciousness raising was thus a critical part of her work, one of her central goals, just as it had been for people like Biegert, Welskopf-Henrich, and many Germans before them, just as it had been for many authors in *Das Ausland* and *Globus*, and just as it clearly was for Hinz-Rosin and Rohrbach.

Without an understanding of that long legacy of thinking, talking, and writing about the American holocaust in Germany, it would have been easy for audience members to have been taken aback by both the free use of the language of genocide and the production of a German slide show, presentation, and book that emphasized one of the great failings of the United States as much as it stressed the impressive efforts of various Lakotas. Viewed from a purely geopolitical perspective, it would also have been easy to read both the film and its reception as an act of gross displacement, a rather specious effort to throw rocks at American misfortunes from the glass house of the compromised German present. The point this chapter has tried to make, however, is that displacement has little to do with the character of Hinz-Rosin and Rohrbach's book and film, their efforts, or the efforts of those who support them. They are, rather, the product of many Germans' long engagement with that part of American history as well as the opportunities presented by a new international arena, which allows contemporary Germans to support American Indians in unprecedented new ways. The prominent interests and concerns that drive those support efforts are not new, as many American Indians, much more than most non-Native Americans, have long understood.

CHAPTER 8

Receptions in Native America

The Red Cloud Indian School on the Pine Ridge Reservation is an oasis on the prairie. Nestled behind a rise just off of Highway 18 about four miles north of the town of Pine Ridge, it makes a stunning impression. Tourists approach it from Hot Springs and Wind Cave National Park on the edge of the Black Hills to the west, drive down from Rapid City or the Bad Lands in the north, come up from Nebraska to the south, or traverse east to west across the reservation on Highway 18 before hooking up north to the school. Regardless of the approach, the vast grasslands they cross make it hard not to notice the trees lining the road to the school buildings, whose clean lines and well-kept grounds compliment the curious faces that often congregate around the main entrance.

People come for a variety of reasons, not the least of which is the Heritage Center Museum, which hosts the Annual Red Cloud Indian School Art Show and boasts an impressive gallery of American Indian art. During my first visit, I came to see Brother C. M. Simon, who not only was responsible for the show's success but also managed to amass one of the country's most impressive collections of American Indian art while directing the museum. In addition, he seemed to know everyone and everything about the reservation, and he was keenly aware of Germans' affinities for American Indians. He had met so many Germans while working there. It was, in fact, Brother Simon who introduced me to the *European Review of Native American Studies*, a journal organized by Christian Feest, which frequently draws out the ironies in interactions between American Indians and Europeans. He had one of the few collections in the United States at that time. He also encouraged me to visit a number of Germans who were living on the reservation, some of whom had been there for many years. He was kind enough to provide me with considerable historical orientation as well, discussing the history of the

FIGURE 33. Arthur Amiotte, "This place reminds us of home . . ."
(Courtesy of the artist.)

show Indians who had been to Germany and naming some of the families whose relatives had been to Europe. He was incredibly generous with his knowledge and his time.

One of the families he mentioned descended from Standing Bear and Louise Rieneck, the Austrian nurse he had met while traveling with Buffalo Bill in 1889. Unbeknownst to me at the time, I was already familiar with one of their descendants, Arthur Amiotte. While surveying Liselotte Welskopf-Henrich's collected papers in Berlin, I had read some of the correspondence between her and Amiotte when he was a young art instructor at the Porcupine Day School on the Pine Ridge Reservation from 1969 to 1971. I had also seen tapes of interviews made during his visit to the Karl-May-Museum in Radebeul over three decades later, where he made a favorable impression with both its personnel and the public who came to hear him speak. I was eager to learn more about him.

As I read up on Welskopf-Henrich's correspondent, I became familiar with his art. His talent immediately transfixed me. I was especially taken by the series of Ledger Art Collages that capture, among other things, the history of his family as well as the history of the many transitions the Lakota negotiated during the early reservation period (1880–1930).

Most striking for me was the mix of European and American Indian sights and symbols in the collages, particularly those he created while working in Europe and those that drew on his relative's own travels there with Buffalo Bill. Standing Bear had returned to Europe several times between his first excursion in 1887 and his last trip in 1891. His tours of palaces, castles, cathedrals, and his encounters with royalty and other Europeans had become part of his family's lore.[1] Indeed, to a certain degree, it was Standing Bear's stories, passed down across generations, that drew Amiotte to Europe and inspired his Ledger Art Collages.[2]

Art historian Janet Catherine Berlo has called these collages "mnemonic works of cultural memory, which unlock narratives of personal and cultural survival."[3] It is an astute assessment; his collages are multilayered historical works of art that combine seemingly eclectic times and places and emphasize the importance of change, transition, incorporation, and persistence rather than radical rupture. They also capture the intertwined nature of Lakota and European lives and life worlds, reminding us that just as ideas, concepts, and notions of American Indians became part and parcel of German cultures through the nineteenth and into the twentieth century, similar kinds of notions, based initially on personal experiences and family narratives, became integrated into the lives and life worlds of many American Indians. In Native America, much as in Germany, encounters engendered stories that took on meaning and encouraged inquiry.

The multifaceted exchanges that often took place across generations in this and other families became clear to me when, years later in the spring of 2008, I had the pleasure of meeting Amiotte in his home in Custer, South Dakota. Traveling into the Black Hills from the Red Cloud School, I was eager to ask him about his family history, his experiences in Germany, and his correspondence with Welskopf-Henrich. I learned that Welskopf-Henrich sought him out during one of her trips to the United States after seeing some of his artwork on display in the Sioux Indian Museum in Rapid City, South Dakota. I learned as well that she made a good impression with her energy and inquiries. He described her as a German Ella Deloria—grandmotherly, kindly, very interested in people, eager to meet his own grandmother, Christina Standing Bear, in her home on the reservation, insisting on drinking coffee with her there, just as she insisted on sampling a whiskey in Rapid City. Most striking to me, however, was his reiteration, during our discussion of Germans' fascination for all things Indian, of the very notions of German tribalism that Welskopf-Henrich had detailed to him in her letters decades earlier.[4] It was at that moment, when he generously shared those recollections, that I recognized the flows of information across the Atlantic between Germans and American Indians captured not only in Amiotte's collages but also in the ways in which he and others tell their stories of interactions with Germans, and how those stories have developed across the twentieth century.

If it is possible to talk about consistencies and continuities in Germans' fascination with American Indians over a long period of time, it is also possible to discuss American Indians' reception of that fascination. It is more difficult; records from the nineteenth century are sporadic and limited. Even the material produced by the many show Indians who traveled to Germany is thin: many of those participants spoke no English; most who did were illiterate; those who could write kept few records; and few of the letters they may have sent home, or those that were dictated by others, were saved over time. Yet the material is there, in oral histories, government and business archives, eclectic collections of private letters scattered across the United States and Europe, and it improves over the course of the twentieth century. That does not mean that we can identify a consensus of what American Indians thought about Germans or their elective affinities any more than we can find a consensus among American Indians about anything else. It does not exist. It is, however, possible to identify a set of consistent opinions and impressions among American Indians that reoccur frequently over the course of the twentieth century in situations in which interactions between Germans and American Indians become frequent or intense. Indeed, stereotypes, clichés, and characterizations of Germans took shape across the twentieth century, and these have much to tell us about the reception of Germans' elective affinities, as well as about Germans themselves.

Diffusion and Cultural Traits

Standing Bear was neither the first nor the last of many American Indians who met and loved Europeans while working in Europe. Nor was he the only one to bring European ideas, customs, and habits back with him to North America. The fascinating research conducted by Lakota anthropologist JoAllyn Archambault on his relationship with Louise and their life together on the Pine Ridge Reservation revealed some of the ways in which Louise's integration into reservation life allowed her to contribute to the ever developing crafts produced by Lakota women. The fact that her parents also accompanied them to Pine Ridge and then relocated among Germans in Chicago helped as well. They were able to supply her with fine cloth, which she and Standing Bear used to line the caskets he made and sold, and which she redistributed to other inhabitants of the reservation. They also supplied her with medicines, which allowed her to become a country doctor of sorts. Thus even as she adapted to life on the reservation, she contributed to it and, in her own way, to Lakota culture.[5]

Such cultural exchanges began decades earlier with the many *Völkerschauen* that toured Germany. The 1885 trip by nine Bella Coolas is the best documented. Adrian Jacobsen, who hired the Bella Coolas, brought them to Germany, and directed their travel and performances there, left an extensive collection of correspondence, notebooks, and photographs. Wolfgang Haberland, a former director of the American section of the Hamburgisches Museum für Völkerkunde, sorted through Jacobsen's letters, placed them in individual plastic sleeves, and organized them chronologically in tidy binders, creating a fantastic archive from the material. He also followed the Bella Coolas back to North America, investigating the impact their trip had on their lives and looking for traces of their experiences within their community in British Columbia.

Haberland published several essays based on that material. They detail the story of the Bella Coolas' venture from its conception in Germany through Jacobsen's efforts to locate the people, the problems he faced getting them to Europe, their experiences performing and traveling, their disappointment upon realizing that they failed to meet the German publics' expectations, and the difficulty of performing the same dances and rituals again and again over many months. That repetition, however, led to innovation, to the manufacture of rituals, and to a show that entertained the performers as well as their audiences. Moreover, as Haberland makes clear, their time in Germany was not limited to their performances. They had plenty of casual interactions with Germans as well.

Indeed, in addition to Jacobsen's photographs of the Bella Coolas dressed in traditional costumes and engaged in performances, there are many pictures of them in the European clothing they wore offstage. Among those is a striking image of Isk-ka-lusta dressed in a European suit with his German girlfriend sitting on his lap, an image that struck Haberland as particularly important because it confirmed the tales he had heard when he traveled to British Columbia in 1978 to seek out the descendants of these men. The most common stories about them turned around their popularity with German women, which he took to be exaggerations typical of young men who had traveled abroad until he saw these pictures. Indeed, Billy Jones, ostensibly the longest surviving of these performers, was later recorded as saying that "German women followed us around," they had frequent liaisons, and many German women wanted to marry these men, but they were unable to return "with their German girls" because of the rules established by Jacobsen and the agreements he had made with the Canadian government. One of these men, however, brought something back: Alec Davis, who spent most of his time with one woman, was reputed to have gained an "amazing fluency" in German that "he retained for the rest of his life."[6]

During their thirteen months in Germany, in fact, the Bella Coolas became quite comfortable with Germans, their manners, and customs. Margarete Cronau, the wife of Rudolf Cronau, wrote an essay in the *Leipziger Tage-Anzeiger* stressing the degree to which they had adopted many German "habits and customs." She invited them to her home for a dinner party and recorded how at ease they appeared in European clothing, using cutlery at German tables, eating German foods with relish (she stressed their ability to consume large amounts), drinking beer, and engaging in polite banter and games.[7]

In addition to these personal interactions—which led to language acquisition, relationships, and the adoption of new forms of dress and diet—they also observed their surroundings and took those observations home with them. That is captured most notably in a house built in the 1890s by the Nuxalk (Bella Coola) chief Clellamin, which was replicated during the 1980s in the Grand Hall of the Canadian Museum of Civilization. According to Janet Catherine Berlo and Ruth Phillips, "the house represents Nusq'alst, the supernatural founder of Clellamin's family, who descended to earth from the world above and became the mountain bearing his name." They also argue that the house "clearly reflects a trip to Germany made by a group of Nuxalk [Bella Coola] in 1885." While they "danced for German audiences," Berllo and Phillips argue, the "German towns they visited provided an architectural spectacle for their eyes, details of which were incorporated into the house built after their return." The most important details are "the towers topped with gold balls (representing rocks to which Nuxalk tied their canoes at the time of a great flood), the blue and white stripes (representing the snow on the mountain peak) and the dormer windows (through which peek animals who inhabit the mountain) also recall northern European houses."[8] Indeed, the blue and white color combination would strike even the most casual observer as a feature typical of many southern German buildings.

Perhaps more important than tracing out the specific manifestations of German culture (which nineteenth-century German diffusionists would have termed "cultural traits") that accompanied individual performers back to North America is acknowledging the vibrant, transatlantic communities of performers and impresarios that took shape during the early reservation period. Even then, the point is not simply to recognize that people like White Buffalo Man established friendships with Germans such as Elk Eber, or that a few, such as Standing Bear, returned home with German-speaking spouses, but to understand that in general, American Indian performers and their German hosts developed a transatlantic performance culture that persisted for decades and resonated on both sides of the Atlantic.

Indeed, if we shift the focus of research from tracing the diffusion of particular cultural traits back and forth across the Atlantic to listening to the communications produced at that time, we learn not only that American Indian performers enjoyed themselves during their travels and asserted themselves in their negotiations but that they also continued to think of themselves as engaged with Europeans long after they returned to North America. Their worldviews, in other words, remained open to Germany and other parts of Europe after their return home, as Amiotte's art documents so well. Germans, in essence, remained on these performers' mental maps—hence the creation of the Nuxalk house, and, more poignantly, the ongoing correspondence received by J. C. Miller, German impresarios, and American Indian performers over decades.

Quotidian Conversations

In the summer of 1913, communications between J. C. Miller and his employee Wayne Beasly, who was in charge of the Miller Brothers' performers in Germany that year, turned around the quotidian. They ranged from discussion of an accident—an American Indian girl was taken to a doctor after being mauled by a tiger—to efforts by Dick White Calf and his wife to break their contract and be sent home early by getting drunk and refusing to work. They also discussed Beasly's own decision to go "on the water wagon," which Miller approved with relief, and Sarrasani's interest in getting more performers. They covered the good business Beasly thought Miller could do with Sarrasani, the poor business suffered by Buffalo Bill's Wild West that year, and the fact that Zack Miller was traveling to Germany to deal with Sarrasani directly. In general, Beasly assured Miller that "outside of the Indians being a little crumby [lice infested], everything is going alright," and then he puzzled over his dilemma: "I will have to get them dipped I guess only I have not got a vat." That comment led to a good deal of amusement in Oklahoma, and a query from Miller about the origins of the lice: "You mentioned that the Indians were crumby, but did not say whether they were United States crumbs or natives of Germany. I spoke to Iron Tail, our chief, about it and he said if they were German crumbs he would like to have you send some of them back over and see what the cross would be."[9]

What we find in such communications, in other words, is less transference than broad, casual interactions in which the discussion of lice among American Indian performers in Bromberg struck Iron Tail in Oklahoma as humorous, but no further from everyday events than their transatlantic discussion of sobriety, business opportunities, or White Calf's efforts to break his contract by violating the rules against drinking.

Indeed, there was plenty of everyday controversy mixed in with the fantastic experiences recalled by Standing Bear and others. In 1925, for example, Beatrice Kent and Frank Charcoal protested against Circus Krone's provision that performers should not leave the circus without permission and refused to work for several days. That led to fines, communications between Joe Miller and Krone, and reconciliation.[10] The following year, Sarah Ghost Dog became ill while working for Sarrasani. As she was convalescing in a tent, a fire broke out and she was severely burned. That provided her son, William Ghost Dog, with an opportunity to write angry letters to the Indian Agent E. W. Jermark in Pine Ridge denouncing Sarrasani and his treatment of American Indian performers.[11]

Ghost Dog complained about their treatment, demanded that his mother, who soon died from her injuries, be buried in Dresden rather than Essen where she had passed away, and he quit the circus in anger over Sarrasani's refusal to follow his wishes. Afterward, he realized he was penniless in Europe with no way home, and he demanded transportation. That led to a flurry of letters inquiring into the conditions of this troupe, which produced photographs of the burial, acknowledgments of thanks from Jermarck to the Miller Brothers for covering the expense of Ghost Dog's solo trip home, and revelations from Germany that much of the contention arose within Ghost Dog's family. He had spent too much time drinking and carousing at night; he had become involved with a young German girl whose parents had begun harassing him, and he had contracted a bad case of venereal disease which infuriated his wife, who had accompanied him to Germany with their two sons, and who also had to accompany him to a German hospital for their treatment.[12]

These quotidian issues were Miller's headache, and something that made the international shows no different from the ones he sent to Buffalo or St. Louis. What set them apart and made them particularly memorable for many performers, however, was the ways in which the everyday combined with the exceptional and standard fare included high standards as performers encountered dignitaries and royalty and received the royal treatment in Germany as well as England and other European states. Certainly Miller became used to hearing, as he did from Sarrasani in 1926, that his most recent troupe had "found good accommodation in especially prepared sitting rooms," in Dresden, and that soon after the performers' arrival they were received by "the Lord Mayor of Dresden, Dr. Blüher, in presence of the consul of [sic] USA."[13] That did not happen in Buffalo.

The important point, however, is that as a result of such treatment, and the fact that American Indians from Oklahoma and Pine Ridge increasingly thought of Germany as a place where they could go and often liked to go, Sarrasani and Dresden became as well known on reservations as Miller and his shows. The Lakotas' mental map accommodated them, and Germany became a place many Lakotas considered going. Many regarded it as a good place to work and a good place to be. Indeed, it was a place to which many performers, such as Jas Sweetgrass from Porcupine, South Dakota, made a point of returning again and again.[14]

Two-Two's Grave

When Sarrasani sent his note to Miller about introducing his 1926 troupe to Dresden's Lord High Mayor, he also remarked on his delight at "greeting old friends," especially Lina Two-Two, the wife of Edward Two-Two, who had chosen to be buried in Dresden twelve years earlier. Much like Standing Bear's descendants, Edward Two-Two's people on and around Pine Ridge retained a connection to Germany across the twentieth century because of his enthusiasm for Germany, his affinity for Dresden, and his choice to stay where, rumor had it, he felt he had been better treated than in the United States.

Edward Two-Two, his wife Lina, his stepson James Garcia, and their daughter Mary Bear Shield were among the famous 1910 group of Lakotas hired by Adrian Jacobsen to work for Carl Hagenbeck in Hamburg.[15] They were also among the performers who eventually agreed to accept a position with Sarrasani after they had fulfilled their contracts in Hamburg. Pleased with the conditions in Germany, they traveled with Sarrasani's circus throughout the country. While performing in Essen, however, Two-Two became ill and eventually he passed away on 27 July 1914 at the age of fifty-six.

The prewar contracts Hagenbeck and Sarrasani signed with the U.S. government and Indian agents on any reservation required them to return the bodies of American Indians who might pass away while in their employ. "In this case," however, as the American counsel George Eugene Eagen explained, "it was the expressed wish of Two-Two that he wanted to be buried in the Catholic Cemetery in Dresden, the home of the circus. His wife, daughter and stepson coincided with this wish," and they "signed a paper in which they waive[d] the right to have the body sent home."

Eagen noted as well that Sarrasani organized "a most imposing funeral" in the circus tent in Essen, in which "all of the members of the circus, employees, and the Directors" took part. "A temporary improvised Chapel was arranged and the coffin wrapped in American Flags placed on a bier draped in black and surrounded with Palms and the many beautiful flower offerings of his friends and admirers in the circus." The service, he wrote, "was performed by three priests from the Catholic Church in Essen-Ruhr," and afterward "the body was carried by the Indians to the entrance of the circus and there placed in a hearse," "conveyed to the railroad," and then to Dresden.[16]

Two-Two was buried in Dresden's New Catholic Cemetery, where his grave has been maintained for almost a century by a succession of German hobbyists. Indeed, decades after his passing, and despite two world wars, these hobbyists continued to venerate his grave, replacing the original, dilapidated stone with a new, clean copy, and transforming the grave into a meeting place during the 1960s. For a time, the Radebeul Club Old Manitou met near his grave as often as twice a week.[17] And it has remained a common rendezvous for such Germans to this day.[18]

Two-Two's descendants have long known that his grave received this treatment, and that too is part of family lore on Pine Ridge, one of the many stories that circulate about the lives and times of show Indians who traveled to the other side of the Atlantic. Over the years, various descendants of Edward and Lina Two-Two have made an effort to visit the grave. In 2004, for example, their great-grandson Clayton Graham traveled to Dresden in search of his family history. Taking part in a film organized by Marc Halberstadt about Germans, Jews, and American Indians, he made a point of traveling to Dresden, visiting the grave, and meeting people such as Hartmut Rietschel, who continues to care for the grave.

Nine decades after Two-Two's passing, Clayton Graham saw that Germans continued to gather feathers to leave at his great grandfather's grave, placing them there together with small American flags, offerings of tobacco, and sometimes sweet grass and bread. Rietschel, who later met Graham while visiting members of the Two-Two family in Pine Ridge, was eager to give him a tour of the cemetery, the surrounding area, and the city. They ate döner

FIGURE 34. Two-Two's grave. (Photo by the author)

kebab together, discussed Lakota history, American history, and Rietschel's extensive efforts to learn more about American Indians while growing up in the German Democratic Republic. Rietschel told him some of the history of the connection between the hobbyists and Two-Two as well as some of the reasons for his own interests in American Indians and his (incredibly successful) efforts to try and locate the graves of all the performers who had passed away in Germany. He showed Graham images of the Elbsandsteinge-birge, outside of Dresden, and he gave Graham the background he sought for his great grandfather's decision to be buried there, near Saxony's Black Hills, and why for Two-Two, Germany was a good place to be.[19]

Hierarchies of Discourse

Clayton Graham's 2004 visit to Dresden caused nothing like the sensation engendered by Two-Two's arrival more than ninety years earlier, but members of the local press were interested in his visit. They wanted to know more about this international connection enjoyed by their city, and they had questions about what the hobbyists had been doing in the New Catholic Cemetery since unification (1990). In particular, when Heidrun Hannusch from the *Dresdner Neueste Nachrichten* interviewed Hartmut Rietschel about his efforts in caring for Two-Two's grave, she asked about the American flags he and others had placed on it. They struck her as rather strong political markers for a cemetery that was located for decades in a state that banned the American flag, and which was now part of a country that had come to eschew gestures of overt nationalism. Rietschel assured her, however, that the flags were not political in that way, rather they were something that belonged on the grave of any American veteran, something Two-Two's grave should enjoy regardless of its location. That was a point his visiting relative understood, and it was something he thought any veteran could comprehend, or anyone who knew about American Indians and their veneration of veterans. Yet the reporter's query is also particularly understandable, given the context of Two-Two's death directly before the outbreak of World War I and the history of the twentieth century that followed. Germany, after all, has not always been regarded as a good place.

Indeed, despite the veteran Two-Two's high regard for Germany and the positive impressions of Germany that his family and other American Indian performers circulated on the reservations before and after the war, American Indians in general exhibited few qualms about engaging the Germans in war. Just the opposite: young men from Pine Ridge and other American Indian reservations volunteered to fight "the Hun" in exceptionally high numbers. As they did so, they exhibited biases, embraced stereotypes, and uttered slanders that were typical of all American soldiers at the time—and which were diametrically opposed to the statements uttered by the show Indians. Indeed, if one can speak of multiple discourses about American Indians circulating in Germany during this period, the same can be said about "the Red Man's German": for many American Indians, the Germans were also quite good to eliminate.

Indeed, although German officers, enlisted men, and civilians followed their British and American counterparts in assigning strong warrior stereotypes to American Indians, there is little evidence that American Indians reciprocated. It is, in fact, striking how consistently they accepted the wartime propaganda about the Germans along with other Americans, and how eager many became to kill, and to discuss killing, German soldiers. When they did this, there was little reverence in their words or tone. The German soldiers were often portrayed as weak, unskilled warriors, or uncivilized beasts.

The eagerness of American Indians to participate in World War I varied from one tribe to the next. The Onondagas are famous for declaring war on Germany independently after a crowd mistreated some of their members in Germany during the outbreak of the war. Their tribal leaders encouraged enlistment; for a variety of reasons, others did not.[20] As Thomas Britten has noted, however, there were many eager warriors among the Lakota who were delighted to travel to Germany for war. Francis Nelson, for example, an Oglala from Pine Ridge, wrote directly to Secretary of War Newton D. Baker Jr. requesting permission to enlist. He explained that he was keen to fight for the United States as a "Real American" and stressed that "if I could only get out in those trenches and scalp a few of this [sic] dirty Germans, I would be one of the happiest Indians living.'" Similarly, another Sioux, John Thunder from Pipestone, Manitoba, "challenged his brethren to demonstrate the courage and bravery of their warrior ancestors," arguing that "'the bad-language people [Germans] are trying to destroy our government and rob us of our homes and so all our men and youth have risen to defend ourselves."[21]

Disdain often accompanied that eagerness. Indeed, a frequently cited Lakota war song contained the following:

> The Germans retreat crying
> The Lakota boys are charging from afar
> The Germans retreat crying
> Lakota boys, the Germans,
> Whose many lands you have taken,
> Are crying like women there
> German, I have been watching your tracks
> Worthless one! I would have followed you
> Wherever you would have gone.[22]

Such sentiments were not unique to the Lakota; they were ubiquitous in the interviews conducted by Joseph K. Dixon among American Indian soldiers.[23] Jesse Lewis, a twenty-four-year-old Choctaw from Bentley, Oklahoma, and a graduate of the Carlisle school, for example, was wounded in the shoulder and the right elbow, the hip, and the back of the neck by shrapnel and machine gun bullets at Verdun in September 1918. Interviewed by Dixon in Greenhut Hospital, Lewis reported that "'if I had it to do over again, I would do it. It ain't much bad. Dutchman, he scared of Indians.'" He reported that he had captured two Germans on one occasion, and he recounted how they shouted "mercy on me" after their machine gun ran out of ammunition. One of the Germans could speak English, and Lewis laughed as he recalled him saying that the "'Indian is full blood American. Indian great men. We are afraid of them. I can fight French and English, but I don't want to fight Americans.'" Similarly, a twenty-two-year-old Pawnee from Oklahoma recounted facing the Germans in "the longest day," and the "biggest day" of his life: "We had had nothing to eat for three days," he recalled, "but I fed upon the satisfaction of knowing that I had fed death into the ranks of the damned Boche. The German under cover is all right," he reported, "but face to face he cannot face cold steel. They might have been brave, but I didn't see any of it."[24]

"Damned Boche" indeed. Many of the men Dixon interviewed called the Germans much worse. Frank Kayser from New York City, who lost one of his legs in the fighting, "said he would have willingly given both legs" because he had seen "what the Boche had done to the women and children."[25] Similarly, Fred Fast Horse from Rosebud recalled that "when they drafted me, I wanted to go because my people were fighters. My father was a chief and fought Custer, and I wanted to go and fight the Germans because they would come over here and destroy our free government."[26] Along with many others, he claimed to "despise" the Germans, or as one recruit from Oklahoma termed them, "the villainous Dutch."[27]

There were then, multiple discourses about Germans among American Indians, and show Indians' positive experiences in pre-war Germany did little to undercut Allied propaganda among American Indian recruits. In fact, those experiences did nothing to prevent young men from the very reservations that produced the most show Indians (e.g., Pine Ridge) from embracing negative stereotypes about German society and culture. At the same time, however, the experience of World War I, even the high casualties among American Indian veterans, and the oft-quoted Lakota war song did little to dissuade performers from Pine Ridge, such as Lina Two-Two, from returning to Germany as soon as possible once the war was over. They easily picked up again on the positive rhetoric about Germans that had been so common earlier and returned home to circulate their favorable impressions of life and work in interwar Germany until another war arrived and the relative hierarchy of the discourses of good and bad Germans switched again.

Postwar Interlude: Heidi and Oscar Howe

The interlude of World War II, and the shifting rhetoric that accompanied it, was also short lived. From the perspective of American Indian servicemen, it was just over three years (7 December 1941–2 September 1945). Here too, anti-German propaganda rose in immediate importance as America entered the war, and American Indians along with other American troops embraced the negative stereotypes of Germans circulated by the Allies. After the Nazis surrendered (May 1945), those ignoble stereotypes dissipated fairly quickly among American Indians as well as other servicemen. To a certain degree, this was part and parcel of the postwar realignments that Peter Novick and others have underscored in their discussions of the American and Western European geopolitical considerations that accompanied the emerging Cold War. Perhaps more important, however, were the many interpersonal relationships on the ground—as the U.S. military high command and their land relations officers knew so well.

Wartime propaganda, for example, did not prevent the American Indian soldier Oscar Howe from falling in love with a young woman who had belonged to Der Bund Deutscher Mädel (League of German Girls in the Hitler Youth). Indeed, after three and a half years in the military, fighting through North Africa, Italy, and Germany, he found her delightful.[28] Oscar Howe met Adelheid (Heidi) Hampel in her father's clothing store in Biedenkopf an der Lahn, in Hessen. By her account, he refused to leave after entering their store: "He just stayed and stayed," persisting even after it was time for the family to close the shop and sit down for a meal. After his death in 1983, Heidi Howe described this obstinate soldier as a man of much endurance, one who immediately struck her as intelligent, but who made his greatest impression by standing fast in the doorway of her home until she would "agree to go out with him." They ultimately did, with dictionaries in hand, struggling to communicate.[29]

In addition to being intelligent and persistent, Howe also revealed during their initial meeting that he was "a Sioux Indian." At first, Heidi Hampel did not believe him. She had "read a lot about Indians," and Howe "did not fit the story image."[30] Indeed, reflecting on their initial meeting years later, she wrote in 1961: "Oscar Howe did not look at all like the Indians I had read about: no feathers, no breechcloth, no hooknose. Instead, he appeared in the uniform of an American soldier and I mistook him for Chinese, or some other kind of Oriental. I must say, I was more than a little disappointed."[31]

Like many other German women and U.S. servicemen who fell in love, they hoped to get married. Her parents tolerated their relationship but assumed it would end after Howe left Germany. It did not. They stayed in contact during the more than two years that separated his departure in late 1945 and their reunion in New York City in 1947. During that time, Howe worked to support himself as an artist and to earn the money necessary to pay for Heidi's flight to the United States. That moment came in 1947, when his painting *Dakota Duck Hunt* won the grand prize in the second Annual National Indian Painting Competition at the Philbrook Art Center in Tulsa, Oklahoma. The $350 prize provided him with the funds he needed to fly her to New York City.[32] From there, they traveled west to South Dakota. Knowing that they "could not get married in South Dakota because he was an Indian," however, they stopped in Chicago and were married by a justice of the peace on 29 July 1947.[33]

If that revelation was Heidi Howe's first indication that racial relations were indeed much different in the United States than they were in Germany, it was certainly not the last. The Howes first lived in Oklahoma, where Oscar Howe worked on a commission to illustrate a book titled *North American Indian Costumes* (1952) before taking advantage of the G.I. Bill and returning to Dakota Wesleyan University in Mitchell, South Dakota. Heidi Howe recalled the bus ride north with their daughter Inge Dawn, who had been born in June 1948: "People really looked at us. An Indian and a white being married you know." They were surprised, if not irritated, and their looks sometimes took on an aggressive edge. That left her exasperated, as did her husband's behavior in response to such racism: "Oscar was afraid to walk on the sidewalk," he would "walk clear around the other side when a white person was walking by." That frustrated her. As a young German who had experienced more liberal race relations in postwar Germany, she felt he "had just as much right to walk on the sidewalk as anyone else." Those prejudices were something that their daughter Inge Dawn had to face as well. As a girl, other "children would make fun of her because Oscar was an Indian."[34]

In South Dakota, Heidi Howe also saw the more general impact of American racism. When describing her surprise at the degree to which her future husband's physiognomy differed from the stereotypes she had absorbed from her youth, she noted, however, that "the greatest let down was yet to come: when I met the Sioux Indians here in South Dakota it was a real shock. Where were the proud, brave, and noble Indians I had read about? Here their once noble spirit had been broken, and they lived on reservations under the most deplorable conditions."[35] She later informed herself about the history that created those conditions, which taught her much about the challenges her husband and others like him had long faced, and like many Germans before and after her, she reacted with a mixture of anger, frustration, and determination, channeling a striking amount of energy into helping her husband develop his talents and pursue his goals. She took care of many bureaucratic responsibilities, helped with his canvases, and ensured that he had time to paint. Most of all, she became an unfailing promoter of his talent. Accepting his wish to stay near his people in South Dakota, rather than move to a center of American Indian art such as Santa Fe, where he surely would have prospered financially, she nevertheless worked to ensure that his national and international reputation grew. Indeed, his biographer John Day assigns her "50% of the credit" for his success—so important were her efforts to promote Howe's work during and after his lifetime.[36]

The result, in this exceptional case, was that a talented artist who was born into poverty on the Crow Creek Reservation in South Dakota was able to pursue an M.F.A. degree in Fine Arts at the University of Oklahoma, become the director of Art at the high school in Pierre, South Dakota (1953–57), then an assistant professor of art at the University of South Dakota, artist in residence and director of the W. H. Over Museum (1957), artist laureate of South Dakota (1960), and then be declared "the preeminent living South Dakota artist" by Governor Ralph Herseth.[37] From there, his career excelled even further, awards accumulated, and he became one of the leading American Indian artists of his generation and a famous American. Most importantly, perhaps, he became what many would describe as an "ambassador between Indian and non-Indian cultures, an inspiration for budding artists and Native Americans, and a revolutionary who broke important barriers through his ideas and artwork."[38]

His biographers often rehearse those facts. Less well known is that he remained well connected to Germany and German America through his family. Heidi Howe's sister, Waltraud, joined them in South Dakota in the 1950s, and the family returned repeatedly to Germany to visit relatives, where the generally reserved Oscar Howe was reportedly more animated than in the United States. His daughter Inge Dawn recalls those visits with some pleasure, as well as the visits they received from German friends and family over the years. As Howe's reputation was established, his studio in Vermillion became a destination for artists and others interested in his art and his insights into Lakota spirituality. Inge Dawn recalled one woman, "a professor from East Germany," who spent a week in her father's studio speaking with him. The grandmotherly Welskopf-Henrich initiated that friendship with the family during one of her tours of the Dakotas and stayed in touch with them until she passed away, corresponding and sending them gifts and packages. As a result, the Howes' was one of the Lakota homes in which her books could be found on the shelves.[39]

Receiving Aid

Many Germans shared Heidi Howe's reaction to the persistent poverty on American Indian reservations and the racism faced by North American Indians, and they sought to help. Most could do so only in minor ways. Nevertheless, a surprising number tried, and increasingly, American Indians noticed those efforts, and remarked on them.

During the 1950s, for example, contacts between German hobbyists and American Indians began where they had left off in the 1930s, with trade in artifacts and goods. Max Oliv, for example, who traveled to Rapid City as early as 1956, even encountered remnants of those earlier contacts. On one occasion, for example, he recognized a picture of a white trapper hanging in a trading post in Pine Ridge as a German collector named Eric Salinsky, posing for the picture in interwar Berlin.

Increasingly, however, as reports about conditions on reservations flowed back to Germany, such traditional collecting trips were combined with efforts to assist the communities with whom hobbyists had contact. Oliv, for instance, became one of the many Germans who began bringing (and sending) money to the Porcupine Day School on the Pine Ridge Reservation, acting as a kind of emissary for different German groups. His first installment of one thousand marks was collected by the Karlsruhe association Zukunft für Kinder (Future for the Children) in reaction to reports they had heard about conditions on the reservation. More installments followed from other concerned Germans. At first these were directed to established institutions and then increasingly to activists such as Madonna Gilbert, as she and others set up the American Indian Movement's now famous survival schools in reaction to the conditions American Indian children faced in government institutions.[40]

Indeed, by the late 1950s politically engaged hobbyists in West Germany, calling themselves "Friends of the Indians," were writing and signing petitions in support of American Indian activism of all kinds, and some exerted considerable energy culling American Indian publications for information about the challenges facing American Indians and then disseminating that information through West German publications and meetings. As they raised awareness, organized petitions, and penned letters to North American governments and associations, they also began raising donations and stimulating associations such as Zukunft für Kinder into collecting efforts of their own. Already in 1958, for example, Senator Paul Douglas from Illinois received letters and petitions from hobbyist movements centered in Frankfurt and Graz (Austria) in support of the National Congress of American Indians' (NCAI) four-point program against termination (the U.S. government's efforts to end its recognition of tribal sovereignty and tribal members' exemption from many taxes and laws), which he recorded in the February 1958 Congressional Record.

As more letters and petitions to the Canadian and American governments followed, Native America took notice and responded, and a dialogical relationship began to take shape that would pave the way for later activism.[41] Indeed, when we examine the hobbyist journals from the 1960s, we not only find ever increasing installments on the state of Native America, reports on the members' current efforts to aid American Indian leaders and communities, and calls for further action but also reprints of letters from people such as George Manuel, a Shuswap from British Columbia, and president of the North American Indian Brotherhood. In 1963 Manuel explained to the German members of the International Friends of the Indians that "it is immensely satisfying to know that people in far Europe have an active interest in the problems facing North American Indians." Referring to a recent talk he had given that sketched out the many challenges his people faced, he stressed "that the help and support—that is the moral support—that I receive from the European friends of the Indians, is exceedingly valuable for me personally and for the members of the Indian Associations who have elected me to represent them." "I am so pleased to be able to tell you," he continued, "that your collaboration has given me much new hope and courage." Recognizing the potential political capital inherent in European aid, he asked them to continue their work, to advocate further on behalf of his cause, and to distribute his talk as broadly as possible. As he explained to the Germans, if the Canadian government recognized that American Indians' concerns were gaining "the world's attention" and that there is a "world opinion" about the "Indian problem," then the "Indian problem could be placed on a new foundation." Indeed, "in this way," he remarked, "the Indian Friends in Europe can do more for us than we can achieve for ourselves here in Canada."[42]

When people such as Manuel welcomed the assistance they could receive from Europeans and encouraged them to do more, they stimulated increased efforts among the "Indian Friends" to spread information across

Germany. That, in turn, led to more volunteers, more petitions and signature drives, and eventually a fairly well-organized effort by some German "Indian Friends" to collect funds to support individuals, associations, and communities and to send money as well as moral support across the Atlantic.

As a result, by the early 1960s Germany was known in Native America as a place not only where one would be treated well as soldier or performer but also where American Indians could appeal for support, and the politically oriented members of the International Friends of the Indians soon began receiving more requests for assistance. In 1960, for example, LaVerne Madigan from the Association of American Indian Affairs wrote them a letter about the Seminole's fight for their land in Florida, requesting that Germans send complaints to Fred A. Seaton, secretary of the interior, to show that people outside of the United States were watching how the government treated American Indians. Receiving a strong response, she wrote a second letter explaining that the problems faced by the Seminole were widespread, that the Oglala and Northern Cheyenne faced similar land disputes, and that they could use the Germans' help as well.

These letters provided the budding German activists with fuel for their fire. They eagerly harnessed the information as well as the anecdotes of ironic resistance and racial juxtapositions. Madigan wrote, for example, that she had recently listened to an "old Cheyenne with long braids and a light in his eye" remark during an assembly that "if they could just hold on to their land a bit longer" everything would be fine, because he had heard that "all the whites want to go to the moon" and once they had bid the last one farewell they could return to their lands and their lives.[43] Sharing such sarcasm and humor about John F. Kennedy's space program and American Indians' concerns with the German activists drew American Indians closer to the people who sought to support them, and such stories stimulated sympathy and admiration among the readers of the German journals and the people the German hobbyists approached for signatures and donations. Thus the German organizers quickly circulated such anecdotes in Germany, reproducing them alongside pointed requests from people such as Father Edwards at the Red Cloud Day School at the Holy Rosary Mission in Pine Ridge, who wrote to them about the many difficulties he faced while caring for the five hundred children at his school who lived with extreme poverty every day, and then asked for donations.[44]

Sometimes individuals sent those donations directly to Father Edwards and others like him. Increasingly, however, during the 1960s, people such as Axel Schulze-Thulin, who became the director of the North American section of the Linden-Museum in Stuttgart and was a central activist and supporter of American Indian political movements during the 1960s, organized broad collection drives for specific causes. In fact, he and his wife Hanni spent much of their time collecting American Indian journals, newspapers, and magazines; translating essays and articles; and reaching out to activists and organizations in Native America. In 1968, for example, he wrote a long essay titled "We Help Indians: The NCAI-Fund and the IFI-Indian Assistance," which described the collective efforts of a small, centralized group to collect donations for causes that had been identified by activists, and then to send, collectively, checks for $500 to the NCAI to support their four-point program of improved education, improved living conditions, concerns with acculturation, and the study of everything from land use to acculturation.[45] To stimulate participation, Schulze-Thulin eschewed romantic notions of American Indians and produced essays and translations from the NCAI *Sentinel* about the everyday issues facing American Indians under the Johnson administration, such as the Bureau of Indian Affairs' role in the continued efforts at termination (ending tribal status).[46]

Schulze-Thulin had some success. Checks and petitions continued to be delivered to the United States, and he and his associates continued to receive letters of thanks from people such as John Belindo, a former director of the NCAI, thanking them for their donations, and Roy Daniels, president of the Indian Brotherhood of the Northwest Territories who, much like George Manuel before him, explained how important it was for him and his associates to receive this international support. All of these responses continued to be printed in the hobby journals as well until, in the early 1970s, the hobbyists split into factions that focused more on the history and material culture of American Indians and those people who, like Schulze-Thulin, sought to focus primarily on contemporary politics and activism (an individual, of course, could belong to both).[47] After that, with the rise of AIM and the spread of support groups in Germany, the tactics persisted and the reception was similar even as the players changed and communications became more intense and more frequent during the 1970s.[48] Many Germans proved eager to help.

Recognized Sincerity

Perhaps because of the sincerity with which many of the German people engaged in American Indian politics and activities, some American Indians grew to tolerate and, on occasion, even appreciate the hobbyists' other activities. In 1956, for example, the Sixth Annual Council of West German hobbyists met in Pirmasens. Among them was Nan Cuz, the Mayan Indian artist whose work would be exhibited in Hamburg and other German cities in 1961. Max Oliv, who compiled a history of these meetings, remarks that she conjured a "gorgeous image" in her "national costume" of "hand-woven clothing and artistic Indian silver jewelry." During the opening ceremony, an unnamed Navajo appeared, and "with great enthusiasm took up a drum and sang songs from his homeland. He also joined the dances." During midday, a third American Indian appeared and was "deeply moved" as he saw the tee-pees and the "German Indians." Nan Cuz spoke for all three of them, when she later wrote to organizers of the meeting: "As an indigenous woman" she seldom had "real contact" with whites. "Among you, however, I had the feeling that I was a member of your council with the same skin color!" She thanked them for their friendliness and sincerity.[49]

Given the number and variety of American Indians who have encoun-tered German hobbyists since Cuz penned those lines, it is not surprising that their reactions have been mixed.[50] Moreover, considering that in 1990 the numbers of German hobbyists ran into the tens of thousands, "enough to stock a mid-sized reservation," as Christian Feest once put it, there have been a wide variety of encounters.[51] Members in hobby clubs have always ranged from part-time participants interested mostly in socialization and play to dedicated enthusiasts focused on the minutiae of material culture, the in-tricacies of microhistory, and the political plight of contemporary tribes. Some enthusiasts have refused to become involved in contemporary politics, while others have abandoned the past to focus on the political actions of the present, forsaking as well their interest in dressing like nineteenth-century Indians in favor of the jeans and T-shirts worn by so many in the western United States today. Individuals who have participated in the hobby for long periods of time have also generally seen their interests and actions shift and change over the years. Consequently, it is impossible to make more than the most simplistic general statements about what American Indians or anyone else might encounter during a "typical" hobbyist meeting, or how that might be received.

One consistency, however, is that American Indians such as Cuz have al-ways been honored guests. They offer the possibility of critical reflection, of authoritative confirmation, or equally imposing condemnation of the hobbyists' goals. Across the Cold War era, the hobbyist journals produced in West Germany—most notably, *Dakota Scout*, *Fährte*, and *Der Indianer-freund*—and the three-volume chronicle of their yearly meetings compiled by Max Oliv, delighted in discussing the various American Indians who attended their local or national meetings.[52] In the East as well, visits by people such as the Lakota Archie Fire Lame Deer in 1983 were sensations that have since become a critical part of hobbyist lore. In 1989 Rudolf Conrad produced a short essay on these meetings with Lame Deer, and during my own visit to the Indian Week in 2006 I heard accounts of his impact on East German associations. What became clear during these discussions was the degree to which the hobbyists bowed to their visitor's authority as an actual American Indian, sought his approval, listened with great attention to his suggestions, and tried to incorporate them into their activities. In Conrad's words, he helped fulfill their "deep wish" to "become acquainted more thoroughly with Indian mentality and religion in order to better understand the Indians' way of life, their culture, history, and present political efforts." He provided them with his own instructional performances, including singing, sweat lodge, and pipe ceremonies, and ingratiated the hobbyists who sought to learn from him. At the same time, Conrad argued that the feeling was mutual: "Archie expressed his pleasure to be here and to see tipis and excellent bead and quill work. This he regarded as a stimulus for his own people to resume some of their old traditions."[53]

That point is critical. As Michael Brown recently remarked, not everyone takes emulation as a compliment. "Indigenous peoples," he stressed, "now perceive themselves as more threatened by outsiders who claim to love their religion than by missionaries dedicated to its overthrow," and "at present" the "critical literature is dominated by the idea that the use of musical and artistic genres by non-natives is theft, the final assault after colonialism has taken away everything else."[54] That position was certainly embraced by Katrin Sieg, who drew liberally on Ward Churchill's condemnations of hobbyists in Europe, and some American Indian scholars who have visited German hobbyists also embraced the notion that they are engaged in theft. American Indians, once victims of colonialism, they write, are now victims of impersonators.

That critical literature, however, has not carried the day, even if it has made many hobbyists more circumspect. There are too many tales similar to Conrad's, and too many positive reports from American Indians such as the Choctaw film director Phil Lucas. Lucas learned about German hobbyists from his friend the Blackfoot director George Burdeau, who had seen hobbyists' teepees during the mid-1970s when he was stationed in Germany. While Lucas was working on the five-part TV series *Images of Indians* with Will Sampson, the well-known Creek actor, he traveled with his crew to Germany in the hopes of locating some hobbyists and including some European clichés about American Indians into the series. After locating some German Yakimas in Cologne, he learned that they had a connection with a Yakima family in North America, that they visited them every other year, and that through those visits they had learned much about songs and dances. He went to their clubhouse, which he described as akin to a museum, the walls covered with objects they had made themselves. There he talked to one of the members about a drum that had been blessed by a Modoc medicine man who had visited their club, and the hobbyist began to demonstrate a drum blessing ceremony. "That's when our dilemma began," Lucas noted, because as he set out to film the event, the hobbyist objected and explained to him that "this is a religious ceremony, 'you can't film it.'" "As Indians, that was quite strange for us to hear," Lucas recalled, "because that is normally the re-action one hears from us." "But what really impressed" him and his film crew, he stated, "was their sincerity." Lucas and Sampson later went on to film some of the hobbyists' activities, but with a completely different perspective than they had initially intended: "What we wanted most to convey was: In order to find genuine appreciation of Indians, one has to travel to Europe."[55]

There are many similar examples of American Indians arriving among hobbyists with strongly mixed emotions but leaving with a generally posi-tive impression. Most notable, perhaps, are the reactions of the Cree couple Joseph and Irene Young and the Ojibwa Barbara Daniels to a group of hobby-ists in the Czech Republic, just across the border from the Elbsandstein and former East Germany. Their experiences among these hobbyists and their reactions to their efforts were captured in John Paskievich's film, *If Only I Were an Indian* (1995). Accompanied by the Canadian anthropologist David Scheffel, these three travelers met a few hobbyists in their home before ven-turing to their group's encampment. On arriving at the campsite, they all professed that they were torn by mixed emotions: "cry, laugh, be angry," one noted, "I was going through a struggle inside of me." As they watched the hobbyists over the next few days and engaged them in activities, however, their opinions solidified: as Frantieisek Stupak told them about life in post-war Eastern Europe and explained that they were "morally defeated people" trying to learn from the Indians, as Joseph Young showed the hobbyists how to capture the best rhythm from the drum and danced with them, and as Irene Young and Barbara Daniels showed them how they make bread in a pan and watched women in a sweat, a consensus emerged. Joseph Young noted how impressed they were with these people's efforts. Barbara Daniels reflected on how watching the Czechs cook food in the ground "brings back good memories." She remarked as well that while much of her culture had been taken away by whites, "these people are different, they use our culture. These things have come alive again." She stated that the visit had taught her that "Indians are not victims, but people who have a lot to offer the world," and she argued as well that "if people in Canada and America would just have a tiny fraction of interest in native culture as these people do, things would be so different than they are." In the end, she issued perhaps the most poignant statement in the film when she commented: "If this is stealing our culture, then I would be happy to see more of it."[56]

What emerges from these and other similar encounters is that many hobbyists recognize their precarious position as people engaged in exploring others' cultures and they seek confirmation that they are "getting it right." For this reason, many are eager to include American Indians in their activities, quickly ceding to them positions of authority and prestige in their subculture.

There have been many incidents where the American Indians they sought out proved inadequate to the task, as in the tale told by the Dakota A. C. Ross in his autobiography. While stationed in Mainz-Gonsenheim with the 505th Paratroop Brigade, Ross was one of the many American Indian servicemen tapped by the military command in its quest to promote German-American relations. One day, Ross's commander told him and "the other Indian boys in the company" to put on their best uniforms and prepare for a meeting. The meeting was with a group of local hobbyists who were delighted to learn that he was a Dakota from Pine Ridge and invited him to attend some of their meetings to discuss his people's history and culture with them. Ross recounts his embarrassment at realizing that these Germans knew much more about those subjects than he did, and he states that "the incident was a great awakening for me. It planted a seed in me to start studying my own history. That's when I started a search for my roots."[57]

In most cases, however, American Indians have something to share, and quite a few have been willing to do so. Some, such as Hopi Lindbergh Namingha, who arrived in Germany under the auspices of the U.S. military in the early 1970s and returned after leaving the military, have become integrated in the scene in official ways. Namingha became the head of the Native American Association of Germany (NAAoG), guiding it for many years, and thus he was active on the edge of the hobbyist scene. The NAAoG evolved out of a series of different associations begun in 1976 to bring American Indian soldiers stationed in Germany together, and since at least 1994 it has been made up of both American Indians and Germans, most of whom are or were hobbyists. The group is well known in Germany for hosting powwows that bring Germans and American Indians together, and for bringing performers from the United States to attend and headline these events. Throughout its history, one of the chief goals of the association has been to educate Germans about American Indians and their traditions. Indeed, a significant amount of its resources have been dedicated to outreach with schools, and its Web site is replete with evaluations of books, cultural events, links to information sites, and tips about exhibitions and events related to American Indians in Germany.[58] Its goal has been to help many Germans "get it right."

On the Rez(es)

If small numbers of German hobbyists and activists traveled to American Indian reservations during the first two decades of the postwar era, the numbers of Germans who arrived in the following decades have been immense. Indeed, in Canada, the Dakotas, and the American Southwest, the numbers of German tourists are daunting. In 2001, for example, Tourism BC reported that "Germans were the highest-spending visitors to British Columbia, responsible for forty-four percent of all European revenues." German tourism, it found, "had almost doubled in the preceding ten years, to become an annual $450 million industry." The Germans came in part for the scenic landscapes, the ocean enclaves, the outdoor activities, but most of all they came for American Indian arts, cultures, and history. Indeed, as journalist Adam Gilders reported, the Aboriginal Tourism Association of British Columbia and the Northern Ontario Aboriginal Tourism Association have generated dozens of studies on these visitors and determined that "of all European tourists," "Germans are most likely to take an interest in authentic Aboriginal cultural experiences." In fact, David Grindlay, the marketing director for Northwest Territories tourism noted: "Germany is currently the fastest-growing European market for the area, and Germans who travel to the Canadian North, while often knowledgeable about native culture, are generally 'fascinated by the pre-contact era, and the era after contact with Europeans,'" and his goal was to provide them access to such information.[59]

Knowledgeable, fascinated, culturally engaged, omnipresent, and able to generate millions of dollars in revenue: these characteristics apply to German tourists throughout Native America. As a result, their place in Native worldviews has gained new connotations. Germans' role on Lakota mental maps, for example, has broadened beyond the interconnections that took shape over the course of a century in Europe and now include the many Germans who flock to reservations each year. Hobbyists and political activists are still among them, and transatlantic connections with both still exist, but they take place within a fundamentally new context: crowds.

Germans' increased presence has afforded both opportunities and conflicts. One opportunity is economic. The production of cultural artifacts for sale or trade has a long history on American Indian reservations, and Germany has provided a recognized market for those goods since the late nineteenth century. Like so much else in this story, however, the scale has changed dramatically in the postwar period. In 2002, for example, Christian Feest noted that in the previous thirty years the prices of American Indian objects increased by four hundred times.[60] Consequently, great profits are possible, and American Indians are increasingly aware that such profits can be quickly realized through Germans and in Germany. Indeed, Quanah Crossland Stamps, who became assistant administrator of Native American Affairs with the U.S. Small Business Association in 1994 and worked with the Bureau of Indian Affairs to develop Tribal Business Information Centers in twenty-one rural reservations, wrote in 2000 in *American Indian Report* that annual sales for American Indian materials in Germany continued to rise, cresting $9 million for jewelry, $2.1 million for moccasins, and $900,000 for pottery and CDs. She stressed as well that "ceremonial or artifact-like items find most attention among those Germans who are particularly well informed and aware of Native American culture and history." As a result, "German distributors offering Native American items usually focus exclusively on this market segment that requires particular knowledge and expertise from the distributor."[61] The German market, American Indians have long understood, is not only extensive but full of connoisseurs.

People's impressions of each other are often channeled and shaped by the contexts in which they interact. American Indians who live on reservations that experience extensive tourism have contact with Germans as traders, artists, guides, hosts, rangers, tribal officials, bureaucrats, and cultural preservation officers. On the Navajo Reservation, when I spoke to park service employees, guides, and craftspeople working in Canyon de Chelly, at the Hubbell trading post, and in the town of Window Rock, their impressions revolved around those moments of transaction. One Navajo woman selling jewelry near the White House Ruins on the floor of the canyon, for example, echoed the comments of the employees at the Hubbell Trading Post and venders I spoke to across the Navajo Nation when she explained to me that she liked German tourists because they "buy good stuff and they always ask about the quality of the materials." They knew what they were seeing. At

Hubbell, the trader in charge was used to Germans coming back every year looking for the highest-quality blankets, and one hears similar comments from the guides and park employees as well. They too stressed that German tourists are much more knowledgeable than the white Americans who visit; as one put it to me, it was easier to talk to them about Navajo ways because "they had already thought about what it meant to have a culture." German tourists, they also noted, generally come prepared, with questions about Navajo culture, history, and politics.[62]

People who work for the Department of Navajo Tourism know this as well, and in their effort to meet the interests of this lucrative segment of visitors, they try to open up interactions that will attract more Germans.[63] They regard German tourists as different: they are often used to traveling and would prefer to "do their own thing" on the reservation; they are eager to purchase translations of hefty archaeology books, not just the simple tour guides; and they frequently seek a different level of experience, with a deeper, more personal level of engagement than other white tourists.[64] Given the degree of engagement with Native America in Germany over the course of the past two centuries, that should not come as a surprise to readers of this book. Nor should it be surprising to learn that Germans make up a significant proportion of the visitors who seek out the "truly authentic" experiences offered up by the tourism organizations located on other reservations or other "aboriginal sites," as the Aboriginal Tourism Association of British Columbia and the Northern Ontario Aboriginal Tourism Association recognized through their studies as well. These Germans, the tourist agencies understand, are more eager to sleep in teepees or hogans, attend ceremonies that last for days, and to seek out personal interactions in small compounds, local get-togethers, and homes where they can experience the everyday.[65]

Thus, there are now market responses to those interests as well. Already in the 1960s there were marketing campaigns for "Winnetours" in West Germany, which took people to the sites of Karl May novels.[66] Similar campaigns continue today, some of them orchestrated by individuals living on reservations, or as joint ventures between residents and German tour agents.[67] Just as important, however, is the marked increase in bed and breakfasts in people's homes and small tour groups organized by American Indians that take Germans into backyards and neighborhoods as much as the big sites such as the Crow Fair, the Bad Lands, and Devil's Tower.[68]

There are also many American Indians who have been willing to open up their religious ceremonies to the Germans they deem to be sincere for nonmaterial reasons as well, allowing some Germans to become regulars in specific locations. Indeed, in 2004 Doreen Yellowbird, a columnist for the *Grand Forks Herald*, attended a slide show about German hobbyists by Birgit Hans, a professor of American Indian Studies at North Dakota University, and a German immigrant. Yellowbird wrote about the experience in her column. Like many other American Indians, she underscored the quality of their work and wondered ironically if these people were better craftsmen and "better at being Indians," "at least in regalia," than her own people.[69] She then reflected: "As I sat there looking at Hans' slides of the German hobbyists, I thought of the Germans who had come each year to the South Dakota Sundance ceremony I attend. A group of about 20 to 25," she explained, "used to fly to the United States each year to attend ceremonies. They had a camp set up at the South Dakota site, just like the rest of us." They did their best to take part. "In our Sundance, each day for each meal of the day, campers feed the camp. The Germans fed, too, and tried to keep with the traditions. One evening before the ceremony," she recalled, "the Germans invited everyone to share a late meal. I sat on a tree stump beside a young woman who looked like she might have stepped out of an executive office. I asked her why the Germans came to these ceremonies. Some in Germany had a culture like this more than 200 years ago, the woman told me. They were trying to get in touch with their ancient culture again." "Hans," she noted, "was skeptical about her comment."[70]

Yellowbird's reflections remind us how common German participation became in Lakota ceremonies and other events during the last decades of the twentieth century. That participation, however, has also been contentious. While some people such as Emerson Spider, the headman of the Native American Church and resident of Pine Ridge, argued that "God does not recognize blood quantum"[71] and favored opening up ceremonies to non-Native participants, others banned anyone outside their community from participating in ceremonies such as the Sundance and condemned the people who were willing to include non-Natives. Tensions grew especially great during the last decades of the twentieth century, when "plastic shaman" began leading non-Natives through ceremonies for exorbitant fees. Names such as Sun Bear and Harley Reagan Swift Bear began appearing in *Akwesasne Notes* and other American Indian periodicals with warnings and condemnations. There was also a quick realization that these people recognized the potential of the German market as well.[72] Indeed, German names were among the pretenders. Some of the most notorious were Karl Scherer, Wolfgang Dahlberg, and Waltraud Ferrari. Scherer, in fact, brought Germans to Pine Ridge to meet Emerson Spider, whom he portrayed to them as a medicine man rather than a headman of a Christian Church (the full name is the Native American Church of Jesus Christ), and he attempted to dupe Emerson Spider into ordaining him into the Native American Church so that he could sell his religious services in Europe. He failed, and other Germans helped to condemn his actions and to police the plastic shamans who set up shop in their country. Nevertheless, abuses, both intentional and inadvertent, based on malice as well as foolishness and arrogance, unsettled Native America and made many American Indians wary of non-Native attentions, German and non-German alike. As Yellowbird noted at the end of her column, the Germans who frequented the Sundance she attended in South Dakota stopped coming. When she asked why, she learned that "the Germans had invited some of the leaders of the ceremony to Germany. The leaders were extremely disappointed when they found the Germans doing their own Sundance, based on what they had learned in South Dakota." "Extremely disappointed" seems a generous understatement.[73]

Such repeated "disappointments" have led scholars such as Hartmut Lutz, who are wary of notions of authenticity and concerned with the commodification of either material culture or cultural experiences, to emphasize that Germans' interests in American Indians can create hazards beyond rude imitation. Reflecting on a meeting of more than two hundred aboriginal artists in Canada in 1998, during which four out of six panelists explained that Germany was the most profitable place for their business, he remarked that because there was so much profit to be made in selling Germans the images they want, Germans gleaned too much influence over the products the artists produce. "In the German cultural market situation," he wrote, "Aboriginal cultures and even individual Native people became representational commodifications of the iconographical construct of *Indianer* or Eskimo." For more than a century, he argued, "First Nations people were either exploited and marketed by non-Native entrepreneurs or they themselves actively and deliberately marketed themselves for the purpose of making profits by (re-)selling to the German public the image the same public had already constructed of the essential *Indianer*." He warned against an emerging dialectic, one in which "the icon generates interest, and the interest generates more of the commodified icon."[74]

Not everyone sees it that way. For many scholars, such as Laura Peers, the power to dictate has long left the hands of the Germans or other tourists and consumers and the "interest" generated by the "icons" that concerned Lutz have opened up more opportunities than anything else. Indeed, in a pointed essay on the topic, Peers underscores that historical reenactors at aboriginal sites in Canada as well as those performers who travel abroad are not simply "giving the tourists what they want." Rather, dressing in a manner that appeals to tourists provides performers with "the hook" they need to begin conversations. Once performers such as Howard Sky have their attention, she notes, he is "free to transmit his own messages." "Yes," she agrees, American Indian performers have often been "forced to deal with externally imposed images and situations of unequal economic and financial power." Even then, however, "they were also actively confronting and manipulating these constraints." Indeed, to her mind, these performances have taken "colonial contests and audiences and turned them into meaningful events designed to educate: using stereotypes to make a living, to teach about the reality of Native cultures and lives, and to build bridges between cultures." Thus along with the "tourists' gaze" that has long concerned academics such as Lutz, she stresses that there is also "a Native performers' gaze," which allows them to see how to work with their audiences' expectations so that they are able to "play themselves" and express "their contemporary identity as persons rooted in their heritage, using the past to validate the present—and vice versa."[75]

That gaze, that ability to read the tourists, to make educated, smart decisions, has allowed many people on reservations to transform tourists attractions into sites of counterhegemonic discourse, in which they can preach their own versions of history and explicate their worldviews, much as Rocky Bear did in Munich more than a century ago.[76] This too appeals to many Germans, or rather still appeals to many Germans, as the tourist agencies have already recognized while mapping out the flows of German tourists into precisely the kinds of sites Peers describes, or noting Germans' interest in archaeological texts as well as "regular tourist guides."

Indeed, what all of these reports demonstrate is a point this book has underscored repeatedly. When it comes to American Indian histories and cultures, Germans distinguish themselves as particularly eager to learn, and American Indians across North America know that. Many now recognize the interest, even the "look" of German tourists. How that eagerness is received, however, varies from place to place, because even if the characteristics most often attributed to German tourists are consistent across many reservations, interpersonal relations and local contexts play critical roles in their reception.

A striking juxtaposition emerges simply by following German tourists along Highway 364 from Window Rock, the capital of the Navajo Nation, up the mesa to Shungopavi village on the Hopi Reservation. There too one hears the same characteristics—knowledgeable, fascinated, engaged, and inquisitive—attributed to German tourists; but the evaluation is different. Whereas Navajo venders and guides generally note with approval that Germans usually arrive well prepared and with pointed questions, the same observations generate disapproval among many Hopi guides. As one artist and guide from the Sun Forehead clan told me, he gets a lot of Germans who want to be guided through the reservation, and they tend to ask "hard questions" that the guides either cannot answer, because they are not privy to the information, or will not answer because it is private information. In many cases it is both, and the questions strike most guides as rude. In an effort to negotiate those inevitable inquiries, he describes the Hopi to the Germans as unit thinkers, whose responsibility for cultural knowledge is dispersed among them. No one, he explains, has all the answers about Hopi culture or religion; that, he clarifies, is a result of living in an environment in which communities survive, but individuals do not, and due in part to the rivalries between villages and clans. Because most whites are focused on their individuality, he explained, they are often surprised that any knowledge might not be open knowledge.[77] And despite Germans' preparatory reading, most do not realize that those divisions apply to much more than the most sacred rights of the Kiva; nor do many of them recognize that their questions often reveal that they already have more knowledge than they should, and that being forced to engage their questions can be tedious. The result is often miscommunication, cultural confusion, and more awkward moments with inquisitive Germans than other, more passive visitors.

Those divergent cultural characteristics only make many of the other behaviors commonly associated with Germans even more irritating among the Hopi than on other reservations. For example, Germans, many American Indians will point out, are immodest: whether the references are to the German women who get out of the big green bus that often brings them to Pine Ridge, so that they can strip down and enter the White River, or the Germans who drive through Monument Valley almost naked in order to take in the heat, the comments carry the same uncomfortable tone. Among the Hopi, however, who often find tourists trying to attend dances, ceremonies, or enter a Kiva in flipflops and a bathing suit, such nudity is disrespectful if not completely offensive. "Imagine them doing the same at the Vatican or in one of their Cathedrals!" traders and guides explain with exasperation.

Such complaints are so common, that Angelika and Jochem Link-Vogt contributed an essay to the *Indianermagazin* in 1993 on how to behave in Indian country. Other how-to guides, such as Father William Stolzman's

How to Take Part in Lakota Ceremonies, exist; but the Link-Vogts' article was written specifically for Germans.[78] They began by underscoring that reception is subjective, and cultural codes vary across Indian Country. Among Lakotas, they wrote, one should "avoid staring people in the eyes," show respect by asking questions, but not interrupt during the answers. Silence in between statements, they noted, is not necessarily "an awkward moment." It can often be a good one. They reminded their readers as well not to make the mistake of being concerned about time; rather, they implored German travelers to learn patience and avoid being pedantic. That, they stated, was a good general rule, but specific rules needed to be observed as well. In contrast to the Lakota, for example, asking too many questions of "Pueblo peoples" can bring an "ice cold silence." Such questioning, they warned, which many Germans regard as "a sign of interest," can easily be received as evidence "of poor upbringing."

A litany of guidelines followed that are worth rehearsing: if visitors have the opportunity to observe ceremonies, they should "remain silent, not approach too closely, remain reserved," and "never clap." Anticipating the comments of the Hopi guides I met a decade later, they counseled: "Imagine someone clapping after a mass!" They also cautioned readers not to enter "private property, a grave yard, Kiva, or sweat lodge!" Indeed, most property on reservations, they instructed, is restricted in some way, and visitors must ask before wandering about in order to avoid trespassing. Moreover, regardless of how tempting the subjects might be, photographs can be taken only after gaining permission. American Indians, they noted, "don't want to be marketed" as exotic objects in their powwow costumes or find themselves "pictured in books and magazines." In some areas, they underscored, "cameras are completely forbidden." And visitors should inform themselves before traveling to those areas.[79]

What this essay reveals, of course, is that by 1993 even well-informed German tourists had done most of those things. Many had offended, some innocently, some with flagrant disregard. What the essay also reveals, however, is that those Germans who were most interested in returning to the reservations had noticed the reactions, listened to the complaints, and tried to control the damage by educating other Germans in potential pitfalls that could accompany any visit. It is a pity that the *Indianermagazin* did not have a wider circulation, for judging from the similarity of the complaints ten years later, their essay had limited resonance.

Another source of irritation in the Hopi context are visiting scholars.[80] In 2003 Leigh Jenkins (Kuwanwisiwma), director of the Hopi Cultural Preservation Office, listed for me a series of German researchers beginning with Heinrich R. Voth who he believed shared "a tremendous arrogance." Many in Europe and North America remember Voth as a Mennonite missionary who was an "excellent ethnographer" of the Hopi and the man who facilitated visits by Aby Warburg and ethnologists such as Karl von den Steinen to the Hopi pueblos. He did the same for many other German tourists as well. Among the Hopi, however, and despite Voth's important support during their many controversies with the government, he is most remembered for his "aggressive practices of gathering and publishing secret ritual knowledge, and his reproducing and selling of sacred objects to museums." The accessibility of the many photographs he took of kivas, altars, and ceremonies in the Mennonite archives in Bethel College, in Kansas, for example, continued to grate.[81] As Jenkins explained to me, Voth and the majority of the researchers who followed him had come to the Hopi with many questions, sought answers for their own uses, but had not "thought of the people who give them information." Thus, many of them had published material about the Hopi that had no business in the public sphere, and by doing so they had done serious damage in Hopi communities. Indeed, many regard their actions as tantamount to theft, and thus they have little reason to look with pleasure upon inquisitive visitors of any kind. As a result of this history, one of Jenkins's goals became to curtail the information that had already been taken and circulated and ensure that no more such violations take place. Jenkins did not issue a blanket statement against researchers but simply argued that research should be conducted in ways that benefited the Hopi.[82]

One of the Germans who tried his best to follow Jenkins's precepts is Hans-Ulrich Sanner, who wrote a dissertation on ritual clowning that he later declined to publish. While Sanner quickly recognized that being a German researcher in Native America was advantageous, because "Germans have a generally good reputation and possess the advantage of not belonging to the oppressors [white Americans],"[83] he also found the Hopi strictures challenging. This was true not only because he became consumed by self-reflection while conducting his research under Jenkins's gaze but also because he became aware of the many stereotypes projected at him as both a researcher and a German.

When I teach the history of Western civilization to classes of some three hundred students at the University of Iowa, I often begin by asking them if they have ever heard of Maximilien Robespierre or a series of famous Germans such as Johann Gottfried Herder, Johann Wolfgang von Goethe, Otto von Bismarck, and Thomas Mann. Occasionally, as many as a dozen hands

rise at one of their names. When I mention Hitler, however, they all rise together, and afterward I ask them why. Why do they all know so much about
this one German and so little about so many others who also had a tremendous historical impact? As many soon learn, the Nazis have been part and
parcel of their lives since they were small children; particular images, tropes,
and ideas about the Nazis are deeply ingrained in American popular culture.
This is true for many American Indians as well. After all, they watched *Raid-
ers of the Lost Ark* too.

Thus it should not come as a surprise that the self-reflective Sanner found
himself the butt of jokes at the hands of the clowns he studied, or that those
jokes often equated him with the Nazis. One even asked him during a performance: "Are you Hitler's son?"[84] What he realized after reflecting on such
judgments, is that the clowns, like other people, rely on stereotypes and clichés when making their observations and commentaries, associating Swiss
tourists with Swiss cheese and Germans with Nazis. Indeed, Sanner notes
that the German New Agers who join their American counterparts in stream-
ing to the Hopi Mesas in search of enlightenment "distinguish themselves in
no significant way" from the Americans "except for their strange English."
And yet that is enough to trigger the "popular and quickly understood con-
ceptualization" of the "German as Nazi." Everyone on the Mesas knows how
to say "Heil Hitler," as do most Americans, and many were willing to describe
to Sanner "how Germans line people up before a wall before shooting them."
Other Hopi drew on the locally generated stereotypes about Germans while
melding them together with the more common tropes. As one Hopi man
told him: "You are a German, so . . . you want to *know*. That's their *nature*. Just
the same way they did to people in the concentration camps: Now let's see
how many degrees he can stand." When the Hopi man saw the discomfort
his comments forced across Sanner's face, he chuckled and stated: "Hey, I'm
sorry I put it to that comparison, but that's exactly what I'm feeling now, you
know, Germans wanna probe!"

And yet, at the same time Sanner endured his "friend's" ongoing and un-
pleasant references to him as his "Nazi buddy," he was also treated to many
stories from other Hopi people about Hopi soldiers who were well treated
in Germany. Some even told him stories of men in prisoner-of-war camps
during World War II who felt their captors "treated them better than their
white comrades," or who, in some cases, were "simply let go" by the Germans
because they were American Indians. At this point, it should not surprise
readers to learn that such seeming antinomies could coexist as contexts in
which many American Indians make sense of Germans or that they could be

combined within a single night's discussion.[85] Discourses about other people can accommodate many antinomies, as evidenced in the German discourse on American Indians over the past two hundred years.

The Seekers

In his best-selling book *On the Rez*, Ian Frazier writes that "the sound of foreign languages on the streets of Pine Ridge during powwow time raises this place to a category of its own among mid-American towns. It reminds you that Pine Ridge village is also the capital of a nation, one that receives emissaries from far away." Among those emissaries are Germans, who baffled him at first: "The fascination many German people, for example, have with the Oglala had seemed merely odd to me until I saw Germans and other foreigners at the powwow. They were excited, all eyes and ears and electronic gadgetry, and they made what surrounded them seem exciting too." On reflection, he decided, "the moment in history when white people and Native Americans first discovered each other was so momentous and fateful and even thrilling for each culture that some of us feel compelled to reenact it again and again." While observing what he deduced was such a reenactment, he argued that the fascination was mutual, and he noted that the ways in which he was perceived on the reservation shifted: some residents wondered if he too was from Europe.[86]

A central problem with stereotypes is that they sometimes are accurate, and sometimes completely off base. Frazier might have been right about some of the tourists he observed at the powwows, but certainly not all of them. In a phone conversation with Richard Erdoes, a well-known author, artist, and photographer who was active in the American Indian rights movement and who helped many American Indians such as Dennis Banks, Mary Crow Dog, Leonard Crow Dog, and Archie Fire Lame Deer write books about their lives and times, he reminded me that he was not a German but an Austrian, who was born in Austria-Hungary. The things that I wanted to know about Germans were not things he could tell me because he was not one. He could tell me a bit about some of the Germans he had encountered, however, such as Liselotte Welskopf-Henrich, who he confirmed was well regarded on Pine Ridge, and he too could recount the stories of the German women who came to the Dakotas to meet medicine men. There were several, he recalled, who sought to have their babies. But not all of them did that, and many who come with other intentions suffer from the misconceptions such stories create. He noted as well the concern some American Indians expressed about the influx of Germans into their ceremonies. If the Germans kept coming, some worried, they might have to start holding their ceremonies in German. Thus some people decided to keep them out. But not everyone did. His implicit point, I think, is well taken. The anecdotes that circulate about Germans on reservations stem from stories that have some accurate antecedents, but they do not apply to everyone.[87]

No one knows this better than Milo Yellow Hair, who spent several years in Germany and Austria acting in many cases as a go-between for his people and the many Germans who wanted, for whatever reason, to travel to Pine Ridge or other reservations in the Dakotas. The reasons do vary. One German woman who arrived as a tourist and stayed, married, and runs a business on the reservation explained to me that her interest came from her love of horses, not any fascination with American Indians. After she had lived there a while, however, she appreciated that life moved at a different pace and that people were engaged in trying to solve challenges and difficulties that were more basic and fundamental than those which concerned the office workers she had known in Europe. Life was more essential on the Rez.[88]

Sitting on the porch in front of his home, Milo Yellow Hair, the former AIM activist, former tribal land director, and well-known narrator of the 1990 documentary *In the Spirit of Crazy Horse*, chuckled to himself when he mentioned Winnetou and Old Shatterhand. "Those two clowns," he remarked. Cognizant of the proliferation of inaccurate and clichéd images of American Indians circulating in Central Europe, but also familiar with Welskopf-Henrich, Erdoes, Biegert, and many others, he, more than most, also knows that there are many sincere people in Germany, some of whom he had been able to meet. Over the years, his interest has been to bring some of those people to the reservation, especially people who leave things. Not necessarily material things. Those wear out. Some bring assistance, ideas, and support of all kinds. The day I spoke with him, he was most interested in organic gardens.

When he turned to my concerns about Germans' affinities for American Indians and their motivation for coming to Pine Ridge, he gestured around, waving his hand at the trailers nearby, the aged lawn furniture, old cars on the grass, the slightly bowed trees, and said: "They want this." By "this" he meant that many would like to live like he does, free of the constraints that bind them daily to rules and regulations, to workplaces, and imposed order, to a kind of life that affords material wealth at an emotional and psychological price. Germans, he noted, are looking for freedom, and much like Jung, they are unnerved by it when they find it.

For him, people who participated in the Austrian and German support groups were people who could distribute information, delegate tasks, harness resources. Like many in Germany and Native America, he noticed that they declined over time in strength and energy, reflecting shifting interests in Germany at the end of the twentieth century. He seems to be keenly aware of the modern dilemma that has recently led to the inordinate production of books on neoliberalism.[89] He understands that there is a clear relationship between property and slavery,[90] a Faustian bargain that lurks at the heart of any civilization and emerges, on reflection, for those who care to contemplate the parameters they have accepted in their lives. What he has seen more than others, perhaps, is how many Germans are engaged in that contemplation and how Germans react when they arrive on the reservation, when they witness not only breathtaking landscapes, disturbing poverty, and realities that clash with ideals, but also the kinds of freedom that come with a different relationship to time, space, and property. Welskopf-Henrich wrote about this decades ago, in her novels and, most earnestly, in her letters to Amiotte and others, when she, much like the executive-looking woman who spoke to Doreen Yellowbird, confessed that Germans were seeking something they felt they had lost, something, perhaps, that was taken away, something identified by Warburg and Jung, something sensed by Grosz and Schlichter, something that some hobbyists, those who have the courage of their convictions, discuss openly. In essence, many seek a release from the tension created by a life of imposed order, a freedom they sense was once there and might be reclaimed; and that, more than the spectacle of feathers and beads, or putative first encounters with the exotic, is what continues to appeal. That is not necessarily irrational, ahistorical, or romantic. For some, it has been thoroughly practical. Indeed, as Milo Yellow Hair stressed, when Germans come and settle on the reservation, when they integrate into the community, it is not as if they stop being German and become American Indians, they just become people in the community, people with a greater experience of freedom: much like Louise Standing Bear did.

Conclusions *What Persists*

The German fascination with American Indians is not over, and I do not expect it to end any time soon. Thus, this book does not conclude, as so many history monographs do, with a rupture, a break, a moment after which everything is different, and yet some traces of the subject remain to be summed up in a tidy epilogue. One of the things this book has demonstrated is that the most radical of political ruptures failed to deter the persistence of many Germans' sense of affinities for American Indians even if those ruptures often succeeded in shifting the meaning of those feelings in the short term. The implications of that point are many, and I have already touched on some of them in the preceding chapters. I am not going to repeat them all again here. I would, however, like to underscore a few points.

To begin with, this book reminds us that many of the preoccupations that surfaced in eighteenth-century German literary culture about Germans' sense of self and their place in the world persisted through all German national governments and their accompanying institutions, and they will certainly persist through the current ones. We know that many Germans' preoccupation with nation building and the emergence of dominant nationalist discourses during the nineteenth century failed to wipe away many local affiliations, particular relationships to land and landscapes, regional dialects, confessional differences, even inter- and intraregional animosities (among many other things). Consequently, it should come as no surprise to learn that eighteenth-century notions of worldliness, articulated so well by Herder and Humboldt, as well as a longing for freedom from the very constraints that nations often solidify as they impose order on landscapes and populations, could persist through these political periods as well.

Persistence is not the same as dominance, and therefore scholars schooled in focusing on dominant discourses and short historical periods easily overlook such tendencies even when they seek continuities. Indeed, one of the implications of this book's story is that there are many things about Germans' actions in particular historical contexts across the nineteenth and twentieth centuries that can only be explained by historical inquiry that pushes back beyond the founding of these various states and recognizes the persistence of multiple, sometimes contradictory, tendencies, traditions, and discourses in German culture. As some scholars have pointed out recently, for example, historians will be better able to explain the quick shift in West Germany away from authoritarian government and toward a federal organization during the immediate postwar era when they accept that both forms of government have histories in German culture. Thus, when National Socialism destroyed the legitimacy of authoritarian regimes, a space opened up for the return of a kind of federalism that was not necessarily new or imposed but drew on older precedents as much as newer imperatives.[1] Similarly, as I have tried to show in the second half of this book, consistent notions of race, masculinity, community, virtuous character, concerns with the American genocide, and a striking degree of empathy for American Indians remained relevant across twentieth-century German cultures. That they coexisted with other, often contradictory notions is undeniable, but so too is their persistence and the ways in which they help explain many Germans' actions and interests.

There is a sense of melancholy in German cultures, shared by many Europeans during the modern period (1789 to the present), which stems from a perception of loss. To return to the question a Lakota scholar at Sinte Gleska University posed to me as she wondered about Germans' eagerness to visit South Dakota reservations and participate in Sun Dances: "Did they also lose what we had before civilization?"[2] In a nutshell: yes. Many Germans felt, and continue to feel, that sense of loss of freedom, of community, of spirituality without bureaucracy, and of the space necessary to develop fully as a human being who belongs to an integrated and coherent world. Such feelings have been repeatedly articulated: in the angry scribbles of a young Rudolf Cronau in his Dakota diaries, the epiphanies of Aby Warburg and Carl Jung during their trips to the American Southwest, the persistent and deliberate writings of Liselotte Welskopf-Henrich, and the offhand comments of "a young [German] woman who looked like she might have stepped out of an executive office" while feeding other members of a Sun Dance.

It is that sense of loss that Milo Yellow Hair identified as well, one that reminds us that Germans have long had a mixed relationship to what William Sewell has called the "the systematic oppressions without which civilization was impossible."[3] As Mack Walker pointed out decades ago,[4] those tortured relationships were often captured in the musings of the millions of Germans who fled Central Europe during the nineteenth century for the putative freedom of places such as New Ulm, Minnesota, where they sought a life free from those oppressions, a place where they hoped their children could develop into whole human beings. The number of Germans who left on that journey with a copy of the *Leatherstocking Tales* in a pocket or satchel is too large to count. So too are the number of references to Cooper's volumes in their letters, official reports, and unofficial memoirs. That many soon encountered and ultimately participated in precisely the kinds of oppressive civilizing processes they had hoped to leave behind is one of the ironies of this history.

Nevertheless, their sense of shared oppression helps to explain why an overwhelming number of Germans have long cheered for American Indians while reading stories of their conflicts with European Americans, while watching those conflicts play out on the wide screen, or while listening to a representative of an American Indian tribe describe his or her people's historical and contemporary struggles. Across the centuries, as they voiced their emotional support, as they rooted for the "Redskins," these Germans were often cheering for themselves, or at least for a part of themselves they longed to regain.

What Germans seem to recall more than any other group of Europeans is the fact that they were both victims and agents of the impersonal forces of civilization and empire that so concerned Herder in the late eighteenth century and continued to obsess Welskopf-Henrich almost two hundred years later. This is a point that is difficult for contemporary scholars to accept. It is much easier to attribute Germans' sense of affinity with American Indians to displacement, projection, or romantic fantasy. For in an age in which the rise of indigenous rights movements have taken shape and gained considerable political traction, the notion that any group of Europeans outside of the Sámi might retain a cultural connection to the land, to tribal orientations, or to any claim of indigeneity strikes most scholars as both intellectually bankrupt and politically incorrect. And yet for decades, American Indian activists such as Jimmie Durham, and countless other American Indians, have been more than willing to entertain the notion of Germans as a tribal people, who, as Welskopf-Henrich and others argued, also fell under missionization, forced assimilation, acculturation, and multiple forms of "systematic oppression," and suffered as a result. Even if we acknowledge that Germans have long lost any claim to indigeneity,[5] it is impossible to refute the sense of loss that many felt by the late eighteenth century (if not much earlier), and which informed both the cultural pluralism of a young Rudolf Cronau and the sub-altern genocide unleashed by National Socialists.

What happens, however, if we take that sense of loss seriously, if we ac-knowledge, as Ben Kiernan has done, that the first victims of the form of genocide that often accompanied European settler colonialism were other Europeans?[6] What happens to German history, or to global history for that matter, if we stop regarding Germans' persistent claims to a sense of loss as forms of projection or displacement, or if we stop rejecting their claims of affinity with American Indians out of hand? What if, instead of smirking when Germans ask about what the United States did to American Indians, we pause and weigh the question? What if, instead of laughing at the notion of a German dressed like a nineteenth-century Yakima performing a drum ceremony, we listen to what he and his counterparts glean from its perfor-mance and recognize the value of their actions? What happens then?

Dirk Moses brilliantly sketches out some of the implications in his analysis of National Socialist genocides. He reminds us that there are many more continuities flowing through German history than the well-researched notion of anti-Semitism—continuities of resistance, concerns with oppres-sion, and a persistent sense of loss—that are too often obscured by scholars' myopic analyses of particular historical moments. But there are even more. After all, not all roads in German history lead to National Socialism, even if many cross through it. That is, implicitly, one of the points of this book.

One of the most troubling aspects of the hobbyists' pursuits, it turns out, is that they may be legitimate, respectable, even admirable acts. In the late 1990s, two photographers, Max Becher and Andrea Robbins, visited a hobby-ist camp near Dresden and produced a photographic display of these people. They combined those photos with images of Leavenworth, Washington, a fake Bavarian village created out of a former lumber town, to create a show that toured with great success in the United States. In the accompanying cat-alog, Jolene Rickard, a professor of art and art history, a member of the Tur-tle Clan of the Tuscarora nation, and a colleague of Paul Chaat Smith who helped create the initial displays in the National Museum of the American Indian, reacted: "The truth is that Indians have been dressing like Europeans since first contact. . . . So why do we think it is so unusual for Europeans to dress Indian? Perhaps," she noted, "this pokes at our latent fear of a regres-sion to some 'primitive' state." Maybe it ties into the fear shared by many colonizing powers that some of their people might "go native." Conceivably the hobbyists, like the central character in Anna Jürgen's award-winning 1950 captivity narrative *Blauvogel,* or the actual Apache captive Herman

Lehmann, might recognize that the price of civilization was paid every day, when they, much like Lehmann, who "was free as a bird" while living among the Apache, became "cramped up in a house and forced to toil for a livelihood" after being "rescued" from the Apache world. Rickard noted that few intellectuals or journalists took the hobbyists seriously; but she did. She recognized that in "a society dedicated to high consumerism . . . these Indian poseurs are resisters" who have something to tell us about "what is missing for these people today."[7]

She was right; but they also tell us something about what persists. German travel cultures, for example, which developed during the nineteenth century, are alive and well. There are good reasons, for instance, that John Sayles included a young German couple in the latest high-tech gear in his 1997 film *Men with Guns*, a film focused on the violent political history of an unnamed Central American country. Young Germans, like those he portrayed backpacking through the forests in his film, continue to take *Bildungsreisen* (trips of cultural edification) across the world, and people like Sayles encounter such German travelers again and again in distant forests, high mountains, and on American Indian reservations.

These are not new impulses. They are rather old, older in fact than the kinds of modern tourism developed by Thomas Cook. So too are the efforts of the hobbyists who could not travel, and thus sought to reach out to a world they might never be able to see. As Petra Tjitske Kalshoven has noted, the kinds of cultural analysis and textual criticism in which serious hobbyists engage are anything but new, even if their particular efforts to harness those techniques strike some scholars as unusual. Few expect to find such things among the hoi polloi.[8] Perhaps, however, it is time to start looking. Because if Kalshoven is correct, and I think she is, there is a *Bildungskultur* that cuts across classes in Germany, which has not seen sufficient attention.

Perhaps it is also time to reimagine German history in a way that recognizes that the "margins of German history," as one set of scholars termed them,[9] are not limited to Europe but extended during the nineteenth century across the Atlantic, deep into the American West, where German colonial history played out just as actively and importantly as in places such as Eastern China, the Pacific, Africa, or Brazil. The point here is not simply to jump on the transnational bandwagon and proclaim the need to study flows of information and ideas that intellectual historians and historians of science have long known had only limited respect for national boundaries. Rather, it is to push back the geographic and temporal boundaries in our heads and follow Germans wherever they went, acknowledging the breadth of Germans' mental maps, and the extent of the German Kulturkreis, as it ebbed and flowed across various geographies, often without respect for national borders. As C. A. Bayly recently quipped, "All historians are global historians now, even if they have not quite realized it."[10] This applies to historians of Germany as well.

Despite that verity, the intertwined history of the United States and Germany has not yet received the attention it deserves by historians of either state. Many remain too quick to recapitulate the categories of their respective nationalist historians of the past when thinking in cultural as much as geopolitical terms. Indeed, a quick look at current American history textbooks makes it hard to see the older Rudolf Cronau as a man obsessed by conspiracy theories. There is a noted Anglo-centrism in American history even today, one that pays even less attention to the expansion and contraction of the German Kulturkreis during the nineteenth century than the German texts of either the present or past.

If, however, we follow the flows of people, institutions, and ideas, quite literally the diffusion of the German Kulturkreis as it ebbed back and forth over various political borders and reached across the Atlantic, we see a different Germany, one not always already bound by national borders. We see a much bigger Germany in which the points of multiplicity and difference are not limited to the Kashubians and Masures on the Polish border; the "world that nationalism lost," as Helmut Walser Smith once characterized it, was much bigger and more diverse than he indicated, or perhaps imagined.[11]

This was a Germany where, during the late nineteenth century, expansion through official colonies was a weak second thought compared to the expansion of German cultures that had already taken place in the United States. It was a Germany made up of cultural traits, not just political and material ones. It was a Germany in which much of what it meant to be German in the heyday of nation making was expressed and pursued well beyond the national borders, where transnational people such as Cronau lived an easy existence on two continents and felt comfortable calling both places home. This was a Germany filled with people ever cognizant of the price of modern civilization and the virtues of remaining in tune with the natural world, the merits of spirituality without institutions, the freedoms and fulfillment enjoyed by individuals and cultures that exist in organic landscapes, and the intrinsic worth of sincere searching. This was a Germany tied to a German America and American Indians, which begot a German memory captured in the advertisements produced by the German Historical Museum in Berlin for its 2004 exhibit of *America Portraits* by the photographer Reiner Leist. It

FIGURE 35. Advertisement in Berlin for Reiner Leist's photo exhibition *American Portraits* at the Deutsches Historisches Museum. (Photo by the author)

focused on two faces: the German American Henry Kissinger and Curly Bear Wagner, a member of the Blackfoot Nation from Browning, Montana. That Germany is still with us.

Most of all, this was a Germany in which a significant proportion of the population thought frequently about a group of non-Europeans as people they would like to emulate, people with whom they chose to feel kinship. It was and remains a Germany in which those people, American Indians, were hailed as resisters, freedom fighters, complete individuals, who were often regarded as inspirational. It was and is a Germany in which representatives of those people continue to be welcomed, in which those representatives have actively engaged Germans in debates about notions of "Indianness," and through those debates they have influenced German notions of human difference. In Susanne Zantop's introduction to the 2002 volume she edited together with Colin Calloway and Gerd Gemünden on *Germans and Indians*, Zantop posed the question: "Why, after all, *should* Native Americans be interested in Germans?"[12] The answer, as readers must know by now, is that there has been a long reciprocal fascination and at least a century of pointed interaction between these two summative groups of people. Germans continue to stream into Native America even today, and they continue to be received with as much wonder as they bring. If this book helps to facilitate understanding during those ongoing interactions, then it will have served one of its central purposes.

Notes

PREFACE

1. See, for example, Benjamin, "Goethe's Elective Affinities"; Richard Herbert Howe, "Max Weber's Elective Affinities"; and McKinnon, "Elective Affinities of the Protestant Ethic."

2. Hobsbawm, *The Age of Extremes*.

3. Helmut Walser Smith, *The Continuities of German History*.

4. Confino, "Reflections: A World without Jews," 547–48; Langewiesche, "Rezension von: Helmut Walser Smith."

5. Confino, "Reflections: A World without Jews," 548.

6. See, for example, Applegate, *A Nation of Provincials*; Applegate, "A Europe of Regions"; and Confino, *The Nation as a Local Metaphor*.

INTRODUCTION

1. Rossbacher, *Lederstrumpf in Deutschland*.

2. Tower, *Envisioning Amerika*.

3. Warburg, *Images from the Region of the Pueblo Indians of North America*, especially 50–54.

4. Fest, *Hitler*, 615.

5. For example, Kimmelman, "Karl May and the Origins of a German Obsession."

6. Rubin, "Germans Emulate American Indians."

7. E. U., "'Manitou' unter Radebeuls Himmel," clipping number 19722000 3, Karl-May-Museum Archive, Radebeul. The title of the newspaper is missing. Similarly, see also KKN, "Kinder Manitous."

8. "Wenn der Papa zum Sioux wird," *Kölner Stadtanzeiger*, 1966, cited in Oliv, *20 Jahre Indian Councils*, 1:185.

9. E.g., Belden, "War Whoops in the Schwarzwald." Similar essays appeared in the *Wyoming State Tribune*.

10. See, for example, Aeppel, "At One with Indians"; Neuffer, "Germans Make a Hobby Out of Cowboys and Indians."

11. Zantop, "Close Encounters," 5. See also Bolz, "Indians and Germans."

12. Lott, *Love and Theft*.

13. Sieg, *Ethnic Drag*, 13.

14. For recent examples of efforts to locate older notions of colonial fantasies at the heart of relations between Germans and American Indians, see, for example, Grewling, "Fighting the Two-Souled Warrior"; and Guettel, "Reading America, Envisioning Empire." For a refreshing alternative that follows Lott's recommendation that we seek out the political range of such performances, see Weber, "'Indians' on German Stages."

15. Borries and Fischer, *Sozialistische Cowboys*.

16. "Das rote Reservat: Indianerkult der DDR," blickpunkt, 16 May 2010, http://blickpunkt.zdf.de/ZDFde/inhalt/28/0,1872,8072188,00.html.

17. The best efforts to engage the relationship between Germans and American Indians have been Bolz, "Indians and Germans," and Calloway, Gemünden, and Zantop, *Germans and Indians*.

18. Hansotto Hatzig, Mannheim, "Zur Leserumfrage: 'Für oder gegen Karl May,'" Bundesarchiv Lichterfelde West, Berlin, DR1 6240, pp. 179–82.

19. Cf. Philip Deloria, *Playing Indian*.

20. Vine Deloria Jr., *Custer Died for Your Sins*, 3–4.

21. This is not to say there were no German-speaking ethnologists working in North America. There were important collectors and collections. The point is that there were few compared to other parts of the world and that those larger collections dwarfed the North American ones. For a short list of ethnologists involved in North America, see Feest, "Germany's Indians in a European Perspective," 40.

22. Boden, *Nordamerika*, especially 7–10.

23. Lampert, "Ein Gang durch das ethnographische Museum des Württembergischen Vereins für Handelsgeographie."

24. Meyen, *Die Kunstkammer und Sammlung*, 72; Hartmann, "Abteilung Amerikanische Naturvölker"; and Bolz and Sanner, *Native American Art*.

25. It is worth noting that even in the postwar period only the University of Frankfurt possessed a chaired position for North American ethnology in West Germany, and even in the GDR there was no place for it at the universities after Lips retired.

26. Penny, *Objects of Culture*.

27. During the same period Sonja Schierle also put on a small but well-organized exhibit in the Linden-Museum in Stuttgart (which has the second largest collection of American Indian artifacts in Germany): "In the River of Time: Mandan, Hidatsa, Arikara; Native Life along the Upper Missouri River," which received significant input from contemporary communities. Similarly, the Munich ethnological museum, which claimed the third largest collection of North American artifacts, also opened up its first permanent exhibition on American Indians, with a strong focus on the Arctic.

28. According to the Hamburg Museum's website, http://www.voelkerkunde museum.com (as of 1 September 2009), "Since 1992, when state-contributions towards the Museum had gradually been diminishing, the Museum's executives had been forced to take self-financing measures. On 1 January 1999, the Hamburg Museum of Ethnology, under public law, was turned into an independent foundation. This inevitably entailed quite some changes for the Museum's research work and its administration." Indeed. The Plains exhibition took place from 31 October 1996

through 31 August 1997 and was described by the administration as "a blockbuster [*Renner*]."

29. Flyer titled "Eine Nacht im Tipidorf," Museum für Völkerkunde Hamburg, 2001. The cost was 105 marks per child, 1,650 marks for a school class of up to sixteen children.

30. The teepee outings were organized in conjunction with Darrell Norman who did something similar in North America. See http://www.blackfeetculturecamp.com/.

31. König, *Indianer.*

32. Feest, "German Medley."

33. David Seven Deers, a sculptor from British Columbia, returned to the Hamburg ethnographic museum in 2004 to carve a giant sun mask in the courtyard.

34. The prayer and interviews were included in the short museum catalog, "Indianer der Plains und Prärien."

35. See, for example, Lutz, "'Okay, I'll be their annual Indian for next year.'"

36. See, for example, L. G. Moses, *Wild West Shows.*

37. See, for example, Deutschlander, "In Search of *Winnetou.*"

38. Ibid., 5, 44.

39. Interview with P. K., Grand Canyon National Park, 12 March 2003.

40. Telephone conversation with I. Q., 3 June 2003.

41. See, for example, LaDuke "Journey of Peace."

42. Quoted in Biegert, *Seit 200 Jahren ohne Verfassung*, 148–50.

43. Deutschlander was told this repeatedly during her interviews in Canada. "In Search of *Winnetou*," 47–50.

44. Zantop, "Close Encounters," 5.

45. Calloway, "Historical Encounters across Five Centuries," 48.

46. See also Otterness, *Becoming German*; and Silver, *Our Savage Neighbors.*

47. By negative integration I mean the unification of disparate German-speaking groups around an objective identity of "German" in response to discriminatory practices or the removal of barriers between them.

48. See, for example, Feest, "Germany's Indians in a European Perspective"; Liebersohn, *Aristocratic Encounters.*

49. Berkhofer, *The White Man's Indian*, 22–25.

50. Welsch and Stekler, *Killing Custer*, 98–102.

51. Berkhofer, *The White Man's Indian*, 25.

52. See, for example, Zahra, *Kidnapped Souls.*

53. See, for example, Helmut Walser Smith, "Prussia at the Margins."

54. Blackbourn and Retallack, *Localism, Landscape, and the Ambiguities of Place*, 4–18.

55. See, for example, Mauch, "Zwischen Edelmut und Roheit."

56. Moore, *Fichte: Addresses to the German Nation*, 109.

57. "Politische Lage der Indianer in den Vereinigten Staaten von Nordamerika," *Das Ausland* (1831): 438–39.

58. See, for example, "Das Fischspeeren der Indianer," *Die Gartenlaube* (1859): 600–602.

59. Banach, "Die Rasse mit der Bronzehaut."

60. The term *Kulturkreis* stems from German diffusionists at the turn of the twentieth century. They often used the term in an effort to establish the boundaries within which putatively unitary cultures developed and then to map out the ways in which they spread. I use the term somewhat differently to capture the extent of a transnational Germanophone world that was uneven, composed of many cultural variants, and had no clearly demarcated borders. What it had was a geographic range within which thicker and thinner concentrations of Germanophone cultures were interconnected, and across which many kinds of Germans moved, communicated, and encountered familiar cultural characteristics—friendly and antagonistic. If we were to try, following the efforts of those diffusionists of the past, to draw lines on a map to show the spread of these German cultures beyond central Europe, those lines would have to be portrayed as inherently frayed and unstable, demarcating areas that easily accommodated both hybridities and indifference. It would be quite messy, and in the end, hardly definitive. The concept is nevertheless useful, for it offers a means to articulate the spatiality of this broad, transatlantic Germanophone world that was not only transnational, in that it extended far beyond Central Europe, but predated and persisted through the creation of the German nation-state and the establishment of the United States' ultimate borders. It was this cultural space that allowed, for example, the contentious German public spheres analyzed by people like Allison Efords to take shape in the United States—it also allowed the stories in this book to develop. See, for example, Efords, "New Citizens."

61. LaDuke, "Journey of Peace."

PART I

1. Plischke, *Von Cooper bis Karl May*, 11, 26, 35, 41.

2. Ibid., 131. Cf. Penny, "Elusive Authenticity."

CHAPTER 1

1. J. B. Rives, "Commentary," in Tacitus, *Germania*. See also See, *Barbar, Germane, Arier*, 44–47.

2. Egmond and Mason, *The Mammoth and the Mouse*, 181–84; cf. Feest, "Germany's Indians in European Perspective," 28.

3. Marchand, *Down from Olympus*, 156–57; See, *Barbar, Germane, Arier*.

4. Marchand, *Down from Olympus*, 162. See also Williamson, *The Longing for Myth in Germany*, 87.

5. Marchand, *Down from Olympus*, 157.

6. Herder, "Treatise on the Origin of Language" (1772), in Herder, *Philosophical Writings*, 160–61.

7. See, for example, Abigail Green, "The Federal Alternative?," 200; van Rahden, "Germans of the Jewish *Stamm*," 28, 36–39; Helmut Walser Smith, *The Continuities of German History*, 174, 181.

8. Ursel Hahn, response to a discussion theme, in *Kalumet* 16, no. 1 (1967): 32.

9. Bollenbeck, *Bildung und Kultur*.

10. Maner, *Germany's Ancient Pasts.*

11. See, for example, Christine R. Johnson, *The German Discovery of the World.*

12. Sachs, *The Humboldt Current*, 26, 93, 10.

13. Daum, *Wissenschaftspopularisierung im 19. Jahrhundert.*

14. Muthu, *Enlightenment against Empire.*

15. Sachs, *The Humboldt Current*, 16–20.

16. Penny, *Objects of Culture.*

17. "Abenteuer unter den Indianern," *Das Ausland* (1830): 1437–38; 1441–42; 1445–46; here 1445.

18. Lutz, *"Indianer" und "Native Americans,"* 266.

19. Ashliman, "The Novel of Western Adventure in Nineteenth-Century Germany,"142; Plischke, *Von Cooper bis Karl May*, 50–51.

20. Barba, "Cooper in Germany," 51–104.

21. Lutz, *"Indianer" und "Native Americans,"* 268.

22. Beebe, "The Search for a Fatherland."

23. Billington, *Land of Savagery, Land of Promise*; cf. Nirenburg, *The Reception of American Literature in German Periodicals*, 61–62.

24. Beebe, "The Search for a Fatherland," 5.

25. Slotkin, *Fatal Environment*, 88.

26. Württemberg, *Travels in North America.*

27. For an excellent introduction into a Native view of the processes of transformation and acculturation these noble travelers encountered and tried to capture, see, for example, David Bernstein, "'We are not now as we once were,'" and the other essays in *Ethnohistory* 54, no. 4 (2007). For a more general introduction to the challenges posed by what is overwhelmingly a non-Native historiography, see Philip Deloria, "Historiography," in Deloria and Salisbury, *A Companion to American Indian History*, 6–24. Perhaps the best introduction to the shifting relationships between these Northern Plains cultures at this time is Hämäläinen, "The Rise and Fall of Plains Indian Horse Cultures."

28. Tyler, "Karl Bodmer and the American West."

29. For more on the tensions they encountered, see Ewers, *Indian Life on the Upper Missouri.* See also Dempsey, "Blackfoot."

30. On Lakota expansion, see White, "Winning the West." See also Denig, *Five Indian Tribes of the Upper Missouri.*

31. For a discussion of the inhabitants of the Great Plains in the 1830s, see David McCrady, "Hidatsa," Frank Henderson Stewart, "Mandan," and the other essays in DeMallie, *Handbook of North American Indians.*

32. Liebersohn, *Aristocratic Encounters*, 148. For an excellent discussion of the Crow at this time, see Hoxie, *Parading through History.*

33. Wied and Bodmer, *Reise in das innere Nord-America.*

34. Tyler, "Karl Bodmer and the American West," 18.

35. Ibid.

36. Ibid., 23.

37. Cited in ibid., 20–21.

38. Penny, "Illustrating America."

39. The use of the original artwork and some, but certainly not all of the reproductions, is detailed in appendix D of Ruud, *Karl Bodmer's North American Prints*.

40. Blackhawk, *Violence over the Land*, 182.

41. Ekkehard Koch, *Karl Mays Väter*, 116–20.

42. Sammons, *Ideology, Mimesis, Fantasy*, 116, 124.

43. Ibid., 3.

44. "Amerikanische Skizzen. Die Indianer. (Von Dr. Gerstäcker)," *Das Ausland* (1846): 213; 218–20; 222–23; 226–27; 230–31.

45. Ibid., 213.

46. This is precisely the dynamic discussed in Silver, *Our Savage Neighbors*.

47. Hämäläinen, *The Comanche Empire*.

48. Gerstäcker, "Amerikanische Skizzen," 230–31.

49. Ibid.

50. Sammons, "Nineteenth-Century German Representations of Indians from Experience," 185–93.

51. The best introduction to those policies can be found in Prucha, *American Indian Treaties*, and Prucha, *The Great Father*.

52. Cited in Sammons, "Nineteenth-Century German Representations of Indians from Experience," 185.

53. Möllhausen, *Tagebuch einer Reise vom Mississippi nach den Küsten der Südsee*; and Möllhausen, *Reisen in die Felsengebirge Nord-Amerikas*.

54. Möllhausen, *Der Halbindianer*.

55. For a partial listing, see Janeck, *Zwischen Gartenlaube und Karl May*, 102.

56. Barba, "Cooper in Germany," 69–70.

57. Cited in ibid., 71.

58. Cited in Sammons, *Ideology, Mimesis, Fantasy*, 94.

59. Möllhausen to Spencer Baird, 21 July 1879, cited in Graf, *Der Tod der Wölfe*, 17.

60. Lutz, *"Indianer" und "Native Americans,"* 238.

61. For further discussion of the Choctaw removal, see, for example, Akers, *Living in the Land of Death*; Wells and Tubby, *After Removal*.

62. Möllhausen, "Blätter aus dem Tagebuch einer Reise vom Mississippi nach den Küsten der Südsee."

63. Based in St. Louis, Catlin became famous for traveling up the Missouri, Mississippi, and Arkansas Rivers capturing images of American Indian tribes and collecting ethnographica.

64. Kort, *I Like America*.

65. "Eine Entführung. Abenteuer," *Über Land und Meer* (1858): 332–34.

66. "Ein Indianerrennen," *Über Land und Meer* (1866): 204.

67. "Indianer, einen Eisenbahnzug überfallend," *Leipziger Illustrirte Zeitung* 52 (1869): 102.

68. Ibid. This is a much different interpretation than one would find in the United States. See, for example, Schimmel, "Inventing 'the Indian.'"

69. "Indianer, einen Eisenbahnzug überfallend," 102.

70. Ibid.

71. See especially Truettner, *The West as America*; and Tyler, *Prints of the West*.

72. See, for example, Glanz, *How the West Was Drawn*.

73. McCloskey, "From the Frontier to the Wild West," 300–301.

74. Glanz, *How the West Was Drawn*, 77–80.

75. Ibid., 64.

76. William S. Talbot, "Oregon Trail"; http://www.butlerart.com/pc_book/pages/albert_bierstadt_1830.htm.

77. McCloskey, "From the Frontier to the Wild West," 302–6.

78. Ibid., 302–3.

79. While this remains the general characterization of Germans of the 1848 generation, the reality was much more complex. See, for example, Levine, *The Spirit of 1848*; and Honeck, *We Are the Revolutionists*.

80. Glanz, *How the West Was Drawn*, 70–71.

81. Ibid., 77–82.

82. Kamphoefner, Helbich, and Sommer, *News from the Land of Freedom*, 2.

83. Walker, *Germany and the Emigration*, 42.

84. Levine, *The Spirit of 1848*, 4.

85. Walker, *Germany and the Emigration*, 42.

86. Calloway, "Historical Encounters across Five Centuries," 47.

87. Kamphoefner, Helbich, and Sommer, *News from the Land of Freedom*, 181.

88. Ibid., 16.

89. Ibid., 23.

90. Walker, *Germany and the Emigration*, 62.

91. Helbich, "Different, but Not Out of This World," 126.

92. See, for example, Conzen, "Peasant Pioneers."

93. Levine, *The Spirit of 1848*.

94. Kreis, *Lakotas, Black Robes, and Holy Women*.

95. Ekkehard Koch, *Karl Mays Väter*, 91.

96. Ibid., 134–35.

97. See, for example, Kautz, *August Valentine Kautz*.

98. Calloway, "Historical Encounters across Five Centuries," 58.

99. Welsch with Stekler, *Killing Custer*, 81, 287–89; Ekkehard Koch, *Karl Mays Väter*, 180; Windolph, *I Fought with Custer*.

100. Brooks, *Captives and Cousins*; Hämäläinen, *Comanche Empire*, 223, 250–51.

101. Quanah Parker was one of the leading Comanche Chiefs of the early reservation period. See, for example, Hagan, *Quanah Parker*.

102. Zesch, *The Captured*, 205, 214; Lehmann, *Nine Years among the Indians*.

103. On *Völkerschauen* in Germany, see, for example, Ames, *Carl Hagenbeck's Empire of Entertainments*.

104. Paul Heydel, "Rothäute in Deutschland," *Leipziger Illustrirte Zeitung* 73 (1879): 112–13.

105. G. S., "The Chippeways-Indianer im Berliner Panoptikum," *Leipziger Illustrirte Zeitung* 80 (1883): 39.

106. For an excellent discussion of northwest coast American Indians' integration into colonial processes, see Raibmon, *Authentic Indians*. For a more general discus-

sion of the transformations in this historiography, see, for example, Blackhawk, "Currents in North American Indian Historiography."

107. F. V. Schirp, "Hagenbeck's Bella-Coola-Indianer," *Leipziger Illustrirte Zeitung* 85 (1885): 388–89.

108. The Sioux are composed of three primary divisions: Dakota (East), Nakota (Middle), and Lakota (West) also referred to in much of the literature as the Santee, Yanktonai, and Teton. There are seven major branches within those groups. The distinctions are linguistic and cultural as well as geographic. For an excellent discussion of these divisions and branches, see Galler, "Sustaining the Sioux Confederation," especially 467–69. See also Gibbon, *The Sioux*.

109. On the transformation of the Great Plains and the Southwest during this period, see especially Hämäläinen, *Comanche Empire*, chap. 7. On the particular resilience of the Lakota, see Gibbon, *The Sioux*; and Hämäläinen, "The Rise and Fall of Plains Indian Horse Cultures."

110. Gustav Schubert, "Die Sioux-Indianer im Berliner Panoptikum," *Leipziger Illustrirte Zeitung* 82 (1884): 91, 94.

111. "Die Siouxindianer," *Über Land und Meer* (1886): 1074–75; Rudolf Cronau, "Die Sioux-Indianer," *Leipziger Illustrirte Zeitung* 86 (1886): 592.

112. A. Oskar Klausmann, "'Wild Amerika' Skizze aus der Reichshauptstadt," *Leipziger Illustrirte Zeitung* 93 (1889): 137. This was not his first time there. "Der amerikanische Kunstschütze Dr. William Carter," *Leipziger Illustrirte Zeitung* 79 (1882): 166–67.

113. In Strasbourg they paused in October 1890 for the winter before resuming their tour again in April 1891.

114. Ames, "Seeing the Imaginary."

115. Before 1877 all of his Indians were played by non-Indians.

116. Warren, *Buffalo Bill's America*, 190–95.

117. Albert Richter, "Buffalo Bill's Wild-Amerika," *Leipziger Illustrirte Zeitung* 94 (1890): 41–43.

118. Fritz Cl. Wolff, "Pertaining to Buffalo Bill," *Leipzig General Anzeiger*, 22 June 1890.

119. *Berliner Zeitung*, 24 July 1890, clipping located in the Harold McCracken Research Library, Buffalo Bill Historical Center, Cody Wyoming Series IX Box 5—Scrapbook from Germany, June–October 1890.

120. Ibid.

121. See, for example, "Ein Indianerkrieg in Sicht?" *Anzeiger und Tageblatt* (Freiburg), 1 June 1890.

122. For example, Dr. Fr. D. "Das Aussterben der Indianer," *Leipziger Zeitung*, 20 June 1890. Cf. *Leipziger Nachrichten*, 17 June 1890; "Buffalo Bill," *Münchner Neueste Nachrichten*, 12 April 1890.

123. "Ansprüche des Rocky Bear," *Münchner Neueste Nachrichten*, 3 May 1890.

124. "Indianergewohnheiten, die Civilization des wilden Westens, Sitten und Gewohnheiten der Rothäute, alles das konnten wir circa vierzehn Tage lang gut studieren," *Dresdner Tageblatt*, 15 June 1890. For an example of an Indian village erected in Dresden only a few years later, complete with performances by Germans, see "Das Albertfest in Dresden," *Leipziger Illustrirte Zeitung* 101 (1893): 267–68.

125. For example, R. Trache, "Pullmann u. Mack's Wild West Show im Zoologischen Garten zu Dresden," *Leipziger Illustrirte Zeitung* 113 (1899): 428.

126. Griffin, *Four Years in Europe with Buffalo Bill*, 80.

127. Sammons, *Ideology, Mimesis, Fantasy*, 229–32.

128. Ibid., 247.

129. See, for example, Kreis, "German Wild West"; Schmiedt, *Karl May*.

130. Kreis, "German Wild West," 253–54.

131. Sammons, *Ideology, Mimesis, Fantasy*, 231.

132. Ibid., 232.

133. Berkhofer, *The White Man's Indian*, 100.

134. Kreis, "German Wild West," 262.

135. See, for example, Penny, "Red Power."

CHAPTER 2

1. The use of the term "massacre" to mean an indiscriminate killing or a wholesale slaughter can be contentious. Within the context of Native American history, "massacre" has a particular resonance, because nineteenth-century European Americans, and many historians well into the twentieth century, frequently used the term to characterize American Indians' victories over settlers and members of the United States military. Those same people, however, generally labeled the indiscriminate killing of large numbers of American Indians by U.S. forces "battles," making them appear somehow more legitimate and less barbarous than similar actions of war by American Indians. This has been true even when the killing by U.S. troops was decidedly one-sided. For that reason, scholars and activists currently use the term with great circumspection. Indeed, the opening of the Sand Creek Massacre National Historical Site to the public in 2007, the first such site in the United States to be labeled in this way, marked a milestone in the shifting discourse over the Plains Indians wars. Within the context of German colonial history, however, "massacre" is a term most-often associated with the actions of Germans against indigenous peoples, such as during the egregious elimination of the vast majority of the Herero people by German colonial troops in German South-West Africa from 1904 to 1907. For the purposes of this chapter, it is important to stress that "massacres" were something Germans both experienced and perpetrated. Therefore I have purposefully used the term to call attention to that aspect of German colonial experience, not in an attempt to revive the term's former usage in American history.

2. The estimate of 600–800 fatalities comes from the classic account of the conflict in Carley, *The Dakota War of 1862*. The exact numbers have been repeatedly challenged. For lower numbers, see Meyer, *History of the Santee Sioux*, especially 120; for detailed accounts, see, for example, Dahlin, *Dakota Uprising Victims*, and Dahlin, "Words vs. Actions."

3. See, for example, the way Ostler incorporated the 1862 conflict into his tight linear history of the Plains Indians Wars, *The Plains Sioux and U.S. Colonialism*.

4. Some have even sought to draw out parallels and logical connections. See, for example, Guettel, "From the Frontier to German South-West Africa."

5. See, for example, Hull, *Absolute Destruction*.

6. A. Dirk Moses, *Empire, Colony, Genocide*, 28–32.

7. For an excellent discussion of their situational ethnicity, see Conzen, "Phantom Landscapes of Colonization," 12.

8. Those positions were set out most explicitly in Cooper and Stoler, *Tensions of Empire*.

9. Osterhammel, *Colonialism: A Theoretical Overview*. The same is true for most of Central and South America.

10. Sebastian Conrad, *Globalisierung und Nation*, see especially 229–78.

11. Indeed, it seems fair to argue that the ties between colonial violence in South-West Africa and New Ulm have less to do with the colonists' shared connections to Germany than with the similarities inherent in these colonial situations.

12. For a recent example, see Brunner, "Der große Aufbruch."

13. It was approximately twenty miles wide and seventy miles long.

14. These treaties were rife with complications and initiated in their inception many of the practices of deception and fraud that would contribute to the conflict a little over a decade later. See, for example, Anderson, *Kinsmen of Another Kind*; and Meyer, *History of the Santee Sioux*.

15. Minnesota became a state on 11 May 1858.

16. Conzen, *Germans in Minnesota*, 11.

17. Hildegard Binder Johnson, "The Germans," 153; Johnson, "Intermarriage between German Pioneers and Other Nationalities in Minnesota," 299; and Johnson "The Location of German Immigrants in the Middle West."

18. The Chicago Landverein (Land Company) was founded by Frederick Beinhorn from Braunschweig. By 1854 it had more than eight hundred members and significant funds, and in June 1855 it acquired land near present-day New Ulm and began clearing and building.

19. Friedrich Jahn founded the first association of gymnasts [*Turnverein*] in Berlin in 1811 as a place to increase the mental and physical strength of the youth and to build nationalism. After becoming the focus of conservative reaction, such associations became centers for Freethinkers and were popular with the 1848 generation. The first American *Turnverein* was founded in Cincinnati 1848 and became a center of agitation in the anti-German riots that followed in midwestern cities in the 1850s. The Turners became popular across the Midwest in the following decades.

20. The Turner Colonial Society in Cincinnati was renamed the Settlement Association of the Socialist Turner Society in 1856. In turn it merged with the German Land Company, retaining that name, in March 1857.

21. Beinhorn and the Chicago Land Company initially restricted attorneys and preachers from membership. Frederick Beinhorn narrative, Brown County Historical Society Archive, New Ulm, Minn. Cf. Hoisington, *A German Town*, 12.

22. Hoisington, *A German Town*, 14–21. Ultimately the depression of 1857 strained the association, and it was dissolved. All joint property was sold off to private individuals and groups in 1858; it left an endowment for the school and the resolution that the money should pay for a teacher and that no Bibles would be found in the library and no religion taught in the classes.

23. Hildegard Binder Johnson, "The Germans," 153. The *New Ulm Pioneer* reported on 6 July 1861 that greater New Ulm had more than one thousand people and 250 houses.

24. For German reflections, see, for example, Walker, *Germany and the Emigration*, 172–73.

25. Wilhelm Pfaender's Letter Urging the Formation of the Turner Colonization Society. "Practical Turnerei" (Gymnastics) appeared in *Die Turnzeitung*, March 1855, in the Pfaender papers collected by Steve Albrecht for the Brown County Historical Society. Similarly, in the spring of 1885, anti-German violence swept across Chicago three weeks before Beinhorn left for Minnesota. Hoisington, *A German Town*, 6–7.

26. For a good introduction to the Turners in general, Cincinnati in particular, and the class background and politics of these men, see, for example, Levine, *The Spirit of 1848*, 91–94. For the slavery question and the American Midwest, see also Honeck, *We Are the Revolutionists*.

27. On the strong class antagonism and diversity of political positions among German immigrants, see Levine, *The Spirit of 1848*. This was not, however, the world of New York City's radical beer hall anarchism, captured in Goyens, *Beer and Revolution*.

28. Conzen, *Germans in Minnesota*, 62. See also Stenzel, *German Immigration to the Minnesota River Valley Frontier*, 27.

29. The *New Ulm Pioneer*, for example, stressed in its first issue on 1 January 1858 that New Ulm was a virtual melting pot of Germans. Cf. Berghold, *The Indians' Revenge*, 53. The *New Ulm Pioneer* was one of the state's earlier papers, and it was recognized as radical. Its motto was: "Free Land, Free Men, Free Work, Free Press!" Its editors claimed to be "independent in everything and neutral in nothing," although they were clear supporters (albeit critical) of the Republican Party. The first German-language paper in Minnesota, *Die Minnesota Deutsche Zeitung*, was initially published on 19 November 1855 in St. Paul. Eventually fifty-one German-language papers were published in the state. Gerhard H. Weiss argues that one finds in the German papers in Minnesota "a great love for America, but not necessarily a similar affection for the Yankee-neighbor." This was true in New Ulm as well. Weiss, "German Language Press in Minnesota."

30. Albert Gregory Schneiderhan, for example, in his narrative "The Day before Yesterday," in the Minnesota Historical Society archive in Minneapolis, stresses that Cooper's books, "read all over Europe at the time" inspired his father to travel to the United States, where he ultimately settled in Scott County, north of New Ulm, in 1860.

31. Hoisington, *A German Town*, 13–16.

32. The *New Ulm Pioneer* was New Ulm's only newspaper from 1858 to August 1862. After the town was largely destroyed, there was no local paper until the *New Ulm Post* was established in 1864. While it is always precarious to regard the local press as representative of the thoughts and opinions of its readers, the *New Ulm Pioneer* is perhaps the best possible source of this kind. It was published by one of the original Turners, Lambert Naegele, and it espoused the political positions that tied the colonists together. Dorothy E. Johnson has argued that the 1860 election returns "prove

that the [*New Ulm Pioneer*] expressed the political opinions of the great majority of the Brown County Residents." Johnson, "Attitude of the Germans in Minnesota toward the Republican Party," 107–16.

33. Also Ojibway and Chippeway, though the more common choice today is Ojibwa. I have chosen to use Chippewa in this chapter in order to retain consistency with the quotations from the primary texts.

34. See, for example, the columns during the first year on Indians passing through for maple syrup, *New Ulm Pioneer*, 18 March 1858; on interactions between the Sioux and Chippewa, 8 April 1858; Winnebago and Sioux, 13 May 1858; half-breeds and polygamy, and the modesty of Dakota women, 22 April 1858; a Sioux encampment near German Park, 17 June 1858; a discussion of the function of the Dakota language, 26 August 1858; a description of Dakota patrons in local stores, 16 September 1858; and the exotic portrait of Dakota passing through on a hunt, which paid close attention to their dress and material culture, 2 December 1858.

35. For a discussion of relations between these three tribes and an Ojibwa view into the conflict, see Treuer, *The Assassination of Hole in the Day*.

36. See, for example, *New Ulm Pioneer*, 17 June 1858, 20 August 1859, and 10 December 1859.

37. *New Ulm Pioneer*, 21 July 1860. Similarly, the paper noted on 7 April 1859 that New Ulm's close proximity to the reservation had "absolutely no downside."

38. The one curious piece of evidence against this is a petition, dated 14 August 1862 and sent to Governor Ramsey from some forty-seven residents of Brown County and the "frontier settlements," complaining that the combination of late payments to the Sioux and the loss of able bodied men through enlistments had created a precarious situation for them, and even stated that they were "in eminent danger to see their families massacred by said Indians." Ramsey Papers, Letters Received, Civil War, Indian Affairs—1862, Minnesota Historical Society. This letter, however, was collected along with several other letters from communities making arguments about wanting to forestall a draft in their local areas, and it is unclear if this threat of violence was used to deter the draft or if it revealed an actual fear. The second is not supported by other materials. However, in August 1861 Gilbraith did express concern that Yanktonais and some others might cause trouble and requested soldiers be placed at the reservation, and on 2 June 1862, Thomas Williamson wrote to Galbraith at the bequest of several Dakotas including Cloud Man and Scarlet Feather, warning him that Indians from outside the reservation may come to cause problems there, and asking for reinforcements, indicating that the troops leaving for the Civil War might encourage Indians from outside the reservation to act out against farming Indians and whites. See Ramsey, Letters Received, Indian Agencies, Military Posts and Units—Aug. 1862, Minnesota Historical Society; neither his request nor the warning led to those reinforcements being placed at the reservation.

39. Despite the petition to Ramsey, this is consistent across essentially all of the personal narratives collected in the Brown County Historical Society in New Ulm and confirmed by soldiers. See, for example, Leonard Aldrich to his brother, 8 October 1862, Leonard Aldrich Papers, P950, Minnesota Historical Society.

40. See, for example, *New Ulm Pioneer*, 18 March 1858.

41. *New Ulm Pioneer*, 10 March 1859.

42. *New Ulm Pioneer*, 13 July 1861. Similar efforts were also lauded. For example, 28 January 1860, 9 July 1858.

43. *New Ulm Pioneer*, 9 July 1859.

44. *New Ulm Pioneer*, 6 July 1861.

45. *New Ulm Pioneer*, 23 February 1858. There is also a further short column on the Sioux being pushed ever further west.

46. *New Ulm Pioneer*, 26 November 1859.

47. *New Ulm Pioneer*, 9 July 1858. Further discussion continued the following year when the annual payments were delayed, 23 July 1859.

48. *New Ulm Pioneer*, 23 July 1859.

49. The working editor of the *New Ulm Pioneer*, Otto Barth, was killed during the siege of New Ulm, and the paper essentially died with him. "Grässlicher Tode des Hrn Barth," *Nord Stern* (La Crosse, Wisc.), 13 September 1862; cf. his obituary in the *Minnesota Staats-Zeitung*, 6 September 1862.

50. For a short but much different discussion of Germans and Dakotas near Beaver Creek, see also Anderson, *Kinsmen of Another Kind*, 241–45.

51. Berghold, *The Indians' Revenge*, 38–44.

52. On the poor surveying of boundaries in the area, see Anderson, *Kinsmen of Another Kind*, 241.

53. *New Ulm Pioneer*, 31 March 1859.

54. Anderson, *Kinsmen of Another Kind*, 242. This was often a point of confusion. See, for example, Tate, *Indians and Emigrants*, 88–89. See also the discussion of similar problems preceding the massacres at Spirit Lake and Okoboji in Northern Iowa in 1857 (approximately one hundred miles south of New Ulm) in Beck, *Inkpaduta*, 41–45, 61–63.

55. Leonhart, *Memories of New Ulm*, chap. 3, "Hunting in Minnesota."

56. Ibid., 34.

57. See, for example, Schneiderhan, "The Day before Yesterday"; Christoph Spelbrink Narrative of the Sioux Uprising, 1912, Brown County Historical Society; and Juni, *Held in Captivity*, 1.

58. Johann Pelzl family narrative, Brown County Historical Society.

59. "Die Indianer Gesetze," *New Ulm Pioneer*, 17 September 1859. There are also a few letters to Ramsey from citizens near the reservations who made similar complaints about the tendency of the Dakotas to help themselves to resources. See, for example, the letter from eleven residents of Renville County to Ramsey dated [1860–1863?] in the Alexander Ramsey Papers, microfilm roll no. 11, Minnesota Historical Society.

60. Minnie Carrigan narrative, Brown County Historical Society.

61. This incident is recalled in both the standard histories of the conflict, such as Carley, *The Dakota War of 1862*, 7, as well as the history based on Dakota perspective, Anderson and Woolworth, *Through Dakota Eyes*.

62. Anderson and Woolworth, *Through Dakota Eyes*, 12.

63. Wamditanka, "A Sioux History of the War: Chief Big Eagle's Story of the Sioux Outbreak of 1862," *Minnesota Historical Society Collections* 6 (1894): 385.

64. Anderson and Woolworth, *Through Dakota Eyes*, 19–20.

65. Wamditanka, "A Sioux History of the War," 388; cf. ibid., 27.

66. Walker, *Germany and the Emigration*, 69.

67. Anderson, "Myrick's Insult." Cf. *The Sisseton and Wahpeton Bands of Dakota or Sioux v. The United States*, Court of Claims No. 22524, 1901, compiled by the Minnesota Historical Society.

68. For an excellent discussion of how, in the Australian context as well as others, settler colonialism along the British model was often inherently ethnocidal and potentially genocidal, see A. Dirk Moses, *Genocide and Settler Society*, 33–34.

69. Ibid., 77.

70. See, for example, Anderson, *Kinsmen of Another Kind*; Anderson and Woolworth, *Through Dakota Eyes*; Board of Commissioners, *Minnesota in the Civil and Indian Wars, 1861–1865*; Carley, *The Dakota War of 1862*; Meyer, *History of the Santee Sioux*; Folwell, *A History of Minnesota*, 109–301; Heard, *History of the Sioux War and Massacres*; Satterlee, *A Detailed Account of the Massacre by the Dakota Indians of Minnesota*.

71. Wamditanka, "A Sioux History of the War," 387. The Turners in New Ulm, like Turners across the United States were well represented on the Civil War battlefields. Levine stresses that one-tenth of the Union Army was German born, and Turners and former Turners were "particularly active in recruiting and organizing these forces." Levine, *The Spirit of 1848*, 256.

72. On contradictions and factions, see, for example, Anderson and Woolworth, *Through Dakota Eyes*; Gabriel Renville, "A Sioux Narrative of the Outbreak in 1862, and of Sibley's Expedition in 1863," *Minnesota Historical Society Collections* 10, no. 2 (1905): 595–618; Wamditanka, "A Sioux History of the War," 390. For Little Crow's time working with the agents to put down Inkpaduta's band of Wahpekutes, see Beck, *Inkpaduta*, 104–6. More generally, see Woolworth, "Little Crow."

73. Carley stresses that given the massive loss of property and "the number of civilian lives lost, the outbreak was one of the worst in American history," and he credits it with unleashing the warfare that continued across the plains until 1890. Carley, *The Dakota War of 1862*, 1.

74. The racialized character of the conflict as a war of extermination has continued to be recapitulated in more current accounts. Carley, for example, terms the event a "holocaust"; ibid., 6, 81.

75. See, for example, "Ein Raubthier attravirt. 'Little Six' gefangen," *New Ulm Post*, 5 February 1864; "Indianer-Greuel," *New Ulm Post*, 12 August 1864; and "Sitzbull, böser Häuptling," *Die Volkszeitung*, 21 January 1881; cf. Weiss, "German Language Press in Minnesota," 54.

76. For a discussion of such structures taking shape, see Silver, *Our Savage Neighbors*.

77. A. Dirk Moses, *Empire, Colony, Genocide*, 26.

78. A. Dirk Moses, *Genocide and Settler Society*, 32–33.

79. Ibid.

80. Indeed, Charles E. Flandrau, who had been the local Indian agent in 1855, and who led the final defense of New Ulm in 1862, made essentially this same point about genocidal massacres being part and parcel of some colonial situations during his pub-

lic statements at the dedication of a monument to the defenders in New Ulm in 1891. See the news clipping from the *St. Paul Daily Globe*, 23 August 1891, collected in the Minnesota Historical Society under the title *New Ulm; Dedication of a Monument to Its Defenders, Aug. 22, 1891*.

81. Typically, the initial accounts of the happenings, such as the column that appeared in *Nord Stern* (La Crosse, Wisc.) 6, no. 10 (23 August 1862), described Dakota violence against whites. Only later, on 13 September 1862, did they discuss the fact that most of the victims were Germans. The same kinds of reporting could be found in other states as well, for example in the columns on 28 August and 18 September 1862 in the *Belleviller Zeitung* (Belleville, Ill.).

82. See, for example, *Pioneer am Wisconsin* (Sauk City, Wisc.), 30 August and 6 September 1862; *Nord Stern* (La Crosse, Wisc.), 13 September 1862.

83. These were extensive. See, for example, "The Difficulty with the Chippewas," *Pioneer and Democrat* (St. Paul), 29 August 1862; "Wisconsin Chippewa Want to Fight the Sioux," *Pioneer and Democrat*, 11 September 1862; and *Pioneer and Democrat*, 24 September 1862. For examples from German-language papers, see "Indianer-Unruhe," *Nord Stern* (La Crosse, Wisc.), 13 September 1862; "Das Freundschaftsbündniß mit den Chippewas," *Minnesota Staats-Zeitung*, 27 September 1862; and untitled column in *Pioneer am Wisconsin* (Sauk City, Wisc.), 6 September 1862.

84. "Indianergreuel im Minnesota," *Nord Stern* (La Crosse, Wisc.), 30 August 1862.

85. The *Minnesota Staats-Zeitung* was a Republican-subsidized paper founded in 1858 and close in tone to the *New Ulm Pioneer*. By this date, the German-language newspapers in Minnesota with Democratic sympathies had been driven out of business. Dorothy E. Johnson, "Attitude of Germans in Minnesota toward the Republican Party," 116.

86. For example, the first clear call for a war of elimination in the *Pioneer and Democrat* appeared in a reprint of a column from the *Stillwater Messenger*, 4 September 1862.

87. *Minnesota Staats-Zeitung*, 30 August 1862.

88. Indeed, Meyer notes that similar calls for a war of extermination went out in the English-language press in 1857 after the massacres at Spirit Lake and Okoboji. Meyer, *History of the Santee Sioux*, 97–102. See also the similar discussion in Beck, *Inkpaduta*.

89. Ramsey served both as territorial governor from 1 June 1843 to 15 May 1853 and state governor from 2 January 1860 to 10 July 1863.

90. This was not an isolated statement. Indeed, it essentially repeated the position voiced a week earlier by Lieutenant Governor Ignatius Loyola Donnelly. "Aus Lt. Gov. Donnelly's Bericht über den Indianer-Krieg," *Minnesota Staats-Zeitung*, 6 September 1862.

91. *Minnesota Staats-Zeitung*, 18 October 1862.

92. "Der Strang der einzig Friedensstifter," *Minnesota Staats-Zeitung*, 15 November 1862.

93. Nix, *The Sioux Uprising in Minnesota*, 91–92.

94. Ibid., 92.

95. Ibid., 139.

96. Indeed, Nix contradicts himself repeatedly on his evaluation of the character of the Dakota. See, for example, ibid., 79.

97. Ibid., 83.

98. Ibid., 77.

99. Berghold, *The Indians' Revenge*, 65.

100. Ibid., 59.

101. Ibid., 117.

102. Ibid., 63, 146.

103. Ibid., 147.

104. Ibid., 160.

105. See, for example, Wilson, *In the Footsteps of Our Ancestors*.

106. Berghold, *The Indians' Revenge*, 54–56.

107. Solomon, it would seem, responded in this manner because he had had trouble with his effort to initiate a draft in Wisconsin. It led to riots. In that sense, the 1862 conflict gave him a reason to mobilize state forces.

108. *Globus* 6 (1864): 8–9. See also "Ausrottung der Indianer in Nordamerika," *Globus* 6 (1864): 287.

109. "Der Indianerkrieg in Nordamerika," *Globus* 8 (1866): 122–23. See also "Abschlachtung von Indianer in Nordamerika," *Globus* 9 (1866): 158, which details the horrific slaughter visited on American Indians at the hands of "pioneers of civilization," a phrase used with great irony and bitterness.

110. Rudolf Cronau, "Um die Erde. Sechster Brief: In Minnesota," 116–18, and "Siebenter Brief: Indianische Dichtung und Wahrheit in Minnesota," 148–50; and "Die Sioux-Indianer," *Leipziger Illustrirte Zeitung* 86 (1886): 591–92. Cronau built directly on coverage in *Die Gartenlaube* during his comments; see the essay from "a German in America," "Erinnerungen aus dem Indianeraufstand in Minnesota," *Die Gartenlaube* (1873): 94–97, 115–19, 162–65.

CHAPTER 3

1. Cronau, "Um die Erde: Sechster Brief: In Minnesota," 116–18.

2. See, for example, Barclay and Glaser-Schmidt, *Transatlantic Images and Perceptions*; Kamphoefner, Helbich, and Sommer, *News from the Land of Freedom*; Kazal, *Becoming Old Stock*; Luebke, *Germans in the New World*; Rodgers, *Atlantic Crossings*; Trommler and Shore, *The German-American Encounter*; Wüstenbecker, *Deutsch-Amerikaner im Ersten Weltkrieg*.

3. Penny, "Illustrating America."

4. Cronau, Tagebuch I, Stadtarchiv Solingen, Na-47-10.

5. Cronau, "Um die Erde: Erster Brief: Aus den Straßen New-Yorks."

6. Cronau, "Um die Erde: Fünfter Brief: Baltimore."

7. Cronau, "Um die Erde: Zweiter Brief: Auf dem Greenwood Cemetery zu Brooklyn"; Cronau, "Um die Erde: Dritter Brief: Das amerikanische Mekka."

8. For a discussion of the political and class factions within German New York, see, for example, Goyens, *Beer and Revolution*; and Levine, *The Spirit of 1848*.

9. Cronau, "Auf des Lebens Wellen und Wogen," 45; Rosenthal, *Leben und Werk eines Deutschamerikaners*, 18–20.

10. Cronau, Tagebuch I, 156.

11. Ibid., 167.

12. Ibid., 168–69.

13. Cronau, "Um die Erde: Siebenter Brief: Indianische Dichtung und Wahrheit in Minnesota."

14. Ibid., 150.

15. Rosenthal, "Leben und Werk eines Deutschamerikaners," 20. Cf. Boyton, *The Story of Paul Boyton*.

16. According to local English- and German-language newspapers, thousands of people turned out for their departure from St. Paul on 30 May 1881. See, for example, "Glückliche Reise: Dr. R. Cronau und Capt. Boyton schwimmen ab," *St. Paul Volkszeitung*, 30 May 1881; "Swimming for St. Louis," *St. Paul Pioneer*, 31 May 1881.

17. See, for example, "Der Schwimmer Paul Boyton," *Buffalo County Republikaner*, 7 June 1881; "Boyton," *Daily News* (La Crosse, Wisc.), 4 June 1881; "Capt. Paul Boyton," *Dubuque Herald*, 8 June 1881, all of which describe entire villages and huge crowds in each town rushing to greet them while landing. "The Famous Navigator," *Davenport Gazette*, 11 June 1881; "Boyton und Cronau," *Davenport Demokrat*, 11 June 1881; "Buoyant Boyton," *Burlington Gazette*, 13 June 1881; "Boyton's Voyage," *Daily Globe* (St. Louis), 20 June 1881; "About 30,000," *St. Louis Republican*, 20 June 1881.

18. Cronau, "Um die Erde: Achter Brief: Ein Monat auf dem Vater der Ströme."

19. Cronau, *Im Wilden Westen*, 13–14.

20. Cronau, "Um die Erde: Achter Brief: Ein Monat auf dem Vater der Ströme," 230.

21. Cronau, *Im Wilden Westen*, 12.

22. Cronau, "Auf des Lebens Wellen und Wogen," 48.

23. Cronau, Tagebuch I, 330.

24. Ibid., 316; Cronau, *Im Wilden Westen*, 51. Steffan was also a Catholic priest and later became the director of the Bureau of Catholic Missions from 1884 to 1901.

25. Cronau, Tagebuch II, Stadtarchiv Solingen, 71, 87, letter from Schenk to Cronau, 24 July 1882, in Tagebuch II between pages 98 and 99.

26. News clippings about Sitting Bull, Standing Rock, the transportation of Sioux prisoners on steamboats, and U.S. Indian policy can be found throughout the diaries next to his notes on those subjects; it is unclear from the notations, however, if the columns were collected before or after he made his notes and had experienced the events recorded in them.

27. Cronau, Tagebuch I, 323–24. See also Cronau, *Im Wilden Westen*, which offers a slightly different rendition of this statement, 60.

28. Cronau, *Im Wilden Westen*, 103.

29. Cronau, Tagebuch II, 72. It is worth noting that Cronau studied Sitting Bull's face in photographs before they met, and his favorable comparison of Sitting Bull to Chingachgook was hardly original. For example, an undated news clipping from an untitled German American newspaper is attached between pages 74 and 75 of Tagebuch II. It too calls Sitting Bull "a much more important personality than Cooper's Unkas or Chingachgook."

30. For an introduction to tensions facing the Sioux at Standing Rock and on other reservations during this tumultuous decade, see, for example, Utley, *The Last Days*

of the Sioux; see also Hoxie, *A Final Promise*; Ostler, "Conquest and the State"; and White, *"It's Your Misfortune and None of My Own."*

31. Cronau, Tagebuch II, 7. Cronau was not the only journalist present. His scrapbook from this early period of his trip, which contains clippings from his trip with Boyton, also includes a long essay on the meeting titled "The Wily Sioux: Great Peace Council at Standing Rock Agency" that appeared in the *New York Evening Telegram*, 9 December 1881. Much of the information matches Cronau's notes, including a shared admiration for the physical presence and oratorical skills of Crow King.

32. Cronau, Tagebuch II, 4–17.

33. Cronau, *Im Wilden Westen*, 62; Cronau, "Auf des Lebens Wellen und Wogen," 52.

34. Cronau's references to Roman senators in his lectures and essays were perhaps even more frequent than his comparisons to Greek gods. See, for example, Cronau, Tagebuch I, 364; Cronau, *Im Wilden Westen*, 52; "Drei Jahre bei den Dakota Indianern," *Kölner Nachrichten*, 27 November 1883. Such comparisons continued well beyond Cronau, especially in the work of Karl May. See, for example, Krinsky, "Karl May's Western Novels and Aspects of Their Continuing Influence," 64.

35. That portrait was located in the Museum of the American Indian in New York City. It is now in the possession of Gerald Wunderlich. See Utley, *Sitting Bull*, 385, n. 11. For a discussion of the photograph, see, Lohausen and Keller, *Rudolf Cronau*, 38–40. For the iconography of Sitting Bull in Germany, see, for example, Feest, *Sitting Bull*; Eggebrecht, "Sitzend inmitten der Prärie." The most recent exhibit on Sitting Bull was organized by Feest at the Museum of Ethnology in Vienna from 10 December 2009 to 15 March 2010.

36. Cronau, Tagebuch II, 75.

37. Ibid., 75–77.

38. Ibid., 77–79. Some of this material is related as well in Cronau, *Im Wilden Westen*, and Cronau, "Um die Erde: Neunter Brief: Ein rother Napoleon."

39. Cronau, Tagebuch I, 24–26; Cronau, Tagebuch II, 75.

40. Berghold, *The Indians' Revenge*.

41. Cronau, "Eine verleumdete Rasse," in Tagebuch III, Stadtarchiv Solingen, NA-47-12, 38, 40, 42.

42. Cronau, Tagebuch I, 24–26; Cronau Tagebuch II, 75; Cronau, "Eine verleumdete Rasse," in Tagebuch III; Dee Brown, *Bury My Heart at Wounded Knee*.

43. Cronau, Tagebuch III, 55. "Taurus Recumbent: Artist Cronau's Highly Colored Pictures of Sitting Bull and His Braves," *Milwaukee Sentinel*, 8 April 1882; "Oscar O'Flahertyism," *Evening Wisconsin*, 8 April 1882; "Der Vortrag des Herrn Rudolf Cronau," *Milwaukee Freie Press*, 8 April 1882; "Rudolf Cronau's Vortrag," *Milwaukee Herald*, 8 April 1882.

44. Cronau, "Auf des Lebens Wellen und Wogen."

45. Cited in Rosenthal, "Leben und Werk eines Deutschamerikaners," 26.

46. Cronau, Tagebuch II, 87.

47. They gave him the name Iron Eyes because of his thick glasses. See the letter from Schenck to Cronau pasted into Tagebuch II between pages 98 and 99.

48. One Bull to Cronau, 12 August 1891, in the possession of Gerald Wunderlich;

this letter was in response to one sent to One Bull by Cronau; Cronau, *New Yorker Staats-Zeitung*, 22 August 1897.

49. Udo Brachvogel, "Zehntausend Meilen durch den Großen Westen der Vereinigten Staaten" *Die Gartenlaube* (1883): 262–66, 375–79, 570–74, 589–91, 760–63; (1884): 160–66, 446–48; (1885): 396–99; (1885): 616–20. Most notable were Cronau, *Von Wunderland zu Wunderland*; *Buch der Reklame*; and *Im Wilden Westen*. All were well received. Theodor Fontane, for example, wrote a glowing review of *Von Wunderland zu Wunderland* in the *Vossische Zeitung*, 26 November 1885.

50. The Stadtarchiv Solingen contains an extensive collection of clippings from these tours in NA-47-8. See, for example, "Lüdenscheid," no title to the paper, 16 February 1886; "Vorträge," Erfeld, 17 February 1886.

51. Cronau offered his audiences the choice of five lectures: "1200 Miles on the Mississippi with Captain Boyton," "A Trip to the Wonderlands of the New World," "Curiosities of American Advertising," "The Decimated Race," and "Three Months in the Land of the Sioux."

52. See, for example, *Solinger Intelligenzblatt*, 6 November 1883, and *Stadt-Anzeiger zur Köln. Zeitung*, 28 November 1883, Stadtarchiv Solingen, NA-47-8. Compare this reception to the news clippings from Buffalo Bill's 1890 tour located in the Harold McCracken Research Library, Buffalo Bill Historical Center, Cody, Wyo., series IX, box 5, for example, *Dresdner Journal*, 7 June 1890, and *Lindener Zeitung* (Hannover), 3 July 1890.

53. See, for example, "Drei Monate unter den Sioux- oder Dakota Indianern," Wiesbaden, 14 December 1884, Stadtarchiv Solingen, NA-47-9.

54. See, for example, "Drei Jahre bei den Dakota Indianern," *Kölner Nachrichten*, 27 November 1883; "Wurtt. Verein für Handelsgeographie," paper title missing, Stuttgart, 25 November 1884; and *Frankfurter Zeitung*, 11 December 1884, Stadtarchiv Solingen, NA-47-9.

55. "Eine Stunde in den Prärien," *Stadt-Anzeiger zur Köln. Zeitung*, 28 November 1883; see also the untitled column from Stuttgart dated 29 November 1884; the clipping from "Verein für Erdkunde zu Halle. Sitzung von 13. Mai 1885"; and from Erfeld, "Vorträge," 17 February 1886, Stadtarchiv Solingen, NA-47-9.

56. "Künstler-Verein," *Leipziger Tageblatt*, 5 October 1885; Haberland, "'Diese Indianer sind falsch.'"

57. "Die Sioux-Indianer," *Leipziger Illustrirte Zeitung* 86 (1886): 592; Cronau, *Fahrten im Lande der Sioux*. Indeed, *Über Land und Meer*, another major illustrated magazine in Germany, credited Cronau with directing the show, not simply accompanying it. "Die Sioux Indianer," *Über Land und Meer* (1886): 1074–77.

58. See, for example, the *Leipziger Zeitung*, 18 June 1890, Harold McCracken Research Library, Buffalo Bill Historical Center, series IX, box 5.

59. Cronau, "Durch Kansas," *Die Gartenlaube* (1893): 152–56.

60. Cronau, *Im Wilden Westen*, v, 42, 169.

61. There are omissions in his tale as well. There is, for example, no mention of his interactions with the Minnesota Dakota; instead his first glimpse of American Indians seems to take place in Dakota Territory, and it is riddled with awed clichés. Ibid., 44.

62. Wüstenbecker, *Deutsch-Amerikaner im Ersten Weltkrieg*, 24, 28, 30, 39, 47, 48.

63. Many of these came under the general title "Verschwindende Gestalten des fernen Westens," in the *New Yorker Staats-Zeitung*; e.g., 1 January 1899.

64. Cronau to Directors of the Bureau of Ethnology, 17 April 1900, Smithsonian Institution Archives, Records of the BAE, box 98, series 1: Correspondence, Letters Received. His dismissal is also discussed in Rosenthal, "Leben und Werk eines Deutschamerikaners," 70.

65. Cronau, "Zum 25. Jahrestag des Custer-Massacres: Ein Rückblick auf ein düsters Blatt aus der Geschichte des fernen Westens," *Kölnische Zeitung*, 23 June 1901.

66. Cronau, "Die Indianische Gewerbeschule zu Carlisle in Pennsylvanien," *Die Gartenlaube* (1904): 31–34.

67. Cronau, *Our Wasteful Nation*; see also Cronau, "A Continent Despoiled."

68. Cronau, "A Continent Despoiled," 640–43.

69. Cronau, *Our Wasteful Nation*, 106.

70. Strand, "The Crying Indian."

71. Cronau, *Our Wasteful Nation*, 106.

72. Cronau, "The Bulwarks of Our Ancestors."

73. Cronau, *Woman Triumphant*, 140–46.

74. Retallack, *Imperial Germany*, 1.

75. So too did the rising American concerns about the dangers of foreign ideologies in the wake of the Haymarket riot (1886), which included a large number of Germans among the participants—as well as essentially all of those who were ultimately executed. Nagler, "From Culture to *Kultur*," 131–54.

76. See also Cronau, "The New Germany—An Object Lesson."

77. Cronau, *Drei Jahrhunderte deutschen Lebens in Amerika*.

78. See, for example, Lears, *Rebirth of a Nation*, 92–132.

79. Cronau, *The British Black Book*.

80. Ibid., 18.

81. Ibid., 59.

82. See especially Cronau, "Does America Need a Third War for Independence?," in *The British Black Book*.

83. Wüstenbecker, *Deutsch-Amerikaner im Ersten Weltkrieg*, 107.

84. Luebke, *Germans in the New World*, 35.

85. Chrislock, *Watchdog of Loyalty*; Wüstenbecker, *Deutsch-Amerikaner im Ersten Weltkrieg*, 161.

86. Wüstenbecker, *Deutsch-Amerikaner im Ersten Weltkrieg*, 219.

87. This was not the first instance of negative integration among Germans and Irish; similar interethnic unity surfaced at other critical moments as well. See, for example, Levine, *The Spirit of 1848*, 134.

88. See, for example, the long discussion of Hall's pamphlet "Lights and Shadows of American Life," on German America in "3,000 TEUTONS MEET AT A WAR CARNIVAL; German Press Club's Entertainment Nets Nearly $12,000 for Relief Work. GRAND OPERA STARS THERE. Some Money Raised at Hotel Astor Fete by the Sale of Curios Made by Prisoners in England," *New York Times*, 20 February 1916.

89. Trommler and Shore, *The German-American Encounter*, xiii.

90. Kamphoefner, Helbich, and Sommer, *News from the Land of Freedom*, 25. See also Luebke, *Germans in the New World*, 42–47.

91. Luebke, *Germans in the New World*, 53. See also Kazal, *Becoming Old Stock*, 171–213.

CHAPTER 4

1. Du Bois, *The Souls of Black Folk*, 2, 13. For the first mention of the color line (1900), see Walters, Brown, Williams, and Du Bois, "To the Nations of the World," 20.

2. Du Bois, *The World and Africa*, 5, cited in John David Smith, "W. E. B. Du Bois, Felix von Luschan, and Racial Reform at the Fin de Siècle"; see also John David Smith, "Anthropologist Felix von Luschan and Trans-Atlantic Racial Reform."

3. Indeed, Du Bois was enamored with Germany before he traveled there. He not only wrote a research paper on Tacitus's *Germania* while at Harvard, his valedictorian address at Fisk University had been on Otto von Bismarck. On Du Bois's intellectual and personal connections to Germany during his formative years, see Barkin, "'Berlin Days.'"

4. Du Bois, "The Present Condition of German Politics, 1893." For extensive discussion of African American intellectuals and their engagement with Germany, see also Zimmerman, *Alabama in Africa*.

5. Indeed, he wrote that while in Germany he "became more human," less governed by his own prejudices, and was "free from most of those iron bands that bound me at home." Barkin, "Berlin Days," 83, 93.

6. This is not to say that no African American intellectuals concerned themselves with American Indians. Some did. See, for example, the material on Booker T. Washington in Zimmerman, *Alabama in Africa*.

7. Conn, *History's Shadow*, 1–2. Cf. David Levering Lewis, who notes that for Du Bois Asians also fell out of his thinking because they were essentially "excluded" from the polity. Lewis, *W. E. B. Du Bois, 1868-1919*, 72.

8. This became clear to Du Bois only after the fact. See, for example, Opel, "W. E. B. Du Bois, Nazi Germany, and the Black Atlantic"; and especially Du Bois, "The Negro and the Warsaw Ghetto."

9. John David Smith, "W. E. B. Du Bois, Felix von Luschan, and Racial Reform at the Fin de Siècle," 25.

10. Francis, *The Imaginary Indian*, 59.

11. Philip Deloria, *Indians in Unexpected Places*, 120.

12. Ibid., 166.

13. http://digital.library.okstate.edu/encyclopedia/entries/M/MI029.html, 2 October 2009.

14. Philip Deloria, *Indians in Unexpected Places*, 68.

15. Penny, "Illustrating America."

16. "1910 Völkerschau; Oglala-Sioux-Indianer. Text von Johs. Flemming," Hagenbeck Archiv.

17. Philip Deloria, *Indians in Unexpected Places*, 69–70. See also Vine Deloria, "The Indians."

18. Wayne Beasly, Bromberg, Germany, to JC Miller, 5 August 1913, and Miller

to Beasly, 16 July 1913, Miller Brothers 101 Ranch Collection M-407 (hereafter 101 Ranch), Western Historical Collections, University of Oklahoma, Norman, Okla., box 3, folder 1.

19. Superintendent at Pine Ridge to Commissioner of Indian Affairs, 21 October 1914, National Archives, Washington, D.C., 50459-14-047 Pine Ridge. See also National Archives, College Park Record Group 59, Stack Area 250, Central Decimal File 1910–1929, 362.11/1317, box 4364.

20. Sarrasani to JCM, telegram, 22 May 1924, 101 Ranch, box 28, folder 2, asking for a troupe for his circus in Buenos Aries; JCM manages it with great bureaucratic challenges: JCM to Sarrasani, 27 June 1924. That venture, however, was not a success.

21. Paul Schultze employee Karl Arthur Volbath (?) to Miller Brothers, 12 November 1924, box 28, folder 6; John Benson at Hagenbeck, N.Y., to JCM, 19 February 1925; Sarrasani in Rio de Janeiro to JCM, 18 July 1925, 101 Ranch, box 30, folder 4.

22. Gleich to JCM, 4 April 1926, 101 Ranch, box 1, folder 1. See Günther and Winkler, *Taschenbuch der Künste*, 128–32.

23. Sarrasani to JCM, 14 October 1926, 101 Ranch, box 41, folder 1.

24. CF Hafley to JCM, 4 January 1926; JCM to Hafley, 21 December 1926, 101 Ranch, box 39, folder 1.

25. Paul Schultze in Berlin to JCM, 6 January 1925, 101 Ranch, box 35, folder 1; JCM to Schultze, 19 April 1926, box 41, folder 2. The Miller Brothers 101 Ranch Wild West Show toured seasonally from 1907 to 1916, and then again from 1925 to 1931.

26. JCM to Sarrasani, 1 November 1926, 101 Ranch, box 41, folder 1; JCM to Schultze, 19 April 1926, box 41, folder 2; Schultze to JCM, 14 January 1927, box 47, folder 5; JCM to Schultze, 19 February 1927, and Schultze to JCM, 8 March 1927, box 47, folder 5, MB 101.

27. Sasse to JCM, 7 February 1927; JCM to Sasse, 10 February 1927; JCM to Sasse, 19 February 1927, 101 Ranch, box 47, folder 5.

28. Schultz to JCM, 18 February 1927, 101 Ranch, box 47, folder 5.

29. The 101 Ranch fell into receivership in 1931; the depression made it impossible for Zach Miller, the one surviving brother of the original three, to save it.

30. A. T. Haeberle, American General Consul in Dresden to the Secretary of State, 1 February 1928, National Archives, Washington, D.C., 11659-28-047.

31. Sarrasani also wrote that "I cannot lay too much stress on the fact that the presence of American Indians with my show, traveling as I do over Europe has aroused tremendous enthusiasm especially amongst the cultured classes and has maked [sic] excellent propaganda for the great and powerful United States of America." Sarrasani to Commissioner of Indian Affairs, 25 February 1931, National Archives, Washington, D.C., 18184-31.

32. Stabber to Eber, 6 May 1936; see also Lone Bear to Eber, 23 December 1934; Stabber (in Brussels) to Eber, 16 June 1935; correspondence in possession of Max Oliv. Stabber and Lone Bear were not alone in their success at establishing relationships in Germany or in their efforts to return to Germany. The Miller Brothers received many letters from other Lakotas on the Pine Ridge reservation asking for assistance in getting work in Germany, or in many cases, such as with Creeping Bear and his friend Watan, wanting to return again. Jas Sweet Grass also found ways to return to Germany once he had been there. On one occasion he returned with a circus from

New York State, and on other occasions after contacting the Miller Brothers and arranging a contract with one of their groups. Creeping Bear to JCM, 11 March 1926, 101 Ranch, box 38, folder 2; Jas Sweet Grass to JCM, 27 January 1927, 29 September 1927, box 47, folder 6; Sarrasani to JCM, 8 February 1926, box 41, folder 1.

33. Warburg, *Images from the Region of the Pueblo Indians*, 60–63.

34. Ibid., 2.

35. Ibid., 6.

36. Ibid., 54.

37. Ibid.

38. Ibid., 66–67.

39. See, for example, Franzke, Haberland, Sanner, and Templin, *Katsinam*.

40. Sanner, "Karl von den Steinen in Oraibi."

41. Jung, *Memories, Dreams, Reflections*, 248–49.

42. Ibid.

43. Ibid., 251–53.

44. Ibid.

45. Czaplicka, "Amerikabilder and the German Discourse on Modern Civilization."

46. Nolan, "America in the German Imagination."

47. Göktürk, *Künstler, Cowboys, Ingenieure*, 164.

48. Farr, "Julius Seyler."

49. Koepnick, "Unsettling America," 8.

50. Ibid.

51. Ibid., 9.

52. Ibid.

53. Scholz-Héansel, "Indianer im deutschen Südwesten."

54. Ibid., 133.

55. Tower, *Envisioning Amerika*, 18, 24.

56. Otto, *Deutsche Amerika-Bilder*, 149, 267, 286–87, 301.

57. See Corn, *The Great American Thing*, 111–12; and Cassidy, *Marsden Hartley*.

58. A partial list of the clubs includes the Munich Cowboy Club (1913), Cowboy Club Buffalo (1919), and Wild-West Club (1921) in Freiburg, First Dresden Indian-and-Cowboy Club Manitou (1928), and the Hunkpapa-Club (1934) in Frankfurt. For a tight discussion of these clubs, see Bolz, "Indians and Germans." Other earlier clubs created from 1894 to 1939 are listed in Oliv, "Geschichts- und Ursachensforschung: Beitrag über Gründung und Entwicklung der ersten Vereine bis zu den Councils," in Oliv, *10 Jahre Indian Councils*.

59. Rudolf Conrad, "Mutual Fascination."

60. Rayna Green, "The Tribe Called Wannabee."

61. E. U. "'Manitou' unter Radebeuls Himmel," clipping number 19722000 3, Karl-May-Museum Archive, Radebeul. See also Seifert, *Patty Frank*, 11.

62. Grosz, *Ein kleines Ja und ein großes Nein*, 81.

63. "Die Indianerschlacht am Little Bighorn," *Karl-May-Jahrbuch*, 1926; Frank, *Die Indianerschlacht am Little Big Horn*.

64. "Die Eröffnung des Karl-May-Museums in Radebeul: Blick in eine alte Kulturwelt," *Dresdner Neueste Nachrichten*, 20 November 1928.

65. "Das Museum der 17 Skalpe," *Danziger Volksstimme*, 29 November 1928.

66. Seifert, *Patty Frank*, 137–39; *Karl-May-Jahrbuch*, 1929.

67. "Die Flucht aus dem Alltag in die Romantik: Cowboy-Club München-Süd. Erwachsene die Wildwest Spielen," *Münchner Illustrierte Presse* (1930): 543.

68. "Die Indianer von München, Wild-West am Sonntag" *Telegramm-Zeitung*, 1 October 1930. See also *8 Uhr Blatt*, 7 September 1963, located in the news clipping file "Cowboy-Club Zeitungen," Stadtarchiv München.

69. "Hau Kola! Hau Kola!—Wildwest jubiliert in München. Münchner Cowboy-Club feiert Geburtstag—Indianerromantik in der Hochstraße," *Abendblatt*, 24 March 1938; "Echter als in Amerika: Fünfundzwanzig Jahre Münchner Cowboy-Club," *Münchner Neueste Nachrichten*, 4 April 1938.

70. Ibid.

71. Unlike most renditions of this battle, the painting places several Sioux, rather than Custer, at the center of the conflict. http://www.thule-italia.org/Arte/eber/eber_2.jpg. It is the image that the National Park Service chose to place on its website for the Little Bighorn Battlefield National Monument because of its putative accuracy. It was also incorporated into the first handbook for the park in the 1950s. http://www.nps.gov/history/history/online_books/hh/1a/hh1a.htm; Seifert, *Patty Frank*, 116.

72. These paintings are well known: http://www.thule-italia.org/Arte/eber/eber_5.jpg; http://www.thule-italia.org/Arte/eber/eber_25.jpg.

73. Stabber-Eber correspondence, in the possession of Max Oliv, Munich. I am grateful to Oliv for sharing these with me.

74. "Elk Eber," *Illustrierter Beobachter*, 1937, series 33, 1227–28.

75. "Indianer und Cowboys im Isartal: Sport, Spiel, und kulturelles Ziel," *Völkischer Beobachter*, 22 June 1934. See also "25 Jahre Cowboy-Club," *Völkischer Beobachter*, 3 April 1938.

76. Otto, *Deutsche Amerika-Bilder*, 92.

77. Speer, *Spandauer Tagebücher*.

78. Klaus Mann, "Cowboy Mentor of the Führer."

79. Gassert, "Without Concessions to Marxist or Communist Thought"; Junker, "The Continuity of Ambivalence: German Views of America, 1933–1945," 244.

80. Parkhill, *Weaving Ourselves into the Land*, 65–74.

81. "Regarding the Sioux as Aryan," undated memo from Dr. Donald Collier, Department of Anthropology, University of Chicago, to an uncited recipient, Office of Indian Affairs, RG 75, box 15, National Archives, cited in Townsend, *World War II and the American Indian*, 33.

82. Townsend, *World War II and the American Indian*, 35.

83. Most recently, see Tooze, *The Wages of Destruction*.

84. Weinberg, *Hitler's Second Book*. While I cite chiefly this book, Hitler reiterated and expanded on these points elsewhere. See, for example, Trevor-Roper, *Hitler's Table Talk*.

85. Weinberg, *Hitler's Second Book*, 18–19.

86. Ibid., 79–80.

87. Ibid., 109–10.

88. Ibid., 116.

89. Tooze, *The Wages of Destruction*, 470.

PART II

1. Oliv, *20 Jahre Indian Councils*, vol. 1; Oliv, *20 Jahre Indian Councils*, vol. 2. These figures do not count all the "lodges" and western style tents that began appearing as well. In 1989, for example, the combined number was 916.

2. Sieg, "Indian Impersonation as Historical Surrogation," 223.

3. Conversation with ethnologist Klaus Fuhrman, 11 March 2004. Fuhrman produced the documentary *Wild West—German Style* and lives in Freiburg.

4. For example, James Hagengruber, in "Sitting Bull über alles," estimated their number at upward of 40,000. http://dir.salon.com/mwt/feature/2002/11/27/indians/ index.html. In 1999, however, Peter Bolz and Ulrich Sanner placed it at 100,000. Bolz and Sanner, *Native American Art*, 14.

5. Haible, *Indianer im Dienste der NS-Ideologie*, 78.

6. According to the Karl-May-Press, the numbers for May's leading novels on American Indians are *Winnetou I* (1939: 360,000; 2010: 3,892,000); *Winnetou II* (1944: 330,000; 2010: 3,307,000); *Winnetou III* (1944: 311,000; 2010: 3,002,000); *Old Surehand I* (1940: 265,000; 2010: 2,696,000); *Old Surehand II* (1940: 250,000; 2010: 2,696,000); *Unter Geiern* (1944: 225,000; 2010: 2,107,000); *Der Schatz im Silbersee* (1944: 485,000; 2010: 3,288,000); *Der Ölprinz* (1945: 212,000; 2010: 1,963,000); *Halbblut* (1943: 244,000; 2010: 1,624,000). Correspondence from Roderich Haug, 16 June 2011.

7. Augstein, "Weiter Weg zu Winnetou," 130. He cites 80–100 million in twenty-five languages, which include those published by presses other than the Karl-May-Press, after copyright expired.

8. Lutz, *"Indianer" und "Native Americans,"* 384–85; Haible, *Indianer im Dienste der NS-Ideologie*, 12, 279.

9. Lutz, "Der edle Wilde auf dem Kriegspfad," 236.

10. Kramer, *Micky, Marx, und Manitu*.

11. See, for example, Borries and Fischer, *Sozialistische Cowboys*, 11, especially n. 3.

12. Weber, "'Indians' on German Stages."

13. *Weekend Journal* of the *Rhein-Zeitung*, 22–23 February 1992, reported visitor figures over 300,000 a year.

14. Walter Scherf, "Die Jugendbande stirbt aus. Zur Sozialpsychologie einer Gemeinschaftsform," in *Jugend in der Gesellschaft* (Munich, 1975), cited in Kreis, "German Wild West," 264.

15. Kreis, "German Wild West," 271.

16. Ibid.

17. Ibid., 265.

CHAPTER 5

1. Nolan, "America in the German Imagination," 12.

2. That has not been unique to Germany. Cf., for example, Berkhofer, *The White Man's Indian*, xvi, 22, 30–31; and Philip Deloria, *Indians in Unexpected Places*.

3. Haible, *Indianer im Dienste der NS-Ideologie*, 92–93.

4. Bolz, "Indians and Germans."

5. Steuben is most well known for his Tecumseh series; Friedrich von Gagern for his *Der Marterpfahl* (Berlin, 1925); *Das Grenzerbuch: Von Pfadfindern, Häuptlingen und Lederstrümpfen* (Berlin, 1927); and *Der tote Mann: Roman der roten Rasse* (Berlin, 1927).

6. Lutz, *"Indianer" und "Native Americans,"* 348–49, 358–59; see also Hohendahl, "Von der Rothaut zum Edelmenschen."

7. Lutz, *"Indianer" und "Native Americans,"* 356.

8. Kreis, "German Wild West," 265.

9. Haible, *Indianer im Dienste der NS-Ideologie*, 131; Heermann, *Old Shatterhand ritt nicht im Auftrag der Arbeiterklasse*, 187; Kreis, "German Wild West," 265.

10. Aley, *Jugendliteratur im Dritten Reich*; Denkler and Prümm, *Die deutsche Literatur im Dritten Reich*.

11. May was jailed twice for petty crimes and began writing while in prison in 1875. True success eluded him until 1893 when *Winnetou* appeared. His history plagued him until his death in 1912.

12. Dr. Bernhart Scheer, "Karl May und die deutschen Jungen," *Siegerländer*, 2 March 1934.

13. Kreis, "German Wild West," 267.

14. The Karl-May-Museum has a selection of newspaper articles from this period, which contain images of soldiers and Hitler Youth moving through the collections. See, for example, *Hamburger Illustrierte Zeitung*, 14 December 1936; and *Dresdener Nachrichten*, 21 February 1937.

15. Haible, *Indianer im Dienste der NS-Ideologie*, 116.

16. Berghold, *Aufstand der Dakota*.

17. For a discussion of this particular continuity, see Penny, "Elusive Authenticity."

18. Feest, "Germany's Indians in a European Perspective," 28.

19. Haible, *Indianer im Dienste der NS-Ideologie*, 162.

20. Gagern, *Das Grenzerbuch*, 171.

21. Steuben, *Der fliegende Pfeil*, 5.

22. Sander, *Volk ohne Land*, 110–13.

23. Beholz, *Tecumtha, der letzte Shawnee*, 280.

24. Lutz, "German Indianthusiasm," 178. Cf. Friedrichs, "Tecumseh's Fabulous Career in German Fiction."

25. "Der letzte Bund der Indianerstämme gegen die Vereinigten Staaten. Tekumseh und sein Bruder Elskwatawa," *Das Ausland* (1832): 1053–54.

26. "Tecumseh, der Shawnee-Häuptling," *Das Ausland* (1860): 201–6; 223–28.

27. *Das Ausland* (1860): 225.

28. Franz Schauwecker, "Bildnis eines Indianers: Die Erhebung der Prärie," *Münchner Neueste Nachrichten*, 10 May 1938. Also popular in the 1930s: Schauwecker, *Thecumseh*.

29. Lutz, *"Indianer" und "Native Americans."*

30. Jacobs, "Todeskampf der Sioux," 3–9.

31. "Versunken! Vergessen?," *Der Pimpf*, October 1938, 15.

32. "Ein Deutscher rettet die letzten Indianer," *Hilf mit!*, April 1937.

33. "Indianer," *Der Pimpf*, October 1938, 1–2.

34. Haible, *Indianer im Dienste der NS-Ideologie*, 138.

35. Weber, "'Indians' on German Stages."

36. Ibid., 229.

37. Heermann, *Old Shatterhand ritt nicht im Auftrag der Arbeiterklasse*, 5–9.

38. Heiner Schmidt from Dresden to Dr. Johannes Dieckmann Pres. der Volkskammer der DDR, 6 August 1956, Bundesarchiv Lichterfelde-West, DR1/6240, p. 66. See also the letters in DR 1/6241. Statewide debates were published as well in the *Mitteldeutschen Neuesten Nachrichten* on 22 July 1956.

39. Werner Baum to Heiner Schmidt, 14 April 1956, Bundesarchiv Lichterfelde-West, DR1/6240, p. 75; and "Betr. Veröffentlichungen von Karl-May-Büchern," 7 November 1961, Bundesarchiv Lichterfelde-West, DR1/6240, p. 3.

40. Neumann, *Indianer-Museum Radebeul*.

41. It remained incredibly popular during all these shifts, attracting no fewer than 250,000 visitors in 1983. "Interessanter Ferienbeginn auch im Karl-May-Museum: Großer Andrang nach Schließzeit in Radebeul am Wochenende," *Sächsische Zeitung*, 6 February 1984, 2.

42. Welskopf-Henrich, "Widerspruch (aber nicht die des Kapitalismus) oder ein junger Autor und der schwarze Mann," unpublished manuscript, Liselotte Welskopf-Henrich Papers (hereafter LLWH Nachlass), Berlin-Brandenburgische Akademie der Wissenschaften, folder 15.

43. *Amaroq—oder Die Schlittenreise* (1957).

44. Bundesarchiv Lichterfelde-West, Berlin, DR1/5014, 91–95.

45. *Tatanka-Yotanka: Ein Roman um Sitting Bull, den größten Häuptling der Sioux* (Berlin: Verlag Neues Leben, 1956); *Der Untergang der Dakota* (Berlin: Verlag Neues Leben, 1957).

46. *Die vier Pfeile der Cheyenne* (Berlin: Verlag Neues Leben, 1957).

47. "Daumann, Rudolf," Bundesarchiv Lichterfelde-West, DR1/3961.

48. "Oliver La Farge," *Die Welt der Indianer*, Bundesarchiv Lichterfelde-West, DR 1/3547, pp. 206–15.

49. "Dee Brown," *Begrabt mein Herz an der Biegung des Flusses*, Bundesarchiv Lichterfelde-West, DR1/3550, pp. 135–46. For a good introduction to Brown's contribution to a new American Indian historiography, see, for example, Wunder, "Native American History, Ethnohistory, and Context," and the other essays in *Ethnohistory* 54, no. 4.

50. On occasion this led to problems. For example, in 1985 the DDR published Steve Talbot's book *Indianer in den USA*, which contained the prefatory citation from the 1948 declaration of human rights: "No one should have his citizenship arbitrarily revoked or be prevented from changing his citizenship." Given that the popular East German performer Wolf Bierman had suffered such a controversial arbitrary revocation in 1976, this was an embarrassing preface that caused the book to be recalled and stripped of the first page.

51. *Die Söhne der großen Bärin* (1966); *Chingachgook, die große Schlange* (1967); *Spur des Falken* (1968); *Weiße Wölfe* (1969); *Tödlicher Irrtum* (1969); *Osceola* (1971); *Tecumseh* (1972); *Apachen* (1973); *Ulzana* (1974); *Kit & Co* (1974); *Blutsbrüder* (1975); *Severino* (1977): *Blauvogel* (1979); *Der Scout* (1983).

52. Peipp and Springer, *Edle Wilde, Rote Teufel*, 163.

53. Cited in Heermann, *Old Shatterhand ritt nicht im Auftrag der Arbeiterklasse*, 83. The historical accuracy was not always better than that evident in their West German counterparts. See, for example, Gemünden, "Between Karl May and Karl Marx."

54. "Östlicher Western," *Der Spiegel*, 7 July 1965. See also "Unter Wilden Mustangs," *BZ am Abend*, 1 July 1965; "Am Lagerfeuer der Indianer: Zu dem DEFA-Film 'Die Söhne der großen Bärin,'" *Neue Zeit Berlin*, 18 February 1966; "Ein Indianer in Babelsberg. Die DEFA (Gruppe 'Roter Kreis') verfilmt 'Dakotas—die Söhne der großen Bärin,'" *Junge Welt Berlin*, 18 April 1965; "DEFA auf neuen Wegen: 'Die Söhne der großen* Bärin,'" *Märkische Volksstimme Potsdam*, 1 August 1965; M. Heidel "Tipi, Wampum, Mokassin," *Neue Berliner Illustrierte*, 3 January 1966, 20–23; and the *Progress Film Program*, 23/66 in Bundesarchiv Filmarchiv, Film Programs Signatur Ba-Fa 15609.

55. *Neue Berliner Illustrierte*, 2 June 1967.

56. Fuchs, "Unverfälschte Wahrheit: Bemerkungen zum jüngsten Indianerfilm der DEFA, 'Die Spur des Falken,'" *Lausitzer Rundschau Cottbus*, 23 July 1968.

57. Such rhetoric persisted in the literature surrounding the DEFA films throughout the 1970s. See, for example, *Film für Sie*, 22/70 in "Tödlicher Irrtum" 17156 (1970), Bundesarchiv Filmarchiv.

58. Schneider, "Finding a New Heimat in the Wild West."

59. See, for example, Moeller, *Protecting Motherhood*; Poiger, *Jazz, Rock, and Rebels*; Schlisser, *The Miracle Years*.

60. Gpfert, "Das Project Indianer."

61. Berkhofer, *The White Man's Indian*.

62. Stephan, *Americanization and Anti-Americanism*.

63. See, for example, Fuchs, "Unverfälschte Wahrheit," and the specific references to genocide in the promotional materials for films like *Tödlicher Irrtum*; for example, *Film für Sie*, 22/70, Bundesarchiv Filmarchiv, Berlin, files: 2315, 12515, 15609, 15985, 16797, 17156, 18772, 19036, 20713, 29625.

64. Hetmann, *Der Rote Tag*.

65. Biegert, *Seit 200 Jahren ohne Verfassung*, 7. The book is dedicated to a list of people who "died since Wounded Knee 1973 in the fight for their people."

66. By 1976, this was no longer radical language. See, for example, in the West, Thilo Koch, "Indianer sein ist schwer," which discusses the "Ausrottung" and "Vertreibung" of the Indians. In the East, "Mündel der Nation: Indianerreservate—Konzentrationslager der Vereinigten Staaten," *Der Morgen* (Berlin) (Ausgabe B), 16 April 1961; "USA lassen Indianer aussterben," *Neuer Weg, Halle*, 28 March 1961.

67. Biegert, *Seit 200 Jahren ohne Verfassung*, 21, 35.

68. Ibid., 69.

69. Ibid., 142.

70. Ingrid Wünsche in Hamburg, AIM support group to LLWH, 28 July 1975, LLWH Nachlass, file 195 Teil II.

71. See, for example, Wagner to LLWH, 31 March 1968, and LLWH to Wagner, 15 July 1968, LLWH Nachlass, Korrespondenz file 174.

72. "Elf Indianer führen Klage: Delegation aus Nord- und Südamerika berichtet über den Kampf um Selbstbestimmung," *Süddeutsche Zeitung*, 3 October 1977.

73. Dietmar Halbhuber, "Zurück zur Friedenspfeife: Hilft das?," *Junge Welt*, 31 May 1975.

74. Bartlet, "American Indian Studies in West Germany."

75. See, for example, Arbeitsgemeinschaft zum Studium der Indianer Nordamerikas "Sitting Bull" in Erfurt, Vorsitzender Günther to LLWH, 21 June 1975, LLWH Nachlass, folder 189.1.

76. See, for example, Giago "The Demise of Aim Caused Nary a Ripple in the Circle of Life"; and for the shifting reception of their delegates in West Germany, Kelly, "A Critical Review of the Support Work for North American Indians."

77. Miriam Geissler, "Indianer auf dem Friedenspfad," *Münchner Merkur*, 30 November 1983.

78. LaDuke, "Journey of Peace," 19–21.

79. "Delegation to Europe Stirs up Controversy," *Lakota Times*, 22 February 1984; "German Parliament Debates Black Hills Issue," *Lakota Times*, 25 April 1984.

80. Peter Bolz, Letter to the Editor, *Das Indianermagazin* (1993). See also Kelly, "Hobby? Hopi!"

81. Schmidt, *Indianer als Heilbringer*, 9–12.

82. Torgovnick, *Primitive Passions*, 155.

83. Liselotte Welskopf, "Lebenslauf," 11 December 1953, Universitätsarchiv der Humboldt-Universität zu Berlin, Liselotte Welskopf Habilitation file.

84. Welskopf-Henrich, "Lebenslauf," 1954, LLWH Nachlass, folder 1.

85. Rudolf Welskopf, "Meine illegale Tätigkeit," 6 April 1947, LLWH Nachlass, folder 6.

86. Welskopf-Henrich (LLWH) to Müller, 12 September 1975, LLWH Nachlass, folder 189 ll.

87. These included the Vaterländischer Verdienstorden in bronze, 1958; the Vaterländischer Verdienstorden in silver, 1961; Orden Banner der Arbeit, 1966; and the Pestalozzimedaille, 1965.

88. Kramer, "'Die Söhne der *großen* Bärin' und 'Das Blut des Adlers.'"

89. It was later published in Swedish, Danish, Dutch, Polish, Romanian, Czech, Lithuanian, Russian, Hungarian, Bulgarian, Slovak, and in West Germany and Austria. Muller, "A Cultural Study of the Sioux Novels of Liselotte Welskopf-Henrich," 107.

90. "Zum Karl May Problem," n.d., LLWH Nachlass, folder 15.

91. "Red point" refers to the markings on the prison uniforms worn by communist inmates in concentration camps.

92. Tokei-ihto is also the name she later gave to Means.

93. Welskopf-Henrich, "Zum Karl May Problem," LLWH Nachlass, folder 15.

94. Thomas Kramer, "'Die Söhne der *großen* Bärin' und 'Das Blut des Adlers,'" 208.

95. Ibid., 210.

96. U. K. to LLWH, 11 December 1971, LLWH Nachlass, file 187; M. G. to LLWH, 11 May 1969, LLWH Nachlass, file 184; R. L. to LLWH, 11 January 1971, LLWH Nachlass, file 185.

97. See, for example, K. B. to LLWH, 11 October 1972, LLWH Nachlass, file 187.

98. R. K. to LLWH, 5 March 1974, LLWH Nachlass, file 187.

99. LLWH to P. S., 12 June 1968, LLWH Nachlass, file 186.

100. LLWH to I and A, 28 February 1969, LLWH Nachlass, file 186.

101. See, for example, G. P. to LLWH, 7 February 1975, LLWH Nachlass, file 190.

102. LLWH to M. S., 13 October 1975, LLWH Nachlass, file 190.

103. LLWH to Berglöwen Children's Association, 6 December 1974, LLWH Nachlass, file 190.

104. LLWH to G. P., 13 February 1975, LLWH Nachlass, file 190; LLWH to N. T., 17 November 1977, LLWH Nachlass, file 192; and LLWH to S., 7 January 1976, LLWH Nachlass, file 195.

105. LLWH to C. O., 17 March 1968/9 [sic], Nachlass, file 174; and Arthur Amiotte to LLWH, 17 April 1971, Nachlass, file 179.

106. D. T. to LLWH, 21 March 1975, LLWH Nachlass, file 174.

107. Chris Spotted Eagle to LLWH, 3 February 1975, LLWH Nachlass, file 179. See also LLWH to Chris Spotted Eagle, 25 November 1974, LLWH Nachlass, file 179.

108. Muller, "A Cultural Study of the Sioux Novels of Liselotte Welskopf-Henrich," 112.

109. LLWH to S. D., 8 January 1975, LLWH Nachlass, file 189.

110. Muller, "A Cultural Study of the Sioux Novels of Liselotte Welskopf-Henrich," 11–112.

111. LLWH to A. K., 20 December 1977, LLWH Nachlass, file 191. Means's visit to her house after the human rights conference in Geneva was their third meeting.

112. LLWH to A. K., 14 March 1974, LLWH Nachlass, file 188.

113. This sort of action continued over the years, for example, B. B. to LLWH, 26 February 1975, and S. D. to LLWH, 27 April 1975, LLWH Nachlass, file 189.

114. For example, H. G. to LLWH, 13 September 1972, LLWH Nachlass, file 187; P. G. to LLWH, 29 March 1973, LLWH Nachlass, file 187; A. K. to LLWH, 12 January 1974, LLWH Nachlass, file 187.

115. For example, LLWH to B. B., 19 March 1975, LLWH Nachlass, file 189/1.

116. For example, LLWH to W. G. in Bulgaria, 11 November 1974; and LLWH to A. H., 12 November 1974, LLWH Nachlass, file 188.

117. LLWH to S. D., 7 April 1975, LLWH Nachlass, file 189.

118. LLWH to F., 11 November 1974, LLWH Nachlass, file 188; LLWH to M. S., 21 January 1975, LLWH Nachlass, file 190; A. H. to LLWH, 7 August 1977, LLWH Nachlass, file 191.

119. H. K. in Cologne to LLWH, 3 November 1973, and LLWH to S., 26 July 1974, LLWH Nachlass, file 188; P. K. to LLWH, 24 May 1975, LLWH Nachlass, file 189/II; I. W. in Hamburg to LLWH, 28 July 1975, LLWH Nachlass, file 195/II; Waltraud Wagner to LLWH, 31 March 1968, LLWH Nachlass, file 174.

120. The correspondence is extensive. See especially her initial letters: I. G. to LLWH, 24 April 1972, and then during the crises on Pine Ridge: I. G. to LLWH, 27 May 1974, 16 July 1974, 6 October 1974, 18 February 1975; LLWH to I. G., 4 March 1975, and 5 May 1975, LLWH Nachlass, file 179.

121. Indeed, she never wavered on this position and continued to argue it in the last years of her life. For example, LLWH to J. G., 22 May 1979, LLWH Nachlass, file 196.

122. LLWH to Amiotte, 1 January 1969, LLWH Nachlass, file 173 (English in the original).

123. LLWH to Rourke, 17 March 1975, LLWH Nachlass, file 179 (English in the original).

124. Geissler, "Indianer auf dem Friedenspfad."

125. LLWH to W., 15 July 1968, LLWH Nachlass, file 174. See similar comments to an American couple in LLWH to V. and E. B., Newport Beach, Calif., 30 October 1977, LLWH Nachlass, file 176-8.

126. LLWH to M., 23 July 1975, LLWH Nachlass, file 195/11.

127. Undated (approximately 1952) manuscript titled "Diskussion um die Bärensöhne," LLWH Nachlass, folder 163; see also LLWH to Müller-Tannewitz, Verlag Neues Leben, 3 January 1950, LLWH Nachlass, folder 162.

128. Grundig, *Zwischen Karneval und Aschermittwoch*, 387.

129. She often underscored those heroic characteristics in public. See, for example, "Vortrag in Plauen," n.d., LLWH Nachlass, folder 15.

CHAPTER 6

1. "'Bill der Rancher' stirbt am Marterpfahl," *Münchner Merkur*, 7 September 1959; "Feuer und Flamme für Schundheftl," *Süddeutsche Zeitung*, 7 September 1959.

2. Newspaper accounts stressed that the American Indians involved included Mohawks, Navajo, and Sioux; a forty-person military band took part, and the proceeds went to a German orphanage. *Münchner Merkur*, 9 October 1959.

3. Copies of the artwork are located in MS-3 Charles J. Belden Collection, in the Harold McCracken Research Library, Buffalo Bill Historical Center, Cody, Wyo. See also the news clipping from the *Münchner Merkur*, 9 October 1959, located in the Stadtarchiv München, "Cowboy-Club-Zeitungen," Trimble interview, 9 July 2003.

4. Indeed, historian Konrad Jarausch stresses in his own personal account that it was "the late 1950s before a semblance of normalcy returned to these shattered lives," a point he clearly feels applies to Germans in general. Jarausch and Geyer, *Shattered Past*, 321. For a general portrait of Germans' desperation at this time, see, for example, Rothenberger, *Die Hungerjahre nach dem Zweiten Weltkrieg*; Stüber, *Der Kampf gegen den Hunger, 1945-1950*; Trittel, *Hunger und Politik*; and Gries, *Die Rationen-Gesellschaft*.

5. *Süddeutsche Zeitung*, 16 August 1951; J. Freudenreich, "München: Cowboy-Träume," *Süddeutsche Zeitung*, 20 April 1953; U. Friedrich, "Wenn der Häuptling Xaverl heißt. . . . Münchens Cowboy-Club feiert Jubiläum—Er ist der älteste der Welt," *Münchner Merkur*, 20 April 1953.

6. K. W. Zachrich, "History of the Cowboy Club in Freiburg," and "History of the Club Sioux West in Freiburg," Charles Belden files, Cody, Wyo.

7. *Dakota-Scout/Fährte* 11, no. 1 (1962): 1–2.

8. *Kalumet* 12, no. 1 (1963): 1–2.

9. National Archives, College Park, Md., RG 549, Records of U. S. Army Europe, General Correspondence Decimal File 1952–1956, box 1041, Baden-Wuerttemberg, file 250/66.

10. Ibid., 21 May 1955: Weekly Civilian Affairs Report for the period 8–21 May 1955

sent to the chief of the Civil Affairs Division USAREUR from LRO Col. Merton E. Munson.

11. Ibid., box 1048, Feb. File 1955, *Spiegel* 8, 16 February 1955.

12. Höhn, *GIs and Fräuleins*, 61.

13. Ibid., 250.

14. Stephan, *Americanization and Anti-Americanism*, 5.

15. "Indianer tanzt für die Münchner," *Abendzeitung*, 4 August 1959.

16. "Rodeo am Nockherberg," *Münchner Merkur*, 5–6 September 1959; *Süddeutsche Zeitung*, 4 September 1959.

17. *Münchner Merkur*, 11 December 1959.

18. Belden, "Heim, Heim on the Range," *Stars and Stripes*, 5 September 1959.

19. *Fährte: Interessengemeinschaft Deutschsprechender Indianerfreunde* 6, no. 1, (1960): 464–65.

20. *Fährte* 7, no. 1 (1961): 8–30.

21. *Fährte* 6, no. 6 (1960): 618.

22. Wolfgang Seifert, "Der indianische Tanz bei den Stämmen Nordamerikas: Nach Tanzdarbietungen und Erläuterungen des amerikanischen Choreographen Leonid Massine," *Dakota Scout* 11, no. 1 (1962): 7.

23. *Kalumet* 13, no. 3 (1964): 123.

24. Wolfgang Seifert, "3. Deutsch Amerikanisches Volkfest, Santa Fe in Berlin," *Kalumet*, 12, no. 3 (1963): 156–57.

25. Cutting from the *Billings Gazette*, 6 August 1966, Harold McCracken Research Library, Buffalo Bill Historical Center, series VI, box 1, file 5, Johnny Baker papers.

26. "Munich Cowboy Club Starts New Building," *SAcom Scene* 8, no. 30 (28 July 1961). "Cowboys und Trachtler," *Abendzeitung*, 24 July 1961; "Cowboy Zentrum an der Isar," *Münchner Merkur*, 10 July 1961. Other American Indian servicemen showed up at the hobbyist councils and the events hosted by the hobbyist clubs. In 1963, for example, Leon Martenac and Gilbert Matthews from Pine Ridge took part in the Munich club's festivities, and more would show up in the decades that followed. Most enjoyed their popularity. *SACom Scene*, 15 August 1963.

27. *Dakota-Scout*, 11, no. 4 (1962): 108.

28. Cited in Höhn, *GIs and Fräuleins*, 13.

29. See, for example, "Germany Meets the Negro Soldier," *Ebony*, October 1946, 5–10, cited in Fehrenbach, "Learning from America."

30. National Archives, College Park, Md., RG 549, Records of U.S. Army Europe, General Correspondence Decimal File 1952–1956, box 1034.

31. Townsend, *World War II and the American Indian*.

32. Britten, *American Indians in World War I*. See also Tate, "From Scout to Doughboy."

33. There were some units composed only of American Indians, but these were the exception, and they were not formed based on principles of segregation. Barsh, "American Indians in the Great War," 282.

34. The Lumbee were known for having harbored escaped slaves.

35. Britten, *American Indians in World War I*, 57.

36. Barsh, "American Indians in the Great War"; Tate, "From Scout to Doughboy,"

430. A greater percentage volunteered, smaller numbers sought deferments, and a larger proportion of adult males served than their white counterparts.

37. Britten, *American Indians in World War I*, 101.

38. Ibid., 40. See also Krouse, *North American Indians in the Great War*.

39. Britten, *American Indians in World War I*, 99. See also the account of Joseph Oklahombi, Tate, "From Scout to Doughboy," 431.

40. National Archives, College Park, Md., General Headquarters American Expeditionary forces, John R. Eddy, 1st Lieut. Infantry to Brigadier General Spaulding, 21 February 1919, RG 120, Records of the American Expeditionary Forces WWI, boxes 3471–73.

41. Joseph K. Dixon Files, Mathers Museum, Indiana University, Bloomington, Ind., file ww-33-01, Camp Dix, 17 May 1919.

42. Townsend, *World War II and the American Indian*, 133, 135. See also Franco, *Crossing the Pond*, 132–33.

43. Townsend, *World War II and the American Indian*, 136.

44. Alison R. Bernstein, *American Indians and World War II*, 40–45.

45. Philip Deloria, *Indians in Unexpected Places*, 236.

46. Garroutte, *Real Indians*, 1–7, 140–43.

47. Ibid., 2.

48. See, for example, Donald B. Smith, *Long Lance*; Clifton, "Alternate Identities and Cultural Frontiers."

49. Garroutte, *Real Indians*, 7.

50. Ibid., 141.

51. Based on accounts from the 1920s, McBride, *Molly Spotted Elk*, 103.

52. On East Germany, see Heermann, *Old Shatterhand ritt nicht im Auftrag der Arbeiterklasse*, 87–88. On the West, *Das Indianermagazin* 3 (1993).

53. Garroutte, *Real Indians*, especially chap. 2, on biology.

54. Warren, *Buffalo Bill's America*, 405.

55. Ibid., 392, 404. This was by no means limited to the Plains. As Richard Slotkin has stressed, the unrequited longing one finds in the *Leatherstocking Tales* was limited to fiction. Slotkin, *The Fatal Environment*, 100.

56. Warren, *Buffalo Bill's America*, 394. Indeed, Paul Chaat Smith has remarked that, given the Comanche's propensity for taking captives, it is hard to know if one can speak of "pure bloods." Paul Chaat Smith, *Everything You Know about Indians Is Wrong*.

57. Katz, *Black Indians*.

58. "Der 107 Jahre alte *Uberhäuptling* der Indianer in München," 6 August 1929, and "Indianer-Empfang," *Bayer Kurier*, 7 August 1929.

59. "Der Oberhäuptling," *Münchner Zeitung*, 7 August 1929; "Die älteste Rothaut der Welt," *Augsb. Abendzeitung*, 8 August 1929; "Ein indianischer Methusalem in München," *Bayer. Staatszeitung*, 6 August 1929; "Der Oberhäuptling der Rothäute beim, Oberhäuptling' der Münchner," *Münchner Augsb. Abendzeitung*, 9 August 1929; "Der Oberhäuptling der Rothäute beim Oberbürgermeister," *Münchner Zeitung*, 8 August 1929.

60. *Wir Indianer*. An English edition appeared in London in 1931.

61. Images of Big Chief White Horse Eagle circulated widely in the 1920s with cap-

tions in English, German, French, and Spanish that often assigned him to the Osagi tribe in Oklahoma.

62. McBride, *Molly Spotted Elk*, 165–66, 193.

63. Donald B. Smith, *Long Lance*, 50.

64. Indeed, that was his claim both in his shop and on his website in 2001: www .winnetou-gallery.de.

65. Anthony Wallace, "Revitalization Movements."

66. That is also characteristic of hobbyist movements outside of Germany that deal with subjects focused on men's actions in the past. See, for example, Horwitz, *Confederates in the Attic*, chap. 1.

67. See, for example, Poiger, *Jazz, Rock, and Rebels*; Moeller, *Protecting Motherhood*; Schlisser, *The Miracle Years*; and the roundtable in *Signs* 21, no.1 (1998).

68. Bederman, *Manliness and Civilization*. For some rethinking of the crises, see the essays in Hagemann and Schüller-Springorum, *Home/Front*.

69. Most of the literature in masculinity studies also tends to agree. It stresses the protean character of masculinity and disavows any putative transhistorical character. See, for example, Whitehead and Barrett, *The Masculinities Studies Reader*; Lengwiler, "Aktuelle Perspektiven der historischen Männlichkeitsforschung im angelsächsischen Raum"; and Adams and Savran, *The Masculinity Studies Reader*.

70. Whitehead and Barrett, *The Masculinity Studies Reader*, 20.

71. For a broader articulation of this point, see Robert Nye's discussion of George Mosse's interest in the Ur-stereotype of serene masculinity in works by Winckelmann and others. Payne, Sorkin, and Tortorice, *What History Tells*.

72. Bederman, *Manliness and Civilization*, 18.

73. "Because individuals do not have biologically fixed identities, any sense of self can only come about through working to achieve a sense of 'belonging' in the social world," ibid., 20.

74. Some of the literature on May has stressed the homoerotic element of his work (wonderfully captured by the recent spoof on the May films of the 1960s and 1970s, *Der Schuh des Manitou*). But the attraction of these tales was never limited to the homoerotic. See, for example, Lutz, *"Indianer" und "Native Americans,"* 313–56.

75. Torgovnick, *Primitive Passions*, 8.

76. See especially Stoler, *Race and the Education of Desire*; and Stoler, *Carnal Knowledge and Imperial Power*. For an explicit discussion of masculinity formation in a colonial context, see Connel, "The History of Masculinity," in Adams and Savran, *The Masculinity Studies Reader*, 245.

77. Jürgen, *Blauvogel*, 55.

78. Lutz, *"Indianer" und "Native Americans,"* 384, see especially n. 58.

79. Undated essay, "Zum Karl May Problem," Liselotte Welskopf-Henrich Papers (hereafter LLWH Nachlass), Berlin-Brandenburgische Akademie der Wissenschaften, folder 15.

80. Stolte and Klußmeier, *Arno Schmidt & Karl May*.

81. Welskopf (LLWH) to Mach, 22 February 1965, LLWH Nachlass, folder 121 "DEFA."

82. LLWH to Dr. Karl, 24 February 1965, ibid.

83. "Ein Indianer in Babelsberg. Die DEFA (Gruppe 'Roter Kreis') verfilmt, Dakotas—die Söhne der großen Bärin," *Junge Welt Berlin*, 18 April 1965.

84. See, for example, Helen Lefkowitz Horowitz, "'Nous Autres.'"

85. See, for example, Sicherman, "Reading and Ambition."

86. Ibid.; A. O. in Munich to LLWH, 7 June 1974, LLWH Nachlass, folder 188.

87. E. B. to LLWH, 9 December 1956, LLWH Nachlass, folder 181.

88. M. de la G. in Weimar to LLWH, 11 May 1969, and N. T. in Wittgensdorf to LLWH, 17 November 1977, LLWH Nachlass, folder 192.

89. See, for example, U. K. in Berlin to LLWH, n.d., LLWH Nachlass, folder 187.

90. See, for example, Dr. Gertrude Hafner's contribution to *Kalumet* 12, no. 3 (1963): 73–78; and Renate Straumann in *Kalumet* 13, no. 2 (1964): 55. Both were engaged in activist activities and outreach to American Indian associations.

91. Warren, *Buffalo Bill's America*, 406.

92. Stadtarchiv Dresden: Bestandssignatur: 17.2.1 A. 122.lll—SARASSANI HEFTE Heft 7, (Sarrasani nach 30 Jahren, Auflage 9); Heft 2, "Two-Two der Häuptling Vier," 26–30.

93. LLWH to A. P., 26 May 1975, and LLWH to R. L., 13 October 1975, LLWH Nachlass, folder 190.

94. Feest, "Europe's Indians," 326.

95. See, for example, the letter to the editor from A. B. in Eppstein, Germany, in *News from Indian Country*, late May 1996, 16A.

96. Ingrid Ostheeren, "Ein kleines Stück Männerglück: No Name City in Poing bei München ist Vernügungspark, Museum und Bühnebild eines idealisierten Wilden Westens," *Süddeutsche Zeitung*, 17 June 1993.

CHAPTER 7

1. Paul Chaat Smith, *Everything You Know about Indians Is Wrong*, 2, 36.

2. Reprinted in *News from Indian Country* 18, no. 3 (9 February 2004).

3. See, for example, Tim Giago, "Notes from Indian Country," *Lakota Times*, 6 January 1983, 4.

4. He wrote, for example: "Holocaust around reservations is: FBI, U.S. Marshalls, State and County police, and including City police; U.S. and County Attorneys; Holocaust is: Federal and State Prisons. Holocaust is: Judge Benson; S[outh] D[akota] Supreme Court (re: White Hawk-Marshall); Native Political prisoners; Marshalls abusing an elderly Native woman, igniting the Custer riot. Holocaust is: BIA education system following the Integration and Assimilation Act of 1883; Holocaust is: the denial of our religion for almost 200 years, i.e. American Indian Religious Freedom Act, dated August 11, 1978, P/1 95–341. Holocaust is: the U.S. ignoring our Sacred Treaties; Holocaust is: the deliberate killing of Oglala men and families by the U.S. Army and other white men. . . . Holocaust is: in lieu of a tattoo or an 'X' on our hand, we are given an 'A' or an 'U,' plus a number at birth. Holocaust is: the hanging of 39 [sic] Dakota by the order of the then President honest Abe Lincoln. He was a true racist (re: Douglas-Lincoln debates)." Punctuation and capitalization in the original.

5. Red Hail (Wasuduta), "Native American Holocaust," *Lakota Times*, 5 May 1983, 5. There are many other examples. See, for example, Gordon Thayer, chairman of the

Lac Courte Oreillis Tribe in Wisconsin, "White America Is Still Using Genocide on Indians," *Lakota Times*, 14 November 1984, 10.

6. http://www.aimovement.org (accessed 11 November 2009). Cf. Lonetree, "Missed Opportunities," especially 644–645, n. 17, which lists the immediate critical press reactions. For a discussion of the relationship between reverence for the Holocaust and a willingness to explain away genocide of American Indian tribes, see, for example, Byrd, "Living My Native Life Deadly." For perspectives on how some scholars attempt to use the rhetoric around Holocaust studies to raise awareness of the challenges faced by American Indians in the United States, see Cook-Lynn, *Anti-Indianism in Modern America*; for some discussion of similar, if extreme, African American reactions, see Michaels, *The Trouble with Diversity*, 55–56.

7. Geyer, "America in Germany."

8. "Von den Indianern Nordamerika's," *Das Ausland* (1874): 228–34, here 228. There are many similar examples. See, for example, "Ausrottung der Indianer in Nordamerika," *Globus* 6 (1864): 287.

9. "Der Indianerkrieg," *Münchner Fremdenblatt und Handelszeitung* 14, no. 11, Stadtarchiv München, Zeitungsausschnitte, 504a "Indianer." (This column appeared in the early 1890s, shortly after Buffalo Bill's tour through Germany; the exact date, however, is missing from the clipping in this collection.)

10. *Meyers Konversations-Lexikon*, 3rd ed., vol. 9 (Leipzig: Verlag des Bibliographischen Instituts, 1876), 252–56.

11. "Vermischte Nachrichten," *Das Ausland* (1832): 860.

12. See, for example, "Der Indianerkrieg in Nordamerika," *Das Ausland* (1836): 829.

13. "Die Vernichtung des Mandanstammes in Nordamerika (Aus Catlins Werk über die nordamerikanischen Indianer)," *Das Ausland* (1842): 23.

14. See, for example, "Das Hinsterben ganzer Stämme im nordwestlichen Gebiet von Nordamerika," *Das Ausland* (1850): 53.

15. See, for example, "Der große Indianerkrieg," *Das Ausland* (1856): 35–37.

16. "Einiges über die Indianerstämme der Westküste der Vereinigten Staaten und deren Behandlung," *Das Ausland* (1860): 676–80; "Amerikaner und Indianer in California," *Das Ausland* (1862): 110–13; 134–37.

17. "Der Indianerkrieg in Nordamerika," *Das Ausland* (1873): 487–89.

18. "Von den Indianern Nordamerika's," *Das Ausland* (1874): 246–51.

19. For examples from other periodicals see, for example, "Der Indianerkrieg in Nordamerika," *Globus* 8 (1867): 122–24. See also "Abschlachtung von Indianern in Nordamerika," *Globus* 9 (1866): 158.

20. Much like in other European states, there was no unitary national reaction to American actions against indigenous people. For a general discussion of reception, see Stein, "And the Strife Never Ends."

21. Guettel, "Reading America, Envisioning Empire."

22. For example, in 1831 the editors focused much of the volume on the removal of the five civilized tribes and produced essays based on Lewis Cass's infamous *North American Review* essay "Removal of the Indians," which supported Andrew Jackson's policies. Guettel, "Reading America, Envisioning Empire," 206–7.

23. Kiernan, *Blood and Soil*, 376.

24. Stauffer, "The Origin and Establishment of Brazil's Indian Service," 50.

25. Helmut Walser Smith, "Talk of Genocide, the Rhetoric of Miscegenation," 114–15.

26. "Kolonialer Vortrag vor Deutschamerikanern," *Deutsche Kolonialzeitung*, 1909, 565; *Jahresbericht der Deutschen Kolonialgesellschaft 1888* (Berlin: Carl Heymanns Verlag, 1889), 1; *Jahresbericht der Deutschen Kolonialgesellschaft 1914/1915* (Berlin, 1916), 29.

27. Blackbourn, "'The Garden of Our Hearts,'" 167.

28. Ibid., 153.

29. Blackbourn, *The Conquest of Nature*.

30. Ibid., see, for example, Sering, *Die innere Kolonization im östlichen Deutschland*; Bassin, "Friedrich Ratzel's Travels in the United States."

31. Cited in Blackbourn, *The Conquest of Nature*, 303–5.

32. Ibid., 293–96.

33. Otto, *Deutsche Amerika-Bilder*, 205–15.

34. Blackbourn, *The Conquest of Nature*, 285–87.

35. Ibid., 306.

36. A. Dirk Moses, "Empire, Colony, Genocide," 31, 37.

37. Zimmerer, "Colonialism and the Holocaust."

38. Palmer, *Colonial Genocide*.

39. Wolfe, "Structure and Event." Cf. A. Dirk Moses, "Empire, Colony, Genocide," 25–31.

40. See, for example, Browning, *The Origins of the Final Solution*.

41. A. Dirk Moses, "Empire, Colony, Genocide," 32–33.

42. Ibid., 38.

43. Ibid., 40.

44. This phrase is borrowed from Friedberg, "Dare to Compare."

45. Rothberg, *Multidirectional Memory*.

46. Novick, *The Holocaust in American Life*, 85–86.

47. Ibid., 101.

48. Ibid., 133, 145, 148.

49. Ibid., 9, 196. Novick is not alone in this pronouncement. See, for example, Rothberg, *Multidirectional Memory*, 9.

50. Rothberg, *Multidirectional Memory*, 119.

51. These have not been pleasant, and irresponsible assertions have resounded on all sides. See, for example, Friedberg, "Dare to Compare." See also Churchill, *A Little Matter of Genocide*; Churchill, *Indians Are Us*; Churchill, *Struggle for the Land*; and Churchill, *Fantasies of the Master Race*.

52. Here too, Novick was not alone. David Stannard has asserted that the uniqueness argument: "willingly provides a screen behind which opportunistic governments today attempt to conceal their own past and ongoing genocidal actions." Cited in Rothberg, *Multidirectional Memory*, 10; cf. Stannard, *American Holocaust*.

53. Novick, *The Holocaust in American Life*, 13–15.

54. Ibid., 190–92; here, Novick relates one of the more disturbing exchanges in

which advocates of the uniqueness of the Holocaust spoke disparagingly of the "ordinary" massacres perpetrated on the Pequots and other American Indian tribes, forcing American Indian scholars to demonstrate the absurdity of their arguments by simply reversing them, substituting "Jews" for "Indians" and "Nazis" for "English." For example, "Commenting on this, an historian of American Indians [David Stannard] wondered what the response would be to the argument that the Holocaust wasn't genocidal because while the Nazis 'could certainly have been less thorough, less severe, less deadly' in their policy toward Jews, after all, some Jews survived, a 'number of whom even live in Connecticut.'"

55. Rothberg, *Multidirectional Memory*, 6. For a nice introduction to some of these issues, see Niezen, *The Origins of Indigenism*.

56. Novick, *The Holocaust in American Life*, 10.

57. Ibid.

58. Paul Chaat Smith, "The Terrible Nearness of Distant Places."

59. Rothberg, *Multidirectional Memory*, 118.

60. On the functions of the "antifascist myth" in the GDR, see Ross, *The East German Dictatorship*, especially 177.

61. For a nice discussion of Freudian notions of displacement in this context, see Rothberg, *Multidirectional Memory*, 12–16.

62. Bundesarchiv Lichterfelde West, DR/1 5104, Lewernz on Rudolf Dauman, *Der Untergang der Dakota*, 10 January 1957, pp. 144–46.

63. Bundesarchiv Lichterfelde West, DR/1 5104, Welskopf-Henrich Druckgenehmigungen, Gutachten #2, Peter Musiolek, Wissenschatlicher Aspirant, Insit. für Allgemeine Geschichte der Humboldt Universität, 5 November 1962, pp. 72–75.

64. Peipp and Springer, *Edle Wilde, Rote Teufel*, 61.

65. Interview over "Problems of the Indian Minority in the USA," 18 April 1973, Liselotte Welskopf-Henrich Papers (LLWH Nachlass), Berlin-Brandenburgische Akademie der Wissenschaften, file 149.

66. For a selection of pamphlets and flyers, see LLWH Nachlass, Korespondenz, 179. On the public use of the rhetoric of genocide at Alcatraz, see Smith and Warrior, *Like a Hurricane*, 18–35.

67. For example, in the West, Thilo Koch, "Indianer sein ist schwer." In the East, "Mündel der Nation: Indianerreservate—Konzentrationslager der Vereinigten Staaten," *Der Morgen* (Berlin) (Ausgabe B), 16 April 1961.

68. B. G. to LLWH, 20 April 1975, and LLWH to B. G., 30 April 1975, LLWH Nachlass, file 190–92.

69. See, for example, I. P. to LLWH, 24 January 1977, and LLWH to I. P., 14 February 1977, LLWH Nachlass, file 192.

70. Rotheberg, *Multidirectional Memory*, 6.

71. Hinz-Rosin and Rohrbach, *Der Letzte Häuptling*. For a glimpse into the popular discussion, which also includes explicit, and rather typical, discussion of the "Holocaust" experienced by the Lakota and other American Indians, see "'Der Letzte Häuptling': Zwei journalisten aus der Region München dokumentieren das Leben der Sioux," *Süddeutsche Zeitung*, 3 and 4 January 2004.

CHAPTER 8

1. Amiotte, "Artist's Statement."

2. Berlo, *Arthur Amiotte Collages.*

3. Ibid., "Giving Voice to the Ancestors through Art."

4. Interview with Arthur Amiotte, 25 June 2008.

5. For a concise discussion, see Warren, *Buffalo Bill's America,* 390–96.

6. Kopas, *Bella Coola,* 236. Cited as "alleged" remarks in Haberland, "Nine Bella Coolas in Germany," 362, 371.

7. Cited in Haberland, "Nine Bella Coolas in Germany," 367.

8. Berlo and Phillips, *Native North American Art.*

9. Wayne Beasly to JC Miller, 29 July 1913, 5 August 1913, 22 August 1913, and Miller to Beasly, 16 July 1913, Miller Brothers 101 Ranch Collection (hereafter 101 Ranch), M-407, Western Historical Collections, University of Oklahoma, Norman, Okla., box 3, folder 1 (101 Ranch).

10. Paul Southerland at Circus Krone to JCM, 15 June 1925, 101 Ranch, box 35, folder 2.

11. Ghost Dog to EW Jermark, 23 September 1925, National Archives, Washington, D.C., 25044-17-047.

12. Jermark to JCM, 14 December 1926, Sarrasani to Jermarck, 11 and 25 November 1926, 101 Ranch, box 38, folder 2.

13. Sarrasani to JCM, 8 February 1926, 101 Ranch, box 31, folder 1.

14. Sweet Grass to JCM, 27 January and 29 September 1927, 101 Ranch, box 47, folder 5.

15. Brennan to Commissioner of Indian Affairs, 17 March 1910, National Archives, Washington, D.C., 17774-10-47; Two-Two's contract is located in file 23412-10-047.

16. Statement by Lena Two-Two, James Garcia, and Mary Bear Shield, and letter from Geo. Eugene Eagen, 30 July 1914, in National Archives, Washington, D.C., 97750-14-736, Pine Ridge, Death of Edward Two-Two.

17. *Spandauer Volksblatt,* 1 September 1968; *Fährte: Interessengemeinschaft deutschsprechender Indianerfreunde* 6, no. 1 (1960): 460.

18. Similar things happened elsewhere in Germany. *Kalumet* 16, no. 5 (1967): 38.

19. "Häuptling 'Kleiner Fuchs' und sein Dresden-Testament," *Dresdner Neueste Nachrichten,* 29 July 2004.

20. Britten, *American Indians in World War I,* 62, 72.

21. Ibid., 64–65.

22. Ibid., 150. Cited and contextualized by Theisz, "The Bad Speakers and the Long Braids." See also Carroll, *Medicine Bags and Dog Tags,* 107.

23. Joseph K. Dixon Files, Mathers Museum, Indiana University, Bloomington, Ind., WW-28-02, Greenhut Hospital Demarcation #3, 27 March 1919.

24. Ibid., notes from Camp Mills, 3 May 1919, p. 29.

25. Ibid., notes from Walter Reed Hospital in Washington, D.C., 10 February 1919, p. 3.

26. Ibid., p. 49.

27. Krouse, *North American Indians in the Great War,* 34.

28. Heidi Howe, "Dakota," 10–12.

29. McKinney, "An Interview with Heidi Howe."

30. Ibid., 26.

31. Heidi Howe, "Dakota."

32. Milton, *Oscar Howe*; Pennington, *Oscar Howe*.

33. McKinney, "An Interview with Heidi Howe," 26.

34. Ibid.

35. Heidi Howe, "Dakota."

36. Sharples, "In the Presence of Greatness."

37. Pennington, *Oscar Howe*, 29.

38. Ibid., 35.

39. Conversation with Inge Dawn Howe Maresh, 11 January 2010.

40. Oliv interview, Munich, 21 June 2007. LLWH to Madonna Gilbert, 1 April 1975 and 14 May 1976 (in reference to Gilbert's trip to Germany), Liselotte Welskopf-Henrich Papers, Berlin-Brandenburgische Akademie der Wissenschaften, file 179.

41. Dr. Gertrude Hafner (Graz, Austria), "Aus der Indianerhilfe der deutschen Indianerfreunde," *Dakota Scout* 11, no. 4 (1962).

42. *Kalumet* 12, no. 3 (1963); see also *Kalumet* 13, no. 4 (1964).

43. *Fährte* 6, nos. 2 and 3 (1960).

44. *Kalumet* 16, no. 6 (1967).

45. *Kalumet* 17, no. 1 (1968).

46. See, for example, the essays in *Kalumet* 18, nos. 1 and 2 (1969).

47. *Kalumet* 18, no. 4 (1969). See especially the essays and letters in *Kalumet* 19, no. 4 (1970).

48. See, for example, "Austrians give Clark a Petition" *News from Indian Country*, 23 May 1984, 1.

49. Oliv, *20 Jahre Indian Councils*, 1:66–68.

50. See, for example, Carlson, "Germans Playing Indian"; Mayo, "Appropriation and the Plastic Shaman."

51. Feest, "Europe's Indians," 327.

52. Local meetings as well, for example, *Kalumet* 14, no. 1 (1965).

53. Rudolf Conrad, "Mutual Fascination"; see also Navajo Elder George P. Lee's comments in "Ein Indianer im Karl-May-Museum," *Sächsische Zeitung*, 6–7 June 1987.

54. Michael F. Brown, *Who Owns Native Culture?*, 23, 63.

55. Interview with Phil Lucas in Peipp and Springer, *Edle Wilde, Rote Teufel*, 269–70.

56. Paskievich, *If Only I Were an Indian*.

57. A. C. Ross, *Ehanamani "Walks Among,"* 92–93.

58. http://www.naaog.de/pageID_5606389.html (accessed in 2008); see also Jennifer Peterka-Hirschfield, "American 'Indians' abound in Germany," *Indian Country Today*, 5 April 2000.

59. Cited in Gilders, "Ich bin ein Indianer."

60. Feest, "Menschen, Masken und Moneten."

61. Stamps, "Germany: Market for Native American Goods."

62. This is not limited to the American Southwest. See, for example, Deutschlander, "In Search of *Winnetou*," 106.

63. Indeed, in 2004 I met some of their representatives to the international trade show during an American Indian dance presentation at the JFK High School in Berlin.

64. Cheryl Cothran and Thomas Eric Combrink at the Arizona Hospitality Research and Resource Center at Northern Arizona University in Flagstaff, who did a study for Navajo Tourism, stressed this point to me during our conversation on 10 March 2003. Venders and guides on the reservation repeatedly confirmed their observations.

65. See, for example, Deutschlander and Miller, "Politicizing Aboriginal Cultural Tourism."

66. The Karl-May-Press in Bamberg conceptualized the notion of "Winnetours" in the 1960s. For advertisements see, for example, *Kalumet* 18, no. 4 (1969): 24.

67. See, for example, the list presented by Verein zur Unterstützung Nordamerikanischer Indianer (Association for the Support of North American Indians) at http://www.asnai.de/frame.htm (accessed January 2010). For a list of Canadian tours, see Deutschlander, "In Search of *Winnetou*," 102.

68. Many of these are also organized by mixed couples, German women married to American Indian men, who market their locations and services in Germany with great success. See, for example, http://www.blackfeetculturecamp.com/.

69. She is not alone. This is a comment I heard repeatedly with reference to German and Czech hobbyists' craft abilities in the Dakotas.

70. The column, and its German translation, can be accessed at http://www.grand forks.com/mld/grandforksherald/news/opinion/8364218.htm?template=content Modules/printstory.jsp. It was posted 6 April 2004.

71. Interview with Emerson Spider, 17 July 2003.

72. See, for example, "Plastic Medicine Men Invade Europe," *Akwesasne Notes*, late Spring 1987, 7.

73. It should be noted that an effort by some Blackfoot living in Germany to set up a Sundance was also not well received on their reserve in Canada. Respect is not simply a question of race. See Deutschlander, "In Search of *Winnetou*," 256–63.

74. Lutz, "'Okay, I'll be their annual Indian for next year.'"

75. Peers, "'Playing Ourselves.'"

76. See, for example, Deutschlander, "In Search of *Winnetou*," 103.

77. Discussion with a member of the Sun Forehead Clan, 11 March 2003.

78. Stolzman, *How to Take Part in Lakota Ceremonies*.

79. Link-Vogt and Link-Vogt, "Andere Völker-andere Sitten!"

80. Sanner, "Confessions of the Last Hopi Fieldworker," 42.

81. Sanner, "Karl von den Steinen in Oraibi." See also, Trotta, "Crossing Cultural Boundaries"; and Michael F. Brown, *Who Owns Native Culture*, 13–41.

82. For more, see McCaffery, "Global Hopi: Local Hippie."

83. Sanner interview, 12 November 2003.

84. Sanner, "'Are you Hitler's son?'"

85. Ibid., 68, n. 98.

86. Frazier, *On the Rez*, 177.

87. Conversation with Richard Erdoes, 5 November 2005.

88. Conversation with R., 20 July 2003.

89. Not just books. A simple glance at the December 2009 program of the American Anthropological Association demonstrates how pervasive the topic has become.

90. See, for example, Michael Mann, *The Sources of Social Power*.

CONCLUSIONS

1. Langewiesche and Schmidt, *Föderative Nation*; Abigail Green, "The Federal Alternative?"; Thomas Nipperdey, "Der Föderalismus in der deutschen Geschichte," in Nipperdey, *Nachdenken über die deutsche Geschichte*; and Umbach, *German Federalism*.

2. Telephone conversation with I. Q., 3 June 2003.

3. Sewell, *The Logics of History*, 116.

4. Walker, *Germany and the Emigration*.

5. For a discussion of the implications of the term and its uses, see, for example, Guenther, "The Concept of Indigeneity."

6. Kiernan, *Blood and Soil*.

7. Rickard, "Alterity, Mimicry, and German Indians."

8. Kalshoven, *Crafting "The Indian."*

9. Gregor, Roemer, and Roseman, *German History from the Margins*.

10. Bayly, *The Birth of the Modern World*.

11. Helmut Walser Smith, "Prussia at the Margins."

12. Zantop, "Close Encounters," 7.

Bibliography

ARCHIVAL SOURCES—GERMANY
Berlin
    Berlin-Brandenburgische Akademie der Wissenschaften
        Liselotte Welskopf-Henrich Papers (LLWH Nachlass)
    Bundesarchiv Filmarchiv, Fehrbelliner Platz
    Bundesarchiv Lichterfelde West
    Bundesbeauftragte für die Unterlagen des Staatssicherheitsdienstes der DDR
    Universitätsarchiv der Humboldt-Universität zu Berlin
        Liselotte Welskopf-Henrich Papers
Dresden
    Sächsisches Staatsarchiv
    Stadtarchiv Dresden
Hamburg
    Hagenbeck Archiv
Munich
    Stadtarchiv München
Radebeul
    Karl-May-Museum
    Stadtarchiv Radebeul
Solingen
    Stadtarchiv Solingen
Stuttgart
    Linden-Museum

ARCHIVAL SOURCES—USA
Bloomington, Indiana
    Mathers Museum of World Cultures, Archive, Indiana University
        Joseph K. Dixon Papers
Cheyenne, Wyoming
    Wyoming State Archive

Cody, Wyoming
 Harold McCracken Research Library, Buffalo Bill Historical Center
  Charles Belden files
College Park, Maryland
 National Archives
Golden, Colorado
 Buffalo Bill Museum
Kansas City, Missouri
 National Archives
Lincoln, Nebraska
 Nebraska Historical Society, State Archive
Milwaukee, Wisconsin
 Marquette University Archives
  BCIM Series, Dakota Territory
Minneapolis, Minnesota
 Minnesota Historical Society
New Ulm, Minnesota
 Brown County Historical Society
Norman, Oklahoma
 Western Historical Collections, University of Oklahoma
  Miller Brothers 101 Ranch Collection
Philadelphia, Pennsylvania
 German Society
  Rudolf Cronau Papers
Pine Ridge, South Dakota
 Pine Ridge Tribal Archive, Oglala-Lakota College
Washington, D.C.
 National Archives
 Smithsonian Institution

SELECTED PERIODICALS

Belleviller Zeitung (Belleville, Illinois)
Buffalo County Republikaner
Burlington Gazette
Daily Globe (St. Louis)
Daily News (La Crosse, Wisconsin)
Dakota Scout
Dakota-Scout/Fährte
Das Ausland
Davenport Demokrat
Der Pimpf: Nationalsozialistische Jugendblätter
Der Spiegel
Die Gartenlaube
Die Zeit
Dresdner Nachrichten
Dresdner Neueste Nachricht
Dresdner Stadt-Rundschau
Dresdner Tageblatt
Dubuque Herald
Fährte: Interessengemeinschaft Deutschsprechender Indianerfreunde
Globus
Hamburger Illustrierte Zeitung
Junge Welt
Kalumet
Kansas City Star
Kölner Nachrichten
Kölnische Zeitung

Lakota Times
Leipziger Illustrirte Zeitung
Leipziger Tageblatt
Leipziger Zeitung
Minnesota Deutsche Zeitung
Minnesota Staats-Zeitung
Mitteldeutsche Neueste Nachrichten
Münchner Illustrierte Presse
Münchner Merkur
Münchner Neueste Nachrichten
New Ulm Pioneer
New Ulm Post
New York Times
News from Indian Country

Nord Stern (La Crosse, Wisconsin)
Pioneer am Wisconsin (Sauk City, Wisconsin)
Pioneer and Democrat (St. Paul)
Sächsische Zeitung
St. Paul Daily Globe
St. Paul Pioneer
St. Paul Volkszeitung
Siegerländer
Süddeutsche Zeitung
Über Land und Meer
Völkischer Beobachter
Wall Street Journal

BOOKS, ESSAYS, AND THESES

Adams, Rachel, and David Savran, eds. *The Masculinity Studies Reader*. Oxford: Blackwell, 2002.

Aeppel, Timothy. "At One with Indians: Tribes of Foreigners Visit Reservations." *Wall Street Journal*, 6 August 1996.

Akers, Donna L. *Living in the Land of Death: The Choctaw Nation, 1830–1860*. East Lansing: Michigan State University Press, 2004.

Aley, Peter. *Jugendliteratur im Dritten Reich: Dokumente und Kommentare*. Hamburg: Bertelsmann, 1967.

Ames, Eric. *Carl Hagenbeck's Empire of Entertainments*. Seattle: University of Washington Press, 2009.

———. "Seeing the Imaginary: On the Popular Reception of Wild West Shows in Germany, 1885–1910." In *I Like America*, edited by Kort, 213–29.

Ames, Eric, Marcia Klotz, and Lora Wildenthal, eds. *Germany's Colonial Pasts*. Lincoln: University of Nebraska Press, 2005.

Amiotte, Arthur. "Artist's Statement." In *Arthur Amiotte: Retrospective Exhibition, Continuity and Diversity*, 5. Pine Ridge: Heritage Center, 2001.

Anderson, Gary Clayton. *Kinsmen of Another Kind: Dakota-White Relations in the Upper Mississippi Valley, 1650–1862*. Lincoln: University of Nebraska Press, 1984.

———. "Myrick's Insult: A Fresh Look at Myth and Reality." *Minnesota History*, Spring 1983, 198–206.

Anderson, Gary Clayton, and Alan R. Woolworth. *Through Dakota Eyes: Narrative Accounts of the Minnesota Indian War of 1862*. Minneapolis: Minnesota Historical Society Press, 1988.

Applegate, Celia. "A Europe of Regions: Reflections on the Historiography of Sub-National Places in Modern Times." *American Historical Review* 104, no. 4 (1999): 1157–82.

———. *A Nation of Provincials: The German Idea of Heimat*. Berkeley: University of California Press, 1990.

Ashliman, D. L. "The Novel of Western Adventure in Nineteenth-Century Germany." *Western American Literature* 3, no. 2 (1968): 133–45.

Augstein, Rudolf. "Weiter Weg zu Winnetou." *Der Spiegel* 49, no. 18 (1 May 1995): 130.

Bakeman, Mary H., and Antona M. Richardson, eds. *Trails of Tears: Minnesota's Dakota Indian Exile Begins.* Roseville, Minn.: Prairie Echoes Press, 2008.

Banach, Berndt. "Die Rasse mit der Bronzehaut, ein Kapitel Menschheitsgeschichte." *Kalumet* 12, no. 2 (1963): 42–51.

Barba, Preston Albert. "Cooper in Germany." *Indiana University Studies* 2, no. 21 (1914): 51–104.

Barclay, David E., and Elisabeth Glaser-Schmidt, eds. *Transatlantic Images and Perceptions: Germany and America since 1776.* Cambridge: Cambridge University Press, 1997.

Barkin, Kenneth D. "'Berlin Days,' 1892–1894: W. E. B. Du Bois and German Political Economy." *boundary 2* 27, no. 3 (2000): 79–101.

Barsh, Russel Lawrence. "American Indians in the Great War." *Ethnohistory* 38, no. 3 (1991): 276–303.

Bartlet, H. Guillermo. "American Indian Studies in West Germany." *Wicazo Sa* 2, no. 2 (1986): 45–50.

Bassin, Mark. "Friedrich Ratzel's Travels in the United States: A Study in the Genesis of His Anthropology." *History of Geography Newsletter* 4 (1984): 11–22.

Bayly, C. A. *The Birth of the Modern World, 1780–1914: Global Connections and Comparisons.* Malden, Mass.: Blackwell, 2004.

Beck, Paul N. *Inkpaduta: Dakota Leader.* Norman: University of Oklahoma Press, 2008.

Bederman, Gail. *Manliness and Civilization: A Cultural History of Gender and Race in the United States, 1880–1917.* Chicago: University of Chicago Press, 1995.

Beebe, Barton Carl. "The Search for a Fatherland: James Fenimore Cooper in Germany." Ph.D. diss., Princeton University, 2008.

Beholz, Robert. *Tecumtha, der letzte Shawnee.* Leipzig: Weise, 1936.

Belden, Charles. "War Whoops in the Schwarzwald." *Farm and Ranch Review,* November 1960, 8.

Belgum, Kirsten. *Popularizing the Nation: Audience, Representation, and the Production of Identity in Die Gartenlaube, 1853–1900.* Lincoln: University of Nebraska Press, 1998.

Benjamin, Walter. "Goethe's Elective Affinities." In *Walter Benjamin, Selected Writings,* vol. 1, *1913–1926,* edited by Marcus Bullock and Michael W. Jennings, 297–360. Cambridge, Mass.: Belknap Press of Harvard University Press, 2002.

Berg, Manfred, and Philipp Gassert, eds. *Deutschland und die USA in der internationalen Geschichte des 20. Jahrhunderts.* Stuttgart: Franz Steiner Verlag, 2004.

Berghold, Alexander. *Aufstand der Dakota: Der Überfall auf Neu-Ulm im Jahre 1862.* Berlin: Grenze und Ausland, 1935.

———. *The Indians' Revenge or Days of Horror: Some Appalling Events in the History of the Sioux.* Edited by Don Heinrich Tolzmann. Roseville, Minn.: Edinborough Press, 2007.

Berkhofer, Robert F., Jr. *The White Man's Indian: Images of the American Indian from Columbus to the Present*. New York: Vintage, 1978.

Berlo, Janet Catherine. *Arthur Amiotte Collages, 1988–2006*. Santa Fe: Wheelwright Museum of the American Indian, 2006.

Berlo, Janet Catherine, and Ruth B. Phillips. *Native North American Art*. New York: Oxford University Press, 1998.

Bernstein, Alison R. *American Indians and World War II*. Norman: University of Oklahoma Press, 1991.

Bernstein, David. "'We are not now as we once were': Iowa Indians' Political and Economic Adaptations during U. S. Incorporation." *Ethnohistory* 54, no. 4 (2007): 605–37.

Biegert, Claus. *Seit 200 Jahren ohne Verfassung. 1976: Indianer im Widerstand*. Hamburg: Rowohlt, 1976.

Billington, Ray Allen. *Land of Savagery, Land of Promise: The European Image of the American Frontier in the Nineteenth Century*. New York: W. W. Norton, 1981.

Blackbourn, David. *The Conquest of Nature: Water, Landscape, and the Making of Modern Germany*. New York: Norton, 2006.

———. "'The Garden of Our Hearts': Landscape, Nature, and Local Identity in the German East." In *Localism, Landscape, and the Ambiguities of Place*, edited by Blackbourn and Retallack, 149–64.

Blackbourn, David, and James Retallack, eds. *Localism, Landscape, and the Ambiguities of Place: German-Speaking Central Europe, 1860–1930*. Toronto: University of Toronto Press, 2007.

Blackhawk, Ned. "Currents in North American Indian Historiography." *Western Historical Quarterly* 42, no. 3 (2011): 319–24.

———. *Violence over the Land: Indians and Empires in the Early American West*. Cambridge, Mass.: Harvard University Press, 2006.

Board of Commissioners. *Minnesota in the Civil and Indian Wars, 1861–1865*. 2 vols. St. Paul: Pioneer Press, 1893.

Boden, Gertrud. *Nordamerika: Die Sammlung des Rautenstrauch-Joest-Museums*. Ethnologica, n.s., 20. Cologne, 1995.

Bollenbeck, Georg. *Bildung und Kultur: Glanz und Elend eines deutschen Deutungsmusters*. Frankfurt: Suhrkamp, 1996.

Bolz, Peter. "Indians and Germans: A Relationship Riddled with Clichés." In *Native American Art: The Collections of the Ethnological Museum Berlin*, edited by Bolz and Sanner, 9–22.

———. Letter to the Editor. *Das Indianermagazin*, 1993.

Bolz, Peter, and Hans-Ulrich Sanner. *Native American Art: The Collections of the Ethnological Museum Berlin*. Berlin: G&H, 1999.

Borries, Friedrich von, and Jens-Uwe Fischer. *Sozialistische Cowboys: Der Wilde Westen Ostdeutschlands*. Frankfurt a. M.: Suhrkamp, 2008.

Boyton, Paul. *The Story of Paul Boyton: Voyages on All the Great Rivers of the World*. Milwaukee: Riverside Printing Company, 1892.

Britten, Thomas A. *American Indians in World War I: At Home and at War*. Albuquerque: University of New Mexico Press, 1997.

Brooks, James F. *Captives and Cousins: Slavery, Kinship, and Community in the Southwest Borderlands*. Chapel Hill: University of North Carolina Press, 2002.

Brown, Dee. *Bury My Heart at Wounded Knee: An Indian History of the American West*. New York: Holt, Rinehart, and Winston, 1971.

Brown, Michael F. *Who Owns Native Culture?* Cambridge, Mass.: Harvard University Press, 2003.

Browning, Christopher. *The Origins of the Final Solution: The Evolution of Nazi Jewish Policy, September 1939–March 1942*. Lincoln: University of Nebraska Press, 2004.

Brunner, Bernd. "Der große Aufbruch." *Zeit Geschichte*, no. 3 (2011): 42–50.

Byrd, Jodi A. "'Living My Native Life Deadly': Red Lake, Ward Churchill, and the Discourses of Competing Genocides." *Native American Quarterly* 31, no. 2 (2007): 310–32.

Cadena, Marisol de la, and Orin Starn eds. *Indigenous Experience Today*. New York: Berg, 2007.

Calloway, Colin G. "Historical Encounters across Five Centuries." In *Germans and Indians*, edited by Calloway, Gemünden, and Zantop, 47–81.

Calloway, Colin G., Gerd Gemünden, and Susanne Zantop, eds. *Germans and Indians: Fantasies, Encounters, Projections*. Lincoln: University of Nebraska Press, 2002.

Carley, Kenneth. *The Dakota War of 1862*. St. Paul: Minnesota Historical Society Press, 2001.

Carlson, Marta. "Germans Playing Indian." In *Germans and Indians*, edited by Calloway, Gemünden, and Zantop, 213–16.

Carroll, Al. *Medicine Bags and Dog Tags: American Indian Veterans from Colonial Times to the Second Iraq War*. Lincoln: University of Nebraska Press, 2008.

Cassidy, Donna M. *Marsden Hartley: Race, Region, and Nation*. Hanover: University Press of New England, 2005.

Chateaubriand, François-René. *Atala and René*. Translated Walter J. Cobb. New York: Signet, 1961.

Chrislock, Carl H. *Watchdog of Loyalty: The Minnesota Commission of Public Safety during World War I*. St. Paul: Minnesota Historical Society, 1991.

Churchill, Ward. *Fantasies of the Master Race: Literature, Cinema, and the Colonization of American Indians*. Monroe, Maine: Common Courage Press, 1992.

———. *Indians Are Us? Culture and Genocide in Native North America*. Monroe, Maine: Common Courage Press, 1994.

———. *A Little Matter of Genocide: Holocaust and Denial in the Americas, 1492 to the Present*. San Francisco: City Light Books, 1998.

———. *Struggle for the Land: Indigenous Resistance to Genocide, Ecocide, and Expropriation in Contemporary North America*. Monroe, Maine: Common Courage Press, 1993.

Clifford, James. *Routes: Travel and Translation in the Late Twentieth Century*. Cambridge, Mass.: Harvard University Press, 1997.

Clifton, James A., ed. "Alternate Identities and Cultural Frontiers." In *Being and Becoming Indian: Biographical Studies of North American Frontiers*, edited by Clifton, 1–37. Chicago: Dorsey, 1989.

————. *The Invented Indian: Cultural Fictions and Government Policies*. New Brunswick, N.J.: Transaction, 1990.

Confino, Alon. *The Nation as a Local Metaphor: Württemberg, Imperial Germany, and National Memory, 1871–1918*. Chapel Hill: University of North Carolina Press, 1997.

————. "Reflections: A World without Jews; Interpreting the Holocaust." *German History* 27, no. 4 (2009): 531–59.

Conn, Steven. *History's Shadow: Native Americans and Historical Consciousness in the Nineteenth Century*. Chicago: University of Chicago Press, 2004.

Conrad, Rudolf. "Mutual Fascination: Indians in Dresden and Leipzig." In *Indians and Europe*, edited by Feest, 455–74.

Conrad, Sebastian. *Globalisierung und Nation im deutschen Kaiserreich*. Munich: Beck, 2006.

Conzen, Kathleen Neils. *Germans in Minnesota*. St. Paul: Minnesota Historical Press, 2003.

————. "Peasant Pioneers: Generational Succession among German Farmers in Frontier Minnesota." In *The Countryside in the Age of Capitalist Transformation*, edited by Hahn and Prude, 259–92.

————. "Phantom Landscapes of Colonization: Germans in the Making of a Pluralist America." In *The German-American Encounter: Conflict and Cooperation between Two Cultures, 1800–2000*, edited by Trommler and Shore, 7–21.

Cook-Lynn, Elizabeth. *Anti-Indianism in Modern America*. Urbana: University of Illinois Press, 2001.

Cooper, Frederick, and Ann Laura Stoler, eds. *Tensions of Empire: Colonial Cultures in a Bourgeois World*. Berkeley: University of California Press, 1997.

Corn, Wanda M. *The Great American Thing: Modern Art and National Identity, 1915–1935*. Berkeley: University of California Press, 1999.

Cronau, Rudolf. *Amerika: Die Geschichte seiner Entdeckung von der ältesten bis auf die neueste Zeit*. 2 vols. Leipzig: Abel & Müller, 1892.

————. *The Army of the American Revolution and Its Organizer*. New York: R. Cronau, 1923.

————. "Auf des Lebens Wellen und Wogen: Fahrten, Kämpfe, Abenteuer und Leistungen eines stets wanderfrohen Überseedeutschen." Unpublished manuscript in the possession of Gerald Wunderlich, New York City, 1939.

————. *The British Black Book*. New York: R. Cronau, 1915.

————. *Buch der Reklame: Geschichte, Wesen, und Praxis der Reklame*. Ulm: Wohler, 1887.

————. "The Bulwarks of Our Ancestors." *Overland Monthly and Out West Magazine* 56, no. 4 (October 1910): 19–26.

————. "A Continent Despoiled." *McClure's Magazine* 32, no. 6 (April 1909): 639–48.

————. "Das Yosemitethal in Kalifornien." *Die Gartenlaube*, 1888, 360–62.

————. *Denkschrift zum 150. Jahrestag der Deutschen Gesellschaft der Stadt New York. 1784–1934*. New York: German Society of the City of New York, 1934.

————. *Die Deutschen als Gründer von New Amsterdam–New York*. New York: Heiss, 1926.

——. "Die Hochfluthen des Mississippi-Gebietes." *Die Gartenlaube*, 1884, 160–66.

——. "Die Indianische Gewerbeschule zu Carlisle in Pennsylvanien." *Die Gartenlaube*, 1904, 31–34.

——. "Die Sioux-Indianer," *Leipziger Illustrirte Zeitung*, no. 2241 (12 June 1886): 592.

——. *Drei Jahrhunderte deutschen Lebens in Amerika; Eine Geschichte der Deutschen in den Vereinigten Staaten*. Berlin: D. Reimer, 1909.

——. "Durch Arizona." *Die Gartenlaube*, 1888, 539–42.

——. *Fahrten im Lande der Sioux*. Leipzig: T. O. Weigel, 1886.

——. *Im wilden Westen. Eine Künstlerfahrt durch die Prairien und Felsengebirge der Union*. Braunschweig: Verlag von Oskar Löbbecke, 1890.

——. "The New Germany—An Object Lesson." *McClure's Magazine* 34, no. 2 (December 1909): 183–89.

——. *Our Wasteful Nation: The Story of American Prodigality and the Abuse of Our National Resources*. New York: Mitchell Kennerley, 1908.

——. *Prohibition and the Destruction of the American Brewing Industry*. New York: R. Cronau, 1926.

——. "Um die Erde: Erster Brief: Aus den Straßen New-Yorks." *Die Gartenlaube*, 1881, 508–11.

——. "Um die Erde: Zweiter Brief: Auf dem Greenwood Cemetery zu Brooklyn." *Die Gartenlaube*, 1881, 577–78.

——. "Um die Erde: Dritter Brief: Das amerikanische Mekka." *Die Gartenlaube*, 1881, 660–62.

——. "Um die Erde: Fünfter Brief: Baltimore." *Die Gartenlaube*, 1881, 879–82.

——. "Um die Erde: Sechster Brief: In Minnesota." *Die Gartenlaube*, 1882, 116–18.

——. "Um die Erde: Siebenter Brief: Indianische Dichtung und Wahrheit in Minnesota." *Die Gartenlaube*, 1882, 148–50.

——. "Um die Erde: Achter Brief: Ein Monat auf dem Vater der Ströme." *Die Gartenlaube*, 1882, 227–34.

——. "Um die Erde: Neunter Brief: Ein rother Napoleon." *Die Gartenlaube*, 1882, 276–79.

——. *Von Wunderland zu Wunderland: Landschafts- und Lebensbilder aus den Staaten und Territorien der Union*. Leipzig: Spohr, 1885, and T. O. Wiegel, 1886.

——. "Winterstürme im Amerikanischen Nordwesten." *Die Gartenlaube*, 1887, 77–78.

——. *Woman Triumphant: The Story of Her Struggles for Freedom, Education and Political Rights; Dedicated to All Noble-Minded Women by an Appreciative Member of the Other Sex*. New York: R. Cronau, 1919.

——. "Zum 25. Jahrestag des Custer-Massacres: Ein Rückblick auf ein düsteres Blatt aus der Geschichte des fernen Westens." *Kölnische Zeitung*, 23 June 1901.

Czaplicka, John. "Amerikabilder and the German Discourse on Modern Civilization, 1890–1925." In *Envisioning Amerika: Prints, Drawings, and Photographs by George Grosz and His Contemporaries*, edited by Tower, 36–44.

Dahlin, Curtis A. *Dakota Uprising Victims: Gravestones and Stories*. Edina, Minn.: Beaver's Pond Press, 2007.

———. "Words vs. Actions." In *Trails of Tears*, edited by Bakeman and Richardson, 35–52.

Daum, Andreas W. *Wissenschaftspopularisierung im 19. Jahrhundert: Bürgerliche Kultur, naturwissenschaftliche Bildung und die deutsche Öffentlichkeit, 1848–1914.* Munich: R. Oldenbourg, 1998.

Deloria, Philip J. *Indians in Unexpected Places.* Lawrence: University Press of Kansas, 2004.

———. *Playing Indian.* New Haven: Yale University Press, 1998.

Deloria, Philip J., and Neil Salisbury, eds. *A Companion to American Indian History.* Malden, Mass.: Blackwell, 2002.

Deloria, Vine, Jr. *Custer Died for Your Sins: An Indian Manifesto.* Toronto: Macmillan, 1969.

———. "The Indians." In *Buffalo Bill and the Wild West,* 54–55. Brooklyn: Brooklyn Museum, 1981.

DeMallie, Raymond J., ed. *Handbook of North American Indians.* Vol. 13, *The Plains.* 2 vols. Washington, D.C.: Smithsonian Institution, 2001.

DeMallie Raymond J., and Douglas R. Parks. *Sioux Indian Religion.* Norman: University of Oklahoma Press, 1987.

Dempsey, Hugh A. "Blackfoot." In *Handbook of North American Indians,* vol. 13, *The Plains,* edited by DeMallie, 604–37.

Denig, Edwin Thompson. *Five Indian Tribes of the Upper Missouri: Sioux, Ankaras, Assiniboines, Crees, and Crows.* Norman: University of Oklahoma Press, 1961.

Denkler, Horst, Sigrid Bauschinger, and Wilfried Malsch, eds. *Amerika in der deutschen Literatur.* Stuttgart: Philipp Reclam, 1975.

Denkler, Horst, and Karl Prümm. *Die deutsche Literatur im Dritten Reich: Themen, Traditionen, Wirkungen.* Stuttgart: Reclam, 1976.

Deutschlander, Siegrid. "In Search of *Winnetou:* Constructing Aboriginal Culture in the Tourist Encounter." Ph.D. diss., University of Calgary, 2006.

Deutschlander, Siegrid, and Leslie J. Miller. "Politicizing Aboriginal Cultural Tourism: The Discourse of Primitivism in the Tourist Encounter." *Canadian Review of Sociology and Anthropology* 40, no. 1 (2003): 25–43.

Du Bois, W. E. B. "The Negro and the Warsaw Ghetto." *Jewish Life,* May 1952, 14–15.

———. "The Present Condition of German Politics, 1893." *Central European History* 31, no. 3 (1998): 155–70.

———. *The Souls of Black Folk: Essays and Sketches.* Chicago: A. C. McClurg, 1907.

———. *The World and Africa: An Inquiry into the Part which Africa Has Played in World History.* New York: International Publishers, 1965.

Effords, Allison. "German Immigrants and the Arc of Reconstruction Citizenship in the United States, 1865–1877." *Bulletin of the German Historical Institute* 46 (2010): 61–76.

———. "New Citizens: German Immigrants, African Americans, and the Reconstruction of Citizenship, 1865–1877." Ph.D. diss., Ohio State University, 2008.

Eggebrecht, Harald. "Sitzend inmitten der Prärie: Indianer in Darmstadt: Wie Sitting Bull und sein Kampf gegen die Weißen zum Mythos wurde." *Süddeutsche Zeitung,* 14 September 1999.

Egmond, Florike, and Peter Mason. *The Mammoth and the Mouse: Microhistory and Morphology*. Baltimore: Johns Hopkins University Press, 1997.

Ewers, John C. *Indian Life on the Upper Missouri*. Norman: University of Oklahoma Press, 1968.

Farr, William E. "Julius Seyler: Painting the Blackfeet, Painting Glacier Park, 1913–1914." *Montana: The Magazine of Western History* 51, no. 2 (Summer 2001): 52–69.

Feest, Christian F. "Europe's Indians." In *The Invented Indian: Cultural Fictions and Government Policies*, edited by James A. Clifton, 313–32. New Brunswick, N.J.: Transaction Publishers, 1990.

———. "German Medley." *European Review of Native American Studies* 15, no. 2 (2001): 55–56.

———. "Germany's Indians in a European Perspective." In *Germans and Indians*, edited by Calloway, Gemünden, and Zantop, 25–43.

———. "Menschen, Masken und Moneten: Ethnologische Museen und Moral." *Museumskunde* 67, no. 2 (2002): 82–91.

———. *Sitting Bull: "Der letzte Indianer."* Darmstadt: Hessisches Landesmuseum, 1999.

———, ed. *Indians and Europe*. Lincoln: University of Nebraska Press, 1999.

———, ed. *Indians in Europe: An Interdisciplinary Collection of Essays*. Aachen: Rader, 1987.

Fehrenbach, Heide, and Uta G. Poiger. "Learning from America: Reconstructing 'Race' in Postwar Germany." In *Americanization and Anti-Americanism*, edited by Stephan, 107–25.

———, eds. *Transactions, Transgressions, Transformations: American Culture in Western Europe and Japan*. New York: Berghahn Books, 2000.

Fest, Joachim. *Hitler. Eine Biographie*. Frankfurt: Ullstein, 1974.

Folwell, William Watts. *A History of Minnesota*. 2 vols. St. Paul: Minnesota Historical Society, 1921–30.

Francis, Daniel. *The Imaginary Indian: The Image of the Indian in Canadian Culture*. Vancouver: Arsenal Pulp Press, 1992.

Franco, Jeré Bishop. *Crossing the Pond: The Native American Effort in World War II*. Denton: University of North Texas Press, 1999.

Frank, Patty. *Die Indianerschlacht am Little Big Horn*. Berlin: Militärverlag, 1957.

Frazier, Ian. *On the Rez*. New York: Farrar, Straus, Giroux, 2000.

Franzke, Andreas, Wolfgang Haberland, Hans-Ulrich Sanner, and Brigitte Templin, eds. *Katsinam: Figuren der Pueblo-Indianer Nordamerikas aus der Studiensammlung Horst Antes*. Lübeck: Museum für Völkerkunde, 2000.

Friedberg, Lilian. "Dare to Compare: Americanizing the Holocaust." *American Indian Quarterly* 24, no. 3 (2000): 353–80.

Friedrichs, Michael. "Tecumseh's Fabulous Career in German Fiction." *European Review of Native American Studies* 11, no. 2 (1997): 47–52.

Friedrichsmeyer, Sara, Sara Lennox, and Susanne Zantop, eds. *The Imperialist Imagination: German Colonialism and Its Legacy*. Ann Arbor: University of Michigan Press, 1998.

Fuhrman, Klaus. *Wild West—German Style*. Anthropo-Filmproduktion, 2004.

Gagern, Friedrich von. *Das Grenzerbuch: Von Pfadfindern, Häuptlingen und Lederstrümpfen*. Berlin: Parey, 1944.

Galler, Robert W., Jr. "Sustaining the Sioux Confederation: Yanktonai Initiatives and Influence on the Northern Plains, 1680–1880." *Western Historical Quarterly* 39 (Winter 2008): 467–90.

Garroutte, Eva Marie. *Real Indians: Identity and the Survival of Native America*. Berkeley: University of California Press, 2003.

Gassert, Phillip. "Without Concessions to Marxist or Communist Thought: Fordism in Germany, 1923–1939." In *Transatlantic Images and Perceptions*, edited by Barclay and Glaser-Schmidt, 217–43.

Gemünden, Gerd. "Between Karl May and Karl Marx: The DEFA Indianderfilme (1965–1983)." *Film History* 10 (1998): 399–407.

Gerstäcker, Friedrich. *Wie ist es denn nun eigentlich in Amerika? Eine kurze Schilderung dessen, was der Auswanderer in Nordamerika zu thun und dafür zu hoffen und zu erwarten hat*. Leipzig: G. Wigand, 1849.

Geyer, Michael. "America in Germany: Power and the Pursuit of Americanization." In *The German-American Encounter: Conflict and Cooperation between Two Cultures, 1800–2000*, edited by Trommler and Shore, 121–45.

Giago, Tim. "The Demise of AIM Caused Nary a Ripple in the Circle of Life." *Lakota Times*, 20 January 1988.

Gibbon, Guy. *The Sioux: The Dakota and Lakota Nations*. New York: Oxford University Press, 2003.

Gilders, Adam. "Ich bin ein Indianer." *Walrus*, October 2003.

Glanz, Dawn. *How the West Was Drawn: American Art and the Settling of the Frontier*. Ann Arbor: UMI Research Press, 1978.

Glasrud, Clarence A., ed. *A Heritage Fulfilled: German-Americans—Die erfüllte Herkunft*. Moorehead, Minn.: Concordia College, 1983.

Göktürk, Deniz. *Künstler, Cowboys, Ingenieure . . . : Kultur- und mediengeschichtliche Studien zu deutschen Amerika-Texten 1912–1920*. Munich: Wilhelm Fink Verlag, 1998.

González, Yolanda Broyles. "Cheyennes in the Black Forest: A Social Drama." In *The Americanization of the Global Village: Essays in Comparative Popular Culture*, edited by Roger Rollin, 70–86. Bowling Green: Bowling Green State University Popular Press, 1989.

Goyens, Tom. *Beer and Revolution: The German Anarchist Movement in New York City, 1880–1914*. Urbana: University of Illinois Press, 2007.

Gpfert, Hans. "Das Projekt Indianer im offenen Geschichtsunterricht als Beitrag zur Friedenserziehung." *Geschichtsdidaktik* 8, no. 2 (1983): 107–25.

Graf, Andreas. *Der Tod der Wölfe: Das abenteuerliche und das bürgerliche Leben des Romanschriftstellers und Amerikareisenden Balduin Möllhausen (1825–1905)*. Berlin: Dunker und Humboldt, 1991.

Green, Abigail. "The Federal Alternative? A New View of Modern German History." *Historical Journal* 46, no. 1 (2003): 187–202.

Green, Rayna. "The Tribe Called Wannabee: Playing Indian in America and Europe." *Folklore* 99, no. 1 (1988): 45–47.

Gregor, Neil, Nils H. Roemer, and Mark Roseman, eds. *German History from the Margins*. Bloomington: Indiana University Press, 2006.

Grewling, Nicole. "Fighting the Two-Souled Warrior: German Colonial Fantasies of North America." Ph.D. diss., University of Minnesota, 2007.

Gries, Rainer. *Die Rationen-Gesellschaft. Versorgungskampf und Vergleichsmentalität. Leipzig, München und Köln nach dem Kriege*. Münster: Verlag Westfälisches Dampfboot, 1991.

Griffin, Charles Eldridge. *Four Years in Europe with Buffalo Bill*. Albia, Iowa: Stage Publishing Company, 1908.

Grosz, Georg. *Ein kleines Ja und ein großes Nein*. Hamburg: Rowohlt, 1955.

Grundig, Hans. *Zwischen Karneval und Aschermittwoch: Erinnerungen eines Malers*. Berlin: Dietz Verlag, 1957.

Guenther, Mathlas. "The Concept of Indigeneity." *Social Anthropology* 14, no. 1 (2007): 17–32.

Guettel, Jens-Uwe. "From the Frontier to German South-West Africa: German Colonialism, Indians, and American Westward Expansion." *Modern Intellectual History* 7, no. 3 (2010): 523–52.

———. "Reading America, Envisioning Empire: German Perceptions of Indians, Slavery, and the American West, 1789–1900." Ph.D. diss., Yale University, 2007.

Günther, Ernst, and Dietmar Winkler. *Taschenbuch der Künste: Zirkusgeschichte*. Berlin: Henschelverlag, 1986.

Haberland, Wolfgang. "'Diese Indianer sind falsch,' Neun Bella Coola im Deutschen Reich 1885/6." *Archiv für Völkerkunde* 42 (1988): 3–67.

———. "Nine Bella Coolas in Germany." In *Indians and Europe*, edited by Feest, 337–74.

Hagan, William T. *Quanah Parker, Comanche Chief*. Norman: University of Oklahoma Press, 1993.

Hagemann, Karen, and Stefanie Schüller-Springorum, eds. *Home/Front: The Military, War, and Gender in Twentieth-Century Germany*. New York: Berg, 2002.

Hahn, Steven, and Jonathan Prude, eds. *The Countryside in the Age of Capitalist Transformation*. Chapel Hill: University of North Carolina Press, 1985.

Haible, Barbara. *Indianer im Dienste der NS-Ideologie: Untersuchungen zur Funktion von Jugendbüchern über nordamerikanische Indianer im Nationalsozialismus*. Hamburg: Verlag Dr. Kovac, 1998.

Hämäläinen, Pekka. *The Comanche Empire*. New Haven: Yale University Press, 2008.

———. "The Rise and Fall of Plains Indian Horse Cultures." *Journal of American History* 90, no. 3 (December 2003): 833–62.

Hartmann, Horst. "Abteilung Amerikanische Naturvölker." In *100 Jahre Museum für Völkerkunde Berlin, Baessler-Archiv: Beiträge zur Völkerkunde*, edited by Krieger and Koch, 219–59.

Heard, Isaac V. D. *History of the Sioux War and Massacres of 1862 and 1863*. New York: Harper, 1865.

Heermann, Christian. *Old Shatterhand ritt nicht im Auftrag der Arbeiterklasse*. Dessau: Anhaltische Verlagsgesellschaft, 1995.

Helbich, Wolfgang. "Different, but Not Out of This World: German Images of the United States between Two World Wars, 1871–1914." In *Transatlantic Images and Perceptions*, edited by Barclay and Glaser-Schmidt, 109–30.

Herder, Johann Gottfried. *Philosophical Writings*. Translated by Michael N. Forster. Cambridge: Cambridge University Press, 2002.

Heritage Center. *Arthur Amiotte: Retrospective Exhibition, Continuity and Diversity*. Pine Ridge, S.D., 2001.

Hetmann, Frederik. *Der rote Tag*. Bayreuth: Loewes Verlag, 1975.

Hinz-Rosin, Peter, and Dirk Rohrbach. *Der letzte Häuptling*. Pößneck: Weltsichten, 2003.

Hobsbawm, Eric J. *The Age of Extremes: The Short Twentieth Century*. New York: Vintage, 1994.

Hohendahl, Peter Uwe. "Von der Rothaut zum Edelmenschen. Karl Mays Amerikaromane." In *Amerika in der deutschen Literatur*, edited by Denkler, Bauschinger, and Malsch, 229–45.

Höhn, Maria. *GIs and Fräuleins: The German-American Encounter in 1950s West Germany*. Chapel Hill: University of North Carolina Press, 2002.

Hoisington, Daniel J. *A German Town: A History of New Ulm, Minnesota*. Roseville, Minn.: Edinborough Press, 2004.

Holmquist, June Drenning, ed. *They Chose Minnesota: A Survey of the State's Ethnic Groups*. St. Paul: Minnesota Historical Society Press, 1981.

Honeck, Mischa. *We Are the Revolutionists: German-Speaking Immigrants and American Abolitionists after 1848*. Urbana: University of Illinois Press, 2007.

Horowitz, Helen Lefkowitz. "'Nous Autres': Reading, Passion, and the Creation of M. Carey Thomas." *Journal of American History* 79 (June 1992): 68–95.

Horwitz, Tony. *Confederates in the Attic: Dispatches from America's Unfinished Civil War*. New York: Pantheon Books, 1998.

Howe, Heidi. "Dakota." *American-German Review* 28, no. 5 (June–July 1961): 10–12.

Howe, Richard Herbert. "Max Weber's Elective Affinities: Sociology, within the Bounds of Pure Reason." *American Journal of Sociology* 84, no. 2 (1978): 366–85.

Hoxie, Frederick E. *A Final Promise: The Campaign to Assimilate the Indians, 1880–1920*. Lincoln: University of Nebraska Press, 1984.

———. *Parading through History: The Making of the Crow Nation in America, 1805–1935*. New York: Cambridge University Press, 1995.

Huhndorf, Shari M. *Going Native: Indians in the American Cultural Imagination*. Ithaca: Cornell University Press, 2001.

Hull, Isabel V. *Absolute Destruction: Military Culture and the Practices of War in Imperial Germany*. Ithaca: Cornell University Press, 2005.

Jacobs, Rudolf. "Todeskampf der Sioux." *Der Pimpf: Nationalsozialistische Jugendblätter*, no. 10 (October 1938): 3–9.

Janeck, Undine. *Zwischen Gartenlaube und Karl May: Deutsche Amerikarezeption in den Jahren 1871–1913*. Aachen: Shaker Verlag, 2003.

Jarausch, Konrad, and Michael Geyer. *Shattered Past: Reconstructing German Histories*. Princeton: Princeton University Press, 2003.

Johnson, Christine R. *The German Discovery of the World: Renaissance Encounters with the Strange and the Marvelous.* Charlottesville: University of Virginia Press, 2008.

Johnson, Dorothy E. "Attitude of the Germans in Minnesota toward the Republican Party to 1865." M.A. thesis, University of Minnesota, 1945.

Johnson, Hildegard Binder. "Factors Influencing the Distribution of the German Pioneer Population in Minnesota." *Agricultural History* 19, no. 1 (1945): 39–57.

———. "The Germans." In *They Chose Minnesota*, edited by Holmquist, 153–84.

———. "Intermarriage between German Pioneers and Other Nationalities in Minnesota in 1860 and 1870." *American Journal of Sociology* 51, no. 4 (1946): 299–304.

———. "The Location of German Immigrants in the Middle West." *Annals of the Association of American Geographers* 61, no. 1 (1951): 1–41.

Jung, C. G. *Memories, Dreams, Reflections.* Recorded and edited by Aniela Jaffé. Translated by Richard Winston and Clara Winston. New York: Vintage 1989.

Juni, Benedict. *Held in Captivity: Benedict Juni of New Ulm Minn. Relates His Experiences as an Indian Captive during the Indian Outbreaks in 1862.* New Ulm: Liesch-Walter, 1926.

Junker, Detlef. "The Continuity of Ambivalence: German Views of America, 1933–1945." In *Transatlantic Images and Perceptions*, edited by Barclay and Glaser-Schmidt, 243–65.

Jürgen, Anna. *Blauvogel: Wahlsohn der Irokesen.* Ravensburg: Otto Maier Verlag, 1968.

Kalshoven, Petra Tjitske. *Crafting "The Indian": Knowledge, Desire, and Play in Indianist Reenactment.* New York: Berghahn Books, 2012.

Kamphoefner, Walter D., Wolfgang Helbich, and Ulrike Sommer. *News from the Land of Freedom: German Immigrants Write Home.* Translated by Susan Carter Vogel. Ithaca: Cornell University Press, 1991.

Katz, William Loren. *Black Indians: A Hidden Heritage.* New York: Simon Pulse, 1986.

Kautz, Lawrence G. *August Valentine Kautz, USA: Biography of a Civil War General.* Jefferson, N.C.: McFarland, 2008.

Kazal, Russell A. *Becoming Old Stock: The Paradox of German-American Identity.* Princeton: Princeton University Press, 2004.

Kelly, Richard. "A Critical Review of the Support Work for North American Indians prior to the Fifth European Meeting of Support Groups." In *Reader for the 5th European Meeting of Indian Support Groups.* Zurich, 1989.

———. "Hobby? Hopi! Some Remarks on the Hopi Reception in Germany." *European Review of Native American Studies* 3, no. 1 (1989): 13–16.

Kiernan, Ben. *Blood and Soil: A World History of Genocide and Extermination from Sparta to Darfur.* New Haven: Yale University Press, 2007.

King, Jeremy. *Budweisers into Czechs and Germans: A Local History of Bohemian Politics, 1848–1948.* Princeton: Princeton University Press, 2005.

Kimmelman, Michael. "Karl May and the Origins of a German Obsession." *New York Times*, 12 September 2007.

Kinzer, Stephen. "Germans in Their Teepees? Naturally." *New York Times*, 2 April 1996.

KKN. "Kinder Manitous: Eine Reportage vom Indianertag in Radebeul." *Dresdner Stadt-Rundschau*, 22 October 1964.

Koch, Ekkehard. *Karl Mays Väter: Die Deutschen im Wilden Westen.* Husum: Hansa Verlag, 1982.

Koch, Thilo. "Indianer sein ist schwer: Wiedergutmachung durch den weißen Mann." *Die Zeit*, no. 18 (1 May 1964): 32.

Koepnick, Lutz P. "Unsettling America: German Westerns and Modernity." *Modernism/Modernity* 2, no. 3 (1995): 1–22.

König, Eva, ed. *Indianer, 1858–1928: Photographische Reisen von Alaska bis Feuerland.* Hamburg: Braus, 2002.

Kopas, Cliff. *Bella Coola.* Vancouver: Mitchell Press, 1970.

Kort, Pamela, ed. *I Like America.* Frankfurt: Schirn Kunsthalle, 2006.

Kramer, Thomas. "'Die Söhne der *großen* Bärin' und 'Das Blut des Adlers': Liselotte Welskopf-Henrichs Indianerbücher 1951–1980." In *Elisabeth Charlotte Welskopf in der DDR*, edited by Isolde Stark, 206–28. Stuttgart: Franz Steiner Verlag, 2006.

———. *Micky, Marx, und Manitu: Zeit- und Kulturgeschichte im Spiegel eines DDR-Comics 1955–1990; "Mosaik" als Fokus von Medienerlebnissen im NS und in der DDR.* Berlin: Weidler, 2002.

Kreis, Karl Markus, ed. "German Wild West: Karl May's Invention of the Definitive Indian." In *I Like America*, edited by Kort, 248–73.

———. *Lakotas, Black Robes, and Holy Women: German Reports from the Indian Missions in South Dakota, 1886–1900.* Translated by Corinna Dally-Starna. Lincoln: University of Nebraska Press, 2007.

Krieger, K., and G. Koch, eds. *100 Jahre Museum für Völkerkunde Berlin. Baessler-Archiv: Beiträge zur Völkerkunde* 21 (1973).

Krinsky, Carol Herselle. "Karl May's Western Novels and Aspects of Their Continuing Influence." *American Indian Culture and Research Journal* 23, no. 2 (1999): 53–72.

Krouse, Susan Applegate. *North American Indians in the Great War.* Lincoln: University of Nebraska Press, 2007.

Kurz, Rudolf Friedrich. *On the Upper Missouri: The Journal of Rudolph Friedrich Kurz, 1851–1852.* Edited and abridged by Carla Kelly. Norman: University of Oklahoma Press, 2005.

LaDuke, Winona. "Journey of Peace: The 1983 Native American Delegation to West Germany." *Akwesasne Notes* 16, no. 2 (1984): 19–21.

Lampert, K. "Ein Gang durch das ethnographische Museum des Württembergischen Vereins für Handelsgeographie." *Jahresbericht des Württembergischen Vereins für Handelsgeographie* 15 (1896–97): xlvi–lxxxv.

Langewiesche, Dieter. "Rezension von: Helmut Walser Smith, *The Continuities of German History: Nation, Religion, and Race across the Long Nineteenth Century*, Cambridge: Cambridge University Press 2008." *sehepunkte* 9, no. 1 (2009), [15.01.2009], URL: http://www.sehepunkte.de/2009/01/15041.html.

Langewiesche, Dieter, and Georg Schmidt, eds. *Föderative Nation: Deutschlandkonzepte von der Reformation bis zum Ersten Weltkrieg*. Munich: Oldenbourg Wissenschaftsverlag, 2000.

Lears, Jackson. *Rebirth of a Nation: The Making of Modern America, 1877–1920*. New York: Harper, 2009.

Lehmann, Herman. *Nine Years among the Indians, 1870–1879*. Albuquerque: University of New Mexico Press, 1993.

Lengwiler, Martin. "Aktuelle Perspektiven der Historischen Männlichkeitsforschung im Angelsächsischen Raum." *Traverse* 5, no. 1 (1998): 25–33.

Leonhart, Rudolf. *Memories of New Ulm: My Experiences during the Indian Uprising in Minnesota*. Translated by Don Heinrich Tolzmann. St. Paul, Minn.: Edinborough Press, 2005.

Levine, Bruce. *The Spirit of 1848: German Immigrants, Labor Conflict, and the Coming of the Civil War*. Urbana: University of Illinois Press, 1992.

Lewis, David Levering. *W. E. B. Du Bois, 1868–1919: Biography of a Race*. New York: Holt Paperbacks, 1994.

Liebersohn, Harry. *Aristocratic Encounters: European Travelers and North American Indians*. Cambridge: Cambridge University Press, 1998.

Link-Vogt, Angelika, und Jochem Link-Vogt. "Andere Völker—andere Sitten!" *Das Indianermagazin* 2 (1993): 53–54.

Lohausen, Hans, and Ruth Keller. *Rudolf Cronau: Journalist und Künstler, 1855–1939*. Solingen: Bergischer Geschichtsverein, 1989.

Lonetree, Amy. "Missed Opportunities: Reflections on the NMAI." *American Indian Quarterly* 30, nos. 3–4 (2006): 632–45.

Lott, Eric. *Love and Theft: Blackface Minstrelsy and the American Working Class*. New York: Oxford University Press, 1993.

Luebke, Frederick C. *Bonds of Loyalty: German-Americans in World War I*. DeKalb: Northern Illinois University Press, 1974.

———. *Germans in the New World: Essays in the History of Immigration*. Urbana: University of Illinois Press, 1990.

Lutz, Hartmut. "Der edle Wilde auf dem Kriegspfad: Indianerbilder für die deutsche Jugend." In *Das Gift der frühen Jahre: Rassismus in der Jugendliteratur*, edited by Regular Renschler and Roy Preiswerk, 235–78. Basel: Lenos, 1981.

———. "German Indianthusiasm: A Socially Constructed German National(ist) Myth." In *Germans and Indians*, edited by Calloway, Gemünden, and Zantop, 167–84.

———. *"Indianer" und "Native Americans": Zur sozial- und literarhistorischen Vermittlung eines Stereotyps*. Hildesheim: Georg Olms Verlag, 1985.

———. "'Okay, I'll be their annual Indian for next year'—Thoughts on the Marketing of a Canadian Indian Icon in Germany." In *Imaginary (Re-)Locations: Tradition, Modernity, and the Market in Contemporary Native American Literature and Culture*, edited by Helmbrecht Breinig, 217–36. Tübingen: Stauffenberg Verlag, 2003.

MacCannell, Dean. *The Tourist: A New Theory of the Leisure Class*. Berkeley: University of California Press, 1999.

Maner, Brent. *Germany's Ancient Pasts*. Chicago: University of Chicago Press, forthcoming.

Mann, Klaus. "Cowboy Mentor of the Führer." *Living Age* 359 (1940–41): 217–22.

Mann, Michael. *The Sources of Social Power*. Vols. 1 and 2. Cambridge: Cambridge University Press, 1986.

Marchand, Suzanne L. *Down from Olympus: Archaeology and Philhellenism in Germany, 1750–1970*. Princeton: Princeton University Press, 1996.

Mauch, Christof. "Zwischen Edelmut und Roheit: Indianer und Schwarze aus deutscher Perspektive." *Amerikastudien* 40, no. 4 (1995): 619–36.

Mayo, Lisa. "Appropriation and the Plastic Shaman: Winnetou's Snake Oil Show from Wigwam City." *Canadian Theatre Review* 68 (Fall 1991): 54–63.

McBride, Bunny. *Molly Spotted Elk: A Penobscot in Paris*. Norman: University of Oklahoma Press, 1995.

McCaffery, Nick. "Global Hopi: Local Hippie: An Anthropological Study of Hopi Identity in Relation to the New Age." Ph.D. diss., Queen's University Belfast, 2005.

McCloskey, Barbara. "From the Frontier to the Wild West: German Artists, American Indians, and the Spectacle of Race and Nation in the Nineteenth and Twentieth Centuries." In *I Like America*, edited by Kort, 299–321.

McKinney, Kathleen. "An Interview with Heidi Howe." *Prairie Winds* (1988): 22–33.

McKinnon, Andrew. "Elective Affinities of the Protestant Ethic: Weber and the Chemistry of Capitalism." *Sociological Theory* 28, no. 1. (2010): 108–26.

Meyen, A. *Die Kunstkammer und Sammlung für Völkerkunde in Neuen Museum*. Berlin, 1861.

Meyer, Roy W. *History of the Santee Sioux: United States Indian Policy on Trial*. Lincoln: University of Nebraska Press, 1967.

Michaels, Walter Benn. *The Trouble with Diversity: How We Learned to Love Identity and Ignore Inequality*. New York: Metropolitan, 2006.

Michalski, Sergiusz. *Neue Sachlichkeit: Malerei, Graphik, und Photographie in Deutschland, 1919–1933*. Cologne: B. Taschen, 1992.

Milton, John R. *Oscar Howe*. Minneapolis: Dillon Press, 1972.

Moeller, Robert G. *Protecting Motherhood: Women and the Family in the Politics of Postwar West Germany*. Berkeley: University of California Press, 1996.

Möllhausen, Balduin. "Blätter aus dem Tagebuch einer Reise vom Mississippi nach den Küsten der Südsee." *Über Land und Meer* 5, no. 9 (1863): 67–69.

———. *Der Halbindianer*. Stuttgart: Boje-Verlag, 1955.

———. *Reisen in die Felsengebirge Nord-Amerikas bis zum Hoch-Plateau von Neu-Mexico*. Leipzig: O. Purfürst, 1861.

———. *Tagebuch einer Reise vom Mississippi nach den Küsten der Südsee*. Leipzig: H. Mendelssohn, 1858.

Moore, Gregory, ed. *Fichte: Addresses to the German Nation*. Cambridge: Cambridge University Press, 2010.

Moses, A. Dirk, ed. *Empire, Colony, Genocide: Conquest, Occupation, and Subaltern Resistance in World History*. New York: Berghahn Books, 2008.

———. "Empire, Colony, Genocide: Keywords and the Philosophy of History." In *Empire, Colony, Genocide*, edited by Moses, 3–54.

———, ed. *Genocide and Settler Society: Frontier Violence and Stolen Indigenous Children in Australian History*. New York: Berghahn Books, 2004.

Moses, L. G. *Wild West Shows and the Images of American Indians, 1883–1933*. Albuquerque: University of New Mexico Press, 1996.

Muller, Elsa Christina. "A Cultural Study of the Sioux Novels of Liselotte Welskopf-Henrich." Ph.D. diss., University of Maryland, 1995.

Muthu, Sankar. *Enlightenment against Empire*. Princeton: Princeton University Press, 2003.

Nagler, Jörg. "From Culture to Kultur. Changing American Perceptions of Imperial Germany, 1870–1914." In *Transatlantic Images and Perceptions*, edited by Barclay and Glaser-Schmidt, 131–54.

Nerburn, Kent. *Chief Joseph and the Flight of the Nez Perce: The Untold Story of an American Tragedy*. New York: Harper San Francisco, 2005.

Neuffer, Elizabeth. "Germans Make a Hobby Out of Cowboys and Indians." *Boston Globe*, 6 August 1996.

Neumann, Peter. *Indianer-Museum Radebeul*. Dresden: Karl May Stiftung, 1962.

Niezen, Ron. *The Origins of Indigenism: Human Rights and the Politics of Identity*. Berkeley: University of California Press, 2003.

Nipperdey, Thomas. *Nachdenken über die deutsche Geschichte, Essays*. Munich: Beck, 1986.

Nirenburg, Morton. *The Reception of American Literature in German Periodicals, 1820–1850*. Heidelberg: C. Winter, 1970.

Nix, Jacob. *The Sioux Uprising in Minnesota, 1862: Jacob Nix's Eyewitness History*. Edited by Don Heinrich Tolzmann. Indianapolis: Max Kade German-American Center, 1994.

Nolan, Mary. "America in the German Imagination." In *Transactions, Transgressions, Transformations*, edited by Fehrenbach and Poiger, 3–25.

Novick, Peter. *The Holocaust in American Life*. New York: Mariner Books, 2000.

Oliv, Max. *20 Jahre Indian Councils (1951–1970)*. Vol. 1. Munich: Western Bund e.V., 1988.

———. *20 Jahre Indian Councils (1971–1990)*. Vol. 2. Munich: Western Bund e.V., 1997.

———. *10 Jahre Indian Councils*. Vol. 3. Munich: Western Bund e.V. 1999, 2004.

Opel, Christian. "W. E. B. Du Bois, Nazi Germany, and the Black Atlantic." *German Historical Institute Bulletin Supplement* 5 (2008): 99–122.

Osterhammel, Jürgen. *Colonialism: A Theoretical Overview*. Princeton: Markus Wiener Publishers, 1997.

Ostler, Jeffery. "Conquest and the State: Why the United States Employed Massive Military Force to Suppress the Lakota Ghost Dance." *Pacific Historical Review* 65, no. 2 (1996): 217–48.

———. *The Plains Sioux and U.S. Colonialism from Lewis and Clark to Wounded Knee*. Cambridge: Cambridge University Press, 2004.

Otterness, Philip. *Becoming German: The 1709 Palatine Migration to New York*. Ithaca: Cornell University Press, 2004.

Otto, Victor. *Deutsche Amerika-Bilder*. Munich: Wilhelm Fink Verlag, 2006.

Palmer, Alison. *Colonial Genocide*. London: C. Hurst, 2000.

Parkhill, Thomas C. *Weaving Ourselves into the Land: Charles Godfrey Leland, "Indians," and the Study of Native American Religions*. Albany: State University of New York, 1997.

Paskievich, John. *If Only I Were an Indian*. Zemma Pictures, National Film Board of Canada, 1995.

Paulson, Robert J. *Franz Massopust, German-Bohemian Pathfinder and Founder of New Ulm, Minnesota: A Tragic Family Saga*. Roseville, Minn.: Park Genealogical Books, 2004.

Payne, Stanley G., David J. Sorkin, and John S. Tortorice, eds. *What History Tells: George L. Mosse and the Culture of Modern Europe*. Madison: University of Wisconsin Press, 2004.

Pearce, Roy Harvey. *Savagism and Civilization: A Study of the Indian and the American Mind*. 2nd ed. Berkeley: University of California Press, 1988.

Peers, Laura. "'Playing Ourselves': First Nations and Native American Interpreters at Living History Sites." *Public Historian* 21, no. 4 (1999): 39–59.

Peipp, Matthias, and Bernhard Springer. *Edle Wilde, Rote Teufel: Indianer im Film*. Munich: Wilhelm Heyne, 1997.

Pennington, Robert. *Oscar Howe: Artist of the Sioux*. Sioux Falls, S.D.: Dakota Territory Centennial Commission, 1961.

Penny, H. Glenn. "Elusive Authenticity: The Quest for the Authentic Indian in German Public Culture." *Comparative Studies in Society and History* 48, no. 4 (October 2006): 798–818.

———. "Illustrating America: Images of the North American Wild West in German Periodicals, 1825–1890." In *I Like America*, edited by Kort, 141–57.

———. *Objects of Culture: Ethnology and Ethnographic Museums in Imperial Germany*. Chapel Hill: University of North Carolina Press, 2002.

———. "Red Power: Liselotte Welskopf-Henrich and Indian Activist Networks in East and West Germany." *Central European History* 41, no. 3 (2008): 447–76.

Peukert, Detlev J. K. *Inside Nazi Germany: Conformity, Opposition, and Racism in Everyday Life*. Translated by Richard Deveson. New Haven: Yale University Press, 1987.

Plischke, Hans. *Von Cooper bis Karl May*. Düsseldorf: Droste-Verlag, 1951.

Poiger, Uta. *Jazz, Rock, and Rebels: Cold War Politics and American Culture in a Divided Germany*. Berkeley: University of California Press, 2000.

Poore, Anne V., ed. *Reflections: Papers on Southwest Culture History in Honor of Charles H. Lorie*. Papers of the Archeology Society of New Mexico 14. Santa Fe: Ancient City Press, 1989.

Prahl, Augustus J. "Friedrich Gerstäcker, the Frontier Novelist." *Arkansas Historical Quarterly* 14, no. 1 (1955): 43–50.

Price, Sally. *Primitive Art in Civilized Places*. Chicago: University of Chicago Press, 1989.

Prucha, Paul. *American Indian Treaties: The History of a Political Anomaly*. Berkeley: University of California Press, 1994.

———. *The Great Father: The United States Government and the American Indians.* Abridged ed. Lincoln: University of Nebraska Press, 1986.

Rahden, Till van. "Beyond Ambivalence: Variations of Catholic Antisemitism in Turn-of-the-Century Baltimore," *American Jewish History* 82 (1994): 7–42.

———. "Germans of the Jewish *Stamm*: Visions of Community between Nationalism and Particularism." In *German History from the Margins*, edited by Gregor, Roemer, and Roseman, 27–49. Bloomington: Indiana University Press, 2006.

Raibmon, Paige. *Authentic Indians: Episodes of Encounter from the Late-Nineteenth-Century Northwest Coast.* Durham: Duke University Press, 2005.

Retallack, James, ed. *Imperial Germany, 1871–1918.* New York: Oxford University Press, 2008.

Richter, Daniel K. *Facing East from Indian Country: A Native History of Early America.* Cambridge, Mass.: Harvard University Press, 2001.

Rickard, Jolene. "Alterity, Mimicry, and German Indians." In *Bavarian by Law/ German Indians*, edited by Max Becher and Andrea Robbins, 30–31. Syracuse: Light Work, 1998.

Rodgers, Daniel T. *Atlantic Crossings: Social Politics in a Progressive Age.* Cambridge, Mass.: Harvard University Press, 1998.

Rosenthal, Heinz. "Leben und Werk eines Deutschamerikaners." Unpublished Manuscript, Solingen Stadtarchiv, GF 184, 1954.

Ross, A. C. *Ehanamani "Walks Among": An Autobiography.* Denver: Bear, 1993.

Ross, Corey. *The East German Dictatorship: Problems and Perspectives in the Interpretation of the GDR.* London: Arnold, 2002.

Rossbacher, Karlheinz. *Lederstrumpf in Deutschland; zur Rezeption James Fenimore Coopers beim Leser der Restaurationszeit.* Munich: W. Fink, 1972.

Rothberg, Michael. *Multidirectional Memory: Remembering the Holocaust in the Age of Decolonization.* Stanford: Stanford University Press, 2009.

Rothenberger, Karl-Heinz. *Die Hungerjahre nach dem Zweiten Weltkrieg. Ernährungs- und Landwirtschaft in Rheinland-Pfalz 1945–1950.* Boppard: Boldt, 1980.

Rubin, Daniel. "Germans Emulate American Indians." *Kansas City Star*, 6 August 2000, A16.

Ruud, Brandon K., ed. *Karl Bodmer's North American Prints.* Lincoln: University of Nebraska Press, 2004.

Sachs, Aaron. *The Humboldt Current: Nineteenth-Century Exploration and the Roots of American Environmentalism.* New York: Viking, 2006.

Sammons, Jeffrey L. *Ideology, Mimesis, Fantasy: Charles Sealsfield, Friedrich Gerstäcker, Karl May, and Other German Novelists of America.* Chapel Hill: University of North Carolina Press, 1998.

———. "Nineteenth-Century German Representations of Indians from Experience." In *Germans and Indians*, edited by Calloway, Gemünden, and Zantop, 185–193.

Sander, Frank. *Volk ohne Land.* Bremen: Burmester, 1935.

Sanner, Hans-Ulrich. "'Are you Hitler's son?' Bilder der Fremden im Spiegel der Hopi-Ritualclowns." In *Konversionen: Fremderfahrungen in ethnologischer und interkultureller Perspektive*, edited by Steffi Hobuß, Iris Daermann, and Ulrich Loelke, 35–78. Amsterdam: Rodopi, 2004.

———. "Confessions of the Last Hopi Fieldworker." In *Mirror Writing: (Re-)Constructions of Native American Identity*, edited by Thomas Claviez and Maria Moss, 41–66. Berlin: Galda + Wilch Verlag, 2000.

———. "Karl von den Steinen in Oraibi, 1898. A Collection of Hopi Indian Photographs in Perspective." *Baessler-Archiv*, n.s., 44 (1996): 243–93.

Satterlee, Marion P. *A Detailed Account of the Massacre by the Dakota Indians of Minnesota in 1862*. Minneapolis: Marion P. Satterlee, 1923.

Schauwecker, Franz. *Thecumseh: Erhebung der Prärie*. Berlin: Safari, 1938.

Schimmel, Julie. "Inventing 'the Indian.'" In *The West as America: Reinterpreting Images of the Frontier, 1820–1920*, edited by William H. Truettner, 149–90. Washington, D.C.: Smithsonian Institution Press, 1991.

Schlisser, Hanna, ed. *The Miracle Years: A Cultural History of West Germany, 1949–1968*. Princeton: Princeton University Press, 2001.

Schmidt, Dorothea. *Indianer als Heilbringer: Ein neues Klischee in der deutschsprachigen Literatur?* Frankfurt a. M.: Brandes u. Apsel, 1988.

Schmiedt, Helmut. *Karl May: Leben, Werk und Wirkung*. Frankfurt a. M.: Fischer, 1987.

Schneider, Tassilo. "Finding a New Heimat in the Wild West: Karl May and the German Western of the 1960s." *Journal of Film and Video* 47, nos. 1–3 (1995): 50–66.

Scholz-Héansel, Michael. "Indianer im deutschen Südwesten." *Jahrbuch der Staatlichen Kunstsammlungen in Baden-Württemberg* 23 (1986): 128–44.

See, Klaus von. *Barbar, Germane, Arier: Die Suche nach der Identität der Deutschen*. Heidelberg: Universitätsverlag C. Winter, 1994.

Seifert, Wolfgang. *Patty Frank— der Zirkus, die Indianer, das Karl-May-Museum*. Radebeul: Karl May Verlag, 1998.

Sering, Max. *Die innere Kolonization im östlichen Deutschland*. Leipzig: Duncker & Humblot, 1893.

Sewell, William. *The Logics of History: Social Theory and Social Transformation*. Chicago: University of Chicago Press, 2005.

Sharples, Riva J. "In the Presence of Greatness: Artist and Educator John Day Has Devoted Much of His Life to Preserving Oscar Howe's Legacy." *South Dakota Magazine* 24, no. 4 (November–December 2008): 35–41.

Sicherman, Barbara. "Reading and Ambition: M. Carey Thomas and Female Heroism." *American Quarterly* 45, no. 1 (1993): 73–103.

Sieg, Katrin. *Ethnic Drag: Performing Race, Nation, Sexuality in West Germany*. Ann Arbor: University of Michigan Press, 2002.

———. "Indian Impersonation as Historical Surrogation." In *Germans and Indians*, edited by Calloway, Gemünden, and Zantop, 217–42.

Silver, Peter. *Our Savage Neighbors: How the Indian War Transformed America*. Princeton: Princeton University Press, 2008.

Slotkin, Richard. *Fatal Environment: The Myth of the Frontier in the Age of Industrialization*. New York: Atheneum, 1985.

Smith, Donald B. *Long Lance: The True Story of an Imposter*. Lincoln: University of Nebraska Press, 1983.

Smith, Helmut Walser. *The Continuities of German History: Nation, Religion, and Race across the Long Nineteenth Century.* New York: Cambridge University Press, 2008.

———. "Prussia at the Margins, or the World That Nationalism Lost." In *German History from the Margins*, edited by Gregor, Roemer, and Roseman, 69–83.

———. "Talk of Genocide, the Rhetoric of Miscegenation: Notes on Debates in the German Reichstag concerning Southwest Africa, 1904–1914." In *The Imperialist Imagination: German Colonialism and Its Legacy*, edited by Friedrichsmeyer, Lennox, and Zantop, 107–24. Ann Arbor: University of Michigan Press, 1998.

Smith, John David. "Anthropologist Felix von Luschan and Trans-Atlantic Racial Reform." *Münchner Beiträge zur Völkerkunde* 7 (2002): 289–304.

———. "W. E. B. Du Bois, Felix von Luschan, and Racial Reform at the Fin de Siècle." *Amerikastudien* 47, no. 1 (2002): 1–37.

Smith, Paul Chaat. *Everything You Know about Indians Is Wrong.* Minneapolis: University of Minnesota Press, 2009.

———. "The Terrible Nearness of Distant Places: Making History at the National Museum of the American Indian." In *Indigenous Experience Today*, edited by de la Cadena and Starn, 379–96. New York: Berg, 2007.

Smith, Paul Chaat, and Robert Allen Warrior. *Like a Hurricane: The Indian Movement from Alcatraz to Wounded Knee.* New York: New Press, 1996.

Speer, Albert. *Spandauer Tagebücher.* Frankfurt a. M.: Ullstein, 1982.

Stamps, Quanah Crossland. "Germany: Market for Native American Goods." *American Indian Report* (April 2000): 21–22.

Stannard, David E. *American Holocaust: The Conquest of the New World.* New York: Oxford University Press, 1992.

Stark, Isolde, ed. *Elisabeth Charlotte Welskopf in der DDR.* Stuttgart: Franz Steiner Verlag, 2006.

Stauffer, David Hall. "The Origin and Establishment of Brazil's Indian Service, 1889–1910." Ph.D. diss., University of Texas, 1955.

Stein, Gary C. "And the Strife Never Ends: Indian-White Hostility as Seen by European Travelers in America, 1800–1860." *Ethnohistory* 20, no. 2 (1973): 173–87.

Stenzel, Bryce O. *German Immigration to the Minnesota River Valley Frontier, 1852–1865: Wir Stammten aus Deutschland nach Hausen Minnesota.* Mankato: Minnesota Heritage Publishing, 2002.

Stephan, Alexander, ed. *Americanization and Anti-Americanism: The German Encounter with American Culture after 1945.* New York: Berghahn Books, 2004.

Steuben, Fritz. *Der fliegende Pfeil: Eine Erzählung aus dem Leben Tecumsehs alten Quellen nacherzählt.* Stuttgart: Franck, 1930.

Stewart, Rick, Joseph D. Ketner II, and Angela L. Miller. *Carl Wimar: Chronicler of the Missouri River Frontier.* Fort Worth: Amon Carter Museum, 1991.

Stoler, Ann Laura. *Carnal Knowledge and Imperial Power: Race and the Intimate in Colonial Rule.* Berkeley: University of California Press, 2002.

———. *Race and the Education of Desire: Foucault's History of Sexuality and the Colonial Order of Things.* Durham: Duke University Press, 1995.

Stolte, Heinz, and Gerhard Klußmeier. *Arno Schmidt und Karl May—Eine notwendige Klarstellung*. Hamburg: Hansa-Verlag, 1973.

Stolzman, Fr. William. *How to Take Part in Lakota Ceremonies*. Chamberlain, S.D.: Tipi Press, 2004.

Strand, Ginger. "The Crying Indian." *Orion* 27 no. 6 (2008): 20–27.

Strong, Pauline Turner. "Transforming Outsiders: Captivity, Adoption, and Slavery Reconsidered." In *A Companion to American Indian History*, edited by Deloria and Salisbury, 339–57.

Stüber, Gabriele. *Der Kampf gegen den Hunger 1945–1950. Die Ernährungslage in der britischen Zone Deutschlands, insbesondere in Schleswig-Holstein und Hamburg*. Neumünster: Wachholz, 1984.

Tacitus, Cornelius. *Germania*. Translated by J. B. Rives. Oxford: Clarendon Press, 1999.

Talbot, Steve. *Indianer in den USA. Unterdrückung und Widerstand*. Berlin: Dietz, 1985.

Talbot, William S. "Oregon Trail." In *Master Paintings from the Butler Institute of American Art*, edited by Irene Sweetkind et al. New York: Harry N. Abrams, 1994. http://www.butlerart.com/pc_book/pages/albert_bierstadt_1830.htm.

Tate, Michael L. "From Scout to Doughboy: The National Debate over Integrating American Indians into the Military, 1891–1918." *Western Historical Quarterly* 17, no. 4 (October 1986): 417–37.

———. *Indians and Emigrants: Encounters on the Overland Trails*. Norman: University of Oklahoma Press, 2006.

Theisz, R. D. "The Bad Speakers and the Long Braids: References to Foreign Enemies in Lakota Song Texts." In *Indians and Europe*, edited by Feest, 427–34.

Thode-Arora, Hilke. *Für fünfzig Pfennig um die Welt: Die Hagenbeckschen Völkerschauen*. Frankfurt: Campus, 1989.

Tooze, Adam. *The Wages of Destruction: The Making and Breaking of the Nazi Economy*. New York: Penguin, 2007.

Torgovnick, Marianna. *Primitive Passions: Men, Women, and the Quest for Ecstasy*. New York: Alfred A. Knopf, 1997.

Tower, Beeke Sell. *Envisioning Amerika: Prints, Drawings, and Photographs by George Grosz and His Contemporaries*. Cambridge: Busch-Reisinger Museum, 1990.

Townsend, Kenneth William. *World War II and the American Indian*. Albuquerque: University of New Mexico Press, 2000.

Trenton, Patricia, and Peter H. Hassrick. *The Rocky Mountains: A Vision for Artists in the Nineteenth Century*. Norman: University of Oklahoma Press, 1983.

Treuer, Anton. *The Assassination of Hole in the Day*. St. Paul: Borealis Books, 2010.

Trevor-Roper, H. R. *Hitler's Table Talk, 1941–1944*. London: Enigma Books, 2000.

Trittel, Günter J. *Hunger und Politik: Die Ernährungskrise in der Bizone, 1945–1949*. Frankfurt: Campus, 1990.

Trommler, Frank, and Elliott Shore, eds. *The German-American Encounter: Conflict and Cooperation between Two Cultures, 1800–2000*. New York: Berghahn Books, 2001.

Trotta, Cathy Ann. "Crossing Cultural Boundaries: Heinrich and Martha Moser Voth in the Hopi Pueblos, 1893–1906." Ph.D. diss., Northern Arizona University, 1997.

Truettner, William H., ed. *The West as America: Reinterpreting Images of the Frontier, 1820–1920.* Washington, D.C.: Smithsonian Institution Press, 1991.

Turski, Birgit. *Die Indianistikgruppen der DDR: Entwicklung, Probleme, Aussichten.* Idstein: Baum, 1994.

Tyler, Ron. "Karl Bodmer and the American West." In *Karl Bodmer's North American Prints*, edited by Ruud, 1–46.

———. *Prints of the West.* Golden: Fulcrum Publishing, 1994.

Umbach, Maiken. *German Federalism: Past, Present, Future.* New York: Palgrave, 2002.

Utley, Robert M. *The Last Days of the Sioux.* 2nd ed. New Haven: Yale University Press, 2004.

———. *Sitting Bull: The Life and Times of an American Patriot.* New York: Macmillan, 2008.

Walker, Mack. *Germany and the Emigration, 1816–1885.* Cambridge, Mass.: Harvard University Press, 1964.

Wallace, Anthony F. C. *Jefferson and the Indians: The Tragic Fate of the First Americans.* Cambridge, Mass.: Belknap Press of Harvard University Press, 1999.

———. "Revitalization Movements: Some Theoretical Considerations for Their Comparative Study." *American Anthropologist* 58, no. 2 (1956): 264–81.

Walters, Alexander, Henry B. Brown, H. Sylvester Williams, and W. E. B. Du Bois. "To the Nations of the World" (1900). In *An ABC of Color: Selections Chosen by the Author from Over a Half Century of His Writings*, edited by W. E. B. Du Bois, 20. New York: International Publishers, 1969.

Warburg, Aby M. *Images from the Region of the Pueblo Indians of North America.* Translated by Michael P. Steinberg. Ithaca: Cornell University Press, 1995.

Warburg Institute. *Photographs at the Frontier: Aby Warburg in America, 1895–1896.* London: Warburg Institute, 1998.

Warren, Louis S. *Buffalo Bill's America: William Cody and the Wild West Show.* New York: Vintage, 2005.

Weber, Alina Dana. "'Indians' on German Stages: The History and Meaning of Karl May Festivals." Ph.D. diss., Indiana University, 2010.

Weinberg, Gerhard L., ed. *Hitler's Second Book: The Unpublished Sequel to Mein Kampf, by Adolf Hitler.* Translated by Krista Smith. New York: Enigma Books, 2003.

Weiss, Gerhard H. "German Language Press in Minnesota." In *A Heritage Fulfilled*, edited by Glasrud, 47–63. Moorehead, Minn.: Concordia College, 1983.

Wells, Samuel J., and Roseanna Tubby, eds. *After Removal: The Choctaw in Mississippi.* Jackson: University Press of Mississippi, 1986.

Welsch, James, with Paul Stekler. *Killing Custer: The Battle of the Little Bighorn and the Fate of the Plains Indians.* New York: W. W. Norton, 1994.

White, Richard. *"It's Your Misfortune and None of My Own": A New History of the American West.* Norman: University of Oklahoma Press, 1991.

——. *The Middle Ground: Indians, Empires, and Republics in the Great Lakes Region, 1650–1815*. New York: Cambridge University Press, 1991.

——. "Winning the West: The Expansion of the Western Sioux in the Eighteenth and Nineteenth Centuries." *Journal of American History* 65 (Summer 1978): 319–43.

Whitehead, Stephen M., and Frank J Barrett, ed. *The Masculinities Studies Reader*. Cambridge: Polity, 2001.

White Horse Eagle. *Wir Indianer: Erinnerungen des letzten grossen Häuptlings White Horse Eagle*. Introduced and edited by Edgar Schmidt-Pauli. Berlin: Verlag für Kulturpolitik, 1929.

Wied, Maximilian von, and Karl Bodmer. *Reise in das innere Nord-America in den Jahren 1832 bis 1834*, 2 vols. Coblenz: J. Hoelscher, 1839.

Williamson, George S. *The Longing for Myth in Germany: Religion and Aesthetic Culture from Romanticism to Nietzsche*. Chicago: University of Chicago Press, 2004.

Wilson, Angela. *In the Footsteps of Our Ancestors: The Dakota Commemorative Marches of the 21st Century*. St. Paul, Minn.: Living Justice Press, 2006.

Windolph, Charles. *I Fought with Custer: The Story of Sergeant Windolph, Last Survivor of the Battle of the Little Big Horn*. Lincoln, Neb.: Bison Books, 1987.

Wolfe, Patrick. "Structure and Event: Settler Colonialism, Time, and the Question of Genocide." In *Empire, Colony, Genocide*, edited by A. Dirk Moses, 102–32. New York: Berghahn Books, 2004.

Woolworth, Alan R. "Little Crow (Taoyateduta or His Red Nation) c. 1810–1863." In *Trails of Tears*, edited by Bakeman and Richardson, 165–67.

Wunder, John R. "Native American History, Ethnohistory, and Context." *Ethnohistory* 54, no. 4 (2007): 591–604.

Württemberg, Paul von. *Travels in North America, 1822–1824*. Translated by W. Robert Nitske. Norman: University of Oklahoma Press, 1973.

Wüstenbecker, Katja. *Deutsch-Amerikaner im Ersten Weltkrieg. US-Politik und nationale Identitäten im Mittleren Westen*. Stuttgart: Franz Steiner Verlag, 2007.

Zahra, Tara. *Kidnapped Souls: National Indifference and the Battle for Children in the Bohemian Lands, 1900–1948*. Ithaca: Cornell University Press, 2008.

Zantop, Susanne. "Close Encounters: *Deutsche* and *Indianer*." In *Germans and Indians*, edited by Calloway, Gemünden, and Zantop, 3–14.

——. *Colonial Fantasies: Conquest, Family, and Nation in Precolonial Germany, 1770–1870*. Durham: Duke University Press, 1997.

Zesch, Scott. *The Captured: A True Story of Abduction by Indians on the Texas Frontier*. New York: St. Martin's Press, 2004.

Zimmerer, Jürgen. "Colonialism and the Holocaust: Towards an Archeology of Genocide." In *Genocide and Settler Society: Frontier Violence and Stolen Indigenous Children in Australian History*, edited by A. Dirk Moses, 49–76.

Zimmerman, Andrew. *Alabama in Africa: Booker T. Washington, the German Empire, and the Globalization of the New South*. Princeton: Princeton University Press, 2010.

Index

CPSIA information can be obtained at www.ICGtesting.com
Printed in the USA
LVOW08s2107290615

444314LV00003B/4/P

9 781469 626444